Praise for *Recovery Options: The Complete Guide*

"*Finally! A no-nonsense, state-of-the-art guide that one can hand to anybody who is having trouble with drugs, alcohol, tobacco, or foods of various kinds. What a gift Volpicelli and Szalavitz have given us: A stupendous, practical way to help the colleagues and loved ones in our lives who are struggling with chemical dependency.*"
—Laurie Garrett, author of *The Coming Plague: Newly Emerging Diseases in a World Out of Balance*

"*Comprehensive, illuminating, easy to read . . . this book points out the diverse paths to the ultimate goal—recovery from alcohol and other drug abuse.*"
—William Cope Moyers,
Vice President of Public Affairs, Hazelden Foundation

"*At last a sensible, clear guide for consumers who are facing the tough choice of seeking treatment for addictive behaviors. In a field long driven by emotion and minimal scientific evidence, Volpicelli and Szalavitz impartially review the options and explain them in clear language. In addition, they take some of the hysteria out of the issues facing substance users and their loved ones by providing a coherent summary of what we really know about alcohol and other drugs. A must read. Bravo!*"
—Fred Rotgers, Assistant Chief Psychologist,
Smithers Addiction Treatment and Training Center

"*Wise, accurate, responsible, accessible, well written. I'm assigning it for my course in drug policy.*"
—Mark Kleiman, Professor of Policy Studies at UCLA
and author of *Against Excess: Drug Policy for Results*

"Joe Volpicelli is one of the most creative research scientists and clinicians in the addiction field. With Maia Szalavitz, he has put together a highly practical and effective book describing a modern approach to the treatment of alcoholism and other addictive disorders. This approach is steeped in pragmatism and soundly based on science. It utilizes techniques that work and that have been adapted to the needs of individual patients. The writing is clear, succinct, and understandable. It should be a very useful guide for patients, their families, and professionals in addressing this terrible disease."
—Charles P. O'Brien, M.D., Ph.D., Kenneth Appel Professor, Department of Psychiatry, VA Medical Center; President, American College of Neuropsychopharmacology

Recovery Options: The Complete Guide

Joseph Volpicelli, M.D., Ph.D.
Maia Szalavitz

John Wiley & Sons, Inc.
New York • Chichester • Weinheim • Brisbane • Singapore • Toronto

The information contained in this book is not intended to serve as a replacement for professional medical advice. Any use of the information in this book is at the reader's discre-
tion. The author and the publisher specifically disclaim any and all liability arising directly
or indirectly from the use or application of any information contained in this book. A
health-care professional should be consulted regarding your specific situation.

Library of Congress Cataloging-in-Publication Data

Volpicelli, Joseph.
    Recovery options: the complete guide / Joseph Volpicelli, Maia Szalavitz.
        p. cm.
    "Published simultaneously in Canada."
    Includes index.
    ISBN 0-471-34575-X (paper)
        1. Alcoholism. 2. Alcoholism—Treatment. I. Szalavitz, Maia. II. Title.

RC565.V63 2000
616.86'1—dc21   99-054733

Printed in the United States of America

10 9 8 7 6 5 4

To my patients
—Joe

To Peter
—Maia

Contents

Preface

My (Maia's) road to addiction is my own. There are countless routes to this destination, and, often, how you get in has a bearing on the best way out. Because there are so many ways to get hooked, there need to be many ways to get free. I hope that this book will give people with alcohol and other drug problems—and their loved ones—a sense of what addiction is and how best to treat it. I hope also to show how it's crucial to recognize the differences among people with substance problems, as well as the similarities. When I attended treatment, the one-size-fits-all philosophy guided care, and I was lucky to get what I needed. Many other people aren't—but this book can help you increase the odds.

I also hope this book can decrease your fears about treatment. I avoided treatment for years because I had heard about how humiliating some types of addiction care are. I didn't want to be broken down—feeling broken was why I'd used drugs in the first place. I didn't know there were choices. I didn't know what to expect. If I had, I probably would have sought help sooner. This book can demystify the various treatment experiences so that you can find the type that will be most helpful.

I wasn't supposed to become a cocaine and heroin addict. My eighth-grade class voted me "Most Likely to Succeed," and in high school, I was known as "Mass Media Maia" because of my obsession with producing the school's cable-TV news show. I wrote for *Seventeen* magazine. My grades and test scores won me admission to Columbia University.

All that early promise didn't make me happy, though. My overweening ambition was a geeky attempt to win friends by offering the promise of future favors. I couldn't imagine that anyone would like me for myself.

Drug education had taught me that tobacco was truly deadly, so I avoided it, and I didn't like the way alcohol seemed to lessen my self-control. As a geek, however, when drug-prevention teachers said that peer pressure will make you take drugs, they were essentially telling me, "drugs are cool." I didn't want to be an outcast, so I felt I'd have to give in to peer pressure on at least one substance. Marijuana and psychedelics began to fascinate me. As soon as I could find a source, I began smoking pot.

Pot and psychedelics caused me few problems. I continued to do well in school—in fact, my social life improved radically. My drug use didn't cause symptoms, it alleviated them—at first.

When I was 17, however, my boyfriend turned me on to cocaine. By the time I started college, I was well on my way to becoming a cocaine addict. The prep-school kids with their perfect clothes and their trust funds intimidated me. I felt as though I always had toilet paper or worse on the bottom of my shoe—like a walking faux pas. I started selling coke so I could make friends by having something they wanted.

Again, it worked—at first. Soon I was part of the in crowd who could get behind the velvet ropes at the hottest 1980s night clubs. I began selling coke to celebrities. But then the late nights started to take a toll on my grades, and the college started to get suspicious about why so many people were visiting my dorm.

At the end of my sophomore year, I was suspended for dealing drugs. I should have been grateful that Columbia hadn't called the police or expelled me—instead, I thought my life was over because I had ruined my academic record.

It was during my suspension, when my life had no structure and I had no hope, that I tried heroin. I snorted the white powder that had been offered to me and found peace. A friend described heroin as being like "warm, buttery love," and that's what it felt like to me.

Junkies' descriptions of heroin read like saints' descriptions of heaven or lovers' descriptions of their beloveds, but the truth is that for most people, it doesn't feel the way it did for me. Heroin kills both emotional and physical pain—so if your life is OK, it feels rather nice, but not worth self-sacrifice. My life was not OK.

Within six months, I'd moved from snorting to shooting. I injected large amounts of cocaine and heroin, often for days on end. In 1986, an arrest left me facing 15 years to life in prison for cocaine dealing—and my response, once I was bailed out, was to use more drugs to escape.

Finally, in the summer of 1988, I hit bottom. I had tried methadone, but I kept using cocaine on top of it and had been cut from the program as a result. I had exhausted my resources. I was starting to withdraw from heroin, and there was a cocaine customer visiting who had some. I found myself begging him for it, figuratively if not literally on my knees. When he refused, I found myself thinking of other ways to get it—such as seducing him or stealing it.

I'd always thought of addicts as people who do things that violate their principles to get their drugs and then can't enjoy them because of guilt. I knew that that was a vicious cycle, and I hadn't seen myself as being in it. Suddenly, I did.

It was as though a camera pulled back and revealed my life for what it was. I was sitting in a filthy, garbage-strewn apartment with blood on the ceiling, dirty laundry, rotting food, and crumpled newspapers everywhere. I weighed 85 pounds; my skin looked ghastly, an ashen gray; and angry red tracks streaked across both my arms and my ankles. I looked like someone with a fatal illness. I knew something had to change.

I went to my mother's house the next day, thinking she'd know where to take me because she'd been suggesting treatment for so long. She didn't. After one hospital turned us away because they didn't "do junkies," we found another. I stayed for seven days, shaking, vomiting, and hardly able to sleep—although they did provide some medical assistance. As I progressed, my counselor suggested I enter an 18-month therapeutic community, but because I'd heard about the rough treatment that takes place in such centers, I refused. He then mentioned a 28-day rehab in Westchester, which had a swimming pool. He listed several celebrities who had attended. Snob appeal worked, and I was off to the ARC-Westchester facility.

I also needed a new sense of purpose, something to do with my life to make me feel useful. I found that purpose in the 12-step programs the rehab introduced me to. Today, I have some problems with the way many treatment centers force 12-step ideology on people. I know that there are many whom it doesn't help—and in this book, we offer a variety of options for recovery. For me, however, at that time, it did the trick. In 12-step fellowships, I found that I could make friends without having to give them drugs and that I could be loved for who I was without being rich or famous. I was terrified that recovery meant working at some low-level job and learning to be content with my misery, but that wasn't the case. In fact, it meant freeing myself from the parts of me that had gotten in my way.

In this book, Joe and I share with you what we've learned about treatment in the course of our work and our lives. He's been an addiction researcher for over a quarter century—and I've now been clean for more than 11 years and have been writing about drugs and addiction since before I quit using. I return to some of my addiction and treatment experiences in more depth in later chapters, where appropriate, to illustrate the topics being discussed. We also detail other people's experiences of treatment, self-help, relapse, and recovery.

We hope that by offering insight on both the science of addiction, which shapes treatment, and the personal experiences of people in treatment, we can give you the best possible guide to care for people who suffer from alcohol and other drug problems. I wish there had been such a book when I needed help. My wish is that we can help you or your loved ones get free.

One thing I can say from personal experience is that life gets better, and that living drug-free is fun, fascinating, and not at all the miserable deadness people with drug problems tend to fear. If it starts to feel that way, there are things that can be done—a recovering person shouldn't accept feeling unremittingly horrible for long because that can lead to relapse. Also, no one should accept treatment that doesn't demonstrate respect or that doesn't treat the addict with dignity. We show you where to start your journey away from drugs and toward a better life. You may well be surprised at how different it can be from what you fear—and at the range of options available to you—from learning to moderate your drinking or other drug use to taking medications that can make the recovery process easier. Knowledge is power.

Acknowledgments

MAIA

Many people find collaborating to involve a clash of egos and a great deal of stress—but working with Joe Volpicelli has been a joy, and I am honored and grateful to have had the chance to be his co-author. I'm also extremely grateful to our agent, Charlotte Sheedy, who never lost faith in me and my work, and to our editor, Tom Miller, whose vision for this book helped shape, structure, and channel some of our more unruly ideas.

I'd also like to thank, in no particular order, the people who have supported me throughout my unorthodox career: Bill and Judith Moyers, Howard Josepher, Charlie Rose, Robert Massa, Laurie Garrett, Kathy Novak, and Gwen Barrett. My parents and siblings—Kira, Sarah, and Ari—have all provided help, intellectual stimulation, and care. My friends Anne Kornhauser, Sue Young Wilson, Joanne Dwyer, and Stacy Horn all added their widely varying perspectives and support, and Marijo Wright was amazing not only at transcribing interviews, but also at understanding subjects and the nonverbal messages they were sending. I want to thank the members of addict-l—particularly Iain Brown, J. Michael Farragher, George Davidson, Ron Roizen, Fred Rotgers, and Robin Room—for challenging my preconceptions and providing a course in addictions that few Ph.D. programs could replicate. I am grateful to all the substance users, alcoholics, and other addicts who shared their stories and their ideas with us. Finally, I'd like to thank Peter McDermott, who enriched both this book and my life in ways too numerous to describe.

JOE

First, I'd like to thank my co-author Maia Szalavitz—her unique ability to understand the science and to put a human face to it never ceases to amaze me. Thank you, Maia, for being patient, yet persistent in seeing this book become a reality. The honor is mine. I'm also grateful to our agent, Charlotte Sheedy, and our editor, Tom Miller, who both gently shaped and guided our writing to lead to a book of which I am quite proud.

I also wish to thank my many teachers, especially Charles O'Brien and Martin Seligman—from whom I have freely borrowed—and my mentor Richard L. Solomon, who is no longer with us, but whose influence and intellectual debt I can never repay. I hope he looks down with pride at his grateful student.

I also thank all my colleagues at the University of Pennsylvania, including Helen Pettinatti, Jan Filing, Tom McLellan, Kyle Kampman, Robert Weinreib, David Oslin, Barbara Flannery, Margaret Rukstalis, John Monterosso, Gail Kaempf, Janice Biddle, Moira Malloy, Louise Epperson, and Peter Gariti, who have challenged my thinking and provided new insights into understanding addiction. I also thank all my students and research assistants for understanding my insistence to "show me the data." I thank Donna Maiuri for transcribing the many interviews and putting up with my craziness. I also wish to thank my parents, Dominic and Mary, for their confidence and support, as well as my friends and my wife, Trisha, and my children, Mike, Katie, and Cristina, who patiently put up with all the long hours to complete this project. Finally, I thank all those people with substance problems, whose passion and compassion inspire me to find a more effective path to recovery. Special thanks go to the many patients who allowed me to share in their recovery and who have also been my most forgiving teachers as I have practiced the art of medicine.

Introduction

My husband is spending too much money on cocaine. How can I get him to stop?

I think I might be drinking more than I should, but I don't like AA. Is there another program that might work for me?

I think my teenage daughter is smoking pot. Should I try to get her into a residential drug program? If so, how do I know which one is the best?

I started using heroin, and now I can't stop. I'm scared of treatment. What can I do?

We wrote this book to answer these questions—to assist those in need of help with alcohol and other drug problems to find not just the kind of care that medical or self-proclaimed experts think is right for everyone, but the type of treatment that best suits a particular person. Remarkable progress in understanding the behavioral and biological causes of addiction has challenged our fundamental assumptions about what addiction is and what the best treatments for it are. There are many more options today than ever before. To take advantage of them, you or your loved one doesn't even need to be ready to give up alcohol or other drugs or to know whether there is a real problem bad enough to require help.

Unfortunately, while research knowledge of what works and what doesn't has grown tremendously, this information has been very slow to reach treatment providers and to affect the care they offer. In fact, many providers deliberately resist change because, they claim, "I know what worked for me, and I'm sure that it can work for everyone willing to do as I say." This attitude has stymied progress in the field and has prevented advances from being available to as many people as they should be. We hope that this book can help people seek the type of care they've decided makes sense for them—and, perhaps, consumer choices will push for change among those who believe that "one size fits all."

I (Joe) am often asked why I have spent the past 25 years of my life trying to understand addiction and how to find the best treatment for it. Contrary to most people's expectations, I have never had a problem with alcohol or other drugs, and no one in my immediate family has an addiction problem. Rather, I first became interested in addiction while a medical student after I received a rather dramatic wake-up call from a Vietnam veteran I treated.

1

I was working in the emergency room late one evening. A man who looked much older than his 40 years was coughing up blood. After a careful history and physical, I diagnosed his problem as "esophageal varices secondary to portal hypertension." Essentially, he had a failing liver, and his swollen fragile blood vessels were tearing. That, along with a deficiency in his blood-clotting system, had caused severe blood loss. I ordered a blood transfusion, and when an endoscopy confirmed my diagnosis, I felt quite satisfied with myself. Knowing that his problem was probably related to drinking, I discharged him when he was medically stable and told him to stop drinking. I even went so far as to get a list of local AA meetings for him. I quite proudly presented this case to my attending doctor the next morning and received a pat on the back for a nice job in diagnosing and treating the patient.

Two weeks later, the same man was back in the emergency room coughing blood and complaining that he'd been thrown out of his apartment. He said he was experiencing daily nightmares and that he needed to drink to knock himself out at night. Not surprisingly, his continued drinking had aggravated his medical condition. His eyes were yellowish, and his abdomen was filled with fluid. This time, I admitted him to the hospital and began a medical-detoxification program. On the second day, while on rounds with the attending doctor, several other medical students, an intern, and a junior resident, I presented this "interesting case." "Hold out your hands," I ordered, "Let's see how those tremors are doing today." He looked up at me frightened, complaining of spiders crawling up his legs. He then shouted, "Doc, I need your help," and held out his hands. As I reached out to his left hand to test for a tremor, he punched me square on the jaw with his right.

After that stunning experience, I developed a healthy respect for the problems associated with addiction. In my arrogance, I had failed to respond this man's pain or his core problem: He wouldn't be able to stop drinking and improve his liver problems unless the posttraumatic stress disorder that was driving his nightmares was also addressed. While many of my colleagues have become angry at patients like the vet, who repeatedly show up drunk in the emergency room, seemingly unwilling to take the good advice the doctors offer, I have found the problem to be an interesting challenge. That man, in the midst of his DTs (delirium tremens) understood more about addiction than did any of the writers of my textbooks. He showed me very literally that addiction hurts not only the person who suffers it but the people around him, as well.

I began to ask about addiction problems among my patients, and another homeless man, named Jim, became my best teacher. While I have been blessed by wonderful mentors, it was my conversations with Jim that most shaped my thinking about addiction. Perhaps the most important lesson was seeing his transformation as he sobered up. Not only did his physical problems improve, but he also seemed to undergo a fundamental healing in his relationships with his family and with himself. I had seen the remarkable effects of heart transplants and the wonder of childbirth, but watching this man's transformation during his recovery was unlike anything else I had ever seen in medicine. With many medical and psychiatric problems, improvement is gradual and often incomplete. Jim's turnaround, however, was dramatic.

I dedicated myself to finding out why this intelligent, good man who cared about his family and society had come to a point in his life where nothing had mattered to him but the next drink. I wanted to know, too, what could help others like him achieve the remarkable recovery Jim had.

During my years in medical school, I also earned a Ph.D. in psychology. I studied animal models of addiction. From my basic research, I learned how stress can make animals drink more alcohol—and how certain drugs, such as naltrexone, can prevent this response. During my residency in psychiatry, I learned more about various treatment options, including cognitive-behavioral therapy and medications such as methadone for drug addiction. Also, while completing my postgraduate fellowship in addiction, I began a clinical trial of naltrexone to treat alcoholism in humans at the Philadelphia VA Medical Center. This research resulted in the discovery of the first new medication approved for alcoholism treatment by the U.S. Food and Drug Administration (FDA) in the past 50 years—and it can cut the risk of relapse by 50% among those who take it.

Why do only a tiny minority of treatment centers offer this drug to their patients, and why haven't we heard more about it? Unfortunately, several factors are involved. A moralistic assumption that addiction is a personal choice seems to underlie most of our treatment for alcohol and other drug problems—even in rehab centers run by people who say they believe that addiction is a disease requiring medical care. One day, while driving to work, I saw a bumper sticker with the Nancy Reagan antidrug motto, "Just Say No," on it. Thinking about the prevalence and belief in the utility of that simple slogan, I realized one reason why it was so hard for treatment providers to begin utilizing the new medication.

If you assume that addiction is a matter of self-control summed up by the "Just Say No" slogan, then there must be a moral, characterological, or spiritual weakness in people who abuse drugs. If this is the case, then measures such as imprisoning them for years, taking their property, and condemning them in prevention campaigns such as the "users are losers" TV spot, make sense. Giving alcoholics and other addicts drugs to ease their craving or withdrawal is not helpful from this perspective. Even if the medications themselves cannot be abused, it is seen as cheating because it makes the hard task of overcoming one's weaknesses easier.

For me, however, this view of addicts as weak and deserving of pain and punishment did not square with what I knew about the many remarkable people I had met who had become alcoholics or other kinds of addicts. They were successful businesspeople, loving fathers and mothers, bright college kids, and many plain ordinary, decent people like Jim, who had just happened to develop a problem with alcohol or other drugs. As they recovered, they were reborn and returned to their formerly positive and productive lives. From my observations working with addicts and from clinical and basic research, it was clear that addiction was not a choice. Instead, the interactions among the drug, the person's life experiences, and the person's brain caused the problem—not some character flaw or moral weakness.

Perhaps nowhere in all of medicine is there a bigger gulf between clinical practice and clinical research than in the field of addiction. Alan Leshner, the Director of the National Institute of Drug Abuse, speaks of the "great divide" between research and treatment practice. Misperceptions about how people become addicted and how to free people from addiction permeate public policy, the news media, and public opinion. I decided that if my research was ever to reach the alcoholics who could benefit from it, I would have to help bridge the gap between what we think we know about addiction and effective treatment, and what addiction actually is and what actually works to treat it.

In order to get a sense of what people who were treating addicts in the community were thinking, I joined an Internet mailing list consisting of a wide cross-section of people interested in the issue. It was there that I met my co-author, Maia Szalavitz. The mailing list, supposedly devoted to "academic and scholarly discussion of addiction-related topics," was, in reality, a battlefield. People who held varying notions about alcohol and other drug problems came to joust with others over the superiority of various positions. There were recovering alcoholics and other addicts who believed in 12-step programs, academics who thought cognitive and behavioral approaches were the only way to deal with substance misuse, people who believed alcoholism didn't exist and that all alcoholics can learn to control their drinking, and even a Freudian psychoanalyst. Few were willing to acknowledge that some people would benefit from an approach other than their own—and few could see that this narrow-mindedness might hurt some of those they so sought to help. The only thing the group seemed to have in common was that none of the treatment professionals offered naltrexone as an option.

Maia came to the list as a journalist who was also an ex-addict. Her position was, "if it helps people, do it," and over time, she became increasingly convinced that those who needed help weren't getting the benefits of treatment advances. The list showed that many longtime drug counselors weren't even aware that research had found their basic beliefs about addiction to be wrong and their practice to be harmful. Despite contrary evidence, they continued to force people to accept the one method they believed was the only possible road to recovery.

In any other field, a discovery like ours, which has been hailed as one of the most important recent contributions to addiction treatment, would be picked up and used by most professionals once it was published. The scientific community recognizes its importance—I was recently awarded the Joel Elkes International Award in Psychopharmacology. The addiction-treatment community, however, is particularly resistant to change.

As a researcher, I have long been frustrated by the alcoholism and addiction field's reliance on miracle cures and horror stories, rather than on science, to guide patient care. After all, most Americans with diabetes or even an emotional problem such as depression wouldn't accept being told by a doctor that praying and "turning your will and life over to the care of God as you understand Him," as AA suggests, is the only treatment for their illness. Why shouldn't alcoholics and other addicts get research-based medicine the way people do for any other disease? While AA and the other 12-step groups have certainly worked well for many, the medical profession has not best served patients or even 12-step programs by claiming that they are the *only* valid method of recovery.

Both Maia and I came to the conclusion that to get the best care, patients themselves need to know what to look for—because many professionals have too much of an attachment to their own ideas of what should work to take into account individual differences. As a result, we decided to collaborate on this book. There is no other book like it—all the previous popular accounts of substance-abuse treatment have been focused mainly on helping patients accept one particular approach to care, rather than informing them about the debates in the field and letting them make up their own minds. All of them tend to be vague in their accounts of what actually takes place in treatment—for fear of scaring people off.

We respect your intelligence more than that. We know that if you are seeking help for yourself or for a friend or loved one, you want clear, concise information to guide you through a very difficult time. We know that most people would rather be informed than left to wonder what the jargon being thrown at them really means. We also know that people are looking for alternatives now in particular. Some have found the "AA one true way" to be unhelpful to them. They have tired of being told that they need to leave their critical-thinking skills behind if they are to recover, and that their families are complicit codependents who have an intersecting disease. They want to know more about getting better than is offered by people whose only knowledge of addiction has been gained from personal experience. While personal experience is crucial to understanding addiction, it's not the only valid source of wisdom. You wouldn't listen only to people who had undergone heart transplants while ignoring what the doctors who treated them said and refusing to look at medical research showing the probability of success in particular types of cases. A person considering treatment should want to know about it from all angles. We hope to put all the conflicting perspectives on alcoholism and other forms of addiction in context.

The good news is that there is effective treatment for alcohol and other drug problems, and the odds are in your favor that if you are seeking help, you will recover. We want to show you how—without sugar-coating the truth or hiding what treatment is really like. We want to demystify treatment so that you know what to expect, what you want for your own recovery, and what is appropriate and inappropriate care.

Our book is divided into three parts. In the first section, "The Problem and the Search for Solutions," we explore what addiction is—and what it isn't. We look at how drugs work, what their real dangers are, and how the dangers can be minimized so that alcoholics and other addicts are as healthy as possible when they are ready to recover. We also examine why some people are particularly prone to alcoholism and other forms of addiction and the genetic and learning mechanisms that help create these conditions.

The remainder of this part provides an introduction to the various types of treatment and the ideas on which they are based. It discusses how effective

treatment succeeds—and which types of treatment are not effective. For loved
ones and families, it lays out the "stages of change" that people go through in
their recoveries and tells how to help people move through them and get what
they need to progress in each phase. We also provide tips for people with drug
problems, to help reduce their fear and motivate them to change. Finally, this
section offers a guide to choosing treatment—and questions to ask to find the
best treatment facility once you have decided on the most suitable treatment
type.

The second part, "The Options," provides more detailed information about
each kind of treatment—including our treatment system at the University of
Pennsylvania, Alcoholics Anonymous and other self-help groups, moderation
programs, methadone, and various kinds of residential treatment. We examine
medications used to detoxify from alcohol and other drugs and to fight cravings.
Each chapter includes stories of patients' experiences with recovery by each
method—both positive and negative, wherever possible. There is also a special
chapter on treatment for teenagers and a chapter on alternative treatment. Each
chapter also summarizes the research on the treatment type it covers and
includes specific things to look for which exemplify the best care in that particular treatment.

Part Three, "Life after Treatment," contains the information you need to
help stay clean and sober and to prevent relapse—and to minimize any damage
caused by slips that do occur. It provides suggestions for dealing with the emotional difficulties that can arise at the start of recovery, as well as information on
what to do if these prove to be clinical conditions such as depression, anxiety
disorders, or posttraumatic stress disorders.

Throughout the book, you will find sidebars with special information for
loved ones and family members—and some that highlight particular points for
people with drug problems themselves. There are diagnostic tests, and other
summaries and tips to underscore important information.

The people who have shared their stories here are real—though their names
have been changed to pseudonyms. In the rare instances where we use com-
posites to illustrate particular points, their names appear italicized at first mention.

Readers of this book shouldn't have to blindly fumble their way into treatment, the way Maia did when she needed help. They'll know the lingo, they'll
know the theories, and they'll know what outcomes research has found about
particular approaches with particular people. They'll have heard from people
who have been there—and learned from their experiences and mistakes. In
rehab, even more than in clothes shopping, an educated consumer is the best
customer.

PART ONE

The Problem and the Search for Solutions

CHAPTER 1

Understanding Problems with Alcohol and Other Drugs

Noah, a man of the soil, proceeded to plant a vineyard. When he drank some of its wine, he became drunk and lay uncovered inside his tent. Ham, the father of Canaan, saw his father's nakedness and told his two brothers outside. But Shem and Japheth took a garment and laid it across their shoulders; then they walked in backward and covered their father's nakedness. Their faces were turned so they would not see their father's nakedness.

Genesis 9:20

Psychoactive substances have fascinated, befuddled, bewitched, and terrified humanity since time immemorial. Some anthropologists (no, not just those found on barstools!) reckon that the invention of beer-making processes was a crucial step in the progress of civilization. Desire for beer may have spurred early tribes to settle down and farm its ingredients. Throughout much of history, alcoholic beverages were the primary source of fluids for city dwellers because water was too contaminated to drink, and alcohol kills many microorganisms. In fact drug use predates human history. Many animal species seek out intoxicating plants and happily consume fermented grain.

We know of no human culture that does not make use of psychoactive drugs—often in a way central to their religious and celebratory rituals. Even the Chukchee, Siberian tribespeople who live in the most hostile Northern regions, rooted out a mushroom with intoxicating properties and learned further (one hates to speculate on how), that these properties were greatly magnified if you ingested the urine of those who ate the mushroom. Urine is few people's first choice as an intoxicating beverage, but with few other available agents to alter consciousness, drinking it became part of Chukchee culture.

It is often hard to admit that there is anything positive about drug use when you are addicted and want to quit or are dealing with an alcoholic or other addict whose life is being ruined by it. Also, most books on treatment and recovery don't mention anything good at all about substance use, for fear of encouraging it. However, it's crucial to learn why these substances are attractive if you want to understand addiction and recover from it. To understand maladaptive drug use, you first need to recognize that use itself is not always wrong or harmful, despite attempts by various factions to convince us otherwise.

It's also important to recognize that the vast majority of drinkers and other drug users—including those who try heroin and cocaine—never become addicted or even suffer short-term drug problems. Just 5% of marijuana users take the drug daily on a long-term basis, and only 10–20% of those who try alcohol, heroin, or cocaine suffer the problems that would define them as "abusers"—an even smaller proportion of these "abusers" can be labeled "addicts" or "alcoholics." The only drug that hooks the vast majority of its regular users is nicotine.

These observations suggest very strongly that pharmacology alone cannot explain drug problems—because if it did, most drugs should hook most people. To understand and recover from addiction, you need to understand not only how drugs affect the brain in general, but also what is different about those who can "take it or leave it," and those who try and fail in their efforts to stop.

Am I an Alcoholic or an Addict?

You would think that there would be an easy answer to the question "Am I addicted to alcohol or other drugs?" which plagues substance users and their loved ones. However, defining and diagnosing alcoholism and other forms of addiction is harder than it sounds. Some examples can illustrate why.

Robert is a 29-year-old website designer. He smokes pot daily—on weekends, four to five joints. His work has been praised by his clients, but he has also lost business because he missed deadlines. His fiancée recently broke their engagement because she felt he wasn't really "there" for her—and that his use was out of hand. He feels that she was just too demanding. He has a 3-year-old son from a previous relationship, and while his former partner does not approve of his lifestyle, she admits that he is wonderful with the boy and never skimps on child support.

Janet is a 47-year-old programmer and mother of two, who suffers from chronic pain due to injuries sustained in a car accident. She has tried everything—from aspirin to electrical stimulation. Nothing has helped but large doses of opiates. Fearing addiction, she weaned herself from the drugs, but after undergoing withdrawal, she was unable to function because of her pain. Two months later, she was doing little more than lying in bed, putting her job in jeopardy and minimizing her ability to care for her kids. When her doctor insisted she begin taking opiates again, she stuck to her prescribed (although large) doses, and her husband, kids, and boss all support her contention that she is happier, healthier, and more productive now.

Chris is a 32-year-old drinker. He drinks almost nonstop from Friday evening through Sunday night. Though most of his drinking is restricted to weekends, he has been missing work on Mondays due to hangovers. His girlfriend is concerned. She says she doesn't like how he acts when he is drunk. When she convinces him to "take a weekend off," he mopes and can speak of nothing but how she's a killjoy and that there's nothing wrong with "hoisting a few."

Virginia, 41, snorts cocaine twice a year as a "celebration." She usually stays up all night and generally consumes about a quarter of a gram. She only uses on New Year's Eve and her birthday and has maintained this pattern since attending college 20 years ago. While in school, she used coke twice a month but cut back when she found that she didn't like the way she felt afterward. She drinks wine with dinner. She also smokes an occasional joint and has taken Ecstasy (MDMA, a popular club drug). Her drinking and other drug use have never interfered with her work, and she believes they are a meaningful part of her social life, to be enjoyed and savored.

Is Janet an addict? What about Robert and Virginia? Is Chris an alcoholic? Simply looking at how much or how often each of them consumes their substance does not tell the whole story. Chris drinks less often than Janet takes her drugs—and he doesn't undergo severe withdrawal symptoms after a binge. Many would argue, however, that despite the fact that Janet is a daily user and is physically dependent on opiates (when she stops taking them, she becomes sick), she shows none of the important signs of addiction. She is not obsessed with drugs, she takes them as prescribed, and her life is improved, not diminished, by them. Meanwhile, Chris, who doesn't drink every day, is experiencing problems as a result of his alcohol consumption, and his life is dominated by thoughts of when he can next indulge. While Robert uses every day, the consequences of his pot smoking are not as clear cut—he might be losing out because he smokes too much, or he might just have a slacker personality. Virginia, however, has not experienced any problems as a result of her drug use.

Many who studied addiction, in search of a way to quantify the problem, often missed much of its essence as a result. *Physical addiction* (or "dependence," as it is properly called) was seen as more important than *psychological addiction* because it could be measured and was visible. As a result, cocaine was seen as "nonaddictive" as late as the 1980s—because it didn't produce the dramatic illness seen in withdrawing heroin addicts. In 1982, *Scientific American* went so far as to compare coke addiction with the desire for more potato chips.

For most people, however, the psychological aspects of addiction—the impaired ability to control the use of the drug, the craving, the depression as it wears off, the life consequences—are far more important than the physical withdrawal symptoms or how often the drug is actually used. People taking painkillers to treat pain due to burns or other painful conditions often withdraw from drugs stronger than heroin with no more discomfort than people suffering the flu—it's only when your psychological comfort and emotional well-being depend on access to a drug that heroin withdrawal becomes hell. If you don't need to have pain killed, you probably won't want painkillers for long, basically. Rather than being trivial then, the mental state of the addict is crucial to understanding addiction. Also, increasing knowledge of how the brain works shows that the psychological *is* physical, and vice versa—because all our thoughts, desires, dreams, and fears must be encoded somehow.

Modern definitions of drug problems try to take all of this into account. The most widely used scheme for defining substance problems is found in the American Psychiatric Association's *Diagnostic and Statistical Manual*. There are two levels of drug problems that can be diagnosed: abuse and dependence.

When Is It a Problem?

The essence of these definitions is that a substance abuser has experienced some level of problems related to his or her use of psychoactive substances, but he or she does not have either the major difficulty stopping or cutting down, or the long-term entrenched problems that an addict does. A substance abuser may be headed for substance dependence, but the vast majority (research estimates about three out of four) are able to outgrow their problems, with little or no assistance, usually by their mid to late 20s. This finding has obvious implications for dealing with teen drug problems, but, unfortunately, because the line between abuse and dependence is so fuzzy, it's almost impossible to predict who will mature out of the problem naturally and who will need help.

Don't worry too much about whether you or your loved one is "really an addict" or "just abusing." What's important is to realize that use has started to become problematic and to recognize and understand the nature of the process that can occur if control over using continues to lapse.

Diagnostic Criteria for Substance Dependence and Substance Abuse

Substance Dependence
A maladaptive pattern of substance use, leading to clinically significant impairment or distress, as manifested by three (or more) of the following, occurring at any time in the same 12-month period:
   (1) tolerance, as defined by either of the following:
       (a) a need for markedly increased amounts of the substance to achieve intoxication or desired effect
       (b) markedly diminished effect with continued use of the same amount of the substance
   (2) withdrawal, as manifested by either of the following:
       (a) the characteristic withdrawal syndrome for the substance (refer to Criteria A and B of the criteria sets for Withdrawal from the specific substances)
       (b) the same (or a closely related) substance is taken to relieve or avoid withdrawal symptoms
   (3) the substance is often taken in larger amounts over a longer period than was intended
   (4) there is a persistent desire or unsuccessful efforts to cut down or control substance use
   (5) a great deal of time is spent in activities necessary to obtain the substance (e.g., visiting multiple doctors or driving long distances), use the substance (e.g., chain-smoking), or recover from its effects

(6) important social, occupational, or recreational activities are given up or reduced because of substance use

(7) the substance use is continued despite knowledge of having persistent or recurrent physical or psychological problem that is likely to have been caused or exacerbated by the substance (e.g., current cocaine use despite recognition of cocaine-induced depression, or continued drinking despite recognition that an ulcer was made worse by alcohol consumption)

Substance Abuse

A. A maladaptive pattern of substance use leading to clinically significant impairment or distress, as manifested by one (or more) of the following, occurring within a 12-month period:

(1) recurrent substance use resulting in a failure to fulfill major role obligations at work, school, or home (e.g., repeated absences or poor work performance related to substance use; substance-related absences, suspensions, or expulsions from school; neglect of children or household)

(2) recurrent substance use in situations in which it is physically hazardous (e.g., driving an automobile or operating a machine when impaired by substance use)

(3) recurrent substance-related legal problems (e.g., arrests for substance-related disorderly conduct)

(4) continued substance use despite having persistent or recurrent social or interpersonal problems caused or exacerbated by the effects of the substance (e.g., arguments with spouse about consequences of intoxication, physical fights)

B. The symptoms have never met the criteria for Substance Dependence for this class of substance.

Addiction

Addiction begins when someone has extreme difficulty controlling, cutting down, or stopping drug use despite repeated negative consequences related to it. Note that this definition does not require physical dependence and that physical dependence doesn't always mean addiction. Here, Janet is not an addict because her use of painkillers is helpful and productive, not harmful. Although some alcoholics and other addicts may claim that their use is a positive thing, if they do have a problem, they will probably not, unlike Janet, be supported in continued drug taking by their family, their workplace, and their doctors! Chris, however, may well be an alcoholic or on his way to becoming one, and Robert, too, has at least a substance-abuse problem and quite possibly an addiction to marijuana, although some may argue that he may simply prefer a slacker lifestyle to achievement. Virginia, however, meets no criteria for drug abuse or dependence and, aside from the fact that some of the substances she takes are illegal, would be considered by most to be simply a recreational, controlled user.

How can you tell where your own drinking or other drug use fits in and what steps you should take to deal with it? Here are some screening tests for alcohol and other drug problems. They can help you determine whether you should see a professional to further assess the problem.

CAGE Screening Test

C　Have you ever felt the need to cut down on your drinking? [drug use]

A　Have you ever felt annoyed by someone criticizing your drinking? [drug taking]

G　Have you ever felt bad or guilty about your drinking? [drug use]

E　Have you ever had a drink first thing in the morning to steady your nerves and get rid of a hangover? (eye-opener) [or a drug to relieve withdrawal]

If you answered "yes" to one or more of these questions, you may have a problem and should consider getting help. As you will see later, a complete assessment to determine the level of severity of the substance problem and to diagnose any other problems that may be driving it is an important first step. To further examine the nature and seriousness of your problem, you may also want to try a second screening test. The first of the following three tests covers alcohol use, the second other kinds of drug use, and the third specifically addresses cocaine use.

Alcohol Use Disorders Identification Test (Audit)

1.　How often do you have a drink containing alcohol?

Never (0)

Monthly or less (1)

2 to 3 times a month (2)

2 to 3 times a week (3)

4 or more times a week (4)

2.　How many alcoholic drinks do you have on a typical drinking day?

None (0)

1 or 2 (1)

3 or 4 (2)

5 or 6 (3)

7 to 9 (4)

10 or more (5)

3. How often do you have six or more drinks on one occasion?

Never	(0)
Less than monthly	(1)
Monthly	(2)
Weekly	(3)
Daily or almost daily	(4)

4. How often during the past year have you found that you were unable to stop drinking once you had started?

Never	(0)
Less than monthly	(1)
Monthly	(2)
Weekly	(3)
Daily or almost daily	(4)

5. How often during the past year have you failed to do what was normally expected of you because of drinking?

Never	(0)
Less than monthly	(1)
Monthly	(2)
Weekly	(3)
Daily or almost daily	(4)

6. How often during the past year have you needed a drink first thing in the morning to get yourself going after a heavy drinking session?

Never	(0)
Less than monthly	(1)
Monthly	(2)
Weekly	(3)
Daily or almost daily	(4)

7. How often during the past year have you had a feeling of guilt or remorse after drinking?

Never	(0)
Less than monthly	(1)
Monthly	(2)
Weekly	(3)
Daily or almost daily	(4)

8. How often during the past year have you been unable to remember what happened the night before because you were drinking?

Never	(0)
Less than monthly	(1)
Monthly	(2)
Weekly	(3)
Daily or almost daily	(4)

9. Have you or someone else ever been injured as a result of your drinking?

Never	(0)
Less than monthly	(1)
Monthly	(2)
Weekly	(3)
Daily or almost daily	(4)

10. Has a relative, friend, or doctor or other health worker been concerned about your drinking or suggested you cut down?

Never	(0)
Less than monthly	(1)
Monthly	(2)
Weekly	(3)
Daily or almost daily	(4)

Record the total score. Eight or higher means you should get a professional evaluation.

Source: World Health Organization (WHO), 1987.

Substance Use Disorders Test

1. How often do you take recreational drugs?

Never	(0)
Monthly or less	(1)
2 to 3 times a month	(2)
2 to 3 times a week	(3)
4 or more times a week	(4)

2. How often do you take enough drugs that your functioning is at least moderately impaired?

Never	(0)
Less than monthly	(1)

Monthly   (2)

Weekly   (3)

Daily or almost daily   (4)

3. How often during the past year have you found that you were unable to stop taking drugs once you had started?

Never   (0)

Less than monthly   (1)

Monthly   (2)

Weekly   (3)

Daily or almost daily   (4)

4. How often during the past year have you failed to do what was normally expected of you because of drug use?

Never   (0)

Less than monthly   (1)

Monthly   (2)

Weekly   (3)

Daily or almost daily   (4)

5. How often during the past year have you needed drugs as soon as you awaken to get yourself going or to avoid withdrawal symptoms?

Never   (0)

Less than monthly   (1)

Monthly   (2)

Weekly   (3)

Daily or almost daily   (4)

6. How often during the past year have you had a feeling of guilt or remorse after taking drugs?

Never   (0)

Less than monthly   (1)

Monthly   (2)

Weekly   (3)

Daily or almost daily   (4)

7. How often during the past year did you experience serious physical symptoms related to your drug use (e.g., for heroin, withdrawal or overdose; for cocaine, overdose, more than 24 hours awake, paranoia, or seriously elevated heart rate; for marijuana, oversleeping or forgetfulness; for multiple drugs, overdose or any of the aforementioned symptoms).

Never   (0)

Less than monthly   (1)

Monthly   (2)

Weekly   (3)

Daily or almost daily   (4)

8.   Have you or someone else ever been injured as a result of your drug use?

Never   (0)

Less than monthly   (1)

Monthly   (2)

Weekly   (3)

Daily or almost daily   (4)

9.   Has a relative, friend, or doctor or other health worker been concerned about your drug use or suggested you cut down?

Never   (0)

Less than monthly   (1)

Monthly   (2)

Weekly   (3)

Daily or almost daily   (4)

Record the total specific items. If you score higher than seven, you should get a further evaluation because you may have a substance-abuse problem.

Source: Adapted from WHO, AUDIT.

Cocaine Withdrawal Severity Assessment

Date:	Date of Last Cocaine Use:	Score

1. OVEREATING: 0 = normal appetite; 3–4 = eats a lot more than usual; 7 = eats more than twice usual amount of food _____

2. UNDEREATING: 0 = normal appetite; 3–4 = eats less than half of normal amount; 7 = no appetite at all _____

3. CARBOHYDRATE CRAVING: 0 = no craving; 3–4 = strong craving for sweets, half the time; 7 = strong craving for sweets, all the time _____

4. COCAINE CRAVING INTENSITY: 0 = no desire; 3–4 = strong desire for cocaine; 7 = unable to resist the temptation _____

5. CRAVING FREQUENCY: 0 = no craving; 3–4 = strong craving for cocaine, half the time; 7 = strong craving for cocaine, all the time _____

6. SLEEP I: 0 = normal amount of sleep; 3–4 = half of normal amount; 7 = no sleep at all _____

7. SLEEP II: 0 = normal amount of sleep; 3–4 = could or do sleep half the day; 7 = sleep or could sleep all the time _____

8. ANXIETY: 0 = usually do not feel anxious; 3–4 = feel anxious half the time; 7 = feel anxious all the time _____

9. ENERGY LEVEL: 0 = feel alert and have usual amount of energy; 3–4 = feel tired half the time; 7 = feel tired all the time _____

10. ACTIVITY LEVEL: 0 = no change in usual activities; 3–4 = participate in half of usual activities; 7 = no participation in usual activities _____

11. TENSION: 0–1 = rarely feel tense; 3–4 = feel tense half the time; 7 = feel tense most or all the time _____

12. ATTENTION: 0 = able to concentrate on reading, conversation, tasks, and make plans without difficulty; 3–4 = difficulty with the preceding half the time; 7 = difficulty with the preceding all the time _____

13. PARANOID IDEATION: 0 = no evidence of paranoid thoughts; 3–4 = unable to trust anyone; 5 = feel people are out to get them; 7 = feel a specific person/group is plotting against them _____

14. PLEASURELESSNESS: 0 = ability to enjoy self remains unchanged; 3–4 = able to enjoy self half of the time; 7 = unable to enjoy self at all _____

15. DEPRESSION: 0 = no feelings related to sadness or depression; 3–4 = feel sad or depressed half the time; 7 = feel depressed all of the time _____

16. SUICIDALITY: 0 = does not think about being dead; 3–4 = feel like life is not worth living; 7 = feel like actually ending life _____

17. IRRITABILITY: 0 = feel that most things are not irritating; 3–4 = feel that many things are irritating; 7 = feel that mostly everything is irritating and upsetting _____

TOTAL: _____

Note. If after a cocaine binge, you use this chart and score above 20, then you should seek medical help for your problem. You may want to ask your doctor for a prescription of a drug called amantadine to help you get through withdrawal. This drug does not have abuse potential and can safely be used in conjunction with outpatient treatment or counseling and self-help groups. A recent study we did found that those scoring higher than 20 had virtually no chance of treatment success without medications to help with withdrawal.

For Family Members and Other Loved Ones: Does the Shoe Fit?

If you are close to someone with a substance-abuse problem, you will probably know it before he or she does. This can lead to friction in your relationship as you try to convince your loved one to stop or cut down, and this person ignores you or becomes angry. Before you take action, first consider the examples of the drug problems described here previously. Try to apply the diagnostic criteria. If they fit, you will find techniques here to help you help your loved one. As you learn how people with substance problems think, you can help them decide for themselves that they need to change.

Joe

Call Your Problem Whatever You Like!

It's amazing how hard it can be for people to admit to having an alcohol or other drug problem that is obvious to everyone else. You might have three DWIs (driving while intoxicated citations), a broken nose from a bar fight, and no money because you spent your last cent on booze, but saying the words "alcoholic" and "I am a" in the same sentence is still difficult. For me, though I was shooting heroin daily, I wasn't "addicted." I just didn't feel like stopping.

Don't worry about whether you are convinced. It doesn't matter. There's no link between saying "I am an alcoholic / addict" and getting better. People who don't say it recover just as often as those who do, surprisingly. The only thing you have to admit to yourself is that something has to change—you don't have to say anything to anyone else. You can go to support groups and just listen, you can keep your decision private, you can try quitting as an experiment, and you can always change your mind. You can call your problem anything you want, so long as you start to think about addressing it. Also, if you do decide to try recovery for a month or so, the decision isn't irrevocable. The alcohol and other drugs will still be out there.

Maia

So how does it all get started? What makes addiction take hold in one person, but allows another to drink or take other drugs casually without problems? What makes someone ready to tackle an addiction problem, whereas someone else has to be dragged from the gutter to the clinic? To answer these questions, we need to understand more about the various types of drugs, the people they appeal to and the effect they have on the brain, and the way that genes can interact with learning to create a cycle of escalating substance use and self-destructive behavior in certain circumstances.

CHAPTER 2

Drugs 101

Many people think they already know how alcohol and other drugs work and what risks they take if they use them. However, both street myths and government propaganda have made the facts about drugs hard to recognize in the midst of stories spun to push various agendas. Because there are so many misconceptions as a result, it's important for everyone involved with alcohol and other drugs—even if only through family members or friends—to know the truth. By understanding what people like about particular drugs, loved ones can gain insights on what addicts need for recovery. Also, if an alcoholic or other addict is not yet ready to stop using, being well-informed about the risks and how to minimize them can mean the difference between life and death. Here are the basics.

How Drugs Work

If drugs are to change your mental and emotional state, they must first reach your brain and interact with the chemicals your brain uses to send signals from one cell to another. Each brain cell is called a *neuron*. Neural signaling is believed to be what allows us to think, feel, and experience.

This sounds simple, but its implications are profound. All of our thoughts and emotions must be represented by brain activity. Because psychoactive drugs affect brain activity, this class of drugs affects how we think and feel. All our experiences change the brain. All we learn must also therefore change the brain—otherwise we couldn't remember and store it—and so another way of affecting brain chemistry can be by talking or having experiences. Reading this book will literally rewire part of your brain—that is, if it teaches you something new.

In terms of treatment, this means that both "talk therapies" (such as AA and most of what goes on in rehabs and counseling sessions) and medications may actually have the same effect when they work. In fact, a recent study supported this idea quite strongly and graphically. The study's authors were trying to help patients with *obsessive-compulsive disorder*, a psychiatric condition that causes people to become overwhelmed by irrational fears and to perform certain repeated rituals in an attempt to dispel them. They treated some patients with medication and others with a type of talk therapy called *cognitive-behavioral therapy*, which taught the patients that their fears were unrealistic and that they could be safe without performing their personal rituals. When the researchers looked at brain scans of the people who overcame the problem—whether they were in the drug group or the talk-therapy group—the same area had changed. Drugs and talk therapy had the same physical effect: to make their brains look and act more normally. The brain can be similarly changed by chemical and psychological means.

Further research has found that simultaneously using talk therapies and drug treatments for mental illness enhances the effectiveness of each type alone. As a result, the state-of-the-art treatment for conditions from depression and obsessive-compulsive disorder to alcoholism and other forms of addiction often involves using medication and talk therapy together.

DRUGS TO FIGHT DRUGS?

I'm often asked whether using drugs to treat addiction simply replaces one problem with another. Is it like using chocolate ice cream to replace chocolate candy abuse? Actually, it's more like using fire to fight fire— there are some situations in which this is the only way to proceed. When you recognize how profoundly addiction affects the brain, it's not surprising that chemical assistance is often useful. Some people get addicted because their brain chemistry was off to begin with. If you don't deal with whatever they were trying to self-medicate, they are highly likely to relapse. Others create a brain-chemistry problem for themselves by using drugs over time. Medications alone rarely offer complete recovery from addiction, but without them, some recoveries would never begin, and others wouldn't last very long.

Joe

The Brain's Complex Cells

Even at the level of a single cell, the brain's processes are complicated. Each nerve cell has an area for receiving messages (the *dendrites*), an area for consolidating them (the *cell body*), and a long projection, which serves like a telephone wire to get the message to where it is needed (the *axon*). The receiving end is a forest of dendrites—branchlike projections—which collect input from thousands of other neurons. This input is in the form of chemical messengers called *neurotransmitters*, which move from one neuron to another in a space called a *synapse*. After they have been squirted into the synapse, these chemical messengers fit into receptors on the receiving neuron. This works like a lock and key—only the correct chemicals will open the lock and affect the second neuron. As with a real doorway, there are various ways to pick the lock, to prevent the door from being opened, and to make it open more easily. Drugs can perform all of these functions—affecting the way neurons communicate with each other and with themselves in the brain's various feedback loops. Over time the brain changes as a result of drug use, and these changes create a need to continue to use drugs.

The most important changes caused by drugs take place in the areas of the brain devoted to emotions. Emotions are the brain's way of motivating us to reproduce our genes—by making things that promote survival, such as food and sex, pleasurable, and by making things that could kill us, such as snakes or sexual rivals, frightening. Taken repeatedly, drugs start to fool these mechanisms by creating intense pleasure—making the brain believe that they enhance survival and that lack of them may be deadly. Let's look more closely at each class of drugs, how it works, what it tells us about addiction, and what potential dangers it poses.

Uppers: Stimulant Drugs

Stimulants—"uppers"—make people feel more alert and excited and less able to fall asleep. Rather than relaxation, they produce a euphoria of expectation and possibility. Drugs in this class include cocaine ("blow," and in smokeable form, "base," "rock," or "crack"), amphetamine, methamphetamine ("speed," "crystal meth"). These are often called "major" stimulants because of their strong and sometimes devastating effects. Methylphenidate (Ritalin), a drug used in the treatment of attention deficit disorder, is also in this group. Caffeine is a "minor" stimulant because its effects are not as pronounced.

How Stimulants Work

Researcher Donald Klein has posited two primary categories of pleasure: the pleasure of the hunt and the pleasure of the feast. Stimulants replicate the pleasure of the hunt—a building excitement, a sense of one's own power and capability, a heightening of awareness, a feeling that you can conquer anything. These feelings are similar to those involved in sexual desire and arousal, while the pleasures of the feast are more like satiation, contentment, orgasm, and afterglow.

This notion has important implications for the problems associated with each class of drugs and for the people most likely to be attracted to them. Stimulants frequently produce an escalating desire for more, but they ultimately prove unsatisfying and frightening, just as escalating sexual excitement without orgasm can soon prove more painful than pleasurable. Intense craving is the result and is most common with the more potent stimulants. One doesn't often see people who drink cup after cup of coffee in the compulsive way a cocaine addict does hit after hit of coke. Cocaine is also particularly addictive because it is *short acting*: Its effects wear off very quickly. Typically, a cocaine high lasts about 30–60 minutes. Smoked crack (or freebase) or injected cocaine is even more addictive than snorted coke because these effects come on more quickly and fall off more steeply.

It seems paradoxical, but the less time a drug high lasts, the easier it is to get hooked. One would think that amphetamine—which keeps you high for about six hours—would be preferred to cocaine because one gets more bang for the buck. Actually, however, getting high tends to be about contrast. You can't have contrast if you go up and stay up—you need to be able to go up, then down, and back up. Some people do prefer amphetamine, but others will try to use it as though it were cocaine and will overdose (OD) or come close to ODing because they take more before they've come down.

Cocaine works primarily by keeping *dopamine,* a neurotransmitter associated with pleasure and motivation, more readily available in the synapse. This is usually felt as euphoria coupled with a strong desire to repeat the experience. As one comic put it, "Cocaine makes you into a new man and the first thing the new man wants is more cocaine."

Cocaine also keeps active two other neurotransmitter chemicals important in the experience of pleasure (serotonin and noradrenaline), though not as strongly as it does dopamine. Amphetamine works similarly, with some additional twists that make its effects last longer. Caffeine, on the other hand, is believed to work by an entirely different mechanism. It blocks the receptor for a chemical called *adenosine,* which modulates brain activity by preventing neurons from staying active too long. Once neurons are stimulated, they keep firing, and the sum of this overall effect is to heighten awareness and reduce feelings of fatigue.

The Down Side

In high doses, cocaine and amphetamines can produce a psychosis nearly indistinguishable from schizophrenia. The person becomes paranoid, hears voices, and feels sensations of bugs all over his or her body. Loud sounds become unbearable—and most situations become overwhelming and filled with a sense of impending doom and terror. Many people decide that they are having a heart attack because their hearts pound so fast. The chances of violence—particularly for those with a history of it—are heightened, though most people without a violent past tend simply try to hide from others. They become extremely irritable and find any demand frightening and threatening.

As the level of the drug in the body drops, the overt paranoia decreases but is replaced by sluggishness, depression, and an ever-expanding feeling of hopelessness. If people have access to more of the drug at this point, they will almost certainly take it—even though it will prevent them from falling asleep and thus recovering, and it may bring back the paranoia. Because the drug itself activates a system telling the body to repeat an action, it is very difficult to get out of the loop even when the users know it will only actually bring more discomfort.

Fortunately, the vast majority of stimulant users who stop taking the drugs do not experience lasting psychosis. Both cocaine and amphetamines do elevate the risk of stroke and heart attack, however, and long-term users can suffer brain damage from tiny, repeated strokes. High doses can also result in seizures. Also, because stimulants cut appetite, users often become malnourished.

Caffeine addiction is far less worrying—even though the drug causes physical dependence, 47.2% of the U.S. population drinks coffee daily. As anyone who has tried to quit drinking coffee knows, headache and irritability are common caffeine-withdrawal signs. Because its negative health effects are so mild, however, most people prefer caffeine maintenance to abstinence; the only negative health effect that has been proven is an increase in panic attacks in those predisposed to them.

Around 10–20% of those who try cocaine and amphetamines will have difficulty cutting down or stopping their use. Those who use these drugs intravenously or who smoke these drugs have the hardest time quitting—and cocaine may hook a slightly larger group than the amphetamines do. The good news about major stimulant addiction is that it tends to run its course faster than opiate or alcohol addiction. The bad news is that this is because it is so wearing on the body and mind and so prone to creating a complete inability to function that within a few years, most either quit, switch addictions, or, unfortunately, die. Over three quarters of cocaine addicts are also alcoholics—and those who run their course quickly with coke may not necessarily give up drinking as fast.

Pay Attention: Attention Deficit Disorder and Stimulants

One group of people at particularly high risk for stimulant addiction is those who suffer attention deficit disorder (ADD). This problem—which is often related to hyperactivity in childhood, but which can occur without that as well—is marked by an inability to focus. About 6% of schoolchildren suffer ADD. Children with ADD often cannot sit still. Others daydream and can't pay attention long enough to do schoolwork. Many are extremely bright but have problems at school because of their inability to follow directions and their distractability.

The highest risk group of children is those with what is called ADD with conduct disorder. These kids behave badly—they are constantly in motion, they break things, and they ignore adult instruction. They seem not only inattentive but also willfully destructive. One mother of a child with the disorder put it this way: "It takes my child to raze a village." If untreated, children with ADD and conduct disorder have a 40% chance of growing up to have a substance-abuse disorder—four to five times greater than normal risk. Physicians used to believe that children with ADD grew out of it, but now it appears that for many, it is a lifetime problem.

ADD is most often treated with stimulants, Ritalin being used most frequently. People with this disorder find these drugs attractive and helpful because the drugs enable them to focus. They tend not to abuse these drugs when the drugs are properly prescribed. Researchers used to think stimulants had a paradoxical calming effect on hyperactive children, but in fact, the drugs increase alertness in these children, as they do in other people. However, the kids do act more calmly because their heightened awareness allows them enough concentration to sit still and stop moving. If, when you take cocaine, you find yourself better focused, mellower, and less frenzied, while others you are using with seem to be talking a mile a minute and increasingly "hyped up," you may have ADD; you should probably avoid further illicit stimulant use and get medically evaluated.

In order to prevent children with ADD from growing up and self-medicating with street drugs, proper treatment in childhood is essential. This can mean using stimulants or psychological therapies that allow the child to sit still and be comfortable. Do not avoid medications here for fear of addiction—addiction is more likely among those with untreated ADD. In fact, recent research finds that treating ADD in childhood reduces the risk of adolescent drug problems by 85%. Some adult stimulant addicts with ADD may need to be maintained on an appropriate stimulant in order to control their ADD, as well.

This does not just continue the addiction—remember, addiction is continued use despite negative consequences. In properly treated ADD, the consequences of proper medication are better functioning and a greater ability to sustain relationships. Active addiction to stimulants has the opposite effect because use goes beyond self-medication into intoxication and is at the mercy of fluctuating street supply, quality, and quantity. If you have a childhood history of ADD or believe that you suffer from extreme distractability, inability to focus (sometimes alternating with periods of intense focus), severe procrastination, and hypersensitivity, make sure you are properly evaluated for ADD when you seek help.

Opiates

Heroin ("junk," "smack," "brown," "china white"), morphine, codeine, methadone, opium, and percodan all belong to a class of drugs called *opiates*. Some are produced from the flower of the opium poppy, others are synthesized to have a shape that has similar effects on the brain.

Whereas the stimulants mimic the pleasures of the hunt, opiates are all about feasting, metaphorically. Rather than increasing awareness and activity, opiates are calming, relaxing, and satiating. In comparing stimulants and opiates, 10 minutes after a shot of cocaine, people tend to be anxious for more, whereas 10 minutes after a shot of heroin, users aren't looking for anything. They are sleepy ("nodding") and may drift in and out of dreams. The experience is one of being comfortable, safe, warm, and content—and beyond caring about emotional or physical pain.

How Opiates Work

Opiates work by fitting into the receptors for one system of the brain's natural painkillers. These natural painkillers are the *endogenous* (meaning "inside the body") opiates, and their effects are similar to those of the drugs. They are called endorphins (for endogenous morphine) and enkephalins (inside the head). When one takes opiates for a long enough time (the period varies, depending on the strength of the drug and the person's own constitution), physical dependence sets in. This is believed to result from a mechanism crucial to understanding addiction, caused by the brain's need to maintain a steady state.

Because the brain is a finely balanced electrochemical system, it is acutely sensitive to changes in its levels of neurotransmitters. Anything that moves a neurotransmitter out of its normal range (even if that range is abnormal but is typical for that person) will be met by an attempt to restore ordinary conditions.

What this means is that no high lasts forever—and that the more of a drug you take, the less effect it will ultimately have as your brain learns to kick in compensatory mechanisms more rapidly and intensely. If you get one big blitz of drug-related joy on Sunday, you may find that you lack pleasure Monday and Tuesday. The brain is very stingy with its "joy juice"—so sneaking out this potion with drugs now means having less of it later.

In the case of opiates, what happens is that as more of the drug is taken, the body reduces its own endogenous opiate production, and mechanisms to cut down on opiate effects are activated. These changes mean that the drug causes less of a high, and the user tends to increase the dose to compensate. Such a user has developed "tolerance." When the tolerant user can't get drugs, these "opponent processes" kick in anyway—assuming that they are going to have to fight against a high level of opiates. These opponent processes result in withdrawal symptoms as the body now confronts a shortage, rather than having to deal with a high level of opiates. Among the common opiate-withdrawal symptoms are nausea, vomiting, diarrhea, insomnia, anxiety, shakes, sweats, and body aches. The worst part of opiate withdrawal typically lasts four days, although in severe cases, symptoms can continue for up to a month.

Although opiate withdrawal has been dramatized by various authorities in order to aid prevention (and by opiate addicts seeking to explain why they couldn't possibly kick!), in fact, the physical symptoms are not much worse than a bad flu, with added anxiety and insomnia. Anyone who has suffered both a severe illness and opiate withdrawal can tell you that most serious illnesses (such as, say, hepatitis B) are far more physically debilitating and painful. Unlike withdrawal from alcohol, benzodiazepine, and barbiturates, withdrawal from opiates is not life threatening. The reason it is so uncomfortable for addicts has more to do with fear of being unable to survive emotionally without the drug and with associated depression than with the actual physical symptoms. Fear and depression are not concerns to be taken lightly, but they need a different remedy than simply dealing with physical signs of withdrawal.

Opiates are particularly attractive to those who are oversensitive to or who suffer high levels of emotional pain and trauma. For such opiate addicts to recover, these issues must be addressed. Also, sometimes, either because long-term use of opiates may permanently damage the system or because some addicts may have been attracted to opiates because they had a preexisting deficiency in this system, some addicts may not be able to live comfortably without long-term or even lifelong maintenance on an opiate drug.

Risks and Dangers

In terms of physical dangers, the major risk of opiate use is overdose, which can be fatal if not treated quickly. There is an antidote to opiate overdose, naloxone (Narcan), which can immediately reverse its symptoms. Prompt medical attention can easily mean the difference between life and death in these cases. Opiates themselves do not damage the liver or other internal organs. The ill health of most street-heroin addicts is related to unsanitary injections, malnutrition, and adulterated drugs, rather than to the pharmacology of opiates. Nonetheless, the death rate among opiate addicts is extremely high—from 6 to 20 times greater than would be expected for other people the same age. No one has yet determined whether this is because a drug with the reputation that heroin has (the "hardest" drug) attracts suicidal people or because the more you expose yourself to the risk of OD, HIV, and so on, the greater your chances of dying are. Either way, despite its relatively benign pharmacology at moderate, steady doses, it kills many of its users and kills them young.

Downers: Depressant Drugs

Drugs in this class include alcohol, the barbiturates (phenobarbital [Nembutal], secobarbital [Seconal], etc.), and benzodiazepines (diazepam [Valium], alprazolam [Xanax], flunitrazepam [Rohypnol], etc.). The term *depressant* can be a bit confusing—it was not meant to be the opposite of the mood-improving "antidepressant" drugs. The "depression" here refers to the fact that these drugs tend to reduce brain activity and promote calmness and relaxation—not sadness or low mood, though they can sometimes do that, as well. Few people deliberately set out to take drugs to make them feel worse, however!

How Downers Work

Alcohol was formerly thought to affect the brain nonspecifically by slowing down all of its processes. While it does affect numerous brain systems, particularly at high doses, its primary sedative effects appear to be related to its impact on a neurotransmitter called GABA (gamma-aminobutyric acid). Alcohol's pleasurable effects are probably due to its impact on endorphins.

Benzodiazepines have a similar effect on GABA transmission but act only on this transmitter, without the global slow-down that high doses of alcohol can cause. They also fit into a slightly different part of the receptor than alcohol does, meaning that they don't compete with each other to enhance GABA action. In practical terms, this means that if you take both alcohol and a benzodiazepine, the effect is synergistic. Not only do the drugs not cancel each other out, but one plus one equals three or more, and this is a common cause of overdose. Barbiturates and opiates also interact synergistically with alcohol. In fact, the vast majority of overdose deaths result from these combinations.

Drugs in the depressant group cause physical dependence. Again, about 10–20% of users become abusers or addicts. Withdrawal from depressants— including alcohol—can be deadly because fatal seizures can result from sudden abstinence by a dependent person. Other withdrawal symptoms include anxiety, hallucinations, sleeplessness, agitation, and disorientation. Medical care is needed to manage detox from depressants to ameliorate these symptoms.

People with anxiety disorders sometimes try to self-medicate their problems with alcohol—as with stimulant addicts with ADD or opiate addicts who have developed an opiate deficiency, maintenance on a benzodiazepine may be needed to treat the underlying condition. However, because alcohol is so socially acceptable and is legal, alcoholics may be self-medicating anything from ADD to schizophrenia. The importance of dealing with the reasons why someone uses—and providing healthier ways of coping with these problems— cannot be stressed enough.

For alcoholics with genuine anxiety disorders, benzodiazepines are prefer- able to continued drinking because these drugs do not cause organ damage and do not produce continued impairment once tolerance has been established. Also, some of the newer antianxiety drugs, such as buspirone (Buspar), don't cause physical dependence and can be tried, too.

Risks and Dangers

Despite the widespread cultural acceptance of alcohol, heavy use of it actually causes more physical damage than do opiates, and it is more likely to produce violence than is cocaine. Unlike the other drugs, however, it has health benefits when taken in moderation. Having one drink a day can reduce the likelihood of heart attack and stroke.

High doses of alcohol over long periods of time are incontrovertibly bad news, however—anyone who has been unable to moderate his or her drinking should not aim for the health benefits of light drinking, given the greater dan- gers from relapse into heavy use.

Alcohol damages the liver and disrupts immune-system function. Over time, large amounts can cause irreversible brain damage (Korsakoff's syndrome). High doses also increase the risk of heart disease and cancer. These effects inter- act synergistically with those of tobacco, making the odds that a heavy drinker who smokes will get head or neck cancer 6–15 times greater than the chances for someone who does neither; odds for throat cancer increase by a factor of 44. Drinking while pregnant is also extremely dangerous to the fetus—about one third of infants born to actively alcoholic mothers suffer some form of mental or physical impairment. Fetal alcohol syndrome is the most common cause of mental retardation.

About half of all accidents on the road and at home involve alcohol—and in 50% of murders, either the victim or the killer or both were drunk.

Nicotine

Our society's other legal drug of choice is the most deadly and addictive drug known, although unlike intoxicants such as alcohol, heroin, or cocaine, it doesn't impair functioning and doesn't usually kill its victims young. These two factors (and, of course, aggressive lobbying by the tobacco industry) have kept cigarettes and their main psychoactive ingredient, nicotine, from being seen as a real drug. The evidence has long shown otherwise.

How Nicotine Works

Nicotine is an unusual drug in several important ways. First, it actually enhances productivity and concentration—so long as you continue to take it. Nicotine isn't just a stimulant, however—it acts as a calming, tension-reducing drug, as well. The drug also has antidepressant and antipsychotic qualities, which is why so many people with serious mental disorders smoke and have extreme difficulty quitting. A cigarette will bring smokers up when they need a lift and down when they need to relax. Because of this, and the fact that it is short-acting and allows one to function while using, it is devilishly difficult to stop smoking.

Among regular cigarette smokers, 90% are physically dependent on nicotine. People who have quit both heroin and nicotine report that it is harder to stop smoking. Nicotine's brain effects are related to its similarity to a neurotransmitter called acetylcholine. By blocking one type of acetylcholine receptor in the brain—a type located on nerves near the midbrain dopamine tract—the drug increases the release of dopamine and serotonin. Smoking a cigarette is thus pharmacologically comparable to a very small hit of cocaine or amphetamine, with an additional relaxing component that results from the drug's peripheral effects on muscle tension.

Severe Consequences

Most people can reel off the negative effects of smoking without much thought: cancer, heart disease, death. What's not so widely known is the power of its impact. For example, smoking and heavy drinking interact synergistically, making each drug more harmful. More alcoholics die smoking-related deaths than die from drinking. Smoking increases the odds of heart disease by 5–19 times over the rates for nonsmokers. The odds of lung cancer increase by a factor of 10–30. Half of all smokers will die a smoking-related death, and it is estimated that each cigarette reduces the smoker's lifetime by 14 minutes. Smoking has also been linked with increased risk for emphysema, bronchitis, bladder cancer, pancreatic cancer, throat and mouth cancers, voice-box (larynx) cancers, cervical cancer, and even reduced penis size and impotence. It also has significant negative effects on fetal development—smokers' babies are more consistently harmed than are "crack" babies. Each year, about 435,000 people die tobacco-related deaths, and smoking is the number-one preventable cause of death in the United States.

SHOULD YOU QUIT CIGARETTES AND OTHER DRUGS SIMULTANEOUSLY?

Traditionally, drug-treatment providers have tolerated smoking. AA meetings are notorious for being filled with chain-smoking coffee drinkers. When most hospitals went smoke-free, they made exceptions for the detox patients. However, recent research has shown that nicotine kills more alcoholics than alcohol does and that banning smoking in detox while providing nicotine patches does not increase dropout rates.

If you are going to detox from alcohol or other drugs as an inpatient and are a smoker, you may have no choice but to kick the cigarettes, at least while hospitalized. Try to avoid relapsing on cigarettes, but if it is a choice between that and your other drug of choice, have the smoke. Smoking takes much longer to kill you, so you have a longer time in which to quit before it does so. Don't put it off indefinitely, however. I tell my patients,"We don't go through all this trouble to get you off alcohol just so you can die of smoking."

Joe

Controversial Cannabis

Marijuana ("pot," "reefer," "grass," "chronic"), a product of the *Cannabis sativa* plant, is the most commonly used illicit drug in the world. An estimated 74 million Americans have tried it—more than one third of the U.S. population over age 12. Among baby boomers and younger Americans, more than half the population has taken this drug. Fortunately, of all the recreational drugs, including alcohol, marijuana is the least addictive.

How Cannabis Works

Pharmacologically, marijuana is in a class by itself. The primary psychoactive ingredient in marijuana is THC (for tetrahydrocannabinol), although there are others that can affect the drug experience. At low doses, THC produces sedating effects similar to alcohol, with a mild, dreamy quality. At high doses, it can produce visual hallucinations similar to those caused by LSD, with euphoria and sensory distortions. It increases appetite ("the munchies") and often produces a sense that everything is funny. THC also has painkilling properties.

Over time, users tend to experience a growing sense of paranoia while high—which may be one reason most people tend to stop taking it after a few years. The positive effects diminish, and the negative ones become more prominent, so most just swear off when the negative effects become bothersome.

THC's effects on the brain are not yet well understood. Researchers have discovered a THC receptor where the substance acts, as well as a new neurotransmitter, anandamide, which has similar effects to those of marijuana. This neurotransmitter system is found in very different places from those affected by other drugs—primarily in the cerebellum, an area involved in the control of complex, learned activity; in the cortex, associated with higher thought processes; and in the hippocampus, associated with forming new memories.

Studies of rats on THC are confounded by the fact that the little critters just don't like pot, for some reason. Two studies have found that THC releases dopamine in rats forced to consume it, but years of previous experiments failed to produce similar results.

We do know that about 5% of those who use marijuana regularly experience severe difficulties controlling or stopping their use. They may smoke daily and may experience irritability and sleep disturbances when they try to quit. Most adult rehab centers, however, are dominated by alcoholics, cocaine and heroin addicts, even though there are far fewer people who use cocaine and heroin than there are who smoke pot.

Teen treatment centers do report a high percentage of patients whose main problem is marijuana, but because so many teens are forced into treatment, with little evidence that their problems are more severe than those who are not treated, it is difficult to know what to make of these statistics. Most teenagers who are heavy pot smokers do not continue their habits into adulthood. Studies have found that heavy drug use in teens does not predict heavy drug use in adulthood in most cases.

The Down Side

Marijuana's negative effects have been greatly exaggerated by the government and the media, but the drug is not harmless. While high on pot, coordination is impaired, short-term memory formation is disrupted, and learning is reduced. Driving or schoolwork can't help but be affected—although marijuana's effects on both are less impairing than being drunk on alcohol.

Government reports have stressed that today's pot is different from the mild drug used in the 1960s, but this research is suspect because of a sampling bias. The samples from the 1960s and 1970s were taken from cheap Mexican pot— not from the high-quality marijuana that was even then available. Modern samples are taken from highly bred, top-of-the-line smoke. This comparison is like looking at beer at one time and examining whisky the next and saying, "Alcohol is now more dangerous."

Much attention has also been given to the "amotivational syndrome" seen in some long-term pot smokers. Research has found that marijuana use is more probably a symptom than a cause of this disorder. Slackers are likely to use pot—but pot doesn't turn highly motivated people into unproductive couch potatoes. It doesn't cause brain damage (in fact, recent research has found that a chemical in marijuana may help prevent the harm resulting from stroke), and it doesn't reduce fertility, except if you happen to be a sea urchin (it seems to harm the sperm of these creatures).

A great deal of research has gone into trying to find a link between marijuana smoking and lung cancer. While it is logical to assume that someone who smoked 20–40 joints a day for 40 years would be at least as prone to cancer as a cigarette smoker, even the heaviest pot smokers don't begin to approach such a level of use. Research examining the link between marijuana smoking and mortality in a population of 65,000 Kaiser Permanente health-plan members in California failed to find a connection, although the study's subjects are only now reaching their 50s, when a large number of lung-cancer cases would start showing up. Nonetheless, similar tobacco studies had already shown real harm by this time. There is also evidence that marijuana may affect the immune system, but actual harm has not been documented.

Reefer Madness: Gateway or Pinhole?

Many people are concerned about marijuana smoking, not because of the effects of the drug itself, but because of a popular idea that marijuana use predisposes kids to try other drugs. There is this frightening statistic: A marijuana user is 85 times more likely to try cocaine than a nonuser.

This is a classic example of a basic error in interpreting science: confusing correlation with causation. Here's another: When retail sales in New York hit their annual peak, drowning deaths in Australia increase. Does this mean that New Yorkers' shopping sprees cause deaths down under? Obviously not—it just means that Christmas in New York occurs during summer in Australia.

The Institute of Medicine (part of the National Academy of Sciences) recently reviewed the data on the presumed gateway effect as part of a study for the President's Office of National Drug Control Policy. They found no evidence that marijuana use leads inevitably to other drug use.

However, marijuana can be very difficult to kick for that small group that does get hooked, so it's important not to throw out all the negative information about it. In fact, marijuana addiction can be particularly insidious because of its relative mildness. Motivation to quit isn't so strong when a drug doesn't threaten every aspect of your life, and marijuana addiction can simply cause a subtle decline in life quality, rather than the huge drama that surrounds cocaine, heroin, and alcohol addiction. You don't bankrupt yourself on it, you're less likely to have car accidents than drunks do, you don't go through gut-wrenching withdrawal, and you are unlikely to start abusing your kids. As a result, while marijuana addiction can cause slow, progressive harm to your career and relationships, its effects are far less obvious, so change may be more difficult. The plus side of this, however, is that if you do decide you have reason to quit, doing so isn't as uncomfortable or life-disrupting—and if you don't quit, you won't be losing out as much as someone who stays an active alcoholic or a junkie.

"Trip" Drugs: Psychedelics

The psychedelics of the 1960s—LSD (lysergic acid diethylamide—"acid"), mescaline, and psilocybin ("shrooms")—frightened a generation of parents with their ability to produce extremely weird, sometimes psychotic-seeming states. For most people, these effects end as the drug wears off, but a small percentage do have lasting aftereffects from experimentation with these drugs.

Even more than marijuana, the psychedelics are self-limiting, with vanishingly few reports of anything approaching addiction. Though some users may take the drugs frequently for a time, this tends to become too physically and psychologically exhausting to continue.

How Psychadelics Work

The effects of psychedelics are well-known: visual hallucinations, perceptual distortions, *synesthesia* (hearing colors or seeing sounds—sensory mixing), emotional *lability* (rapid mood swings), time distortions, a sense of connection with the universe, and euphoria. There are also "bad trips," in which users experience fear, paranoia, depression, and nightmarish illusions. Some people who take these drugs frequently will experience *flashbacks*, momentary reentrances into the drug experience. Most of these are mild, but some people do experience disruptive problems.

LSD works by affecting one type of serotonin receptor. Why tiny amounts of LSD cause such profound effects is still a mystery. Because the serotonin system is involved in filtering perceptions, however, it's not surprising that hallucinations and sensory changes are common.

MDMA (methylene dioxymethamphetamine; Ecstasy, "X") is a psychedelic that has become popular recently. Unlike the others, its primary effect is not visual hallucinations, but rather a physical sense of euphoria and close connection with and empathy for other people.

The Down Side

Aside from flashbacks and individual bad experiences, some research suggests that heavy LSD use may be associated with increased likelihood of depression. Though it is not certain that LSD caused this depression (it may be that depressed people are particularly prone to taking LSD), it certainly suggests that the drug may have extra dangers for those who are depression prone. There is no evidence that LSD damages chromosomes—the original research in this area was flawed. LSD "freakouts," which required hospitalization, have diminished even as use has remained steady—suggesting that they were a product of high doses and of drug taking in detrimental situations, which have decreased as users taught each other the best ways to deal with the drug. Also, there is probably a small group of people who have a predisposition to mental illness, which is worsened by psychedelics, but no one has yet been able to predict who will respond this way.

MDMA seems to be more dangerous than the earlier drugs, even as its acute effects are not as frightening. Animal and human studies have found that the drug can destroy serotonin-producing neurons. Because these nerves are crucial in maintaining positive mood, loss of them can increase the odds of depression. MDMA users report that the drug's effectiveness declines over time and depression after use is common. This could potentially lead to a real gateway effect—as depression does increase the odds of addiction to alcohol, cocaine, and heroin, particularly for someone already immersed in a drug-using subculture.

Also, a small proportion of users seems to have an allergic reaction to the drug, which can be deadly. No one has discovered what makes people prone to this reaction—and someone could take the drug safely one night and die from it the next. One theory links it with a deficiency in the liver enzyme that breaks down MDMA. Between 3% and 10% of the white population (numbers are unknown for other races) have extremely low levels of this enzyme, and this may account for the findings that someone who took a regular dose can be found dead with 10 times the expected amount in his or her bloodstream. Recent human data also links MDMA use during pregnancy to birth defects.

Inhalants: Gasoline, Glue, and Other Household Products

Every few years, the media rediscovers the "hidden dangers" of products that kids can use to get high, such as airplane glue and gasoline. In these stories, they tend to list particular products—and coverage of inhalant use tends to be followed by increases in it. Kids see the part that says "you can get high on this" and ignore the warnings because they are inundated by so many other exaggerated warnings about drug dangers. Unfortunately, inhalants are actually extremely dangerous—they can kill suddenly, and if they don't kill you outright, they do destroy brain cells and can cause lasting intellectual impairment.

Oddly, however, inhalants are one of the few drug types more popular with 12- and 13-year-olds than with older kids. Few adults or even older teens bother with them. The truth is, they don't really get you high. If inhalants had real advantages, why wouldn't they be a drug of choice among addicts, who would love the low price and the legality?

In truth, inhalants simply cause unpleasant symptoms such as headache, dizziness, and nausea, which those who aren't familiar with other drugs interpret as a high. For most kids, one or two tries is enough—only extremely disturbed people with little money and limited access to other drugs tend to do them with any type of regularity.

One note: Sometimes, people include "whippits" (small containers of nitrous oxide intended for use in making whip cream) as inhalants. These actually do contain a psychoactive drug: nitrous oxide, which is used in dental anesthesia. It's a safe drug when mixed properly with oxygen, but when inhaled in uncontrolled doses, in "whippits," it can lead to loss of consciousness and even death if access to air is withheld for long enough. Fortunately, this is a relatively rare occurrence. Few people aside from dentists actually become addicted to nitrous oxide. It's hard to get much more than a momentary buzz from whippits because they contain only small amounts of nitrous gas and are not mixed with oxygen. You use one, take a breath of air, and lose the high—which doesn't happen with medical nitrous oxide because it provides a continuous dose mixed with oxygen.

SHOULDN'T WE TELL KIDS THAT ALL DRUGS ARE BAD?

Some people who work in prevention programs try to stress the dangers involved in the use of any drug and minimize the differences among them. This ploy can backfire when a kid sees his or her friends using pot without problems and thinks, "They must've lied about everything else, as well." Most people would prefer that their loved ones took no risks at all — but because this is impossible, it's important for people to know the real dangers and their likelihood so that they can manage risks accordingly. The following chart lists the hazards associated with each class of drugs and the related harms:

Drug	Loss of Control	Intensity of High	Physical Withdrawal	Medical Consequences	Psychosocial Consequences
Nicotine	+++	++	+++	++++	+
Marijuana	+	++	+	+	+
Cocaine and amphetamines	++++	++++	++	++	++++
Alcohol	++	++	++++	+++	++++
Opiates	+++	+++	+++	+++	+++
Barbiturates	++	+++	++++	+	++
Benzodiazepines	+	+	+++	+	+
LSD	+	++++	+	++	++
Inhalants	+	++	++	+++	++

Note. + = little or none; ++ = moderate; +++ = a great deal; ++++ = extreme.

Why is it that some people experiment with drugs and get on with their lives, while others fall in love with a particular substance or with the whole state and culture of intoxication? We've already hinted at some of the reasons—such as self-medication of mental illnesses or emotional problems. There is more to the process of addiction and the requirements of recovery, however, and the following chapters explore these more closely.

CHAPTER 3

What Causes Addiction?

John seemed angry but looked defeated as I greeted him for his first session. It was a week before Christmas. He and his wife had had a fight the night before, which he feared could end their marriage. Several months earlier, John had lost his job. His finances were in complete disarray. He couldn't even afford to buy presents for their eight-year-old son and five-year-old daughter. John didn't know how to express his disappointment and frustration. For the first time in their relationship, he began to push his wife and threatened to hit her if she continued to nag him about his drinking. She responded by saying he could either get help or get out. He told me he could tell by her look that she meant it.

Tearfully, John related that he hated the holidays. While growing up, he and his brother were continually disappointed when their father, a police officer missed most of Christmas Eve. Christmas Day wasn't much better, because Dad would be hung over and irritable. At times, he would shout abuse at and hit John's mother. On more than one occasion, John tried to protect her, but then he himself became a target. A little boy against a drunk, raging police officer wasn't much of a match. Each year, John hoped it would be different, that a decorated tree and presents would welcome the family on Christmas morning, that the family would be together, full of joy the way he imagined his friends celebrated the holiday.

As it happens, a window in my office looks out on a graveyard. (It must not inspire confidence in my patients to see a graveyard there, but I saw a chance to make a point.) I asked John to look out the window and imagine 20 years into the future. He said he saw a young man, obviously intoxicated, staggering over a grave—cursing at his father for dying and leaving the family, angry because his father abused his mother, and angry because this young man has just been kicked out of his house because of a fight with his wife. He laughed and asked whether I was the ghost of Christmas past or future.

Then John's tears flowed again as he recognized the pattern his life had taken. He had always promised himself he would never be like his father—that he would treat his wife and kids well, and that they'd have the best Christmases ever. But here he was, seeing the same fear in his son's eyes that he knew his father must have seen in his own. How could he change? He'd thought he was in control of his drinking, but obviously something had gone terribly wrong.

John later thanked me for what he called an early Christmas present. He saw then that just as one drink lead can lead to the next drink, an alcoholic parent can have an alcoholic child, and a pattern of abuse can be passed from one generation to the next. The cycle had to be broken. At that moment, John began treatment for his alcohol addiction. He knew that he needed help, and he wanted to do better for his children. The bravado and all the reasons that he "needed" to drink seemed to evaporate, though I knew that they would be back as he got better and that this was only the beginning of a slow and often frustrating recovery process. To understand it, you have to understand how the addiction started.

What had led to the vicious cycle in John's family? Why did John cross the boundary from recreational use into alcoholism, while his brother was able to drink normally? Why do some people learn alcoholism and others learn control?

We don't yet have all the answers to these questions, but we now understand the addictive cycle better than ever before. When John looked out over the graveyard that Christmas week, he already knew that his father had been an alcoholic, and that his grandfather had also had a love affair with liquor. A liquor bottle might well have been the family emblem.

You might think that if John hadn't been raised by his alcoholic father, he wouldn't have learned the negative drinking pattern so well. While that may be true in some cases, research suggests that in people with John's history, genetics plays a crucial role—and that sons of alcoholics who have been adopted by non-alcoholics are almost as likely to develop drinking problems as those who stay with their alcoholic parents. Like musical children raised by nonmusicians, children predisposed to alcoholism raised in an abstinent family still have a higher than normal chance (unfortunately, in this case) to find the "training" and the "instruments" they need.

Research finds that between one third and one half the variance in the risk of becoming an alcoholic is accounted for by genes. Compared to many other traits that can be affected by both genes and environment, this is a large role for genetics. Children who have one alcoholic parent have about four times greater likelihood of becoming alcoholics themselves, as compared with children whose parents don't have a drinking problem. Someone whose parents are both alcoholics has odds six times greater of getting hooked on booze.

The odds vary slightly with gender—and there is evidence that in some families, boys are susceptible to alcoholism while girls have an elevated risk of depression. While statistics for other drugs have not yet been worked out, evidence suggests that susceptibility to other addictions has a similarly large genetic component.

How Is Alcoholism Passed from Generation to Generation?

We know that alcoholics can't possibly inherit a gene that says, "find alcohol and drink it frequently," so what could it be that they are actually inheriting?

There are four mechanisms that have been discovered so far, which suggest what an "alcoholism gene" could be doing. Please note that there is probably more than one gene involved, so these mechanisms aren't mutually exclusive. One person's alcoholism might be explained largely by one set of causes, while another might become an alcoholic via a totally different route. The same is probably true for other addictions. This is one of the reasons why it is important to have a variety of treatments because some may work for one type, while others work for another.

These are the gene-influenced factors that have been found in alcoholics so far: Some people who become alcoholics are less sensitive to the sedative effects of alcohol—so they can "hold their liquor" better than other people. Because this is often a source of masculine (and recently, feminine) pride, it can lead to support for such drinkers making drinking an important part of their lives.

Another gene seems to make alcoholics more sensitive to the pleasurable effects of alcohol—so the sensations that drinking elicits are more attractive. These people find that they normally have difficulty experiencing pleasure—but when they drink, they get euphoric. Research has found that they start off with a lower-than-normal level of endorphins and that drinking increases the amount of this brain chemical, so they feel greater pleasure and less pain—an outcome that would obviously make drinking compelling. Interestingly, as we show in Chapter 11, naltrexone can remove the extra buzz that alcohol gives alcoholics—in some sense, reducing the influence of this gene.

Another gene works the opposite way: Those who have it are at lowered risk of alcoholism. A large percentage of Asians carry a gene that makes their livers less capable of handling alcohol, and in this group, there is a significantly lower alcoholism rate.

Finally, alcoholism can also be a result of genes that influence personality, by making someone more or less likely to take risks, to do well socially, to be depressed, to seek to feel better, and so on. Those who like taking risks and who are socially inhibited are at high risk. Depression and other mental illnesses also raise the odds of addiction, including alcoholism.

Beyond Genetics: Emotional Learning

Environmental factors also increase the odds of alcoholism and other forms of addiction. Few parents deliberately set out to make their children into addicts such as alcoholics—though once you know how addiction can be acquired, you can see that an unfortunate minority, such as John's father, seem to have done exactly the "right" things. Addiction is what might be called an emotional learning disorder. Emotional learning—influenced by both genes and environment—is at its core.

Just as a gene can reduce the level of the chemicals the brain makes to experience pleasure, so can environmental factors. The most important of these are stress and trauma. The more that children's lives include traumatic and stressful experiences, the more likely their brains are to become stuck in a dysfunctional high-alert anxious or depressed state. In such circumstances, people spend their lives in fear, anticipating more negative events and continuing to feel stress. This stressful anxiety increases the chances that they will seek relief and find it in substances.

In John's family, the constant fear of his father's drunken rage made his already-alcoholism-prone nervous system even worse. Whether he was actually hiding while his father screamed at his mother—or just waiting for his father to come home and wondering whether his father would be his good sober dad or a strange, angry drunk—he had a hard time relaxing and refraining from worry.

Also, doing almost anything repeatedly, in itself, is moderately rewarding. The brain likes to channel repetitive tasks to systems that don't require conscious thought. If you get in the habit of brushing your teeth every morning, or walking the dog at the same time each night, chances are you will start to feel uncomfortable when you try to stop. A voice in your head will nag, "Isn't it time to do it?" A new habit can be developed simply by repeating an activity for 90 days.

The more John drank, the more the voice in his head, which wanted a drink, spoke to him. This emotional conditioning is powerful. People learn to avoid a hot iron automatically after touching one once. A new mathematical theorem doesn't stick in the mind as well, however. What makes something stand out is emotional significance. You might forget everything you learned in eighth grade, but you'll always remember being teased or your first crush. The pain and the pleasure linger.

So alcohol, with the powerful pleasure it offers to those who are vulnerable, gets marked in the brain as a positive factor in survival and linked with the same chemicals that motivate us to stay alive and reproduce. Because they produce artificially high levels of pleasure chemicals, drugs can feel even better than sex, food, or companionship. For the same reason, they can divert us away from other activities. They teach a seemingly easier way of getting rewards. Of course, there is often a price to pay for this shortcut. The systems that try to maintain balance always kick in and spoil the fun at some point.

The Two Paths to Recovery: Fear and Hope

How does recovery ever start? There are two major paths out of the narrow space where addiction traps people: fear and hope. The first path emerges from a threat to the addict's basic value system. If this happens, the addict realizes that drug use is putting everything else at risk, and the addict begins to make changes as a result. In many recovery programs, this is called "hitting bottom." For Maia, it came when she begged a man for heroin and realized that she was willing to do anything to get it. This behavior conflicted with her morality, so she recognized that she needed help. "Hitting bottom" is a moment when you recognize that change is necessary, and you seek out what you need to make it possible. Fear of staying in the same situation overcomes fear of change.

John also had such an experience in my office that Christmas week. He'd found that alcohol had gradually taken over his life because it was so helpful in changing emotions that made him uncomfortable. Like his father, he had found that alcohol was a good anesthetic. If he was anxious about work, a drink would calm him down. If he was worried about his marriage, a few beers would relax him. Soon, however, every choice he made seemed to require a drink. He was afraid to stop. His control was impaired not just by alcohol itself, but by a skewed decision-making system that emphasized relief now at the expense of future trouble and that told him that drinking was the only solution. When John was in my office that day, he had a sudden revelation about the path his life was taking. It was too similar to that taken by his father for him to accept it. He was moved to act when not only his marriage, but also his whole sense of himself, was threatened.

The second path to recovery involves a reawakening of hope, which improves your vision of your options. For example, an addict may fall in love and realize that the relationship won't last if she or he doesn't quit, or the addict may get a job opportunity that requires sobriety and may find the career chance more compelling than the drinking life. Sometimes, a threat to your values can-not push change without the re-entrance of hope—an alcoholic may want to stop but may not be able to see the possibility of stopping without someone showing that it can be done.

Anita, whom we hear more from later, had a recovery inspired by a new, hopeful development in her life. She was 42-years-old—and had been drinking heavily since her late teens. She became involved with a program in which she worked closely with people who had kicked alcohol and other drugs. Seeing that others had done it and were happy and functional gave her hope that she could do it, as well—and she has now been clean for more than six months.

Both paths are important to treatment, and different treatment methods place emphasis on one or the other. Some try to scare you about the dire conse-quences of continued substance use—others try to attract you into recovery by showing how life without alcohol and other drugs can be better than continued indulgence. Once we've explored the basics of each kind of treatment and how it works, we'll be able to see how to find out what's right for whom and when. Of course, understanding the ideas on which the varying treatments are based and how well they work in practice is also crucial to selecting the best care.

Knowledge Is Power
- Addictions such as alcoholism have both genetic and learned aspects.
- Alcohol and other drugs are more attractive to those who, for whatever rea-son, have more pain and stress—and less comfort—in their lives than do other people.

- Alcohol makes many alcoholics feel, at least at first, a more intense high than that attained by other drinkers.
- There is no alcoholic or addictive personality per se, but certain traits do increase your risk of addiction.
- Learned aspects of alcoholism and other forms of addiction narrow addicts' views of their choices and of their control over their lives.
- Hope of a better life or fear of a worse one can motivate recovery.

CHAPTER 4

Addiction Treatment Philosophies

Charles, in his mid-20s, came from a well-to-do family. He had attended private schools and was in line to take over his family's business. While in college, Charles developed a well-earned reputation as the "life of the party." After having several beers, the normally shy Charles felt confident, talkative, funny, and generally euphoric.

He would often have a dozen or more beers on Friday and Saturday nights, and while he felt miserable on Sunday mornings, he did not see drinking as a problem. One Saturday night, however, his life changed forever. While driving home from a party, Charles crashed his car into a telephone pole. He wasn't seriously injured, but the car was totaled, and a Breathalyzer test showed twice the legal level of alcohol. He lost his driver's license for several months and was mandated to receive treatment.

While Charles acutely felt the sting of disappointment from the look on his parents' faces when they heard about his accident, the hurt was nothing like the shame and fear he experienced on his first day in the treatment program. He found himself with people from every social class. There were homeless men in shabby, dirty clothes and a crack-addicted woman, no older than himself, trying to maintain order among three noisy children. There were also older men in suits carrying cell phones and briefcases—and a woman in her late 50s who reminded Charles very much of his grandmother.

Charles was terrified. His friends had told him that treatment would throw him in with "lowlifes" and that it would be humiliating. They said he could expect to be told what to do and when to do it—and that he shouldn't ask any questions or raise any challenges because that would mark him as a trouble-maker and could possibly reflect badly on his court case. He wished he had a drink so that he wouldn't be so embarrassed and afraid. He was greatly relieved when a kind nurse told him that there would be no "encounter sessions" or "moral inventories." When she asked him what he wanted from treatment, he began to feel that maybe, just maybe, treatment might actually help him deal with the stress and fear that he'd always used alcohol to fight.

In many areas of medicine, you don't have to think much about your doctor's philosophy of treatment. Taking out a gallbladder is taking out a gallbladder—it doesn't matter what your doctor's views on morality and values are, so long as he or she performs the operation with skill and care. You choose a surgeon for surgical prowess, not by delving into her or his spiritual beliefs about why good gallbladders go bad. Though people are becoming more aware of the need for holistic treatment, this doesn't play a significant role in the majority of medical decisions.

Things are different with addiction treatment. As you may have noticed when you read the definition of addiction, the diagnosis tells you little about how the problem is caused, how long it will last, or how it should be treated. It doesn't even tell you whether total abstinence from all drugs is necessary for recovery. This lack exists because those issues are still hotly debated by providers. Even though many of the questions still fought over have been settled by research, unfortunately, this information has not filtered through much of the treatment community. As a result, you need to know how a center views addiction before you can determine whether treatment there will be right for you. You will be treated very differently by a counselor who believes that you are a weak-willed person who brought the problem on yourself, for example, than by one who sees addiction as a medical illness like diabetes or cancer.

In this chapter, we look at the major ideas about treatment and how they shape today's care. We explore the differences and similarities among these approaches, so that you can decide whether a particular approach makes sense for you.

There are several important ideas about alcohol and other drug problems that guide the way America deals with substance problems. While some are old and have little basis in science, they continue to influence public policy and the treatment of alcohol and other drugs. Many treatment centers combine views on addiction or give lip service to one position while treating patients as if they believed another. If you enter treatment knowing about these various views and choose treatment based on the one that makes the most sense to you, the process will be less confusing and more productive.

The Moral Perspective

Addiction is not an ordinary biological illness. . . . There is a moral dimension to addiction that is not present in asthma or pneumonia. . . . People who are oriented to immediate reward rather than to delayed gratification, people who are self-centered rather than concerned with the needs of others, people who lack religious values, people who are impulsive and extroverted are all more at risk of addiction. . . . One inescapable element of addiction is dishonesty. A person can-

not be an addict without being a liar—to oneself, to those who care, to the community at large.

Robert DuPont, former head of the National
Institute on Drug Abuse, in a 1997 book, *The Selfish Brain*

One of the oldest and most entrenched ways of viewing addictions is to see the problem as moral failings, or sins. From this point of view, addicts use drugs and alcoholics drink because they are more hedonistic and self-centered than other people. They continue using or drinking to excess because they choose to place their own selfish need over and above the needs of their families, jobs, and communities.

Moral concepts about substance problems place the blame for addiction squarely on the addict—the addict has chosen to use dangerous substances, and the addict's weak will has made her or him fail to stop or cut down. Alcoholics and other addicts are simply bad people.

Obviously, this perspective is highly stigmatizing toward people with substance problems. It is also what might be called a "folk" model, rather than a scientific one, because it is based on values alone, rather than on data, despite having some scientists as proponents. Although many alcoholics and other addicts behave more selfishly than other people, on closer inspection, the moral differences between them and others tend to be more linked to childhood experiences and to genetic and personality factors than they are to their use of substances. For example, people who have been physically abused as children are both more prone to violence and more prone to addiction—but this does not mean that addiction has made a nonviolent person into a violent one. The addiction can exacerbate, but rarely create, a violent tendency in most cases. As one crack addict put it, "If you are a treacherous bitch, conniving all the way and a sweetheart on the outside and you take this drug, it will make sure that your treachery and your conniving come right out. This drug brings out the one you don't want others to see."

To take another example: Most people wouldn't say that starvation causes immorality because some poor people steal food—but they would recognize that appetite and lack of resources make theft more likely. The same is true for addiction, but the moral perspective confuses the presence of excess appetite itself with the increase in immorality that it can sometimes cause. There is no scientific evidence that alcoholics and other addicts are inherently more selfish, dishonest, or immoral than people who do not take drugs or those who take them and don't get hooked. You do not need to buy these ideas about yourself—or about an addicted loved one! They are based on myth, not fact.

Fortunately, few treatment centers—aside from those with overtly religious affiliations—explicitly rely on the moral model to shape their treatment. However, as you can tell from the fact that the former head of the National Institute on Drug Abuse sees addicts as selfish liars, the moral model lurks in the background of many types of treatment.

The Drug Made Me Do It! Pharmacological Determinism

The earliest scientific models of addiction focused on the effects of the drug, not on the personality of the addict. Physicians observing opiate users discovered that after a period of daily use, those who tried to quit would experience unpleasant withdrawal symptoms. Because these symptoms are instantly curable by more of the drug, doctors believed that the desire to avoid them was at the root of addiction and that this caused people to do things they otherwise would never consider. If you've ever seen Frank Sinatra playing "The Man with the Golden Arm," you can see this belief in action, as the bad drug takes a good man down.

This idea has been given the unwieldy name "pharmacological determinism." Here, the problem resides in how a drug affects the body. From this point of view, normal and decent people who take dangerous drugs can easily become enslaved and driven to immorality by the power of the chemical. They say, "I couldn't help myself—I was high," or "It wasn't me, it was the drink talking."

As regards illicit drugs, this soon became intertwined with the moral perspective. The public conception of the addict now went something like "good people almost never take these drugs, but if they do, they can 'go bad' like the weak people who ordinarily use them." For alcohol, too, this perception changed over time.

In the Temperance Movement (which sounds like it supported moderation, but actually advocated abstinence), Americans came to believe that alcohol itself was a dangerous substance, which could pervert and undermine anyone who drank it. As these sentiments gained popularity, so did support for Prohibition, which was enacted in 1919. In the same way as most people now believe that no one can control their illegal drug habits, the Prohibitionist position on alcohol was that there is truly no such thing as moderate or safe drinking for anyone.

After the repeal of Prohibition (and adding to support for this repeal), another notion about alcoholism came to prominence: the idea that alcoholics are not bad people, but rather are afflicted with a disease that makes alcohol irresistible to them. Unlike the pharmacological-determinist perspective, it made room for both moderate and addicted drinking. Thus, alcohol could be legalized because it was only harmful to a small minority of the population, who couldn't handle it. This position was championed by supporters of the first successful and hugely popular alcoholism-recovery program, Alcoholics Anonymous.

The Twelve-Step / Disease View

In 1935, a New York stockbroker and a proctologist from Akron, Ohio, created the best-known treatment for alcoholism in the world. Hospital coworkers said of "Dr. Bob" Smith that if you went for surgery with him, "you really bet your ass." The broker, Bill Wilson, had been a hopeless alcoholic. He'd lost job after job as a result of his drinking, and he had been hospitalized dozens of times. Right before creating Alcoholics Anonymous, he had been panhandling in the street, cursing religion.

Wilson revised his views after he had a spiritual awakening during detoxification in a hospital in 1934. He had been told by members of the Oxford Group, an organization that had had some success in reforming drunks, that change was not possible without faith. In what he later jokingly called his "hot flash," he felt God's presence. As he described it, "My depression deepened unbearably and finally it seemed to me as though I were at the bottom of a pit. I still gagged badly on the notion of a Power greater than myself, but finally . . . the last vestige of my proud obstinacy was crushed. All at once I found myself crying out, 'If there is a God, let Him show Himself. I am ready to do anything!' Suddenly the room lit up with a great white light. I was caught up into an ecstasy which there are no words to describe. . . . God comes to most men gradually, but His impact on me was sudden and profound."

It was so sudden, in fact, that Wilson asked his doctor if he had gone insane. The doctor replied, "Something has happened to you I don't understand. But you had better hang onto it. Anything is better than the way you were."

Five months later, Wilson found himself in an Akron hotel room—alone on a business trip, bored, restless, and craving a drink. The idea came to him that if he tried to help another alcoholic, it might take his mind off his own desire for booze. When a woman he telephoned suggested he try to help the fast-declining Dr. Smith, a movement was born. The basic idea behind Alcoholics Anonymous is that only someone who has been there can understand what alcoholism is like—and that by helping a fellow alcoholic to stop drinking, recovering alcoholics can keep themselves sober. Its famous 12 steps are the way to achieve this aim.

There are several other crucial ideas that AA members have promulgated, which have been adopted by the treatment centers based on 12-step ideas. Hazelden is the best known of these centers, and because the program grew first in Minnesota, AA-based treatment centers are called "Minnesota Model" or "Twelve-Step/Disease Model" programs.

These programs do not consider alcohol itself to be problematic for everyone, nor do they think everyone is equally likely to be negatively affected by it. A minority of people—alcoholics—simply aren't able to handle it. Based on the ideas of alcohol researcher E. M. Jellinek, 12-steppers call this difference a "disease" or "allergy." They do not believe that alcoholics are less moral than other drinkers, but alcoholics are simply physiologically incapable of ever drinking moderately. Alcoholics are "powerless" over alcohol—and once the drug is in their system, they have no control.

According to AA, if alcoholics and addicts are to get better, they have to live a highly moral and spiritual life. They must make amends for wrongs done and help other alcoholics recover. These principles are embedded in the 12 steps. By taking these steps, alcoholics can find a new source of pleasure and purpose to replace the solace of drinking. Their self-concept and self-esteem improves as they begin to see themselves acting morally and doing God's will. Though alcoholism is seen as a disease, there is a moral dimension in this model because recovery is seen as impossible without making reparations for past bad behavior and avoiding the guilt involved in continuing to behave badly.

Members of AA tend to see the disease as incurable—it can only be arrested by continuing commitment to the program and lifelong abstinence. Relapse is believed to occur when people are not working the program properly—when they have not been honest with themselves or taken the steps as suggested. Some AA members believe that relapse can happen even if you are vigilant about your recovery—but most talk about it as a result of a personal lapse or failure, albeit one that the person may not have been aware of before it was too late. Many AA members believe that alcoholism is largely genetic and therefore deeply ingrained.

Also important here is the idea that alcoholics and other addicts cannot safely take *any* potentially dependence-producing psychoactive substance without close supervision (even substances that they haven't previously abused) because this may lead them to a new addiction or may create urges that lead them back to their drug of choice. Exceptions are made for caffeine and nicotine, however.

The disease model, and variants of it, are the most widely accepted ideas about alcoholism and other forms of addiction in the American drug-treatment community. Alcoholism has been declared a disease by the American Medical Association. The American Society of Addiction Medicine concurs with the 12-step/disease model notion that the illness is "chronic, progressive and frequently fatal." However, as we show, research evidence in support of the next model provides a strong challenge to some disease-model claims.

Addiction as a Bad Habit: Learning Models

> *An addiction is an experience that takes on meaning and power in the light of a person's needs, desires, beliefs, expectations and fears. Compulsive, dependent attachments arise from the contrast between the barrenness and anxiety people sense in the rest of their lives and the immediate fulfillment they expect to feel when engaged with the addictive object or sensation. Everyone has habits and dependencies of varying degrees of severity. An addiction is a habit that gets out of hand.*
>
> Stanton Peele and Archie Brodsky,
> 1991 preface to their 1976 book, *Love and Addiction*

While 12-steppers have keyed in on the idea of alcoholism and other addictions as inherited, genetic disorders, learning perspectives on substance misuse focus on the environmental differences that separate those with drug problems from other people.

For example, factors such as child abuse, poverty, and neglect are all linked with significantly elevated levels of alcohol and other drug problems. Also, whether people around you use drugs and how and when they take them can certainly influence your own desires and habits. Learning models of addiction spotlight the fact that many habits are acquired in a social context. They look at the processes—like those discussed in the previous chapter—that move someone from being a casual drug user to becoming someone who cannot live without booze or other substances.

Treatments called "motivational enhancement" and "cognitive and behavioral therapies" work with people at different stages of recovery to teach people with drug problems how to handle the cues and triggers that might cause them to desire drugs. They try to expand people's perceptions of their options and help them make better choices. Rather than claiming that people with substance problems are powerless over their desire to use and over their behavior if they do take a drug, these programs focus on the factors that an alcoholic or other addict can control—such as whether to go into a bar.

When looked at as learned behaviors, substance disorders occur on a spectrum—and it is only at the very far end, among a tiny minority of people, that control over use is lost forever and moderation is an impossible goal. Disease, moral, and pharmacological perspectives stress factors that alcoholics and other addicts can't control—such as their genes, their moral character, and the chemical properties of drugs—so they inherently rule out a return to moderate use. What is learned, however, can be changed in most cases. As a result, some treatments based on learning models work with alcoholics (and some even with addicts) to achieve moderate use rather than abstinence. Though most Americans haven't heard about the research on these treatments, they are as successful as abstinence-focused treatments in reducing drinking and related negative consequences.

DON'T BLAME YOURSELF!

The shame and guilt associated with alcoholism and other forms of addiction are compounded by the social stigma attached to them. Most of this stigma is based on a moral vision of addiction; that is, addicts are stigmatized because we are seen as lazy, weak, selfish people who choose to harm ourselves and others.

Viewing addiction as a disease helps lift this burden—but it doesn't totally remove it. For me, that could only be done by considering the choices I had made in my life, understanding why I had made them and trying to avoid repeating the mistakes. Other people find relief in seeing addiction itself simply as a series of bad choices, which they are now working to overcome.

However you do it, recovery is much easier when you feel good about yourself and refrain from seeing yourself as bad, worthless, or wrong. No one chooses to get trapped in a destructive cycle of drug use—and you are not to blame for trying to make yourself feel better in the one way you found that worked. Intoxicants are a part of human life, no one would really want a "drug-free America," and a substance itself cannot be "moral" or "immoral." What matters is to get yourself into a position where you can find comfort and safety and live up to your own values without being caught up in a pattern of drinking or other drug-taking that gets in your way. A first step toward doing that is to stop blaming yourself or chastising yourself for having gotten stuck in the first place—and to start considering the best ways out.

Maia

FOR FAMILY MEMBERS AND OTHER LOVED ONES: JEKYLL AND HYDE

It's painful to watch the transformation that someone close to you may undergo when he or she becomes an alcoholic or other kind of addict. The person may have been open, kind, caring—and now seems only focused on getting high. He or she might avoid you, or even lie to you or steal from you. It gets hard not to see such behavior as a slap in the face, as a self-centered, willful betrayal. Try not to blame the person, however, or focus on how shameful her or his behavior is.

Most alcoholics and other addicts already feel guilty and unworthy of love because they know that what they are doing is wrong. The problem is, they often see no choice. They just feel that life would be impossible to take if they didn't take drugs. So, they rationalize and avoid.

The more you can help them recognize that you love them and care about them and that you are not out to take away what they need but to replace it with something better, the easier it will be to help motivate them to change. Don't let them slide if they do something that hurts you—let them know about it, but also let them know that you think it is related to their drug use. Focus on the negative aspects of the behavior, not the negative aspects of the person. The more they see the connection between their substance use and your pain and the more hope you give them that there is an alternative, the more likely it will be that they will get help.

Joe

The Biopsychosocial Perspective

Our final view is a synthesis of what we consider to be the best aspects of these models. All of its elements are supported by research data. This view borrows from the pharmacological-determinist model the notion that different drugs affect the brain in different ways, and that these ways must be recognized and dealt with in order to effectively treat addiction.

From the 12-step/disease perspective, the biopsychosocial view takes the idea that the social support of other recovering addicts and alcoholics is helpful for those wishing to overcome addiction—and that addiction is a medical, not a moral, problem. It also agrees that there are genetic differences among people, which predispose them to problems with alcohol and other drugs, although the exact nature and extent of the genetic contribution has yet to be worked out. A life of recovery often requires finding new sources of meaning and purpose, and those who have these issues need ways of dealing with the issues if they are to recover.

From the learning models, the biopsychosocial perspective takes the notion that addiction is a disorder of learned behavior, and that unlearning this behavior is some of the main work of recovery. Some people may be able to learn moderation; others need to work toward abstinence by understanding the emotional, social, and physical cues that push them back toward their old behavior patterns.

The treatment that we offer at the University of Pennsylvania Treatment Research Center (U Penn) is based on this three-part model. A stepstool would fall over if it lost any one of its three legs, and we believe that recovery is best sustained by dealing with all of the biological, psychological, and social problems related to drink and other drugs.

CHAPTER 5

What Works, What Doesn't

Almost everyone knows someone who has gone to the best or the most expensive rehab and returned immediately to heavy drinking or other drug use. As a result, the public has a very jaundiced view of substance-abuse treatment—which hasn't been helped much by treatment providers' lack of clarity about what treatment can and cannot do.

The problem is that many providers themselves began with an overly inflated view of their ability to help people. They thought they had the answer—all they needed was to spread the word. Few entered the field with the scientific spirit of "let's see what works and dump the rest"; rather, most providers sought to evangelize for a method in which they personally believed. To make matters worse, their own ideology set them up to measure success in a way that almost guaranteed failure.

The Chronic Problem

As late as the early 1990s, experts dealt with addiction as though what mattered most was breaking the habit and taking the initial steps away from booze and other drugs. While they said addiction was a lifelong disease, they also said that if you did as you were told, you'd beat it. Just follow directions. When addicts relapsed, however, the professionals started moralizing—blaming relapsers for not following instructions, rather than considering that if 80% of treated patients failed, perhaps the problem was with the program and its standards, not the patients.

The heart of the matter turned out to be this: If you consider alcoholism and other forms of addiction to be acute conditions, like pneumonia, which will clear up with a round of antibiotics and bed rest and will never recur, addiction treatment will rarely succeed. At least 80% of addicts are not cured by one treatment: They relapse, and without addressing the causes of relapse and offering tools for coming back afterward, there is little chance of helping most people with substance problems.

American treatment providers initially defined anything other than instant lifelong abstinence following one treatment as failure. Someone was either free of alcohol and other drugs 100% of the time—or treatment hadn't worked. Even today, if you slip and use alcohol or other drugs even once in any program based on the 12 steps, you go back to square one. You have to count your days afresh. You are just as much a beginner as someone who never tried to get sober—at least in your AA meetings. Reductions in use or other life improvements don't count.

However, when you understand the deep roots of addiction and the fact that relapse is more the rule than the exception, you can't help but see it as a chronic, often lifelong condition. Recovery requires a complete and sustained lifestyle change—not just a quick stay in a hospital and it's done. Assuming that addiction is an acute illness is like expecting a schizophrenic to be treated once and totally restored to sanity. If we measured the outcome of schizophrenia treatment this way, it would be seen as useless, as well, despite our current ability to help many schizophrenics attain significant periods of normal functioning. It makes no sense to call schizophrenics or diabetics who require more treatment "failures"—they simply have chronic illnesses.

Also, because of the learned aspect of addiction, recovery is an educational process, as well as a medical one. Few people learn without making mistakes. Treatment-center clinicians have now discovered that their own expectations of

Treatment Compliance and Relapse Rates for Various Diseases

Disease	Compliance with Routine and Rates of Relapse (%, for first year)
Insulin-dependent diabetes	
Medication compliance	<50%
Diet and foot care compliance	<30%
Relapse (ER visit needed)	30–50%
Hypertension	
Medication compliance	<30%
Diet compliance	<30%
Relapse	50%
Asthma	
Medication compliance	<30%
Relapse (ER visit needed)	60–80%
Addiction, including alcoholism	
Treatment compliance	10–50%
Slip	50–70%
Complete relapse	30–45%

sudden and sustained cures had failed both them and their patients. Most know now that for the majority of people, recovery rarely occurs without any backsliding—and try to teach their patients to view relapse less harshly. It's like dieting and exercise—almost no one does it perfectly, but if you change your lifestyle to include more healthful habits, you can lose weight and keep it off.

Also, compared to treatment of other chronic illnesses, addiction care has an excellent record. My colleague Thomas McLellan is a leading researcher on treatment effectiveness. He realized that recovery from addiction, like successful treatment of asthma, diabetes, and high blood pressure, often requires major lifestyle changes. With all these illnesses, there is often a large component of *denial*. The person doesn't want to admit to having the problem, or that it's bad enough to require a difficult diet or unpleasant medication. As a result, people often drop the diet and forget the meds—frequently leading to hospitalization.

McLellan decided to study how well people followed treatment recommendations and how often treatment failed for these three conditions, as compared with the problems people have during addiction treatment. As you can tell from the accompanying chart, addiction care did quite well. In some cases, it achieved even greater success than treatment for the other illnesses.

Alcohol Treatment

Reid Hester and William Miller of the University of New Mexico have conducted the most exhaustive review of the alcohol-treatment literature available. They concluded that while there is no single superior treatment, an array of demonstrably effective approaches is now known. Individualizing treatment is crucial. What works for you may not be best for your best friend, and vice versa. Unfortunately, some of the most effective treatments are also the hardest to find and the least well known—while the least effective are the most commonly used.

THE GREAT AA DEBATE

Minnesota Model, 12-step treatment providers tend to fervently believe that their method is superior to all others. People who recover without attending AA are viewed suspiciously, and if they have any problems, these are attributed to their lack of AA-nurtured spiritual growth. People who stop attending meetings are seen as being in danger of relapse, and those who stay sober for long periods of time without the program are seen as "dry drunks." They are believed to have given up alcohol, but not negative personality traits related to their alcoholism.

There is no evidence that people who recover through AA or other 12-step groups are morally, emotionally, or spiritually superior to people who get clean and sober by other methods. While it may be helpful for people who like AA to believe it is the best way, this can hurt people for whom AA doesn't work. Chronic relapsers, for example, can actually be harmed by the 12-step/disease-model view that once a slip has started, you are powerless to stop. Research shows that the stronger one's belief in this perspective, the longer and more damaging the relapses are. I myself got clean in a 12-step program, but I think saying "AA is the only way" is harmful. We all have different needs.

Maia

What Works

Hester and Miller's Top Ten Alcoholism and Alcohol Abuse Treatments with the Most Research Support

1. Brief interventions
2. Social-skills training (a type of cognitive and behavioral therapy—CBT)
3. Motivational-enhancement therapy
4. Community reinforcement approach (basis for CRAFT, Community Reinforcement Approach Family Therapy)
5. Behavior contracting (another behavioral approach)
6. Nausea-aversion therapy (behavioral treatment pairing nausea with drinking)
7. Client-centered therapy (another CBT approach)
8. Relapse prevention (CBT based)
9. Self-help manual (CBT based)
10. Cognitive therapy

The treatments with the best research support are all cognitive/behavioral approaches to the problem—which means that they focus on the learned aspects of addiction and how to change your behavior to avoid slipping back into old patterns. You'll notice that 12-step programs and Minnesota Model treatment are not on this chart. This doesn't mean that they don't work, but simply that there hadn't been enough well-controlled research at the time of the review to support them as well as the other programs. Recently, two large studies compared a treatment called "12-step facilitation" (which is similar to Minnesota Model treatment) to two different cognitive approaches and found that it was equally helpful. In fact, for people who do not have additional mental disorders, 12-step facilitation was slightly more effective. When choosing treatment, you should consider the facts about research support but also decide which approach you feel most comfortable with. Research shows that those given a choice of treatment do better than those who are forced into what is available.

Motivational Enhancement

Motivational enhancement therapy (MET, sometimes called "motivational interviewing"): A type of talk therapy designed to help people become motivated to quit or cut down on drinking or other drug taking.

The best antidotes to addiction are joy and competence—joy as the capacity to take pleasure in the people, activities and things that are available to us; competence as the ability to master relevant parts of the environment and the confidence that our actions make a difference for ourselves and others.

Stanton Peele and Archie Brodsky

While studying the treatment of alcoholism, Bill Miller uncovered a startling fact: The confrontation and infantilization commonly thought necessary to help alcoholics and other addicts overcome their problems actually often hinders change. As in treatment for other psychological conditions, how well the counselor relates to the client and empathizes with the client actually predicts how well that person will be doing six months later. Those who bark orders and "confront denial" find that more of their clients are drinking and taking other drugs than those who are sympathetic and kind.

Would you rather admit your most humiliating problem to someone who understands and offers support—or to someone who will tell you what an idiot you are for having ruined your life, and who will respond with great disapproval to any admission that you have not done as he or she suggested? Motivational treatments are based on the assumption that given the right support and choices, people will want to recover. Rather than being treated like babies, people coming for treatment should be treated as adults with a problem. No one likes being told what to do, and people are far more likely to change their behavior if they realize that doing so is in their own interests. Which would you prefer—taking a course in computing because your parents or employer insist on it, or taking one because you love programming and realize you can make good money in the field? Helping people realize that they want recovery for themselves and strengthening their internal resolve to do the work necessary to achieve it is the name of the game here.

Motivational enhancement therapy (MET) or motivational interviewing are the techniques Miller and others have developed to best prepare alcoholics and other addicts to change their lives. Using empathy and encouragement, MET therapists focus on the patients' own goals and try to help them see how substance use may be hindering their achievement of these aspirations. Motivational techniques were also in the top five research-supported treatments in Hester and Miller's review. We rely heavily on them in our treatment at U Penn. Over a dozen studies have found them to be more effective than comparison treatments.

Cognitive and Behavioral Therapies

Cognitive and behavioral therapy (CBT): A nonconfrontational type of talk therapy that focuses on changing negative thoughts and behaviors to help prevent relapse and enhance recovery.

Many people try to cope with their urges by gritting their teeth and toughing it out. Some urges, especially when you first return to your old drinking environment, are just too strong to ignore. When this happens, it can be useful to stay with your urge until it passes. This technique is called "urge surfing."

Urges are a lot like ocean waves. They are small when they start, grow in size and then break up and dissipate. You can imagine yourself as a surfer who will ride the wave, staying on top of it until it crests, breaks and turns into less powerful foamy surf. The idea behind urge surfing is similar to the idea behind many martial arts. . . . By joining with the opponent's force, one can take control of it and redirect it to one's advantage. . . . [You feel what parts of your body are experiencing the craving, think about the negatives of drinking and devise ways to get relief without it.]

Cognitive-behavioral coping skills
therapy manual from Project Match

Cognitive and behavioral therapies (CBT)—which are often used in conjunction with motivational enhancement—work to help people unlearn what alcoholism and other forms of addiction have taught them. They focus on the thoughts (cognitions) and behaviors associated with the desire to drink and how to recognize them and avoid acting on them. CBT offers specific techniques (like the one described in the preceding extract) to change negative thinking patterns that can lead to anxiety, depression, and relapse.

Almost all of Hester and Miller's top 10 alcoholism treatments can be described as cognitive techniques. When compared with 12-step facilitation, both CBT and motivational enhancement perform quite similarly—and some people find them more attractive because they don't require a lifetime commitment to attending 12-step meetings. Many of AA's slogans, such as "Keep It Simple" and "One Day at a Time," actually encapsulate similar cognitive techniques, though the program doesn't label them as such.

While CBT and MET can be used to help people abstain from alcohol entirely, there are also treatments using these techniques for those who wish to learn to moderate their drinking, as well.

What Doesn't Work

Hester and Miller's Bottom Ten Alcoholism and Alcohol Abuse Treatments with the Least Research Support

1. Psychedelic medication
2. Unspecified standard treatment (usually 12-step)
3. Videotape self-confrontation (using video to show people their bad behavior)
4. Antianxiety medication (as treatment, not detox)
5. Metronidazole (a medication)

6. Relaxation training
7. Confrontational counseling
8. Psychotherapy
9. General alcoholism counseling
10. Educational lectures and films

The preceding chart lists the least effective treatment techniques studied in Hester and Miller's review. Unfortunately, it reads like a description of what the vast majority of alcoholics now in treatment receive. As noted previously, confrontational counseling is not only ineffective (not one study showed a positive effect), but it can also be harmful. Films and lectures tend simply to fill time in treatment—they don't have much impact on recovery.

Traditional psychotherapy (Freudian, Jungian, psychodynamic, etc.) is also not useful in treating alcoholism. Its emphasis on insight into problems that may have spurred someone to start drinking doesn't seem to help him or her stop. Also, general one-on-one alcoholism counseling—where the counselor has not received specialized training in specific, demonstrably effective techniques such as CBT or MET—does not improve recovery rates.

FOR FAMILY MEMBERS AND OTHER LOVED ONES: TOUGH LOVE OR TOUGH LUCK

When someone close to you has an alcohol or other drug problem, you are bound to be angry and frustrated with the person for not dealing with it sooner or for behaving badly while high or withdrawing. The person may have made and broken promises, borrowed money and never repaid it, even stolen from you or otherwise betrayed your trust.

As a result, you might think that treatment has to be harsh and blunt in order to snap them out of it. You may have read the sections on CBT and MET and thought, "That sounds very nice and politically correct, but how are alcoholics going to change if they never confront their bad behavior?"

MET, CBT, and other motivational therapies don't avoid dealing with tough issues. If someone is, for example, missing sessions or continuing to drink or take other drugs, the therapist will ask about it and try to find out what is going on. The difference is that these therapies don't view confrontation for its own sake as positive. They don't see active alcoholics and other addicts and as manipulative liars who need to be "broken" before they can be treated as adult human beings. Motivational therapists find that the best way to get people to tell the truth is to treat them with kindness and dignity. As your mom may have said, you catch more flies with honey than you do with vinegar.

Joe

Addiction Treatment

Sadly, there is currently no study comparable to Hester and Miller's review of alcoholism treatment, which has examined treatment for other addictions. However, many of the basic findings carry over—and there have now been three major federally funded studies that explored the effectiveness of the most common addiction treatments: Minnesota Model treatment, methadone maintenance, and therapeutic communities. As we mentioned before, Minnesota Model treatment is based on AA's 12 steps and the disease concept of addiction. It is traditionally conducted in an inpatient setting for 28 days, although now there are many outpatient programs, as well. Methadone maintenance is a treatment for heroin addicts, which involves provision of the drug methadone, often for life. Therapeutic communities (commonly called TCs) are long-term residential treatment centers—usually lasting 18 months—aimed at breaking down the antisocial behavior related to addiction and remodeling the addict's personality by allowing her or him to work up through a rigidly structured hierarchy.

Another type of care for addicts is called *harm reduction*. This is not directly comparable to other treatment because it focuses on reducing the damage done to addicts while they use, rather than getting them to quit, but it is an important option for saving lives. The most common example is needle exchange. These programs offer clean needles to addicts to fight the spread of AIDS and other illnesses. Research has shown that needle exchange cuts HIV rates, can help addicts improve their health, and can be a source of referrals to other treatment. The idea of harm reduction is similar to the ideas behind MET and controlled-drinking programs.

The large federal studies—DARP (Drug Abuse Reporting Program), TOPS (Treatment Outcome Prospective Study), and most recently DATOS (Drug Abuse Treatment Outcome Study)—all found that drug-addiction treatment dramatically reduces drug use, crime, and other health problems associated with addiction. Although they didn't include control groups, there is evidence from comparisons to other methods of dealing with addiction that for those with serious drug problems, treatment is more effective than no treatment or prison.

As with alcoholism, there is no one treatment that is clearly superior for all addicts, but there are a number of techniques and medications known to be effective. The best addiction treatment—just like the best alcoholism treatment—uses a variety of proven techniques and shapes treatment to meet your own individual needs.

Knowledge Is Power

- Addiction and alcoholism are chronic conditions, all treatment fails if it focuses on seeing these as acute, short-term problems.
- There is no one superior treatment.
- The least confrontational treatments are usually the most successful.
- Twelve-step/disease model approaches are the most common substance-abuse treatments in America. Some are confrontational, some aren't.

CHAPTER 6

For Families: Stages of Change and Ways to Make a Difference

Ann called me early in January. She was distraught about her sister, Lisa. As is the case in so many families with an alcoholic member, the holidays had been a disaster. Lisa had spoiled Thanksgiving and Christmas by stumbling around drunk, insulting Ann's in-laws and instigating arguments with everyone. New Year's Eve was worse. Ann had to physically fight her sister to get the car keys out of her hands to prevent her from driving drunk. Ann said that Lisa's drinking was completely out of control, but despite her pleas and those of other family members, Lisa did not believe she had a problem. Ann asked, 'What can I do, how can I get her to see that she needs help?"

If you have an alcoholic in your family, Ann's situation is probably painfully familiar. It can be simultaneously infuriating and frightening trying to live with an active alcoholic or other addict—infuriating because their behavior seems willfully selfish, but frightening because they don't seem to see how they are harming themselves and others. If you yourself are drinking heavily or taking large doses of drugs, you may believe that your family is exaggerating and simply wants to control you or deny you the few things that make life bearable. This chapter focuses on the processes by which substance misusers come to recognize whether they do indeed have a drinking or other drug problem—and how families can help encourage someone they love to move from this recognition through the other stages of change.

The idea of *stages of change* is a concept that is slowly revolutionizing addiction treatment. It was developed by researchers James Prochaska, John Norcross, and Carlo DiClemente, who worked with people who quit smoking. They discovered that there are distinct, common phases people go through when changing any behavior. When you recognize that people don't change instantly and magically, but go through a predictable series of stages that can be altered by events, you can tailor your approach to what works best in each particular period. Many attempts at treatment fail because they use techniques not appropriate to the person's motivational stage—and this can actually make the person more likely to relapse.

By understanding which stage a person is in, treatment professionals and loved ones can learn to use specific strategies to move them toward recovery. Ann's story has a happy ending. One year later, she and her sister returned to my office. Lisa smiled broadly as she related her journey during the year and how grateful she was for her past six months of sobriety. She described her initial reluctance to acknowledge that drinking might be a problem and her failed attempts to cut down on her own. She told me how she anxiously awaited her first appointment with me and about the joy she experienced as she successfully completed her first month sober. She also detailed her shame and embarrassment when she had a relapse on her birthday. Each of these events reflected a transition through the stages of change. The support of her family, her friends, and her treatment providers has brought her to the point where now she states, "I know the past six months have been good but I am careful not to become overconfident."

The notion that people are not uniformly motivated to begin treatment helps us to understand why addicts often ignore the advice of friends and family members and why the process of recovery is often marked by fits and starts. The six stages of change are illustrated in the accompanying diagram.

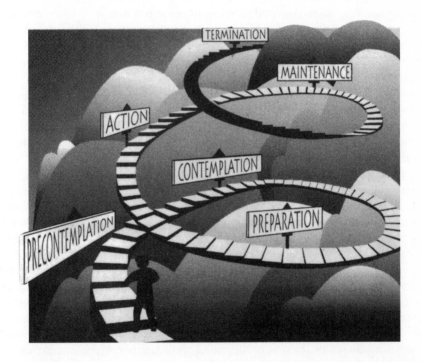

The figure is a spiral because change is rarely linear—people cycle through the various stages, often many times before they get a handle on their problem. The stages start with *precontemplation*, when change isn't even considered, and *contemplation*, when someone ruminates on whether to change. The next phase is *preparation*, when a person gets ready to make a move, then *action*, when the person goes ahead and does it. Finally, there is *maintenance*, when efforts are taken to sustain the change, and, for some, even *termination*, when maintenance efforts aren't necessary any more because the change is so ingrained.

Relapse is also one of the stages of change. When you recognize that relapse is actually a part of the recovery process, not a sign that recovery has ended, your options for dealing with addictions greatly expand. The challenge for someone who is trying to help a loved one deal with a substance problem is to speed up the process by which the person moves through the stages until achieving a stable and long-lasting recovery.

Next, we look closely at each stage, at how to determine the current stage of a loved one, and at what you can do to help.

Precontemplation

Precontemplation: The first stage of change, when someone isn't aware that change is needed; sometimes called "denial."

In Lisa's case, like those of most alcoholics and other addicts, at first she didn't believe there was a problem. When she was given a phone number to call for treatment, she put it in her desk drawer, along with other papers she never used. She ignored Ann's pleas, demands, and suggestions that she get help because she did not believe she needed it. This stage is called "precontemplation."

People in precontemplation do not believe that their substance use is troublesome — so why should they want to change it? Of the 15 million alcoholics in this country, only about 10% are involved in treatment at any given time. Sadly, even most people in treatment are not fully aware of how much alcohol is harming them, and they are not convinced that their addiction is actually the cause of their medical or other life problems. Even in the face of adverse consequences such as a drunk-driving offense or accident, these people maintain that there is nothing wrong with the way they drink or how they behave when drinking.

Perhaps the majority of alcoholics and other addicts do not realize when they have crossed the line between recreational use and addiction. While this may seem inconceivable to those who are not addicted, it is important to keep in mind that addiction can progress very slowly. Frogs that are placed in water slowly heated to boiling could escape — but they don't try to jump out until it is too late because they are unaware of the gradual change. Similarly, people using drugs may slowly escalate their use and not realize when they are in "hot water."

In Chapter 1, we looked at how to determine whether someone has an alcohol or other drug problem. If you are concerned about a friend's or a relative's drinking or other drug taking, you should try to have the person take a self-test before assuming automatically that the person needs help. If you live with the person and can accurately answer the questions yourself without needing to ask the person to take it, you can do it this way, as well. Otherwise, if you want to have someone take a self-test, approach the person in a neutral and nonconfrontational matter. Do so at a time when you are not involved in other conflicts or arguments related to his or her problems—the best time is when you both are as relaxed as possible, given the situation. Stress that you aren't asking her or him to take this test because you think that the outcome is a foregone conclusion—but that you are concerned, and wonder whether he or she should be, as well. Let your loved one look at the questions and answer silently or in writing—not out loud for you to hear. Be supportive and kind, and reassure the person with the problem that you will not compel him or her to take any action. Let your loved one know that you just want her or him to be aware of whether alcohol or other drugs are causing trouble and that you would like to help if possible.

If he or she is willing to share the results with you, and the test does indicate a problem, try to discuss how his or her drinking or other drug taking has affected you. Do not be accusatory or try to inspire guilt—use simple statements such as, "When you got drunk on Saturday and weren't able to attend Jennifer's soccer game, I felt awful because Jennifer really wanted you there, and there was nothing I could do about it." Try not to say things like "You drunken bastard—why couldn't you even stay sober for a few hours for your daughter's soccer game?"—much as you may want to!

Try to help the substance misuser recognize the impact of the drinking or other drug taking on your loved one's own health and work, as well. Again, don't accuse—just try to show that there is a problem, and that there are options for change. Feedback like this can be the most important step in helping someone recover. A recent study illustrates this dramatically. Patients visiting their family doctors for a checkup were tested for alcoholic liver damage. Those who had an abnormal test were told about it and instructed to cut back or abstain. Compared to a group of drinkers with similar damage who were not given advice, those who were told were more likely to take action. The results were so impressive that the mortality in the group given feedback was less than 50% of that for the control group.

If you feel uncomfortable about asking your loved one to take a self-test, you may want to ask his or her doctor to administer one as part of a general checkup, like the aforementioned physicians did. Sometimes, people can hear advice from a health professional and take it more seriously than they do when the same advice comes from a partner or a relative.

Also, if the person you are concerned with is willing to try a few counseling sessions to determine whether she or he has a problem and what to do about any problem that exists, you should refer him or her to a counselor who practices motivational enhancement therapy, MET. The first type of MET to try is the "brief intervention." Typically, this consists of a session or two with a counselor or doctor who provides feedback about drinking or drug taking and its effects on the person's own health. Various suggestions are offered, based on the goals most important to your loved one. Some university research programs and alcohol-awareness groups offer days when drinkers can come in for a "Drinker's Checkup," which is similar. Each year, the National Institute on Alcoholism and Alcohol Abuse has a national screening day for alcohol problems, as well.

For those with more serious problems, however, awareness of the problem and a small dose of feedback on how to deal with it may not be enough. Even when Ann told Lisa how much trouble her drinking was causing, Lisa blithely ignored her at first, for example. In Minnesota Model and TC models, the treatment places much emphasis on such denial. This denial is believed to be an actual symptom of the disease of addiction. Research reveals a more complicated picture. Denial is not unique to addicts—in fact, it is a normal human coping mechanism. Elizabeth Kübler-Ross, in her work with dying people and their loved ones, laid out a series of psychological stages common to dealing with death. These stages include denial, bargaining, depression, and finally acceptance. They are similar to those for coping with addiction.

Unfortunately, some people in the drug-treatment field have pathologized denial and placed a great deal of emphasis on the idea that it needs to be broken down. Such counselors believe that a person needs to admit that he or she is an alcoholic or other addict before recovery can begin. Interestingly, research has found that this is actually not true—those who agree to call themselves "addicts" or "alcoholics" are no more likely to get clean and stay that way than those who do not.

Proponents of traditional treatment methods often also tend to believe that nothing but "hitting bottom" can successfully end denial and start recovery. Unfortunately, "bottom" cannot be defined until after someone has already changed—making it impossible to predict recovery. For example, Lisa did not begin treatment after her disastrous behavior on New Year's Eve, but months later. In retrospect, she may say the party was "rock bottom," but that concept has no real utility because there is no obvious or consistent point when people actually stop using. No one can predict what circumstances will make someone say, "enough is enough."

If you want to try to help someone "hit bottom" by doing things such as refusing to give money or shelter any more, you need to be aware that the consequences may not be recovery, but homelessness or worse. While it is certainly appropriate to withhold money that will be used for buying drugs, or to tell someone who is disrupting your household to leave if the person isn't willing to get sober, it is impossible to know whether this will prompt recovery or a more dangerous life of addiction. As a family member, you should decide on such remedies for your own sanity—not because it may fix or save your loved one.

In his moving memoir of his daughter's struggle with alcoholism, *Terry*, former senator and presidential candidate George McGovern details his regret about ending emotional support for his daughter after she had a series of treatment failures. Counselors had told him and his wife that this might bring her around. Unfortunately, she was soon found dead, frozen to death after collapsing drunk into a snowbank. The McGoverns regret having taken this advice—and wish that even if they hadn't been able to prevent her death, they had at least had more contact with her before she died. The problem with "tough love" is that you can't predict whether it will make matters better or worse.

Also, contrary to the idea that the more people lose, the more likely they are to recognize that recovery is necessary, research finds that those who have lost the *least* are the most likely to recover. It's easier to get help, after all, if you still have a job and good insurance than if you are living on the street and have lost everything. In fact, having something left to lose is a better incentive to staying clean than having lost everything. Doctors faced with losing their license have an amazingly high chance of recovering, but those who have already ruined their chances of ever practicing medicine again do far worse. Threats and punishments may help those whom they deter, but they may actually decrease the odds of recovery for those who fail to heed them.

What is the best way to help someone recognize that they have a problem? Ann first attempted a *Johnson-style intervention*, which is probably what you think of first when you hear the term *intervention*. You've probably seen this technique used in movies and on TV. Ann sought the help of a professional counselor trained in this type of intervention and arranged for Lisa's friends and family to meet and confront her. Lisa was not told the nature of the meeting— Ann lured her to it under the pretense of a shopping trip.

> **Johnson-style intervention:** A technique pioneered by Vernon Johnson, in which family members and significant others meet with a counselor and together confront the person with the substance problem. Negative consequences are instituted (for example, marital separation) if the person refuses to enter Minnesota Model treatment immediately.

Once Lisa was present, she was told to sit quietly and listen to what those who cared for her had to say. Family members told her point blank, "You're an alcoholic and you need help." They discussed how Lisa's drinking had affected them and how concerned they were about her future. Lisa initially reacted with anger and fear—and cursed her sister for lying to her about "shopping." However, by the end of the session, she agreed to go into a residential 28-day program.

At first, it seemed as though the intervention had succeeded. Lisa was a model patient. Unfortunately, she relapsed less than a week after discharge. Looking back, Lisa said, "I really didn't believe I was an alcoholic then; I just did the program to get my family off my back." While the Johnson technique does help some people (and has recently been improved to decrease the intensity of the confrontation involved), research finds that interventions designed to fit the person's stage of change are much more effective.

One recent study compared the effects of a motivational approach called CRAFT (community reinforcement approach family therapy) with the Johnson technique. The results were startling. Alcoholics with family members trained in CRAFT were more than twice as likely to enter treatment as those who used the Johnson technique—64% versus 30%. Other research has found that those who entered treatment following a Johnson-style intervention were more likely to relapse than those who entered treatment either by their own choice or because of other types of coercion. Lisa's experience bears this out.

A Parent's Experience of CRAFT

Juanita, who just turned 65, is a homemaker who lives in New Mexico. Her daughter Diana, who had excelled at school, began using drugs when she was

14 years old. "She was a freshman in high school and was very anxious about being thrown into this new, big school." Diana seemed OK at first. She was elected to the student council, and her friends were other student leaders, "but they led her in the wrong direction," said her mom.

Juanita's husband is a child psychiatrist, so he referred his daughter to a colleague. "She went high on pot and he didn't know it," her mom said. "She was very depressed, I think she was trying to self-medicate it. But between her sophomore and junior year of high school, I realized that this was just a different person from the daughter I had known. She was out of control, she wouldn't come home until two hours after her curfew, or she'd come in at 7 A.M. —we had a lot of fights. Her sister, who is a year younger than she is, was so turned off by all of it because Diana treated her horribly."

Diana dropped out of high school at age 17. "She just wasn't doing her work or going to class," her mom said. She soon married a drug dealer, who "had been incarcerated most of his life." They quickly had two children. Diana managed to stay clean during her pregnancies, but just after her second baby was born, "I went with her for the baby's second checkup and she was nodding. I didn't know then that that was a sign of heroin use. I tried to get her to go to AA, to NA—I knew she was using something. She was never in a good mood, but there were times when it was more terrible than others.

"I don't remember how we heard about CRAFT at the University of New Mexico, but my husband and I started going. And I don't know, maybe she thought that if they think my problem is bad enough that they are getting help for themselves, maybe I will try it.

"CRAFT taught us so much. They were saying that we had to have our own lives, that we need to realize that we can't save her or fix her, that we couldn't do it for her. We were taking care of both her boys and she'd say she would be home at six and then we'd see her in a week. They said, 'Get a sitter and go out. Get your life back.' "

The treatment mainly consisted of couples therapy, although Al-Anon meetings were recommended. "The therapist was very attentive—we did most of the talking. We'd vent and she'd offer suggestions. She showed us some charts and graphs—like that wheel with the stages of change on it. She said, 'Here's where Diana is in the stages of change. She also taught us to see it as a disease, and that lecturing wouldn't help. I was so mad at Diana for having these two kids and not taking care of them. I'd say, 'Why won't she respond to me?' and the counselor said, 'Her brain's not working right.' And that helped."

CRAFT first helped Diana to enter a methadone program. "We'd been going for a while and she said she would try it. Bob Myers, who directs CRAFT said, if she wants to come in, we'll get her in and he went out of his way and met with her that morning. I thought that was a turning point for her, but if you ask Diana, she'll say it was a little better, but she was still consumed with her habit.

"One of our main problems was that we demanded nothing of her. We had given up, we treated her as part of the couch. CRAFT taught us to ask, 'Why should I give you a ride into town if you aren't giving anything back?' We had to set limits. It helped us get our lives together so that when she was ready for help, we were ready to be there for her."

Finally, Diana wound up in jail on a drug-related charge. She was given the option of attending a residential treatment center with her children—or staying in prison. She called her mother and said, "I think I've hit bottom." She went into treatment that day.

Diana has now been clean for a year and a half. Juanita says, "CRAFT helped me get into the grandmother role and her into the mother role for my grandchildren. I have to bite my tongue 20 times a day not to take over as mother, it's not easy. But now I'm really enjoying being Gramma."

First Steps

So how do you deal with someone, like Lisa, who remained in precontemplation despite an intervention and an attempt at treatment? As this research suggests, rather than force a dramatic jump into intensive treatment, the first step should be more modest. That is, try to help the person see that drinking is problematic before broaching the idea of treatment. This is best accomplished in a loving supportive way but with clear and direct continued feedback on how the addiction is adversely affecting the person's health, relationships, and ability to function.

After Lisa's relapse, Ann began to try the motivational-enhancement approach, which I helped her adopt. First, she consistently and firmly presented feedback to Lisa about how her drinking was causing difficulties. When Lisa didn't show up for a family event or was rude because she was drunk, Ann didn't ignore it, as her family had previously done, but said things like, "We really missed you yesterday," or "That was really inappropriate—I've never seen you do anything like that sober." It can be difficult to maintain composure when you see a loved one continue to engage in drug abuse and not admit the problem. Nonetheless, it is rarely productive to simply nag someone about drinking or use these occasions to elicit shame. Instead, as Ann did, the most useful thing to do is to repeatedly present examples of the relationship between drinking and bad consequences and to show how life could actually be better, not worse as Lisa feared, without drinking.

During this time, while Ann continued to present Lisa with examples of the relationship between drinking and trouble, Lisa went through similar stages to those elucidated by Kübler-Ross. After a period of denial, she began to bargain, "If you stop hassling me and talking about it every time I mess up, I will cut back on my drinking," she said. Because she was afraid that she would fail at this, however, she instead drifted away from Ann and the rest of her family so that they wouldn't have a constant supply of evidence about the issue. She became lonely and depressed and felt abandoned, but Lisa was causing her own isolation. Ann didn't avoid her, and when she visited, if Lisa had binged, Ann once again talked to her about the consequences of heavy drinking. In addition, Ann presented a vision of the happiness Lisa could experience if she stopped drinking. She used examples of friends who had overcome drinking problems and had become much more satisfied and more productive.

By spring, Lisa had accepted that she needed help—and had moved from precontemplation, where there is no awareness of the problem, into contemplation, where she began to consider changing.

Appropriate Care for People in Precontemplation

The best approach to people in precontemplation is the use of MET techniques. These are used by many counselors and are also used by harm-reduction programs such as needle exchanges and moderate-drinking programs. The key for moving people from precontemplation into contemplation is to help them see the positive effects of change—to offer hope.

Contemplation Phase

Contemplation: The second stage of change, in which a person recognizes there is a problem and considers whether to deal with it.

When Ann continued to express concern, Lisa began to ask herself whether there was anything beyond her older sister's usual annoying attempts to dominate her in her insistence that she had a drinking problem. She decided, "I'll cut down a bit, get her off my case." This was the start of the second stage of change for her: contemplation.

Substance misusers in the contemplation stage are considering whether they really have a problem. They often test themselves and make elaborate plans to keep their drinking or drug taking under control. In the contemplation phase, an individual is aware that there is a problem but has not made any real commitment to take a particular action to deal with it.

Reaching This Stage

This phase may last for an extended period of time. In Stan's case, it lasted over a year. The 31-year-old single man had been arrested for driving under the influence. Initially, he denied he had a problem. Then, he began bargaining, saying he would cut down if only his mother and other family members and friends would get off his back. When his attempts at controlled drinking failed, he became depressed and discouraged. He would now admit to his friends and family that he was an alcoholic—but he believed that that might mean that he'd never be able to stop. He had moved from precontemplation into contemplation but didn't seem able to progress.

During his first appointment with me, Stan focused on the fact that his liver-enzyme tests were not abnormal. "How bad of an alcoholic can I be," he asked, "if my liver is normal?" Despite consistent feedback from his mother and friends, and my recommendation, Stan refused to attend AA meetings or other support groups or to take medications to control his urges to drink. He wanted to think about his options and perhaps cut down on his own. He recognized that if he continued to abuse alcohol that it would interfere with his goals for life, which were to find a wife and start a family. However, when he drank, Stan experienced such profound joy and energy that he was not sure he wanted to completely give it up. So back and forth he went—wanting to avoid the problems associated with drinking, yet not wanting to give up the positive things that he still believed alcohol gave to him.

For about a year, Stan unsuccessfully tried to cut down on his own. One evening, returning from a bar, he was stopped again for drunk driving. Facing jail time, he scheduled another appointment with me.

During the contemplation stage, people are engaged in an internal debate about whether to give up drinking or drug taking and how to do so if they decide to stop. There may even be times when they slip back into denying the problem (precontemplation), but often the danger is recognized. Nevertheless, the next step may be avoided. In order to get out of this ruminative state, the addict needs to become convinced that recovery is better than continued drug use. While from the outside, it may be clear that the crack pipe or the liquor bottle is wrecking a person's life, from the vantage point of the person who is using, the situation looks different. To an addict, drinking or taking other drugs may seem like the only way to achieve emotional comfort and social connection—and no one wants to give those things up. To make matters worse, the part of the brain that sets emotional priorities can be profoundly affected by drugs. This means that drugs may seem better than they are, and life without them may seem far worse because of the distortion in the system.

To move forward, the person needs to feel as though the balance has shifted in favor of recovery. Threats such as losing a job or being faced with prison can sometimes do this—by making it look better to give up drinking than to lose work or freedom—but ultimately the addict needs to develop the sense that life without drugs is intrinsically better than life with them.

One way to help develop this sense is to offer attractive options—to show the person who is contemplating change how recovery has improved the lives of others. The promise of improved relationships and well-being, the hope of a new love or a more challenging job, a pregnancy—these are some of the situations that have moved people from contemplation into the next stage of change, preparation. If someone you care for is in contemplation, the way to help is to show over and over how the consequences of drinking or other drug taking are harmful, not helpful—and that recovery can be rewarding and exciting, not dull and threatening, as they may fear. Here, it is most important to stress the positive aspects of change—and help reduce the person's fear of the negative things about recovery. To move from precontemplation into contemplation, people need to increase their perception of the pros of recovery; to move from contemplation into preparation and action, they need to decrease their fears about changing.

Appropriate Care for People in Contemplation

Contemplators can benefit from similar interventions to those used for people in precontemplation: MET, moderate-drinking programs, and harm reduction. At this phase, however, counselors or relatives who are trying to help them should focus on the cons of continued drinking or other drug using—as well as on the attractiveness of sober life and the ability of the person to achieve it.

Information that offers hope about recovery and facts about the dangers of continued use is particularly valuable, so long as it is realistic and not exaggerated.

Preparation Stage

Preparation: The third stage of change, in which the person has decided to change and is getting ready to do so.

The preparation stage combines intent and modest steps toward actually changing. During this stage, people make appointments to see a health-care provider, find out when support-group meetings take place, or start to monitor their drug use. This is a fragile step in recovery because these beginning changes can be easily extinguished. For example, about 15% of people who make an appointment to begin treatment for alcoholism at our center never make it here. For cocaine addiction, the results are worse—nearly half of those who schedule an appointment never show or drop out in the first couple of days. Like a seed beginning to take root, the person in the preparation stage needs a lot of support and nurturing. Unfortunately, for many people, preparation does not take hold and they fall back into contemplation.

Reaching This Stage

For Lisa, after she called to make her appointment, she experienced strong feelings of anxiety and shame. "What if I fail again?" "What will people think of me that I have to be in a treatment program twice?" She even wondered whether she should reconsider needing help: "Maybe I can do it on my own." Fortunately for Lisa, Ann helped allay her fears and reduce her shame. She told her that she was proud of her, and that getting help was nothing to be ashamed of—in fact, it was a sign of strength. Ann even drove her to her first appointment.

When we started to talk, I could see that Lisa felt relieved. She had expected to be judged and told how bad she was for drinking so heavily and for relapsing. She had figured there would be nothing we could—or would—be willing to do to ease her symptoms of withdrawal. Instead, our treatment team supported her, calmed her, and helped reduce her fears. We told her what treatment would entail, what medications we could prescribe to reduce symptoms and craving, and what she could expect from treatment.

Appropriate Care for People in Preparation

People in preparation need hope and support above all. Confrontational or aggressive approaches can do a great deal of damage here because they may frighten addicts away from care. Similarly, approaches emphasizing the negative qualities and shame of addiction may also backfire by making people feel that they are failures and that treatment will be impossibly painful. MET, harm reduction, moderate-drinking programs, and other types of empathetic counseling are all useful. Family members should stress that recovery is possible, that they have faith that the alcoholic can recover, and that they support their efforts to change. Talking to someone in recovery who is satisfied with her or his own life without booze or other drugs can also be helpful.

Action Stage

Action: The fourth and most visible stage of change, in which a start is made to actually deal with the problem.

By asking for my phone number, making the call, and attending the appointment, Lisa began to take action to deal with her drinking problem. She was anxious about whether to call, whether it would help, and whether she could live without drinking. Nonetheless, she psyched herself up to pick up the phone — and then she came to see me, entering treatment.

In the past, almost all treatment centers required people to be ready for action or they wouldn't accept them. You had to be drug free when you entered care or immediately thereafter — or you "weren't motivated" and might be expelled. Never mind that on one hand, they were saying you had a disease and the symptom was drug use; if you exhibited that symptom, you weren't deemed ready and would often be kicked out. Relapse rates were extremely high because only 20% of alcoholics and other addicts are at the action stage at any given time. Interestingly, this figure coincides with the percentage who succeed in achieving sustained abstinence after one shot at treatment.

Reaching This Stage

Lisa called me when she was prepared to try sobriety. During the action phase, she took part in treatment. Her birthday slip was a fall into the relapse phase, but she quickly recovered and now is in the final stage of change, maintenance.

In the action stage, the individual makes real and substantial changes in his or her life. Typically, this involves an initial stage of detoxification in which the addictive cycle is broken, followed by a period of rehabilitation in which the person learns to recover from the long-term consequences of addiction. Once someone is in the action stage, what has typically been seen as "treatment" begins. Anything from a therapeutic community to a moderate-drinking program to Minnesota Model treatment can be used here.

For individuals such as Lisa or Stan, one of the major challenges during the action stage is to repair damage caused by the addiction. For Stan, it meant coping with the consequences of a second DWI. This included not only legal costs but also getting around without a driver's license. It also meant repairing his relationship with his loved ones, who had grown mistrustful of him and remained angry about his behavior while he was drinking. More importantly, for Stan, it meant learning to feel better about himself and gaining confidence to attend social events without drinking.

In Lisa's case, she discovered that her drinking had begun to damage her liver, so part of her rehabilitation was to recover medically. Lisa had the unconditional support of Ann, who was thrilled at her progress, but she had a tougher time repairing her relationship with her brother. She also had to learn to support herself without relying on her family.

As you will see, there are many alternative approaches to recovery. Each effective method, however, addresses not only the early stages of treatment but also the long-term consequences of addiction. Early interventions and treatment can make it easier to recover, but it is rarely the case that simply giving up alcohol or other drugs is all that is necessary. Indeed, avoiding a return to drug addiction is a bigger challenge, which requires a considerable commitment of time and energy. The final stage of recovery is the maintenance phase.

Appropriate Care for People in the Action Phase

Almost all treatment can be effective for people who are ready to change. Minnesota Model programs, AA meetings, Rational Recovery, therapeutic communities, cognitive-behavioral therapies: All of these are explicitly aimed at people who wish to become abstinent. Motivational counselors are also almost always trained in cognitive and behavioral techniques to help people who have become ready to quit. These include relapse-prevention techniques and social- and coping-skills training. Moderate-drinking groups can support those who are working to cut down; methadone can be used for heroin addicts for whom it is appropriate. Harm-reduction programs are less useful here because they are largely aimed at helping active addicts.

Maintenance Stage

> **Maintenance:** The stage at which someone has dealt with the initial challenges of changing and now continues to work to avoid relapse.

The final stage in the cycle, maintenance, is the phase in which people work to sustain the changes they have made. However, even after people have been sober for months, the risk of relapse remains high. Until they have achieved five years of abstinence or trouble-free controlled use or drinking, it is really hard to say whether they are out of the woods and have exited the wheel and entered the phase known as "termination." Some people—like those in 12-step fellowships—don't believe that termination is possible and recommend lifelong vigilance. It is certainly true that relapse remains a very real possibility for a very long time.

Appropriate Care for People in Maintenance

People in maintenance will probably have ended or drastically cut back on formal treatment and may rely only on support groups such as AA or NA or the occasional counseling session. At this point, they have learned much of what they need to know to avoid returning to alcoholism or other forms of addiction and are simply practicing it in their daily lives. Don't stop supporting them—they need to know that you are still proud of them and that you recognize that they are still working hard. Change takes a long time, and people in recovery often are rewarded a great deal for early steps but are ignored later, and this can lead to resentment and anger. Also, during maintenance, it is very important for addicts to be able to recognize serious threats to recovery—like a break-up, the death of a loved one, a fall into depression or other mental illness—and to deal with them appropriately without relapsing. Another important maintenance skill is to deal with any relapses that do occur as quickly as possible by getting additional help or doing whatever is necessary to return to recovery (i.e., getting help for depression or other mental illnesses or getting therapy to cope with grief or any other precipitating factor). Family members should try as much as possible to remain supportive, but if their loved one relapses, they should not flinch from returning to the reminders of the connection between substance use and trouble, which helped move the person along while in precontemplation and contemplation.

Relapse

> **Relapse:** An episode of addictive substance use (i.e., five or more drinks during one drinking occasion, an "all-nighter" or more with cocaine, a day of heroin or marijuana use), which can occur at any point.

Lisa had a relapse about six months into her recovery. At this point, she began to wonder if just one drink would be OK. On her birthday, her coworkers took her out to celebrate. When they all ordered drinks, Lisa joined in, not wanting to have to explain why she was abstaining. Although she only drank three drinks on her birthday, she found her craving for alcohol was high the next day. She stopped at a liquor store and thought to herself that she could now control her drinking since she had only had three drinks the day before. Later that night after numerous drinks, an intoxicated Lisa went to a bar, picked up a man, and went home with him. The next day, after waking up in a strange bed with a severe headache, Lisa called me and told me what had happened. She quickly regained her sobriety but retained a healthy skepticism about her ability to control her drinking.

How to Determine Whether Someone Has Relapsed

When people relapse into alcoholism or other forms of addiction, they often attempt to hide it from loved ones or support groups. However, because they often haven't practiced this skill for a while, the symptoms are usually quite obvious. An increase in secrecy, signs of intoxication (for alcohol, alcohol on the breath, slurred speech, stumbling, etc.; for cocaine, paranoia, jumpiness, dilated pupils; for heroin, pinpoint pupils, "nodding out"; for marijuana, spaciness, red eyes, paranoia, giggling), and a return to irregular and unpredictable behavior are often seen. However, family members and friends have a tendency toward denial, as well—and so they may ignore this evidence because they really don't want to believe that their loved ones have slipped. Don't jump at the first possible hint, but if you are reasonably sure that there is trouble, gently and calmly ask about it. Try not to leap to conclusions—the more willing you are to listen to their side, the more likely you are to hear the truth rather than to elicit defensiveness.

Appropriate Care for People in Relapse

If people relapse and admit it, ask them how they feel and what they plan to do about it. If they are ashamed and afraid to return to their counselor or support group, remind them that relapse is often a part of recovery and that if they discuss it with those who support them, they can learn from it. Stress that they are not failures, and that few people learn anything new without making mistakes. However, if people who have slipped become defiant and believe that they can now "handle" their drug use, return to the feedback techniques used for dealing with people in precontemplation.

How to Determine What Stage of Change a Person Is In

1. Did the person solve the problem more than six months ago?
   Yes   No
2. Did the person take action on the problem in the past six months?
   Yes   No
3. Does the person intend to take action in the next month?
   Yes   No
4. Does the person intend to take action in the next six months?
   Yes   No

No to all questions:	Precontemplation
No to all but question 4:	Contemplation
No to only 1 and 2:	Preparation
Yes to 2, No to 1:	Action
Yes to 1	Maintenance

Source: Adapted from *Changing for Good*, by J. Prochaska, J. Norcross, and C. DiClemente.

Codependence No More

Living with an alcoholic or other addict can be an utter nightmare—those close to the eye of the storm are often almost as damaged as the addicted person. As a result, it's very important that you not only try to help the addict, but also remember to take care of yourself. Pop psychology has adopted the term *code-pendent* for the significant other of an alcoholic or other addict, but the term has become so debased by its use as a description for any type of caring behavior ("loving too much," etc.) that it has become almost meaningless.

Nonetheless, there is a real danger that those close to addicts will become so wrapped up in dealing with the substance problem that they won't take care of their own mental and physical health. This enmeshment is why many treatment programs include family therapy in their treatment. If family members are using their "care-taking" of an addict as a way to hide from their own emotional troubles, they might unconsciously undermine the addict's recovery because recovery forces them to look again at themselves. Also, unresolved resentments and family issues can trigger relapse, so it is important to help everyone around the addict to become as healthy as possible so that such problems are minimized.

HOW DO I KNOW IF I'M "ENABLING" SOMEONE'S ADDICTION?

Traditional views of codependence have stressed that the people close to alcoholics and other addicts actually make their drinking and drug use easier. They offer excuses to the boss when the addict is late or missing from work, they pay to bail the addict out of jail. Essentially, they help addicts avoid the consequences from their substance misuse, when these consequences might have made them recognize that they have a problem. Another form of "enabling" is nagging or fighting with the alcoholic or other addict—this can give her or him an excuse for further indulgence.

From this perspective, it looks as though a partner can do no right. If she tries to talk her husband out of drinking too much, she's giving him an excuse; if he tries to protect her job and keep her from ruin, he's helping her avoid consequences. What is the best thing to do?

First, take care of yourself. Make sure that you have support for dealing with the problems that living with an active alcoholic or other addict can bring. This can be as simple as talking to friends, or you may want to get counseling or attend a support group such as Al-Anon.

Second, make decisions about consequences based on what you feel is right. It's easy to decide, for example, that you don't want to pay for someone's drinking—but much harder to make the decision whether to separate from an alcoholic spouse. Make this decision based on your own needs—not on the idea that it will bring your loved one to his or her senses. It might—but it also might just make things worse for your loved one. Also, though it is tempting to think that getting the police involved might be a good wake-up call, you have to seriously consider the effects this will have on someone's future. Possession of certain amounts of drugs can lead to life in prison; and even lesser drug convictions can significantly narrow employment opportunities. This can be a real problem because decent employment is one of the best relapse-prevention tools ever found. Many parents and partners have seriously regretted calling the cops on their addicted loved ones when they find that getting them into the system is much easier than getting them out, and that drug treatment is rarely on offer for most drug crimes. Involving the police should be a last resort—unless you are concerned about your own safety, of course. If your concern is with the addict's health, call a treatment professional instead.

Finally, learn how to talk to your loved one about the problem in a way that is as nonjudgmental and "non-nagging" as possible. Discuss how concerned you are, how the behavior makes you feel, what your fears are, and why you think there might be a better way. Talk about how the drug use is causing problems that he or she may not have noticed. Remember, addicts often think that drugs are the solution rather than the problem—try to help them see otherwise.

For example, if your partner says that drugs are the only thing that makes him feel good, remind him of other things that he used to enjoy (music, sex, work, friendships, sports, etc.). Stress that the nature of addiction is to push out all other sources of pleasure and then present the illusion that nothing but drugs is fun. If your loved one says that coworkers would think less of her if she didn't drink at company parties, point out that not only will not drinking keep her sharper and prevent embarrassing behavior, but that most people pay little attention to the drinks in other people's hands. Also, whenever there is an incident where alcohol or other drugs have caused trouble, be sure to point it out in as calm and sensitive a manner as possible. This is not the time for "I told you so," but rather, "I want you to recognize for yourself whether this is a problem for you. You drank last night, and you were late to work this morning again. Yesterday, when you stayed sober, you were on time."

Joe

If the addiction is seemingly intractable and relapses go on for years, family members may need long-term support to handle their sadness and anger over the situation. While cutting off contact with an addict may or may not move the person toward recovery, it may be necessary for family members to do so for their own emotional health. The feelings evoked by this process are very painful—and support from others who have been there can be crucial in taking and maintaining this stance.

The best-known support group for significant others of alcoholics is Al-Anon, which was founded by Lois Wilson, the wife of AA's cofounder. Al-Anon is not designed to change the alcoholic's behavior, and in fact, research shows that attending Al-Anon as a way of trying to get an alcoholic into treatment is five times less effective than CRAFT. However, the same study showed that Al-Anon attendance (as well as CRAFT) significantly improved the functioning of family members who attended. Particularly if you are dealing with someone who keeps relapsing, it is important to have a place to go to deal with your own concerns, and Al-Anon—and its sister program Nar-Anon (not to be confused with any other similarly named organization) for those dealing with other drug problems—has been very useful to people in this situation.

The next chapter includes information for people with substance problems to help them move toward recovery.

Knowledge Is Power

- Know what stage of change someone is in before trying to decide on a particular treatment. Unless the person is ready for action, programs such as AA, Minnesota Model treatment, TCs, and CBT are not appropriate.
- Be aware that motivational family therapy techniques—such as CRAFT and MET—are more effective at getting people engaged in treatment than are traditional Johnson-style interventions.
- To help a family member move forward, use techniques appropriate to his or her stage of change.
- For those in precontemplation, help them recognize the consequences linked to their drinking and other drug taking.
- For those in contemplation, help them recognize that change won't be as scary as they fear and that the consequences of not changing are worse.
- For those in preparation, reinforce the notion that alcoholics and other addicts will feel better and be happier when they have overcome their addictions.
- Support your loved ones' treatment decisions even if you disagree with their choice of care.
- Don't chastise relapsers—help them get back on track by stressing that relapse is not the end, but can be a learning opportunity.
- If your loved one is a chronic relapser, get support and help for your own problems—Al-Anon is one good place to start.

CHAPTER 7

Overcoming Barriers
to Recovery

*One time I had a seizure and I had an internal struggle going on
while I was having the seizure: "I'm not going to get high anymore but
how can I not get high anymore because that's all I know." During the
seizure, it was like this lightbulb kept going on and off, "I can do
that." "But you can't do that.". . .that was probably a few months
before the last time I used."*

Barton, a recovering cocaine addict

We doubt that you are in precontemplation if you are reading this chapter: If
you don't think you have a problem (and aren't dealing with a loved one's, of
course), why would you? Contemplators, however, often look for information
about change, so we will start here and move through the stages and the fears
that are most common to those with substance problems.

If you have been kicking around the idea of dealing with your problem for a
long time, you may feel as though it's impossible to make a real decision to
change. You worry about what people will think of you, or about failure, or
about the loss of the comfort you associate with drugs. To help yourself out of
this seemingly endless rumination, there are specific things you can do to allay
your fears and enhance your motivation.

First, expose yourself to all kinds of negative information about your habit
and about its consequences. Watch films that show alcoholism destroying families, read novels about the children of alcoholics and other addicts and how it
affects their lives, and make a conscious effort to focus on the negatives rather
than the positives of your substance. If you tend to dismiss such negatives as
Puritan propaganda, find reports by people you respect, which talk about the
harms that really are associated with addiction. Get liver tests, look at the physical harm you may have visibly done (i.e., tracks, malnutrition, etc.), and try to
force yourself not to use excuses to explain them away. Try to allow yourself to
experience the worries and fears you usually push aside about addiction. Look
in the mirror, and ask yourself whether you look as good as you could or feel as
good as you should about yourself. Does it take a tremendous effort just to do
ordinary things and feel "normal"?

DENIAL AND RATIONALIZATION

When I first started using cocaine, my boyfriend, who had gotten me into it, began to worry about his own use. We went to an NA meeting together. I found the experience horrifying. It seemed to me as though the people there were brainwashed. They never mentioned having enjoyed their drug use, and any reason they discussed for using in the past was now called "rationalization." I felt as though they thought all drug use and drinking was wrong, and they sounded like crusading Nancy Reagan types to me. If every reason for using from "I wanted a spiritual experience" to "I wanted to have fun" was considered rationalizing, how could there ever be a legitimate desire? I felt then and still feel that there can be positive reasons to alter consciousness with chemicals, so what they were saying rang false to me. I also didn't like the way NA members seemed to use the same clichéd catch phrases over and over.

If you said you didn't have a problem with drugs, they said you were "in denial." This baffled me. By that reasoning, whether you have a problem or not, you actually have one because you say that you don't. As we left the meeting, I said to my boyfriend, "They think that everything I think or say about drugs is denial or rationalization."

While my story might have been very different had I identified with someone at that meeting, at the time, there was really nothing to indicate that I had a drug problem. I had used cocaine maybe 10 times and could do perfectly fine without it. I had taken a lot of psychedelics but was getting tired of them and did not have any problem giving them up. Alcohol, pot—all of it I could take or leave. You might say that I was in pre-precontemplation—as I hadn't developed a problem that required change yet! It was only later that it became true that I was using numerous defenses to avoid looking at my addiction.

With cocaine, it was, "I'm just selling it to make money," or "It helps me do schoolwork and have friends and get invited to parties," or "I could stop, I just don't want to." With heroin, my favorite one was, "I'm only physically addicted. I can stop anytime I want I just don't feel like being sick today." When I became aware of these defenses, I began to get ready to recover.

Maia

At the same time, continue to gather information about recovery. Look for evidence that people in recovery can have productive and exciting lives—think about what in your own life will improve if you do quit. For example, you might think about spending more time with your partner or children, about the money you'll have that you won't be spending on drinking or other drugs, or about not having to fear running out of drugs or not worrying about the police. Think about how your health will improve, how you will have more energy to devote to other pursuits and how you will learn to appreciate the pleasures of other things in life, which may have fallen away during the single-mindedness of serious addiction. Stress to yourself the positive advantages of recovery.

Also, work to minimize your fear. Ask yourself, What do I most fear about attempting to confront my substance problem? Is this fear realistic? How can I either reduce the chances that I will have to face these fears or overcome them? You may be surprised to learn that you can avoid many of the things that have made you feel as though you need to avoid recovery itself. You have many choices—not just AA, but also SMART and cognitive/behavioral therapy, not just abstinence but also moderate-drinking and harm-reduction programs, not only confrontation but also kind and empathetic treatments. As you become more aware of the cons of not changing, and the desirability of changing, you will become more committed to recovery. Eventually, you'll say, "OK. I'll try it."

Be Prepared: The Forgotten Step

Many people rush headlong into treatment, not realizing that it is important to lay the groundwork for any major life change. You wouldn't move into a new neighborhood without first checking out what it's like there—otherwise, you may find that you wind up somewhere that doesn't meet your needs. In the case of alcoholism and other forms of addiction, this lack of information often leads to relapse. Of course, if it is an emergency situation where you can't bear your old life another minute, do seek help right away. Don't use preparation as an excuse not to act when you feel you should, but if you genuinely feel very shaky about your commitment to change, preparation can make a real difference.

One of the first things you can do before even entering treatment or starting to attend self-help groups is to try to begin to distance yourself from the world of alcohol and other drugs. Spend less time at bars or with the friends that you use drugs with, and spend more time with those who tend to make you minimize your substance use. Begin imagining yourself as someone who "used to" do that, rather than as a "drinker" or "drug user." You don't have to picture yourself as an uptight, party pooper: The idea is to see over time that you can meet your goals better without alcohol and other drugs, and that you can even accept that other people may have fun with them, but that in your own case, it is no longer helpful but harmful. Cut down if you can, but don't beat yourself up if you can't: This is why you are seeking help. Some people find it useful to imagine that they had a certain lifetime quota of psychoactive substances to consume, they exceeded it, and now it's time to leave it to others. You don't have to decide that drugs are the devil to say that they are no longer right for you—though if that is helpful, go right ahead!

To allay your fear of treatment, talk to people about it. Ask whether you can visit the treatment center you are considering ahead of time, to see whether it is right for you. Talk to people who have been helped there. Get a friend or loved one to escort you to a self-help group meeting if you are afraid to go on your own. The more conscious you are of what you fear about recovery, the more steps you can take to make it less frightening. Often, the biggest fear is not knowing what to expect or what will be expected of you. Finding out is almost always a relief because the unknown is nearly universally much scarier than heading into a situation in which you know what will happen and how to behave.

Also, some people fear being shamed about having become addicted. If you already feel bad about yourself, you may be terrified of opening up to others. Talking to a counselor at a treatment center before starting care can help you determine whether it will be a safe place for you. Most addiction professionals take steps to stress that addiction is a disease or other nonwillfully caused disorder, that it is not your fault that you got hooked, and that people in recovery deserve support and sympathy, rather than shame. Having an empathetic counselor actually reduces your relapse risk—so if the one you speak to isn't, find another.

Other people's fears may be focused on groups. They may have been teased or ostracized by peers and don't like the idea of sitting with others who could scapegoat them again, especially without any refuge. They may have become very isolated during their addictions—or started drinking and using other drugs because social interaction was always difficult for them. The best way to deal with this is, again, to talk about it. If you enter a group in a rehab and say, "I'm terrified of being here. Please help," you are highly unlikely to be attacked. Rather, the group will support you in learning how to overcome your fear and relax. In most cases, even in confrontation-oriented programs, it is only when you act superior or refuse to try that people get on your case. Further, if the idea of proconfrontation programs bothers you, choose others.

Pace Yourself

If the notion of making a huge change all at once is too much for you, try taking smaller steps toward quitting. Slowly stop seeing your drinking buddies and other drug pals, gradually expose yourself to the negative side of your problem, and get beyond your defenses. Over time, build up your positive perceptions about recovery and your belief in your ability to achieve it. Congratulate and reward yourself for doing this—the more comfortable you are, the more competent you will feel about taking scarier actions. Alone, any particular step may seem insignificant, but just as alcoholism and other forms of addiction develop as a result of a series of smaller, seemingly unimportant decisions, so can recovery.

Fear of Withdrawal Pain

Another common fear people have regards withdrawal. Marijuana, for the vast majority of people, has no withdrawal symptoms, though some extremely heavy users who quit abruptly may feel out of sorts for a while. If heroin, alcohol, or benzodiazepines or other depressants were your drugs of choice, withdrawal can be pretty difficult. Cocaine withdrawal isn't fun—but at least you aren't physically ill. Even with the best medications we have now, however, there will still undoubtedly be some discomfort when you quit any substance. The thing is not to blow your fear of discomfort out of all proportion. Anyone who has suffered through hepatitis B or has had major surgery or an illness requiring hospitalization has probably been through much worse suffering than the vast majority of alcoholics and drug addicts experience in withdrawal. With proper medical treatment, you should feel only minor discomfort—certainly a piece of cake compared to childbirth, surgery, or chemotherapy.

The real problem with kicking drugs is not the physical symptoms, anyway. Fear that you will never feel good, fear that you will have a pleasureless life, filled with depression and anxiety contribute more to the problem. You can counter these fears by reminding yourself that it is withdrawal that feels rotten and that doesn't mean that recovery always feel like this. Just as you tell someone who is having a bad acid trip that "it's only a drug, you'll feel better soon," remind yourself that it's only withdrawal and that the worst will be over in less than a week. As AA puts it, taking it "one day at a time" or even "one second at a time" can make almost anything bearable. Try not to worry about what will happen next, or what has happened in the past. Distract yourself with TV, baths, reading, and so on. You won't have to feel like this forever, and if you carry on feeling hideous after a week or so, you should ask your doctor to reexamine you for undiagnosed psychiatric or physical disorders. It does take your brain some time to readjust after drug dependence, and this is bound to cause difficulties with feeling pleasure, as well as some outright depression in the first few months. Most people find that improvement is rapid, however, and it's not as bad as they feared. In fact, a real problem is that once you are over the really nasty bits, you often think, "Damn, that wasn't so bad. I'm cured. I can use once in a while now. . . ." and start the whole cycle again.

The Long-term Fears:
Boredom, Discomfort, and Uselessness

> *People are so afraid that the fun will go away. They have the attitude from looking at other people who have been high for so long, people like Jimmy Page and Keith Richards and whoever else has been doing it for all these years. These guys may be rock and roll legends, but they are sad, miserable, bloated pigs when it comes right down to it. . . . For me being awake and alert and just invigorated by the fact that you're standing in a field of grass beneath a blue sky is a lot more special than being in a hotel room with a needle in your arm.*
>
> Anthony Kiedes, of the Red Hot Chili Peppers,
> on his recovery from heroin addiction

Many people don't want to start recovery because they fear that it will be like life before they found substances: bleak, frightening, and unpleasant. They like the camaraderie of the bar, the outcast hipper-than-thou cynicism of junkiedom, or the rush, rush, rush world of cocaine. Being straight or sober just isn't something they ever aspired to. In fact, the very thought can be depressing for such people.

Worry not—these barriers are not as insurmountable as they may seem. Though early recovery can certainly be difficult, the people you find in recovery are some of the same wild people with whom you drank and used other drugs. You don't have to be uptight, antidrug, or boring to be in recovery. You don't have to want "serenity." You just have to want to stop a behavior that may once have been fun and exciting but now is destroying you. At first, you may indeed have to avoid some of the "cool" places where you drank or used other drugs. You may have to stay away from your old friends and drinking buddies for a while. You won't lose your real friends, though, and you won't have to avoid bars and clubs forever. Most people find that their life in recovery is actually fuller and more interesting because they are no longer trapped in the repetitive rut and narrow life that addiction so often ends in. They find that their senses are renewed, that they take new enjoyment in everyday activities, and that they can finally do some of the things that fear had kept them from. We can't stress enough that recovery is not about deprivation. Rather, recovery is about getting rid of something that is no longer useful and instead developing better ways of coping, which can make you more able to love, work, and enjoy life. If recovery isn't better than using (after the initial adjustment period), you should seek additional help. It should be about feeling better, not worse.

Of course, it's hard to believe this when you are still addicted because if you believed it, you'd probably have kicked already. The pull of habit, the culture surrounding drinking and other drug using and the distortion in your pleasure circuitry has probably got you convinced that there is no other way. You may also feel useless and that it is too late to change.

Self-hate: The Ally of Addiction

Self-hatred and defeatist thinking are among the biggest barriers to recovery. When you think about trying to deal with your drug problem, you tend to run up against such thoughts as, "What an idiot I am! How could I let it get this bad?" or "If I admit I'm an addict, that means accepting that I am like those others—a lousy, evil lying cheat who is not worth anything and who will always be defective." Try not to go there. A common phenomenon among addicts is that they hate themselves for hating themselves—and this can trap them in a cycle as vicious as the addiction itself. This occurs because the more worthless you tell yourself you are, the worse you feel, and the worse you feel, the more you need escape, and the more you need escape, the more you want to get high, and the more you want to get high, the more you do, and the more you do, the more out of control you feel, and the more out of control you feel, the more worthless you feel, and so on.

Instead of engaging in these thoughts, try to disconnect yourself from them and observe them. Rather than going with "I am worthless," say, "I seem to be putting myself down now. Why?" The more you examine these thoughts and recognize that they are not "truths" or anything necessarily connected with reality, the less control they will have over you. The less credence you give these thoughts, the better you will feel and the easier it will become to let go of the drugs. Because most people ultimately use drugs to avoid pain, the less pain you have, the less need you will have of avoiding it. This is why a crucial part of recovery is learning to be nice to yourself, as silly as that may sound. Support groups are often really crucial to learning about self-hate because when you see, for example, a gorgeous, brilliant woman who thinks she's ugly and stupid, you begin to recognize that your own ideas about yourself are probably equally distorted. There is really nothing like the comfort of finding that you are not alone in your fears and troubles.

LISTEN, LEARN, AND SHARE

When I was in treatment, the idea that sitting around and talking about drinking and drugging could make you *not* want to do it baffled me. I'd seen people go to AA or NA and come right back to get high. Some people do find that meetings in which people linger on "war stories" about drug use increase their cravings—if this is the case with you, you should attend different meetings, such as those in 12-step programs, which focus on the steps or readings, rather than personal stories ("Step Meetings" or "Big Book" meetings, as opposed to "Discussion" meetings).

However, most people find that listening to others talk about their addiction is helpful—because it reveals the same distortions in thinking and pain and fear that they themselves have. Seeing people who have been clean five or more years talk about how awful they felt when they first got into recovery and hearing them describe how they got better can be inspiring. It is also really good to hear other people discussing how they think about life and its problems. Where else but in a self-help group can you hear people discuss their obsessions, fears, and dreams openly and honestly? Your own insanity seems much less out there when you hear that others share it and some are even loonier.

Maia

Another technique for dealing with this problem was pioneered by 12-step programs. In AA, they say, "If you want self-esteem, do estimable actions." This idea—that your attitudes are changed by your behavior, rather than the reverse—has a long history in psychology. If you find yourself doing good things, it gets harder and harder to believe the voice inside that says, "you're a bastard." Also, just as the negatives build on themselves, so do these positive actions.

Now, Take Action

OK, so you've done it. You've decided to confront your substance problem, you're ready to choose care and take definitive measures. What can help you most during this key time? First, once you know what type of treatment or recovery group you want to try, set a date to start. Be prepared for last-minute "I don't want to do this," and "Don't I need to go on a business trip that week?" and other objections that will come up in your head. Just set a date and stick to it.

Once you have done this, tell your family, friends, and others you care for and whom you trust about it. This will help them help you maintain your commitment. It will make it harder for you to back out, and it will help them prepare to deal with some of the ups and downs that come when someone is kicking an addiction. You can skip this step if you feel that they will stigmatize or undermine you, but if that is the case, you will need to be sure to get extra help setting up other support during your treatment.

If possible, you should try to plan exactly how you will go about dealing with your problem. For example, if you are quitting drinking and need inpatient detoxification, you should set that up, as well as a plan for continuing care in an appropriate program and make plans to join some kind of support group. If you are trying moderate drinking, you should allow yourself a certain time period to do so with a support group or a counselor—and also, a plan for what you will do if you find you cannot moderate. Steps for dealing with any kind of relapse should also be considered in your planning.

Of course, in emergency situations, you will not be able to do any of this, but the better prepared you are, the more likely it is you will be able to achieve your goals. Now, you are ready to go for it! The next chapter will help you determine the best treatment type for you.

Knowledge Is Power

- Examine your defenses to help determine whether you are hiding information from yourself about the severity of your problem.
- To spotlight the connection between your drug use and the trouble it causes, make a list of the worst things you've experienced lately, and determine whether they are possibly related to your habit.
- If you have decided that you have a problem but don't know whether you want to deal with it, try to expose yourself to more information about the down side of drinking and using other drugs and about the up side of recovery.
- Find out in advance what is expected of you in treatment—this will allay your fear of the unknown.
- Don't blow withdrawal out of proportion—it's not the worst thing you can go through, and it won't last forever.
- Keep reminding yourself that recovery will be better than your present life—not dull and awful as you may fear.
- Attack self-hate by recognizing it and detaching yourself from it.
- To gain self-esteem, do estimable actions.
- Make a recovery plan, and help yourself stick to it by telling people close to you about it.

CHAPTER 8

How to Choose Treatment

When you or someone you care for is sick or in trouble, the first impulse is often to rush to deal with it and try to make it all better instantly. You just want it fixed, cured, resolved. While this makes sense for most emergencies, because alcohol and other drug problems are complicated and often chronic, it is important to think carefully before choosing a course of action. Remember that treatment must match a person's stage of change in order to be most effective. Also keep in mind that addiction can be deadly, so choose care as thoughtfully as you would for cancer or HIV. Don't jump at the first straw that is offered. Think long term. Another consideration is to be cautious: Sadly, a large number of charlatans will be happy to take your money and promise a cure, without any evidence that their particular treatment is effective.

First, Do No Harm

In general—and counterintuitively—it almost always makes sense to try the least intensive option first. The only exception is a genuine emergency: an overdose or severe withdrawal. Obviously, if someone is kicking and screaming on the floor in a withdrawal seizure, trying to take them to an AA meeting or outpatient counseling is ludicrous—and issues about whether they want help and will stay clean are of secondary concern. Someone this sick should be taken to a hospital detox immediately. Decisions about continuing care can be considered during the four to seven days while the person is hospitalized.

Detox programs are largely similar. Some claim to be painless (see Chapter 10), and new medications are always being tested, but in the long run, research shows that the method of detox doesn't make the difference in whether a person stays clean and sober. The nearest hospital will probably be fine for emergency detox; if you have time and want to be selective, choose based on how sympathetic the staff seems and what medications are available to ease symptoms. A caring staff can make a huge difference to someone who will be suffering at least a few days of discomfort, despite even the best medical care now available.

Please note: Hospitals often have arrangements with particular treatment centers for treatment following detox. These may be excellent, or they may be not so great, but you shouldn't accept a recommendation from a hospital detox counselor as the last word on what's best. Frequently, there is a financial incentive for them to refer to particular places, so make sure that the suggested option is genuinely the best one by checking out alternatives and deciding for yourself.

For someone who is just starting to have alcohol- or other drug-related problems, although it may be tempting to throw them into inpatient treatment for 18 months, this is generally not the best idea. This thinking is based on the Hippocratic oath: First, do no harm. In ordinary medicine, you wouldn't start with a heart transplant at the first sign of chest pain. You would try nonsurgical options first, then the least invasive surgical options, and so on. The only way you would start with extreme measures would be if the patient were at immediate risk of death—and while many may think this is the case with any drug use at all, this can actually make a minor problem worse.

Just as a heart transplant causes all kinds of complications with increased vulnerability to infections and a complex, lifelong medication regimen, which are best avoided if at all possible, overintense addiction treatment can actually increase the odds that someone who has had only a few episodes of drug abuse will get worse. Treatment centers are filled with people who have serious addiction problems and who have used every drug imaginable. They need to talk about it to recover—but in doing so, they can expose a curious, beginning user to a whole new range of temptation. In many teen-treatment centers, this is unfortunately a more common result than recovery is. A kid may enter as a heavy pot smoker and leave determined to find and inject heroin.

Step 1 for All Treatment Seekers: Complete Assessment

One of the first things anyone seeking treatment should get is a thorough assessment. Unfortunately, many detoxes and treatment programs don't emphasize assessment—they assume that all alcoholics and other addicts are the same. Everyone entering treatment needs to have a complete psychiatric and medical workup. If this step is missed, a problem that can lead to relapse could go untreated and complicate later recovery. Keep in mind that the majority of female alcoholics and other addicts have additional psychiatric problems that need treatment and that a significant minority of males have such troubles. Also, assessment needs to be ongoing. Even the experienced addiction specialists often can't tell which glum and immobile alcoholic with three days clean is seriously depressed, and which is just suffering withdrawal.

To make sure a treatment center or detox program is doing proper assessment, ask about how often the patients see a psychiatrist and what conditions are ruled in or out. Don't be afraid of seeing a psychiatrist: If you do have an underlying psychiatric condition that is leading you to self-medicate, you will feel much better in most cases when using medications that actually do treat the symptoms you have.

Choose What's Right for Your Stage of Change

In selecting any nonemergency treatment, a crucial question to ask is what stage of change you are in. If you are in precontemplation or contemplation and haven't decided for yourself that your use needs to stop, entering an action-oriented program can do more harm than good. Your loved ones may try to push you to shoot for abstinence immediately, but if you truly don't believe that this is right for you or aren't genuinely convinced that you have a drug problem, you should probably start with a program designed for people with these questions.

For people in precontemplation, harm-reduction programs (controlled drinking, MET, or—for IV drug users—needle exchanges and user support groups) are the best bet. These may not satisfy the family's need to get the drinking and other drugs stopped instantly, but they are likely to be the best way to get the alcoholic or other addict to the place where stopping is possible.

Controlled or Managed Alcohol and Other Drug Use: Threat or Menace?

Some people fear that controlled-drinking programs or other therapies that don't instantly force abstinence will (a) enable alcoholics and other addicts to use drugs longer than they otherwise would have done, and (b) prevent the consequences of their addiction from becoming severe enough to make them "hit bottom." There is no evidence that these programs do this, and in fact, a version of them was recommended by AA's founder Bill Wilson, in his AA-conference approved book, *The 12 Steps and 12 Traditions.*

Wilson explains that at first, AA only attracted members who had lost everything. As it became better known, however, people who entered the program didn't have to "hit bottom," as hard as the first members had:

> To the doubters, we could say, "Perhaps you're not an alcoholic after all. Why don't you try some more controlled drinking, bearing in mind meanwhile what we have told you about alcoholism?" This attitude brought immediate and practical results. It was then discovered that when one alcoholic had planted in the mind of another the true nature of his malady, that person could never be the same again. Following every spree, he would say to himself "Maybe those AA's were right. . . ." After a few such experiences, often years before the onset of extreme difficulties, he would return to us convinced. He had hit bottom as truly as any of us. John Barleycorn himself [alcohol] had become our best advocate.

Most people who start in moderation programs, in fact, wind up choosing abstinence—but the fact that they do so with firsthand evidence that their use is unmanageable increases the odds of success. Research finds that more people believe that they have chosen something for themselves, rather than being forced, the more likely they are to succeed.

Abstinence-Focused Treatment: A Range of Options

For people who have already decided that their drinking or other drug use has to stop, there are many options. The first question is whether to be treated in a residential center or on an outpatient basis. Again, for most people, the least intensive option is the best thing to try first. Most people can start with a medical and psychiatric assessment, and if this shows that there are no conditions that require inpatient care, the best place to begin is with your regular primary-care physician and a simple self-help group. If you find you need additional support, you can add outpatient counseling or, for even more treatment, an intensive outpatient program that meets daily for several hours. Why go away and spend extra money (or have to fight your managed-care company) if you can get the same results for free and sleep at home?

Inpatient or Outpatient?

At the University of Pennsylvania, we've developed a way of determining who has the best chances of success in an outpatient treatment center and who really needs inpatient care. We call it ICU—the name is easy to remember because the same acronym stands for intensive care unit. The test determines which alcoholics and other addicts need our version of "intensive care."

Please note: Many insurance companies and hospitals use the Patient Placement Criteria devised by the American Society for Addiction Medicine to determine whether inpatient treatment is necessary. Our research shows that these criteria don't really predict who will do well in either setting. Surprisingly, factors such as living with an active drug user or in a drug-saturated environment don't rule out success at outpatient care. Nor does previous inpatient treatment failure. Here's what does:

- *Inability to Avoid Intoxication for at Least One Day.* If you or your loved one is using alcohol and other drugs daily, particularly many times a day, and cannot maintain abstinence for 24 hours, outpatient care is not likely to be enough to begin recovery.
- *Convulsions.* If alcohol, barbiturate, or benzodiazepine dependence is severe enough that the person has seizures when he or she tries to abstain, inpatient care is strongly encouraged because such seizures can be fatal. Also, if heroin or other opiate dependence is severe enough that withdrawal is intolerable without medical support, inpatient care or methadone maintenance is needed.
- *Unemployment.* If you or your loved one is unemployed, outpatient care may not fill enough time or space to occupy the position presently taken by alcohol or other drugs.

Having one of these factors should not rule out outpatient care, but for people with more than one factor, inpatient care is likely to be preferable. There is one exception here: For people with heroin problems, outpatient methadone maintenance can be used and is actually the best option for the most severe cases. Also, note that our criteria suggest that the higher your level of social and psychological functioning, the less intense your treatment needs are. Because those who are doing well economically can generally afford better treatment, however, they have typically been offered or sometimes even forced into longer stays in treatment. This makes little sense: Someone like a doctor or dentist, for example, who has managed to continue working while addicted, does not need to spend months in an inpatient facility learning vocational skills or being forced to confront denial. Medical and other professionals should steer clear of excess treatment and, like anyone else, start with the lowest level of treatment first. Unfortunately, some people have had their careers threatened and spent needless extra months, even years in care because greedy treatment facilities believed that people with a "high bottom" need the most treatment. Isn't it interesting that these high-functioning professionals happen to be those who can afford to pay for more treatment?

Also, be aware that inpatient care on its own is rarely enough to end alcoholism or other forms of addiction serious enough to require it—aftercare (follow-up counseling and groups) on an ongoing basis for at least six months or involvement with some type of self-help and support group is needed to reinforce the changes begun away from home. When choosing inpatient treatment, always be sure to ask about aftercare and what arrangements are made for the transition from treatment to home, which, if not handled properly, can lead to relapse.

Alcohol Treatment

Once you have determined which setting is right, many of the rest of the decisions vary, depending on what substance is the primary drug of abuse. For people with alcohol problems, the choice is between philosophies of treatment based on AA and those that use cognitive and behavioral strategies. Also, you must choose whether you want to attend a program that offers medication. For inpatient treatment, this choice is limited: Virtually all inpatient alcoholism treatment in America is AA focused and limits medication use. Almost the only exceptions are research programs affiliated with major universities such as ours, Columbia, Yale, New York University (NYU), University of California at Los Angeles (UCLA), University of New Mexico, Rutgers, and the University of Washington, to name some of the most important addiction-research centers. If you live near one and have decided that AA is not right for you, your best bet is to try to enroll in a study, though be aware that most studies use outpatient treatment. Even if you turn out to be in a placebo or control condition, most studies at some point offer the full, free treatment to participants, and control subjects often actually get some treatment, just not the new type under investigation.

Given the predominance of the AA philosophy, it pays to be open-minded about it. Read about the AA experience—talk to people about it. Even if you think you will hate it, don't rule it out automatically. You may find that some of the things—such as talking in groups and the "God stuff" that you are sure you disagree with—can actually help, and if you don't like them, you can always disregard the program's recommendations once you have finished the inpatient portion of treatment and are clean and sober. If you need inpatient treatment, you may have to deal with a dose of AA.

Also, if you do find that you can't stand it, be sure that your reasoning for not going to meetings after treatment is sound. Early recovery is difficult—if you aren't going to use AA or the AA-oriented aftercare that some treatment programs offer for support, find an outpatient, cognitive or motivational-style counselor to help, and join an alternative support group such as Rational Recovery or SMART recovery. AA's ideas may not be for everyone, but most people with drinking problems serious enough to require inpatient treatment need some support and help in learning to live sober afterward.

Treatment for Cocaine, Heroin, Marijuana, and Other Drugs

For people with other (nonalcohol) drug problems, there are two primary types of inpatient treatment: therapeutic communities (TCs) and Minnesota Model treatment. In Minnesota Model treatment, the alcoholics and other addicts are thrown in together because the disease of addiction is believed not to be specific to any particular drug. TCs will take addicts who have alcohol problems, as well as other drug problems, but rarely are used for people with alcohol problems alone. TCs typically last for 6–18 months and are the most intensive form of addiction treatment; Minnesota Model rehabs generally treat patients for 10–30 days.

The key difference here is the emphasis on confrontation: TCs are big on it for the most part, and Minnesota Model treatment tends to be more gentle, though there are exceptions in both directions. As always, research suggests it's better to start with the shorter, kinder program.

If You Want More

If you have started in a Minnesota Model program for either alcohol or other drugs, and you feel that you need more time away from home—or can't afford to stay in a Minnesota Model rehab as long as you would like, you might also consider a halfway house. These programs are similar to Minnesota Model treatment, in that they emphasize 12-step recovery, but they provide less counseling and support than an inpatient rehab. People who live there generally work during the day and pay a low fee for room and board. Most people stay between three and six months. Halfway houses are a good option for people who feel that they need to stay away from their old life for longer than a few weeks, but who do not wish to deal with the heavy confrontational style of therapeutic communities. Another, similar option is called an "Oxford House." These are simply group residences occupied by people in 12-step recovery. Some have formal programs, others just offer a sober environment and buddies to go to meetings with.

However, if you have not worked for years, have few job skills, or have been homeless and unaccustomed to regular work and family life, a therapeutic community may be the right choice for you. People who have spent the greater part of their lives using drugs and hustling to get them may need to spend the 6–18 months in treatment that TCs offer in order to get reacquainted with structure and work.

Outpatient Drug-Addiction Treatment

Outpatient treatment for addiction, with the exception of methadone, is similar to outpatient treatment for alcoholism. There are 12-step-oriented programs, and then there are counselors and centers who work with cognitive techniques. The 12-step-oriented programs are more common and easier to find; for those who don't like this approach, outpatient research programs are also a good bet.

Criteria for Selecting Treatment

Once you have located some centers that provide the type of treatment you want, here are some issues to raise to help you choose among them. Considerations for choosing an individual addiction counselor also follow.

Check the Licensing Credentials

When considering any medical treatments or professionals, check out their credentials with the state or local authorities and with local professional organizations. Many states now offer such information via the Internet—and you should never select a treatment center or counselor who is not, at the very least, state licensed. The only exceptions are Oxford houses and halfway houses—which, because they are often run by nonprofessionals, may be excellent, despite lack of credentials. State licensing, however, is a bare minimum for professional treatment, and there are many licensed facilities that nonetheless provide substandard or even abusive care.

For inpatient or intensive outpatient treatment, accreditation is a sign that the center cares about outcomes and quality care. Two U.S. organizations accredit drug-treatment facilities, and the processes are involved and somewhat arduous and expensive, which is good if you are trying to tell whether a center actually does what it says it does. Of course, because most accreditation-determining visits are announced ahead of time, centers can still cheat, but it is less likely that someone will take the time and effort to attempt to be accredited and then cheat than it is that a center will just not bother because so few people know how to make informed choices about treatment.

The Joint Council on the Accreditation of Health Care Organizations (JCAHO) is the larger of the two accreditors, and it has a long history of inspecting and examining hospitals and other health-care facilities. States will shut down hospitals, and insurers will not cover care if they fail to reach at least the lowest level acceptable to JCAHO—so they have long experience in checking up on medical institutions, not just drug treatment. See the appendix for their website (and other contact information), where you can find out whether a rehab is accredited. Please note: Unless you ask specifically, JCAHO may not offer negative information beyond whether a center is accredited, so ask about legal troubles and patient-care problems particularly.

The other group that now accredits rehabs is called CARF (the Rehabilitation Accreditation Commission), and it does its work predominantly in the Western United States. CARF is a newer organization and accredits physical rehabilitation programs as well as drug rehabilitation ones, but the methods it uses to evaluate programs are similar to JCAHO's. Contact information for CARF is also in the appendix.

Find Out the Ombudsman/Complaint Procedure

A quick and easy way to find out a program's patient-centered orientation is to ask about the procedure for dealing with complaints. The best centers have a patient ombudsman or advocate who deals only with patient-counselor conflicts and who is there to represent the point of view of the person in treatment. Centers that don't have such an employee but have a procedure where a patient with a problem can appeal decisions made by counselors or rules they think are being applied unfairly to someone in management are also likely to be good. Accreditors always require a documented and thorough complaint procedure because it is a hallmark of good institutional medicine.

Any center that responds nervously to a prospective patient or family member's question about the issue is probably not the one to pick. Also definitely avoid a center that responds, "Patient complaints? They're all whiners and liars—we know what's best and they need to learn that in order to get better," or anything similar. Many treatment centers post a "patient's bill of rights" prominently in their hallways, but that is all the thought they give to the issue. Some explicitly prevent patients from talking to anyone other than the counselor assigned to them, which is an open invitation to abuse of power. If a woman is being sexually harassed by her counselor but is not permitted to speak to other staff members, how can she get help?

Talk to Treatment Graduates

An excellent way to find out what a particular treatment center is like is to talk to some of its graduates. Graduates who are still in touch with the program are likely to be those who had a positive outcome, but if you speak with them away from the center, they are likely to honestly answer questions about what the regime is like and how it worked for them. Graduates who now work at the center, however, are likely to represent the counselor's perspective, rather than the patient's. Be sure to ask how confrontational the treatment is, whether it deals well with people who need additional help, and whether there are types of people for whom the treatment is not suited.

A way to find people who have had bad experiences with particular treatment centers and who will give you another perspective is to do a search of the Internet. Several sites have been put up by disgruntled treatment participants, and there are Usenet newsgroups and mailing lists for those who did not like the care they received (try alt.recoveryfrom12steps, for example). Remember that not all complaints may be justified, but also take into account that not all praise may be earned either. Be skeptical, and be aware of biases. Questions: What was a typical day in treatment like for you? Is there anyone you think this treatment might be harmful for? What advice would you give to someone considering going there?

Find Out the Center's Beliefs about Relapse and the Nature of Addiction

Another area to explore when looking at a treatment center is its philosophy of care. Understanding how a center sees addiction can tell you a lot about how it treats patients. Some providers will tell you explicitly that they think addicts are all liars, cheats, and manipulators. Most people will wish to avoid such a center—although if they feel that this description applies to them and that they need help breaking free of it, they may wish to try it. The biggest proponents of this view tend to be TCs, but some Minnesota Model providers also subscribe to it.

How a center views relapse is also an important key. If a center sees it as willful misbehavior to be punished, you probably don't want to go there. If it views relapse as an unfortunate, but sometimes useful, part of recovery, you are likely to have located a compassionate provider. Also recommended are providers who see relapse as not just the patient's mistake, but also evidence of a possible misstep by a counselor or another aspect of treatment.

Find Out the Center's Beliefs about Research and Outside Evaluations

Some treatment providers believe they already know the best way to treat addiction and are highly skeptical of any advances in the field. Others constantly study their techniques and try to improve them based on the latest data. Unfortunately, the former are far more common than the latter, but this is slowly changing. Obviously, a university treatment center will base its care on research. If you are getting treatment in a study, there is no need to ask about this. For other centers, you should ask whether the center has been evaluated by an outside team of researchers or whether such evaluations are planned for the future. You should ask what level of education the counselors have, and how often they are required to update their education or training. It's not a problem if a few of the counselors have little education other than their own addiction experience—in fact, some recovering people are among the best counselors, but if there are none with master's degrees or more education, you may want to look elsewhere.

Ask About Medication Use

Addiction treatment centers tend to be overly conservative about the use of medication—so much so that even though there is replicated research showing that drugs such as naltrexone can reduce relapse by 50% in alcoholics, most centers don't offer it. Despite the fact that half of alcoholics and other addicts suffer an additional psychiatric diagnosis that can lead to relapse, many treatment centers still either don't allow the use of antidepressant medication or are very stingy with it.

If a center offers patients access to antirelapse medications such as naltrexone and others, it is likely that it is in touch with research and following guidelines for state-of-the-art care. Avoid centers that have blanket prohibitions on psychiatric medications unless you are absolutely sure that the person needing help does not suffer depression, attention deficit disorder (ADD), panic disorder, schizophrenia, bipolar disorder, or any other condition best treated with medication. A center that bans such drugs is generally not acting in the best interests of its patients. Of course, in psychiatry more generally, there has also been a problem of overmedication. A rehab that puts everyone on the same dose of the same medication regardless of circumstances is also not likely to be the best.

Investigate Special Concerns

Dual Diagnosis

If you already know that the person who needs treatment has a psychiatric disorder, it is particularly important to make sure that the rehab center will deal with it properly. You may want to check out rehabs that specialize in people with dual diagnoses (see Chapter 22). For centers that don't specialize, you should ask about the amount of psychiatric help offered and how accommodations are made to deal with issues that may arise (for example, if a depressive patient cannot participate in a group or cannot wake up in time for scheduled breakfast—or if someone with ADD cannot focus on lectures).

Women

Women also have special needs in treatment. Because there are more male than female alcoholics and other addicts, most treatment centers have a very male environment. If a center does not offer any female-specific groups or resources, avoid it. Also, because research finds that between 40% and 80% of women who need inpatient treatment for alcoholism or other forms of addiction were sexually or physically abused as children, be sure that the treatment center you choose has appropriate groups to deal with these issues—as well as treatment for posttraumatic stress syndrome, which is common among those who have been abused. People who were sexually or physically abused can be reinjured by many of the coercive techniques used in therapeutic communities, so be careful if a TC is the treatment you select.

Sexual Orientation

Gay, lesbian, bisexual, and transgendered people may also not be comfortable in the straight-male-dominated environment of many treatment centers. Because it is very stressful to have a stigmatized sexual orientation, particularly for young people, homosexuals, bisexuals, and transgendered people are more likely than others to develop substance problems. Also, in many places, gay meeting spots are primarily bars, so exposure to heavy drinking is increased, and people often fear recovery because they think they will no longer be able to socialize.

There is at least one Minnesota Model treatment center specifically for gays and lesbians: the Pride Institute, which has several locations around the country. Cities such as New York and San Francisco also have specialized AA meetings for gay men and lesbians. Gay community centers also often have substance-abuse counseling available, and many AIDS organizations offer help to people with or without HIV who have substance problems, as a prevention strategy.

Race

African Americans and Latinos—particularly if they come from poor communities—may need treatment that is sensitive to their cultures and economic needs. If you are involved with political activism for racial equity, for example, being told that you are "powerless" by some white treatment counselor may not exactly be therapeutic. You may want to check whether your church, mosque, or synagogue offers any drug treatment or support groups. Many have developed wonderful, politically empowering programs for people with substance problems. There are even several congregations run by ministers in recovery and devoted particularly to serving people with alcohol and other drug problems. The Nation of Islam also has a program to help people overcome addictions. For Latinos who have trouble with English, it's obviously important to be sure that any treatment center has enough Spanish-language therapists and groups to be useful. You'd be surprised at how many treatment centers put people who don't speak English into English-language AA and other groups, which cannot help those who don't understand the language.

Ask about the Daily Routine

Whether treatment is provided on an outpatient or an inpatient basis, most centers offer a fixed schedule. Hester and Miller's evaluation found that some of the most common features are actually the least effective. Lectures and films, for example, seem to do little to help people recover, though they are a common part of many rehab routines.

On the other hand, you cannot spend eight hours a day in therapy without going nuts, so what you should look for is balance. A center that offers a schedule that is mostly group work with some individual counseling, time for lunch, and the odd lecture or film is likely to be fine. One that fills the day with films and lectures and has very little time spent in interactive situations such as group therapy or one-on-one counseling is less likely to be helpful. The more individualized a center's care is, the more likely it is to be useful, as well.

Find Out about Family Involvement

Finally, most treatment centers now recognize that family members can either be part of the problem for alcoholics and other addicts or part of the solution. Most Minnesota Model centers and TCs offer at least some family therapy. Many motivational counselors also seek family involvement. It is a useful part of treatment for many, so, if possible, choose a center that offers it.

With all family programs, the idea is to uncover and defuse any issues that may be helping to support the addictive behavior. The other thing they seek to do is to visibly show people in treatment how much their substance problem has affected others, and how much these others care about helping the patients to stop it. By dealing with problems while someone is in treatment, many relapses can be avoided.

Many treatment centers, particularly Minnesota Model rehabs, suggest that family members become involved with Al-Anon and accept that they have the "disease of codependency." There is no research suggesting that this is helpful to the addict. If family members find it useful, they should attend, but if not, it shouldn't be a big concern.

Selecting a Counselor

In most treatment programs, counselors are assigned to patients, and there is little choice in the matter. However, if you do get a choice or are looking for someone to work with on an outpatient basis, for either initial or ongoing care, here's what to look for:

As always, you will want to know about licensing and educational credentials—in general, more education is better than less, but this isn't necessarily the key factor here. You will also want to know about the therapist's philosophy of care: It makes little sense for someone who wants to try to moderate to go to a counselor who believes that abstinence is the only way. Conversely, someone seeking support for 12-step work will probably not do well with a therapist who has an exclusively cognitive-behavioral therapy (CBT) orientation and thinks AA is nonsense. Someone trained in CBT and motivational interviewing who also supports 12-step participation for those so inclined is probably your best bet.

The most important factor here, however, is the way you feel about the therapist. We've stressed that caring, supportive, and empathetic counselors have patients who stay clean longer, drop out of treatment less often, and relapse less frequently than those who are cold or confrontational. If you find someone you like and feel safe with, all of the educational and philosophical stuff may not matter because you relate to the person and believe the person can give you what you need.

Such empathetic counselors are often idolized by their patients: They tend to have large, thriving practices, and people adore them. By all means, get recommendations from friends, family members, and your physician: If one name keeps showing up, that's an excellent sign. However, even if your best friend tells you she or he knows just the person for you, be sure to talk to the counselor yourself before committing to treatment. It's a highly individual matter, and someone you "click" with may do nothing for your friend, and vice versa. Visit several before making up your mind, unless you find someone right away that you know you will be comfortable with. Trust your gut, basically.

Some people insist that only ex-alcoholics and other ex-addicts and can really empathize with those kicking alcohol and other drugs. Research, however, finds that it's not whether counselors have had personal experience that determines whether they work well with people with substance problems, but again, how kind and caring they are. If you feel that someone in recovery will be better for you, then use this as one of your criteria, but be careful to look for empathy, as well. Some counselors in recovery become very rigid and strict, and this approach is not usually successful.

Choosing treatment for substance problems can be a daunting task because of the controversies in the field and because of the stigma still attached to people with drinking and other drug habits. It's worth the effort to select carefully, however. If you find the right treatment on the first try, you can reduce the odds of relapse dramatically. In the rest of the book, we lay out exactly what the various types of treatment are like, what to expect, what to avoid, and how they work. So many people seeking help are scared of the unknown. That's one fear you can avoid by reading this book.

Top Ten Questions to Ask Treatment Providers You Are Considering
1. Are you state licensed?
2. Are you accredited?
3. What is your patient-complaint procedure?
4. What is the role of confrontation or "breaking denial" in your treatment?
5. When do you use medications?
6. What is the cause of relapse, and how do you deal with it?
7. What is your position on 12-step programs?
8. What do you provide in terms of aftercare?
9. How do you deal with [women, cultural issues, sexual-orientation issues, language differences, etc.]?
10. What research is your treatment based on, and has it been evaluated by outside researchers?

PART TWO

The Options

CHAPTER 9

BRENDA: The Penn Paradigm

Connie, a 32-year-old mother of one, was referred to our treatment center after numerous failed attempts to quit crack and booze. The authorities had just taken her 2-year-old son into foster care. Distraught at the loss of her child, Connie left her group home at 3 a.m. that night and smoked some rocks. She got drunk to come down. The next few days were a blur but when she returned to the group home, she was battered, intoxicated, and hopelessly depressed. She was asked to leave the home—but fortunately, she found shelter with a friend who brought her here to U Penn.

Stephen is a 63-year-old successful lawyer who came to see me at the insistence of his daughter, who believed he was an alcoholic. While Stephen admitted that he had a few drinks after work each day, he thought his daughter was overreacting. At a recent family gathering, however, Stephen drank heavily and began telling off-color jokes. Embarrassed, Stephen's daughter vowed not to invite Dad to any more family parties until he got treatment. Stephen agreed he acted foolishly that night but denied that he had an alcohol problem. He did agree to an evaluation.

Although Connie and Stephen have very different substance problems, both of them found help here at the U Penn Treatment Research Center. Because we carefully evaluate all patients—looking not only at their drug use, but also at their family and social network, their employment, and their psychiatric and emotional problems—we are able to tailor our approach to each patient. Connie and Stephen's experience with at our center illustrates how our treatment works. We start treatment with four basic assumptions:

1. Addiction is a chronic disease characterized by a tendency to relapse.
2. Those who begin treatment and stay in treatment generally get better.
3. A variety of biological, psychological, and social factors lead to addiction, and these factors also offer strategies for recovery.
4. Individualized treatment programs are more effective than those assuming that "one size fits all."

From this treatment philosophy, we have developed a program of treatment that can be used in almost any setting. It can be initiated by a general practitioner, a clinical psychologist, or by a psychiatrist, or it can be conducted in a specialized treatment center. We combine MET, CBT, medications, self-help, good medical and nursing practice, and a large dose of Marcus Welby. The idea is really to treat our patients the way we would want to be treated ourselves. Our system has six components and is easily recalled through the use of the acronym, BRENDA. The steps generally proceed in chronological order.

B — Biopsychosocial Evaluation (Assessment)
R — Report to patient on assessment
E — Empathetic understanding of the patient's situation, offering support to him or her
N — Needs (a determination of key needs to be met in order to spur recovery)
D — Direct advice to the patient on how to meet those needs
A — Assessment of reaction of patient to advice and changes in strategy to address problems

As we discuss each stage in more detail, you'll see how the system works and how each step is designed to build on the preceding one to create an environment of trust and understanding. Unlike many of the other treatments described in this book, we take a genuinely eclectic approach and fit the treatment to the person, rather than the other way around. It's often been said of traditional treatment that "If your only tool is a hammer, everything around you looks like a nail." At U Penn, we recognize that square pegs don't comfortably fit into round holes and try to tailor our approach accordingly. Even if you can't come to us, we hope that you can use what you learn here to best utilize whatever treatment you do choose — and to recognize when there is something that you need in treatment that you aren't getting.

Biopsychosocial Assessment

Biological or Medical Assessment

Because we know that not all alcoholics and other addicts are alike, we begin with a really good sense of what a person's particular problems are, and how deeply the person's substance use has affected the various aspects of her or his life. We include a physical exam — with particular attention to symptoms and physical signs of alcohol and other drug abuse, such as liver enlargement or tenderness. Blood tests for liver enzymes are also conducted. We look for bruises, tracks, abscesses, jaundice, malnutrition, and other symptoms that can indicate physical damage related to addiction. If a severe physical disorder is discovered, referral to the appropriate medical specialist is given.

Psychosocial Assessment

The psychological component of the assessment includes a thorough assessment of past emotional problems, including a history of depression, anxiety disorders, and psychotic disorders. Often, this reveals a story of childhood abuse or a more recent trauma. The health-care provider is sensitive to signs that the patient may be defensive about revealing too much initially, particularly regarding traumatic experiences. However, many people find it a relief to know that these issues are not off limits and can be brought into treatment later. We try our best to ask embarrassing or potentially upsetting questions in a way that makes people feel comfortable enough to respond honestly. Current psychological symptoms such as changes in appetite, sleeping habits, energy level, concentration, sex drive, and other interests are assessed. Panic attacks, irrational fears, obsessions, compulsions, and paranoid symptoms are some of the other things we look for.

A social evaluation is also important to determine the patients' support for recovery in their daily lives. The health-care provider reviews the amount and quality of social interactions in the patients' past and present life experiences. We look at such things as marriage, friendships, family relationships—any kind of social relationship that may be used to help, or in some cases to hinder, recovery. People with a stable job and several good, close relationships are much more likely to recover than those who lack these vital supports. If we see that these factors are present, we work to bolster them—and if not, we try to help the person develop supportive relationships through self-help groups and to move toward employment through such things as job-training programs, volunteer work, GED classes, college, and so on.

Alcohol and Other Drug Abuse Assessment

An important part of the alcohol and other drug abuse assessment is to look for relationships between drug use and life problems. We use scales such as the tests presented in Chapter 1, and then other more detailed questionnaires to try to figure out where drink and other drugs have done the most damage. When these tests are completed, both the patient and the provider should have a good sense of how severe the problem is. Rather than get hung up trying to convince a patient that he or she is really an alcoholic or another kind of addict, we simply try to identify areas where drug use has interfered with physical and emotional health and general functioning.

We're very big on assessment here—and though it sometimes makes people crazy to have to fill out so many forms and answer so many questions, ultimately, they tend to end up thanking us for it, because it helps them to understand their own difficulties. Another thing we look at is high-risk behavior for HIV. If someone is injecting drugs, we will want to be sure that they know how to protect themselves from HIV until they stop—and we will try to encourage them to get tested so that they can begin treatment for that disease, if needed.

Continuing Assessment

The biopsychosocial evaluation begins with the first visit and continues throughout treatment. Changes in physical and psychological symptoms can indicate clinical improvement, and feedback about improvement in these areas can help people become more motivated. Conversely, deterioration in any area can be a sign that relapse may be imminent and more aggressive treatment may be needed.

In Connie's case, on her first visit, she saw a social worker who performed an initial assessment. Next, she was examined by Gail, a nurse practitioner who completed a medical history and a physical exam and took blood samples. Connie was surprised when Gail asked her for a urine sample to test for drugs because she hadn't expected that expectations of recovery would start on her first visit. Gail reassured her that we weren't trying to punish or scare her—we just wanted to know what she was using and to help her chart her progress over time.

Nevertheless, that first day was a challenge for Connie. She spent several hours in our center being asked numerous highly personal questions. Though it seemed like a long day, Connie told us later that she always felt respected and hopeful. She told Gail that she had been experiencing stomach pains recently but otherwise felt healthy. Gail noted that except for a tender liver and elevated liver enzymes, Connie seemed physically fine.

As she got to know Gail, Connie began to open up. Later that first day, she talked about how she felt hopeless and despairing. She was surprised at how easy it was for her to relate her past history of sexual abuse to the nurse-practitioner—even though it did bring tears to her eyes when she described being raped at age 12 by her stepfather. Connie was well aware that her alcohol and other drug use had begun as a way to deal with the pain of this abuse and betrayal of trust: she said that using "stopped the nightmares." Because Gail could see that Connie had significant emotional problems, she explained that it would be wise to have a more complete psychiatric evaluation, so the next day, I examined her. I found that in addition to alcohol and cocaine dependence, Connie suffered from depression and posttraumatic stress disorder.

Connie told me she'd been very anxious about seeing me. She had seen psychiatrists before and had been previously diagnosed as schizophrenic. She had been prescribed antipsychotic medication, but, she said, "it made me feel like a zombie," so she stopped taking it. At the other treatment programs she'd attended, when she described feelings of hopelessness and her recurring, dreadful nightmares, drug counselors had told her that they were "just symptoms of addiction" and would go away if she just stopped drinking. Connie knew better, however—she'd started drinking to stop the nightmares, and every time she tried to quit, they returned.

Stephen's biopsychosocial assessment was much different from Connie's. While Connie had significant psychosocial problems—including a psychiatric disorder and being homeless—Stephen's evaluation revealed less serious difficulties. He had elevated liver enzymes and reported some difficulty maintaining an erection. While he still didn't think he had really needed to be evaluated for alcohol problems, he felt satisfied that at least he had had a thorough medical exam. He was also grateful that he had had a chance to discuss his impotence problem with a physician, he had been too embarrassed to seek help for it previously.

Report

On their next visit to our clinic, both Connie and Stephen received a full report on their condition, based on their answers to the questionnaires and the results of their other medical tests. Connie already knew that she was an addict and had emotional problems. Her discussion with Gail was reassuring to her, however, because she didn't feel like she was being judged or bullied. It was a relief for her to find out that she was not HIV positive and the abdominal pain was not viral hepatitis and would clear up as she stopped drinking.

She was also relieved to learn that we did not think she had schizophrenia. When Gail explained that her nightmares and depression and flashbacks were all symptoms of posttraumatic stress disorder, for the first time, Connie felt that her experience made sense. She wasn't going crazy because she used drugs—she was using drugs to keep herself from experiencing unpleasant symptoms. She was also glad to learn that there were treatments that could help reduce these symptoms without her having to resort to cocaine or alcohol. She told us she felt that Gail understood, and she began to feel reassured that perhaps she would be able to turn her life around and be a good mother to her child. For the first time in a long time, Connie began to feel hopeful.

Stephen's reaction to his report was very different. He sat in my office with his arms folded across his chest, waiting to be told the same thing every other program his family had pushed him to try did: that he was alcoholic and "in denial." I avoided this trap, however, and made no effort to confront him or to suggest that he accept that diagnosis. As I reviewed the report with Stephen, I noticed his reaction to specific items. While he was not particularly concerned about the effect alcohol was having on his relationship with his daughter, Stephen seemed genuinely worried that the elevations in his liver enzymes and his impaired ability to obtain erections were related to excessive alcohol use. By understanding what mattered to Stephen, I could help him work on achieving the goals that he found important.

After years of ignoring his daughter's accusations that he was "alcoholic," followed by occasional attempts to give in and seek the help she thought he needed, he began to realize that alcohol was actually preventing him from doing things that he cared about—and that it might actually be visibly shortening his life. He still wouldn't accept the idea that he was an alcoholic, however: He saw this admission as a defeat and an insult. Stephen saw alcoholics as constantly intoxicated, unemployed, lazy, and shiftless, and he did not believe he had anything in common with such people. Therefore, despite the pleas of his daughter, he could not understand why she thought of him that way, and he would not stick with any treatment requiring him to say that he was. To avoid this dilemma, in the Penn Paradigm, we focus on the relationship between alcohol or other drug use and real-life problems. In a spirit of working collaboratively and offering encouragement, during the report stage, we initiate a discussion of how changes in drug use can result in improvements in the areas that matter most to a particular person.

Empathetic Understanding

The importance of empathetic understanding cannot be overemphasized. Throughout this book, we've seen how crucial it is for people to feel safe and understood if they are to recover. If you can find a counselor who empathizes with you and supports you, no matter what her or his philosophy of treatment is, you will be ahead of the game. Being understood helps in every aspect of the treatment cycle. To maximize empathy, the health-care provider listens closely to the client and tries to get a sense of what is most and least important to him or her. The provider doesn't impose his or her own agenda—even if I thought that, say, Stephen should care more about his daughter than about his sex life, that wouldn't mean I should try to tell him that. Doing so would only make him feel judged and demeaned—it wouldn't do anything to solve his problem, and it could make him drop out of treatment entirely.

To empathize best, the provider has to attempt to see the world as the patient does. We ask ourselves—what would it be like if someone just told me I had to give up the love of my life? Would I go along and just say "OK," or would I fight and try to prove wrong this bearer of bad news? What would convince me that the love of my life was really bad for me—being told so by my friends and family, or finding out for myself by really examining how this person treats me?

Empathetic practitioners avoid power struggles with their patients by allying themselves with their patients' needs and desires and recognizing that the more someone feels understood, the more likely it is that he or she will take advice and suggestions. Once an empathetic relationship has been established, then both parties can get what they want. Patients get help dealing with the problems they care about—and the practitioner can guide treatment to take these wants into account.

Take Stephen's case. Someone looking at him with empathy can recognize that he is willing to explore changing his drinking habits but is not willing to call himself "an alcoholic." With that, as well as his employment status in mind, certain treatment options—such as inpatient rehab—make no sense, even though his insurance would cover it.

In Connie's situation, Gail stressed that she understood why her pain and distress over her childhood led her to use alcohol and other drugs. She told Connie that it is perfectly normal for people to seek to escape pain—and that it is, in fact, a healthy sign of a desire to survive. Connie then expressed her shame and guilt about how her drug use had led her to neglect her son, and how he'd been taken away from her. Again Gail listened—and explained how untreated depression can leave someone paralyzed and unable to take care of others. She said that what was important now was that she was getting help so that she would never be in that position again. Gail talked about how drug use can go from being a coping tool to an overwhelming need, and how people who have been traumatized are particularly vulnerable to this problem. She said that she'd had many patients who had had their kids taken—but that many were now reunited and learning to form families again.

As Gail offered hope that recovery was possible and that Connie did have a chance of getting her son back, Gail saw an obvious change in Connie's disposition. For the first time, Gail saw a slight smile cross Connie's face. During those first few sessions, Connie said, "I feel understood in way that no other program has understood me." By looking at the addiction from Connie's perspective, Gail saw that attention to Connie's psychosocial problems—particularly getting her a safe home, managing her depression, and initiating parenting classes and the custody case—was going to be critical in Connie's treatment program.

Needs

As you can see, for treatment to progress, the practitioner must find ways to meet the unique needs of the patient. One of the real advantages of the BRENDA system is that it is essentially a "case-management" approach: While we may not provide all the services that our patients need, we will recognize that these needs exist and work to hook them up with someone who does. We aren't wedded to getting everyone into AA or putting everyone through job training—we just try to offer what's needed.

The results of the assessment, the response to the report, the practice of empathy—all of these should lead naturally to a sense of what the key needs are. The Penn Paradigm—taking its lead from motivational enhancement and harm-reduction approaches—assumes that it is what the patient considers important, not what the treatment program is pushing, that matters.

Looking at Stephen's situation from the outside, for example, you might think that giving up drinking entirely is the most sensible course for him to take. That was not what he wanted to do, though, and if we had tried to force him to do that, he probably would have dropped out of our treatment, as he had done in all his previous attempts.

For Connie, the issues were different. Gail discovered that getting her child back was her most important concern. Because she saw clearly that her cocaine and alcohol use had caused her to lose custody, she was motivated to try anything to have her son returned. She had no problem accepting that she would have to become totally abstinent if she was to convince a judge that she was the fit mother that she so wanted to be.

FOR WOMEN: YOUR NEEDS COUNT

There is no doubt that women often have very different treatment needs than men do. The most common problems include being survivors of sexual and physical trauma and being depressed. There is also a more severe stigma attached to female alcoholics and other addicts: Men can be funny drunks, but women are seen as ugly or sexually loose.

Women-only therapy groups and self-help groups can be a crucial aid to recovery (AA has "women's meetings," as do several other 12-step programs; there is also a recovery group for women only, called Women for Sobriety). Many women with substance problems haven't had close female friends and use flirtations with men to avoid paying attention in mixed-gender meetings. Many fear that sharing about sexual abuse or relationship issues in mixed meetings may invite more abuse, and they simply don't feel safe. Women's meetings and groups avoid these problems and, in my own experience, are much more intense and open. Lesbians and bisexuals are welcomed in most women's meetings, but there are some groups that are homophobic, so gay and bisexual women may want to attend either gay women's meetings, where available, or lesbian and gay men's meetings. Gay community centers are often a good source of information about such groups.

Continuing evaluation is of particular importance for women because a majority do have other psychiatric problems. Posttraumatic stress disorder is often overlooked or misdiagnosed, so if you have suffered from serious trauma such as child abuse, rape, spousal or partner abuse, or witnessing a violent crime or other tragedy, try to mention it to your counselor and doctor.

If you have children, you may also have to deal with custody issues, child-care issues, and behavioral problems, which can plague children of alcoholics and other addicts. Parenting classes and family therapy can help, and making such efforts is bound to help if you have lost or are in danger of losing custody. Lack of child care can also be a real barrier to treatment. Many treatment programs are beginning to provide on-site child care, which U Penn has found to be very helpful. Some inpatient centers now even allow children to stay with their mothers. Before you rule out treatment because of child-care problems, get more information. Since the late 1980s, treatment centers have become much more responsive to women's needs.

Maia

Direct Advice

Given all of the preceding considerations, we begin to offer advice. Research shows that patients given a menu of treatment options do significantly better than those who are simply told what to do. This principle is incorporated into the BRENDA approach, and the direct advice is given in the form of options, not dogmatic demands.

Following the guidelines we've shown you here about choosing treatment, we sometimes refer people to inpatient detoxes—or to a study that another group here is working on, which seems appropriate. Sometimes we recommend self-help groups, and other times group or individual counseling. If we do refer someone out, we ask the person to keep coming to us for checkups, as well. If these outpatients have any problems, we want to be able to help them get back on track and, if necessary, refer them to additional services. Also, of course, we always keep in mind what the patient can afford and what services are available when making treatment plans.

In Stephen's case, we told him that the best and safest approach would be to abstain entirely, but when he balked at this, we recommended that he try the Moderation Management support group and that he take naltrexone. Even as he began his treatment program, however, he continued to feel harassed by his daughter. We suggested that he try a brief period of family therapy. A few sessions with both the father and the daughter present showed that Stephen's daughter was genuinely worried about the health of her father and did not trust his recovery. With support, Stephen was able to explain what his treatment goals were and what he would do if he didn't achieve them by working the moderation program. Stephen also offered ways that his daughter could express her concern without it feeling like nagging to him. With the tension in their relationship lessened, Stephen felt more competent and better able to pursue his goals.

For Connie, we recommended a women-only therapy group with other survivors of sexual trauma. It was here that she did the real work of facing her emotional issues—and here where she began to feel the effects of recovery. She told us that it was this group—where she realized she wasn't the only one who'd been through the things she had, and where she finally felt safe enough to discuss the things that had been tormenting her for years—that really made the difference. When she felt hopeless about ever regaining custody of her son and questioned her ability to care for him, others in the group related their own successful experiences in regaining custody. They reassured her that a clean and sober Connie was a caring and loving person who would be a wonderful mother. When Connie attained three months of complete abstinence, she was given a certificate by the program at our "Family Night." With tears streaming down her cheeks, Connie hugged each member of her group as she clutched the piece of paper with proof of her hard work. A year earlier, she would never have believed it possible to go three months without alcohol or crack.

Assessment of Reaction to Advice

As treatment continues, we constantly assess how the patients have reacted to our advice—whether they have done what they said they would, whether they've missed appointments, and, of course, whether they have suffered relapses. During the course of treatment, increasing responsibility is given to the client to direct the specific components of treatment. This helps our system self-correct: Treatments or suggestions that are not used by clients or do not move them closer to their goals are reexamined and often discarded. While typical treatment programs treat nonadherence as "resistance" and leave the responsibility to the client to find the motivation to continue treatment (i.e., "he just hasn't hit rock bottom yet"), the Penn Paradigm looks at resistance as a starting point to examine why the person didn't follow recommendations and to determine whether there is another approach that might be better for the person in that particular situation.

This constant evaluation of our approach doesn't mean that we never have dropouts or people who don't succeed in treatment. Sometimes, even though each step of the BRENDA approach has been used, the client objects to every single option offered. Any advice is met with, "Yes, but I can't because . . ." Often, reassessing the situation is important.

For example, when Stephen was told that his elevated liver enzymes were signs that his liver had started to be damaged by alcohol, and perhaps he should abstain from alcohol, Stephen protested, "Yes I should stop drinking, but I can't not have a drink or two in front of my colleagues when we go on business dinners," or, "Yes, I should stop drinking, but sometimes I need a drink or two to get to sleep at night." Even though the illogic of each objection was pointed out to him—not drinking at business dinners might sharpen his competitive edge, and alcohol-induced sleep is not particularly restful—Stephen had a but each time total abstinence was mentioned.

It turned out that in his mind, he equated the idea of abstinence with giving in to his daughter. If Stephen agreed to abstain from alcohol, in his eyes, it meant that his daughter was right and he was an alcoholic. I then asked Stephen what he wanted to do about the problem of his elevated liver enzymes and his inability to sustain erections. He replied, "I'll cut down a little in my drinking." Eventually, we agreed that Stephen would abstain for two weeks to "give his liver a break and detoxify from alcohol." After that, Stephen could drink but no more than five drinks in a single day, and preferably less. Also, Stephen agreed to take naltrexone to help him refrain from bingeing. He also agreed to take careful notes on the number of drinks he had each day, and if he could not refrain from having five or more drinks, then he would go with plan B, complete abstinence.

Another problem we sometimes have is that patients don't take their medications. BRENDA was actually developed because we realized that naltrexone worked amazingly well when taken regularly—but that if patients missed even just 20% of their pills, relapse was as common as without medication.

We have identified several factors that keep people from taking their medications—and have included at the end of this chapter a list of tips that can help you remember to do so if you are in a program that offers naltrexone or other meds.

Another common difficulty that some patients have is missing appointments. Connie's recovery was not straightforward—she had one major relapse, which was followed by a period in which she was not in treatment. When she had started our program, Gail discussed the schedule with her, including our policy for missed appointments. If someone repeatedly misses appointments without canceling and without a good explanation, we sometimes start a treatment "sabbatical." This is a period of a month during which we will not restart treatment.

About two months into treatment, Connie learned that her first request to regain custody of her son had been denied. Although this did not mean that she would necessarily lose him forever, Connie began a week-long binge on alcohol and cocaine. Attempts to contact her were unsuccessful, and her mother reported that Connie, who had moved in with her during treatment, had not been home for some time. When Connie was contacted two weeks later, she was invited back into treatment and underwent a second detoxification with Gail.

A pattern emerged, however, in which Connie did not show up for treatment in weeks in which she used cocaine or drank. When Gail pointed out that these lapses were opportunities to learn what triggers led to drug use and that it was especially important to come to sessions after a slip, Connie began to feel less shame about her slips. Still, at this point, she missed more appointments than she met. At times, she would come to the center without a scheduled appointment, while at other times she would cancel at the last minute.

Eventually, we sent a letter to her home, during which a "treatment sabbatical" was scheduled. She was told that due to a pattern of missed visits, she would not have an appointment scheduled for at least 30 days. When her sabbatical was concluded, she could call us and reenter treatment. The door remained open to Connie, but we wanted her to come when she really wanted to make an effort, not when she wasn't sure about getting better. Paradoxically, being told that she could not come into treatment for a month motivated her. She really liked Gail and other members of the treatment team and did not want to drop out. She circled on her calendar the date when the sabbatical ended and called us that same day to reschedule.

From that point on, her attendance was excellent. Not only did she attend her individual sessions with Gail but she also became a consistent participant in the group therapy, attending at least twice a week. It was at this point that she was able to develop the supportive relationships she needed in the group to really work through her fears and pain about her past and about how she would deal with her life no matter what happened in her battle to get her son back.

FOR FAMILY MEMBERS AND OTHER LOVED ONES: WHAT YOU CAN DO

Family members can help people who are undergoing treatment in our system in many ways. One of the most important things they can do is just to let the people in treatment know that they recognize how hard their loved ones are working and are glad that they decided to deal with their problems. It's important not to criticize their treatment choices. There may be reasons that you are not aware of that make these choices best for your loved ones, and the more you encourage them to continue working on their problems, the more likely they are to be able to do so.

Another thing you can do is participate in family therapy if it is indicated—and to attend treatment-related functions designed for family members to help them support the person with a drug problem in their family. Attending family therapy or support groups or other treatment-related programs does not mean that you are "crazy" or "have a disease" or are "codependent." It just means that you have chosen to learn as much as possible to make your loved one's recovery easier.

Try not to criticize your loved one for slips or relapses. Stress that slips are not failures, and just like a horseback rider needs to get back up after a fall, your loved one should go right back into recovery efforts. Mistakes happen—what you make of those mistakes is up to you, and you don't have to let them defeat you.

Finally, if treatment requires medication, and your loved one is willing to let you help her or him take it, you can do so. Don't pester your loved one about it, though. Just ask once at an agreed-upon time each day whether he or she has taken it, and leave it at that. Some people may ask a significant other to call the doctor or counselor if the medication is not taken. If you are going to do this, you must agree about it ahead of time, and you must both be willing to have this rule in place. If the person with the problem already feels "nagged" or "controlled" by her or his significant other, this may not be a good arrangement. Whatever you do, have very clear rules and consequences, and follow through on them.

Joe

Slips and Relapses

At U Penn, using the research findings on relapse prevention, we find it important to distinguish between a small slip—where someone has a glass of wine or a sniff of cocaine but then stops—and a relapse involving a full-fledged return to excessive use. Because people tend to have so much shame about relapse, they often let a slip become much more because they figure they have already blown it anyway. By using the notion of slips, we allow people to feel that recovery doesn't end with just one mistake, but that there are a series of decisions involved, which can be stopped at any point.

We use slips and relapses as learning opportunities—and do not expel patients who are making a sincere effort to recover because they don't do it perfectly as soon as they enter treatment. We recognize that addiction is chronic and often marked by relapses, and we try to remove the shame attached to this and allow the person a sense that each slip followed by a return to treatment is a step away from addiction. By combining a variety of proven treatment approaches, we allow them to synergize—for better effects than any one approach alone could achieve. Research so far shows that BRENDA is effective in reducing drug use and drug-related harm, helping patients stay in treatment, and helping them take their medications properly. We are continuing to study and improve it.

MEDICATION TIPS

In order to get the best results from treatment, it is important to take medication exactly as prescribed. Here are some tips to help you avoid missing doses or forgetting whether you have taken your medication.

1. Have your prescriber provide the drug in a blister pack, labeled so that you will know whether you took each day's dose. If these are not available, get a pill box with compartments for each day, and place the pills into them immediately after you have your prescription filled.

2. Take your dose at the same time every day. Make it part of your routine. If you are going to be taking it in the morning and you eat breakfast or have coffee, put the pills on your kitchen table and take them with your meal or your morning cup. If you prefer, take them when you brush your teeth in the morning or at night. If you have any other specific routine—such as choosing your clothes in the morning or preparing the kids for school, you can incorporate the meds there, as well. Just be sure to associate them with something that you do every day.

3. If you feel comfortable with it, ask your partner or spouse to help you remember your medication and to help you think of this as part of his or her routine, as well. Only do this if you won't see it as "nagging," however.

4. Put a note on your refrigerator, medicine cabinet, or anywhere else where you will see it regularly to remind yourself to take your medication. Move the note around so that it doesn't fade into the background and cease to be an effective reminder.

5. If you feel like deliberately missing a dose, call your doctor or counselor to discuss why. Be honest about your feelings related to medication—and about possible side effects. Your doctor can help you work out whether the effects are medication related.

6. If the reason you want to skip a dose is because you are experiencing urges to drink or use other drugs, call someone you trust from a self-help group, or call a counselor, or get to a self-help meeting. The urge will pass—and if you take the medication, it will pass faster.

Knowledge Is Power
• Complete and continuing evaluation is one of the most important parts of successful treatment.

- If your treatment provider isn't empathetic — kind, caring, supportive — you will probably not get the most out of treatment.
- While it is best to avoid slips if possible, they don't need to become full relapses and can help you learn to have a more stable recovery.
- Understanding what someone's reasons for not wanting to stop drinking or using other drugs can help the person to find other ways to get those needs met and thereby become ready for recovery.
- Self-medication — using drugs to help deal with pain and trauma — is one of the most common causes of addiction, particularly among women. Post-traumatic stress disorder (PTSD), depression, and other problems must be dealt with in order to improve sufferers' lives and increase their odds of recovery.

CHAPTER 10

Getting Off:
Medications to Help You Quit

*At the end, I was drinking faithfully, a pint a day, sometimes more.
[When I detoxed,] I had the Serax, but I had no withdrawal symptoms. I had no problem. I think that was all I needed.*
                          Gordon, an alcoholic treated at U Penn

Many alcoholics and other addicts—particularly those who use alcohol or
heroin—have a terrible fear of withdrawal. In the past, most treatment centers
would only alleviate withdrawal symptoms if a patient was in danger of death
or—at the very least—begging and pleading. They argued that it served an
addict well to experience the uncomfortable feelings of withdrawal. "They will
think twice about using again," the care providers said.

This approach is cruel and without merit, however. For example, one of my
alcoholic patients had gone through detoxification many times, including once
while he was incarcerated. In jail, he experienced severe cramps, nausea, vomiting, panic attacks, and insomnia. After three days, his symptoms improved.
Within 24 hours of leaving prison, however, he was drinking again. Because of
the way addiction is learned—pleasure is associated with having the drug, pain
with *not* having it—awful withdrawal symptoms can actually *increase*, rather
than decrease, drug desire. Worse, repeated abrupt detoxifications without medications can lead to sensitization of the nervous system, making each successive
detoxification more severe than the preceding one. Fear of withdrawal can then
become a real barrier to treatment.

Fortunately, many of today's detox programs recognize that a "let 'em sweat it
out" approach leads to dropout, rather than to increased recovery rates. In this
chapter, we examine the types of medications that are most useful in easing the
transition from addiction to recovery; in the next, we look at those medications
that are helpful over the longer term.

Treating Physical Dependence

Once your body has adapted to the continuous presence of a drug, removing it
throws your whole system off and creates unpleasant symptoms. Physiological

dependence is not unique to drugs of abuse. Withdrawal symptoms can occur if you abruptly stop some high blood pressure medications, for example. To prevent this, these drugs are slowly tapered when they are discontinued. Unfortunately, it is extremely difficult to slowly taper your drug of choice. When you start to take a little, you tend to want more, not less. People don't crave drugs that lower blood pressure, but a drug that offers comfort is a different story. Slowly cutting down, in anything but a highly controlled setting, is often impossible.

Detox medications tend to be different—they have similar effects to the abused drug, but produce less of a high while taking the edge off of withdrawal symptoms. Using such medications allows addicts a safer and more comfortable means of quitting, and detox can now even be done in many cases without hospitalization. The remaining sections describe some medications that can help with various withdrawal syndromes.

Detox from Alcohol and Other Sedatives

One night I was sitting in the lab alone . . . listening to dreamy Hawaiian music on the radio. Slowly, a pile of pineapples started to build up on the table. They got bigger and bigger and nearer and nearer, as if they were going to fall and crush me. Two of them leaped from the table and crashed into my head. I was knocked to the floor, swinging madly at the faces of those pineapples. I swung, I swore, I started throwing beer cans at the advancing hordes of pineapple faces. I cut my hands, my face, my legs. I had D.T.'s.

from a personal story in the *Big Book*, p. 427

The most dangerous symptoms of alcohol withdrawal are related to its sedative effects. Alcohol depresses the central nervous system, and over time, your body adapts to this chronic sedation. If long-term excessive alcohol use is abruptly stopped, your nervous system will rebound and be hyperactive. In mild cases, this can mean "the shakes," sweating, anxiety, difficulty sleeping, and rapid heart rate. In more severe cases, it can include withdrawal seizures and hallucinations. In the most severe cases, death can result.

In principle, any sedative can be used to treat withdrawal from any other sedative. The safest and most effective medications are benzodiazepines—but some are more prone to abuse than others. Unlike Valium, for example, Serax and librium both have low abuse potential. Serax is not metabolized by the liver (which is often impaired in alcoholics) and thus has an additional safety benefit.

In my clinical experience over 25 years, I have supervised the detoxification of several thousand alcoholics. Nearly all of them received Serax, but I have never seen anyone who became a "Serax addict" after our detox. Over 80% of patients successfully complete detoxification on an outpatient basis at our center—and the vast majority of them, like Gordon, who was quoted at the beginning of this chapter, experience significant relief from withdrawal symptoms within 24 hours.

Treatment of withdrawal from other sedatives is similar to alcohol treatment. However, withdrawal from certain drugs, such as Valium, which stay in the body longer than others, can take weeks. If a person with an anxiety disorder has begun to abuse such medications, a slower detox may be warranted to prevent the reemergence of anxiety symptoms.

Detox from Cocaine and Other Stimulants

Most of them are here for cocaine or freebase but there's also a sizable opiate contingent. The cocaine people sleep all the time because by the time they get here, they haven't slept in weeks. We opiates have been sleeping a lot, so now we roam the halls at night, twitching through our withdrawals. I think there should be ball teams: the Opiates vs. the Amphetamines. The opiates scratch and do hand signals and nod out, and the amphetamines run around the bases and scream.

from Carrie Fisher's *Postcards from the Edge*

Physical withdrawal symptoms from stimulants such as cocaine and amphetamines are not nearly as dramatic or life threatening as those seen with sedatives. In fact, for years, researchers thought cocaine didn't cause physical dependence because they couldn't measure significant withdrawal signs. However, just as stimulants cause general excitation of the nervous system, stimulant withdrawal produces an opposite reaction. When you take stimulants, you feel a reduced need for sleep, your heart rate jumps, and you experience, at least initially, feelings of energy and excitement. Stimulant withdrawal is associated with a slower heart rate, feelings of low energy and interest, and increased need for sleep. Perhaps the most important symptoms of stimulant withdrawal are mental: extreme craving for the drug, anxiety, fear, lethargy, and depression.

As one coke addict put it in Terry Williams's study, *Crackhouse*, "My friend calls the [crack] pipe the devil's dick because the more you smoke, the more you want. . . . When people say they don't get the same physical addiction as heroin addicts, that's a piece of shit, too because you always want this drug. You want it when you are sleeping, you dream about it. The cloud [of crack smoke], the blizzard is on your mind when you wake up in the morning. Now you don't usually get the physically violent convulsions and all, but so what?"

Because stimulant withdrawal is not life threatening, however, and doesn't have any physical symptoms to be alleviated, physicians usually suggest simply waiting out the three- to four-day period that it takes for the body to readapt. For many people, particularly binge users, this is probably the right strategy. Recent research suggests, however, that there is a subgroup of chronic users of cocaine who have more severe withdrawal symptoms and who can benefit from medications.

If you have used large quantities of cocaine daily over a long period of time and score over 20 on the cocaine-withdrawal test in Chapter 1, you may want to try a medication called amantadine, which increases dopamine activity in the brain and may be able to help you quit. It is not a controlled substance and can be prescribed by any physician. We know that cocaine causes an overrelease of dopamine—so it is likely that there is a shortage of this substance for people in cocaine withdrawal. If cocaine use is daily, this shortage may become severe—and people with problems this bad often cannot even stick out three to four days without cocaine to begin treatment. We've found that amantadine can help such people stay in treatment—and that it significantly relieves the distress they feel during cocaine withdrawal.

Detox from Opiates

Opiate withdrawal lies between sedative withdrawal and stimulant withdrawal in severity, though addicts often battle each other over whose suffering is the worst, and heroin addicts tend to make the most dramatic case. There are obvious physical symptoms, including "goose flesh," rapid heart rate, diarrhea, muscle cramps, vomiting, nausea, aches and pains, and general malaise. For heroin, acute physical withdrawal is unpleasant but not life threatening and usually lasts about a week. Opiate withdrawal is often compared to a severe flu—but because most flus aren't combined with insomnia, anxiety, and emotional pain similar to losing a love, many addicts don't find that this description adequately conveys their experience.

Two Medical Approaches

There are two general medical approaches to dealing with opiate withdrawal. One is to substitute the opiate of abuse (i.e., heroin) with a longer-acting opiate such as methadone, and then to gradually reduce the methadone dose. This method has the advantage of effectively reducing withdrawal symptoms and craving and helps keep patients in treatment. However, simply providing heroin addicts with 21 days of methadone treatment on an outpatient basis is rarely successful—even though many methadone clinics offer this program. This time period is just too short to allow addicts to stabilize their lives as longer-term maintenance can. Most tend to simply increase their heroin use as the clinic drops the dose of methadone. Inpatient methadone detox, done properly, however, can be very helpful. One note: If you are admitted to a hospital that uses this approach, make sure that you will receive no opiates for the last few days before you are discharged. Otherwise, you will be comfortable in the hospital but will have to deal with the worst of withdrawal afterward—which can be a real problem if you are at home rather than in further inpatient treatment.

Another method is to use nonopiate medications such as clonidine to reduce withdrawal symptoms, also while the person is hospitalized. During opiate withdrawal, the brain's noradrenaline system is overactive because one effect of the brain's opiate systems is to damp down this system. Lack of this "damper" causes symptoms such as anxiety and restlessness and nausea. Clonidine can block most of the physical symptoms, but unfortunately, it does little for the craving or anxiety. In combination with liberal use of antianxiety or sleeping medications, however, someone who is hospitalized can be kept relatively comfortable with clonidine, and this detox is one of the most commonly used to ready heroin addicts for more intensive drug-free treatment.

Clonidine is safe enough to be used on an outpatient basis, and the detox process takes three to four days—but only the most highly motivated patients seem able to withstand it.

MY DETOX EXPERIENCE

When I entered detox, I was well into my first day of heroin withdrawal. I had been shooting 5–10 bags a day, as well as up to a gram of cocaine. I was underweight and probably malnourished—the only thing I can remember eating at the end was Boston cream pie and the odd chocolate milkshake. I weighed 85 pounds.

My mom had had to call several hospitals before finding one that provided heroin detox. I was eventually admitted to Harris Hospital in upstate New York, near where she lived. When I arrived, I was given an injection of naloxone—I guess in the hopes of getting the last of the heroin out of my system and speeding up the withdrawal process. If I had known it was naloxone, I would have refused it. It made me immediately much sicker. I was then given clonidine to help treat the withdrawal symptoms. Though it did not make me any less anxious, and though I did throw up a few times and felt pretty nauseous, it did make me somewhat groggy and less shaky. Because the detox I attended had an ideological stance against giving any potential drugs of abuse to addicts, they didn't give me anything to help me sleep, and I think I was probably awake for most of the first four days I spent there. I was achy and uncomfortable and terrified—but oddly, I also had moments of euphoria. I had resisted getting help for so long, and my life had gotten so bad that even being in withdrawal somehow seemed like relief. The euphoria brought me a brief sense that life without drugs wouldn't be so bad and that perhaps I might still somehow salvage my life. I still whined and complained, but the hospital did let me take long baths, which helped, and the other addicts who were kicking were very supportive. I slowly began to feel better.

Oddly, my withdrawal symptoms briefly returned when I entered a private rehab facility in Westchester, after seven days in the hospital. I threw up and shook, and the rehab staff thought I might be bulimic because I had actually lost weight in the detox. Withdrawal seems to fluctuate with environment and does not get better steadily; rather, it's bad, it gets a bit better, it gets a bit worse, then better again until it's done. Each day sees some progress, but when you have another bout of symptoms, there's a tendency to fall into despair and feel as though you are getting nowhere. It's just an uneven process, and scary new situations such as moving from a hospital to a rehab can bring some of it back on. The most important thing to keep telling yourself is that withdrawal will be over soon, the worst of it doesn't last very long, and each second you've gone through is one closer to being through with it.

Maia

Ultra Rapid Opioid Detox (UROD)

In an effort to overcome the disadvantages of clonidine detox, a new approach has been introduced, in which opiate detoxification takes place under general anesthesia. The promoters of this technique claim that they can condense days of withdrawal discomfort into just four hours by using high doses of opiate-blocking drugs such as naloxone and naltrexone. These drugs (often used to treat overdose) remove opiates from your system, but they also make opiate withdrawal more intense.

Proponents of UROD say that flooding the system with antagonists prompts a shorter withdrawal period. Because the person undergoing detox is anesthetized while the drugs are administered, they also claim that the method is "painless." After the procedure, the patient may be discharged or may stay one night in the hospital for observation. The patient is referred to an outpatient program and given naltrexone to reduce relapse risk. There are several major drawbacks to this approach, however.

First, we don't really know if the procedure actually does condense withdrawal. Some addicts who have undergone it claim that it does. For instance, Juan, a 44-year-old fashion executive whom Maia interviewed for a story she wrote for *Newsday*, had been addicted to prescription painkillers and had previously tried to quit on his own. "It cut the withdrawal time by one third, easy," he said. "Within 48 hours, I felt fine, and I was sleeping and leading a normal lifestyle within a week."

Not so, said Neal, another patient Maia spoke with. He had been using a half gram of heroin daily, on top of 100 milligrams of methadone. "It was the worst withdrawal I ever had, by far," he said. He reported not being completely unconscious during the procedure and having terrifying hallucinations. When he came to, he said, "I was choking on a plastic tube with vomit coming up, I was [having a bowel movement,] and I couldn't stand I was so weak." The procedure Neal underwent also involved the implantation of time-release naltrexone under his skin. Several days later, still experiencing nausea, diarrhea, severe anxiety, and dehydration, he had the implant removed.

Because there have been no controlled studies comparing UROD to traditional inpatient detox, we have no way of knowing which of these stories is the more common and whether it actually is more comfortable for most people. The fact that after the procedure, patients are often given clonidine and sedatives to take home suggests that even supporters of the process recognize that ongoing withdrawal is common.

There are also other potential dangers. Anesthesia itself carries a small, but real risk of death. The reason people are discouraged from eating before major surgery is to decrease the risk that they will vomit during anesthesia and will choke on their own vomit. Because opiate withdrawal itself produces vomiting, particularly when exacerbated by antagonists, the risk of death is increased. There has been at least one death from this complication in the United States— and dozens of others around the world from other complications within 48 hours of the procedure.

Given the high risk of this procedure, and the fact that opiate withdrawal is not life threatening, it is probably better to wait until more research has been done before considering it. If really you feel that you cannot stand four days of withdrawal and want to wake up able to take naltrexone so that you cannot slip back into dependence, you may want to consider it (though you may suffer the four days anyway!). However, it is expensive—usually $3,000–$5,000, not covered by most insurance carriers.

Detox from Marijuana

While the vast majority of even heavy pot smokers quit without experiencing significant withdrawal symptoms, some do experience several days where they feel under the weather, with symptoms such as headache and nausea. Marijuana detox is almost always done on an outpatient basis, unless there are other drugs that produce more significant physical dependence involved. Over-the-counter medications such as acetaminophen (Tylenol) can help with the headache (and this has the advantage of not irritating the stomach). For nausea, you can take any of the numerous over-the-counter remedies available. In most cases, these symptoms are not long lasting or incapacitating. If you are having overwhelming difficulties, you should seek medical attention, to be sure there is not another physical or psychological disorder involved.

Maintenance Drugs and Craving Fighters

Though most detox drugs can get you through the transition from active addiction or alcoholism to recovery, most cannot help with the most important part of the process: reducing craving for drugs and helping you avoid relapse. Research has found that the type of detox you undergo—whether it's medically managed for comfort or "cold turkey"—does not determine whether you will stay clean. Basically, all addicts can get clean by locking themselves in for a week—the real trick is staying away from the drugs and the booze afterward. In the next chapter, we look at medications that can help with relapse prevention. Detox drugs and those used for maintenance, such as methadone, often have similar effects to the drug of choice; craving fighters tend either to reduce the high resulting from slipping or to use other mechanisms to help the addict avoid the drug, without producing a new drug dependence. You would think that the treatment community would embrace such medications, but once again, providers that do so turn out to be somewhat hard to find.

Detox Medications Currently Available and Recommended

For alcohol: Serax or librium

For cocaine use that is severe and associated with difficult withdrawal symptoms: amantadine

For heroin: clonidine with a sleep medication protocol for inpatients; inpatient methadone detox; or buprenorphine detox, if available (can be done on an outpatient basis)

Knowledge Is Power

- A number of medications can now make detoxification easier, though none make it painless.
- Some medications help with detox or maintenance by mimicking the action of the drug of choice; others help by fighting drug craving.
- Don't let the prejudice of some recovering people against the use of medications prevent you from getting the best care.
- Two detoxes we don't recommend, due to lack of efficacy or safety concerns are rapid or ultra rapid opiate detox (ROD, UROD, etc. — using anesthesia and antagonists) and outpatient 21-day methadone detox.

CHAPTER 11

Medications to Reduce Craving and Relapse

Bob spent nearly 40 years—from ages 12 to 52—in a drunken stupor. He lost his job, his family, and his self-respect. A dozen treatment programs and over two dozen therapists and psychiatrists failed to keep him from returning to the bottle. He had periods of a week, a month, and even nearly a year once, but Bob found it impossible to stay sober. He blamed himself for his failures, and each failure escalated his self-loathing. Finally, Bob reached his breaking point and bought a shotgun. "I am done," he said, as he pulled the trigger, gun barrel pointed at his forehead. He flinched—but incredibly, he heard a click as the gun misfired. In frustration, he aimed at a wall and pulled the trigger again. This time, the gun fired, and several alarmed neighbors came running. He made excuses about cleaning his gun, then drank himself to sleep.

The next day, he noticed an article in the paper about a new medication to treat alcoholism. A nearby treatment program, in Phoenix, Arizona, was using it. With nothing to lose, Bob decided to give treatment one more chance—and soon took his first naltrexone tablet. Amazingly, Bob found his craving for alcohol diminishing. For once, the treatment groups and the advice they gave made sense—and he was actually able to do as they suggested. He felt free. Two years and one minor slip later, Bob reflected back on how his life has changed. During the six months in treatment when he took naltrexone, he found that the urges did not have the same power over him. He was able to pursue other interests, without the constant nagging thought of a drink dominating his thoughts and decisions. With the help of a supportive therapist, Bob found a part-time job, fell in love, and gained a new sense of self-esteem. "Without naltrexone, I am sure that I would be dead by now. Today I am alive, happy, and sober," he said.

Not everyone finds naltrexone as helpful as Bob did, but the past decade has seen remarkable progress in medication development for the treatment of alcohol and other drug addictions. Naltrexone is the first new medication approved by the FDA for human alcoholism treatment in nearly 50 years. Others are in the pipeline for both alcoholism and other addictions. Research—at our center and others—has found that adding naltrexone to an alcoholism treatment regimen can decrease the risk of serious relapse by 50%. The use of medications offers new hope to millions of people who've been unable to recover using the "talking cure" treatments alone. Unfortunately, there are strong social forces that make getting medications from the lab to patients very difficult.

Using drugs to treat addictions is highly controversial among recovering alcoholics and other addicts, and even most treatment professionals—particularly those who attend 12-step programs or provide Minnesota Model treatment. Such providers fear replacing one addiction with another (even though these drugs can't do that) and don't even mention the option to their patients. This omission is tragic because there are many stories like Bob's, where medication really can make a difference. Also, oddly, though many members of AA and other 12-step fellowships speak out against medication, there is nothing in the program as written that supports this position. In fact, AA's cofounder Bill Wilson supported medication-development efforts. He himself even tried LSD to see whether it could help create the spiritual experiences sought by members. An official AA pamphlet ("The AA Member and Other Medications") stresses that if you have been honest with your physician about your addiction and she or he prescribes medication, you should listen to your physician and not to AA members telling you to avoid all drugs. (A good retort is, "And what medical school is your degree from?") Treatment centers' blanket opposition to medication is beginning to change—but sadly, the majority still don't offer these options. For example, Hazelden only began allowing the use of antidepressants for depression in its patients in 1997—and it still doesn't use any anticraving medications.

In this chapter, we look at some of the recent advances in the pharmacological treatment of addictions. An understanding of both the strengths and the limitations of medication can help you choose the most effective type of treatment to meet your needs. If you find yourself dealing with serious urges and cravings, you may want to ask your treatment provider or your general practitioner for this type of assistance.

Medications for Alcohol Problems

Several types of medications have been used to treat alcohol dependence including Antabuse (disulfiram), lithium, serotonin reuptake blockers (Prozac [fluoxetine], etc.), and most recently, naltrexone. Here's how they work. Antabuse blocks one step in the metabolism of alcohol. This leads to an accumulation of a toxic chemical called acetylaldehyde. It produces symptoms such as facial flushing, nausea, vomiting, and low blood pressure, and in severe reactions, it leads to respiratory depression, heart attacks, or even death. By taking Antabuse, an alcoholic gives him or herself a very good reason not to drink. Unfortunately, the drug does nothing to reduce alcohol craving—so those who crave alcohol just stop taking it or risk the reaction.

Another medication, lithium, helps stabilize mood and is used in the treatment of manic depression (bipolar disorder). Researchers theorized that it might help alcoholics because many drink to regulate mood. More recently, Prozac, Zoloft, and similar antidepressants have been studied because of their effectiveness in reducing depression and in treating other types of compulsive behavior. Placebo-controlled studies have shown that all of these medications have limited effects on relapse, however. While they may help certain sub-groups of patients—like those who also suffer depression, manic depression, or anxiety—they are not effective in reducing relapse rates in general.

The Naltrexone Story

Initial Research

In the 1970s, when researchers were first beginning to understand the brain's opiate system and how alcohol interacts with it, I wondered whether interfering with this system might help reduce alcohol craving. I tested my theory first on rats. Like humans, rats drink much more alcohol after being in a stressful situation. We subjected our rats to the rat equivalent of a very bad day at the office—and then gave one group of them naltrexone, the other, placebo. Next, they were offered free access to alcohol. The placebo-treated rats drank excessively, like most rats do after experiencing stress. The naltrexone-treated rats, however, drank normally—only moderately. It seemed that my theory was right—and that naltrexone was a promising medication to test on human alcoholism.

The first human clinical trial of naltrexone began in 1986 at the University of Pennsylvania/VA Center for Studies of Addiction. After a standard alcohol detox program, patients received either 50mg/day of naltrexone or placebo for 12 weeks. For the first month, both groups got intensive outpatient treatment, and afterward, they received biweekly group therapy.

During the study, we measured alcohol craving and actual drinking weekly, and we measured liver enzymes monthly. People taking naltrexone reported significantly reduced craving, compared to those on placebo. This was the first demonstration that a medication could actually reduce the desire to drink alcohol! Even more encouragingly, the people in the naltrexone group drank much less frequently than those taking placebo—on about 50% fewer days. There was also a reduction in serious relapse—which we defined as an episode of five or more drinks during a single drinking occasion. By this measure, naltrexone cut relapse rates in half. About one half of the placebo subjects relapsed during the study, compared to less than 25% in the naltrexone group. This was also the first study to show that a medication could significantly reduce relapse rates for alcohol-dependent patients.

Interestingly, naltrexone did not have a dramatic effect in preventing subjects from having a single slip. About half the subjects in both groups experienced a slip during which they had one or two drinks. What was really fascinating and exciting, however, was that the medication seemed to help reduce the chance that a slip would become a relapse. Because I had proposed that the addictive cycle seen in alcoholics was at least partially due to the ability of alcohol to stimulate their opiate receptors, I also predicted that naltrexone might block or diminish the loss of control over drinking typically seen in alcoholics.

Happily, results from our study were consistent with my theory. Over 85% of the placebo subjects who slipped went on to relapse, but just 50% of the naltrexone subjects who slipped returned to full-blown alcoholic drinking. Naltrexone may not necessarily prevent someone from picking up the first drink, but it can often prevent that drink from becoming a "drunk."

The reports from people who were taking naltrexone were also remarkable. Several subjects told me that at a party or other social situation, the pressure to drink was too much to resist, and they had broken down and had one. They found, however, that the alcohol didn't have its usual effect on them. They did not feel as high as they usually did, and probably more importantly, they didn't feel a compulsion to have another drink. They reported doing something they had never been able to do before—they stopped drinking, leaving half a beer on the bar.

Stephanie O'Malley at Yale University confirmed our results. She gave alcoholics 50 mg of naltrexone per day for 12 weeks but used much less intensive "talk therapy" than we did. Her population, unlike ours, was mostly white and employed. We were pleasantly surprised to see that despite the differences in the groups studied and the intensity of psychosocial support, the subjects who received naltrexone still had much lower relapse rates than the subjects receiving placebo.

Another of our studies examined people with a family history of alcoholism who were drinkers, but so far not yet alcoholics. They were compared with drinkers who had no close alcoholic relatives. After lunch, they each drank about three beers—having previously taken either naltrexone or a placebo. When the people with the family history took placebo, they reported more euphoria and excitement from drinking than the normal subjects on placebo. When the children of alcoholics took naltrexone, however, their response to alcohol was the same as that of normal drinkers. It was almost as if the drug had reduced the influence of a genetic vulnerability to alcoholism!

Use in Treatment

In late 1994, the FDA approved naltrexone for treatment of alcoholism in the United States. Since that time, double-blind studies both here and internationally have repeatedly demonstrated the efficacy of naltrexone in reducing alcohol craving and relapse. Naltrexone is now approved in dozens of countries and represents one of the most important new advances in the treatment of alcoholism this century.

If you need treatment for a drinking problem, it makes sense to ask your provider for a naltrexone prescription—or to choose one who you know offers it. Any physician can prescribe naltrexone because it is FDA approved, and for most people, there are very few side effects. The most common are nausea (experienced by about 10% of people), headache (7%), dizziness (4%), fatigue (4%), insomnia (3%), anxiety (2%), and sleepiness (2%). Most of these side effects went away quickly and were not severe enough to cause people to stop taking medication.

If you decide to start your treatment with just a self-help group, you can also ask your primary-care physician for a prescription to try while you begin your recovery. For best results, naltrexone should be taken for at least six months— this is enough time for a person to readjust to life without alcohol and for alcohol craving to diminish dramatically. There are no withdrawal symptoms associated with stopping naltrexone, and it has no abuse potential. However, some people prefer to continue to take it for longer, so that they can have an occasional drink without craving more or returning to bingeing. (The effect naltrexone has on the craving for the second drink ceases when you stop taking it.)

There are some limitations to the use of naltrexone and other medications in treating alcoholism and other forms of addiction. A medication is not a cure—and so those who do not want to give up heavy drinking may simply refuse to take it. Alcoholics may also fear that taking anticraving medication will prevent them from experiencing other life pleasures aside from drinking. This is not the case for the vast majority of alcoholics, but if you do experience a feeling of amotivation or pleasurelessness while on naltrexone, we've found that adding a selective serotonin reuptake inhibitor (SSRI) antidepressant such as Prozac or Zoloft can help. Other people fear that they won't be able to be properly treated for pain if they have an accident or other sudden, painful situation while on the drug because it prevents all opiate action. This actually is not true—you just need to warn physicians who treat you that you have taken naltrexone, and they can compensate for severe pain with nonopiate medications or larger doses of opiates. Also, of course—if pain or anhedonia are chronic for you—you can simply stop taking the medication and use other approaches. The goal of treatment is to make you feel better, not worse!

With the type of support and therapy we offer to our patients, we've found that the majority of alcoholics can comfortably and consistently take naltrexone. We have to work hard to help see that a desire to not take it (in the absence of side effects) can be a warning sign of possible relapse, however. Believe it or not, even when faced with blindness as a result of not taking medications, 58% of diabetics consistently miss doses. There is a resistance among most people—even when faced with threats as serious as blindness, or death—to consistent pill taking, so it's not surprising that alcoholics, too, sometimes have difficulty.

When I reviewed the results of our studies, I found that among subjects who were less consistent about taking their medication, relapse rates were quite high in both the placebo and the naltrexone groups. In contrast, among naltrexone subjects who took their medications religiously, relapse rates were less than 10%. The relapse rates for those who took placebo consistently were approximately three times greater than for the naltrexone subjects, again showing a powerful effect of the medication, as well as the importance of helping people be sure to take it.

Drugs for Treating Opiate Addiction

Naltrexone

In theory, naltrexone should be even more helpful for the treatment of opiate addicts than it is for alcoholics. Naltrexone directly blocks the receptors involved with the high produced by heroin. It does not produce physical dependence and has zero potential for abuse. Heroin addicts on naltrexone will experience no high whatsoever if they try to take heroin (unless they manage to get their hands on an exceptionally and usually impossibly expensive large dose). Thus, it should prevent a heroin slip from becoming a relapse into physical dependence.

Sadly, heroin addicts really don't seem to like to take naltrexone. In one study, only 15% of heroin addicts prescribed naltrexone were still taking it one month later. Even when counselors watch people take the pills to ensure that they do so, many addicts request to switch to methadone instead. This is in contrast to alcoholics—most of whom will take naltrexone without reporting problems with side effects.

It may be that for opiate addicts, who are infatuated with a direct opiate high and who may even have been born with deficiencies in their opiate systems, having them blocked by naltrexone is uncomfortable or unpleasant. For some, the addition of an antidepressant can help—but most do not seem to find naltrexone useful. About 20% of opiate addicts, however, do find that naltrexone can cut cravings and reduce relapse for them, without bothersome side effects. One 43-year-old heroin addict said that every time he'd tried to kick before trying naltrexone, he'd always been obsessed with heroin and this would drive him to relapse. On naltrexone, he said "I could see someone nodding [high] and not want to use." He has now been clean for more than a year.

If you have the motivation to take naltrexone to counteract opiate addiction and find it tolerable physically, the results can be excellent. For example, a study of health-care professionals who feared losing their licenses if they relapsed found that if they did consistently take naltrexone, they had a lower rate of relapse than those who did not take it.

Buprenorphine

This drug is one of the most promising new medications discovered so far for detoxification and maintenance treatment of opiate addiction. Buprenorphine can be seen as a cross between methadone and naltrexone—it can produce the calming, opiate effects of methadone, but when people inject additional opiates, it blocks the high the way naltrexone does.

This dual quality—as well as the fact that it is long acting and thus only needs to be taken once a day—makes it ideal for either detox or maintenance. Its advantage for detox is powerful: The withdrawal is shorter and less severe than that experienced following methadone maintenance. Most people in the studies of buprenorphine reported only mild withdrawal discomfort when switching from heroin itself to buprenorphine. The peak time for withdrawal was on the morning of the second day, prior to that day's buprenorphine dose— unlike with methadone or heroin, where withdrawal symptoms are severe for four days or, in very severe cases, longer. Also, if someone wants to switch to naltrexone after detoxing with buprenorphine, this transition takes only one day, compared to more than a week (and often an experience of more severe withdrawal) when trying this switch from methadone.

As a maintenance drug, buprenorphine also seems particularly helpful. One significant advantage is that taking extra buprenorphine to "top up" will only decrease, rather than increase, the opiate feeling—unlike with methadone. This quality also means that overdose is nearly impossible. If you take too much buprenorphine, you may suffer withdrawal symptoms, but unlike with methadone or heroin, you won't die. Even if you take other opiates on top, the naltrexone-like effect of buprenorphine will prevent them from acting, again unless you use exorbitant amounts. Essentially, buprenorphine provides some of the opiate comfort addicts seek, while reducing craving and helping prevent slips from becoming full-fledged relapses. As a result, heroin addicts tend to like buprenorphine far better than naltrexone. In one study, Tom Kosten of Yale University reported that most patients could not tell the difference between buprenorphine and methadone in terms of their daily well-being. In fact, most of his subjects who reported side effects from what they believed to be the experimental drug (it was a double-blind study comparing methadone and buprenorphine) turned out to be on methadone.

In our experience, nearly all patients report that they would like buprenorphine maintenance—or, if they needed to come off of heroin again, they would prefer buprenorphine to other detoxes. Over 80% report that buprenorphine is the best medication they have tried for opioid dependence. When the FDA makes buprenorphine available clinically (which is expected to happen soon), it will mark an important advance in the treatment of opioid dependence—and not only for pharmacological reasons. Buprenorphine, unlike methadone, is likely to be made available from any physician by ordinary prescription. People on buprenorphine maintenance will not have to deal with the restrictions and hassles of the current methadone system. Buprenorphine probably won't replace methadone entirely because individual differences mean that some people will still do better on methadone, but it is an important new option.

Drugs for Cocaine Abuse

The history of attempts to find a "methadone" or "naltrexone" for cocaine has been marked by disappointment. Cocaine's pleasurable effects are believed to result from its enhancement of the action of one of the brain's pleasure chemicals: dopamine. Earlier, we discussed how amantadine, a medication that increases dopamine activity, can reduce withdrawal symptoms, especially for those on the more severe end of the cocaine-addiction spectrum. Like most detox medications, it mimics the effect of the drug of choice, though without producing a sharp high. For heavy cocaine users, longer term use of amantadine can work as a sort of maintenance to help with longer-lasting dopamine deficits.

Dopamine Blockers and Other Cocaine-Action Blockers

In theory, then, dopamine-blocking drugs might prevent cocaine from working and reduce craving for it. This turns out not to be the case because the blocking of dopamine cuts strongly into the normal experience of pleasure. Dopamine blockers are used as antischizophrenic drugs, and schizophrenics have long been notorious for not wanting to take their medications. This is not "crazy" on their part, given that the side effects of these drugs can be joylessness and amotivation, not to mention drooling and a jerky-movement disorder called "tardive dyskinesia," which can be irreversible even after they stop taking the drug. New antischizophrenic medications are better, but dopamine-blocking drugs have so far not been of much use in mitigating cocaine addiction.

As a result, researchers have tried instead to create a methadone-like drug—one that could maintain cocaine patients with some of the feeling they wanted, but without the dysfunction related to their drug of choice. This, however, merely produced synthetic stimulants with abuse potential. Because stimulants are inherently not satiating (for all but those with ADD, who can be maintained on them), this tactic seems unlikely to result in useful drugs.

Cocaine Vaccine

Some researchers are now working on a vaccine to block cocaine action, which has definite advantages over a dopamine-blocking drug. The vaccine would cause antibodies to eat up cocaine before it ever got to the brain, preventing it from producing a high. However, it would have no effect on natural dopamine—so it wouldn't cause pleasurelessness. Nonetheless, this idea, too, has some serious problems. For one, the antibodies could become saturated if someone was determined to get high—and though the presence of more cocaine would cause the immune system to produce more antibodies, these wouldn't be ready in the instant it takes an injection of coke or a hit of crack to be taken. The variable presence of antibodies might also cause a variability in tolerance—which could make overdose more likely. Finally, because cocaine addicts are at high risk for HIV, and many are already infected, using the immune system to fight cocaine might be either less effective in people with already-impaired immunity, or dangerous to them.

Do Antidepressants Help?

Because many people who have chronically used cocaine suffer depression during and immediately after withdrawal, it was anticipated that antidepressants might reduce relapse. While some uncontrolled studies suggested that antidepressants were helpful, carefully controlled clinical trials failed to confirm these findings. These findings do not mean that those suffering depression following heavy cocaine use shouldn't be treated for it, but simply that this treatment alone cannot be counted on to reduce relapse.

Some Promising New Medications

One of the reasons that drug development is so difficult is because the brain is complicated, and neurotransmitters interact with each other in often unpredictable ways. One important interaction is the relationship between dopamine and gamma-aminobutyric acid (GABA). GABA is an inhibitory neurotransmitter that blunts the release of dopamine in some areas and increases it in others. Studies in both animals and humans suggest that the anticipation of using cocaine causes a small increase in the release of dopamine. This acts like an appetizer for a meal or the sight of a sexually appealing person—and increases desire. Reminders of cocaine thus increase craving and the possibility of relapse.

However, if GABA is being released at the same time, the ability of reminder cues to stimulate release of dopamine is lessened. Studies in our laboratory show that GABA-enhancing drugs significantly cut the craving for cocaine elicited by cues such as seeing your dealer, a razor normally used to chop coke, or a crack pipe. Therefore, medications that increase GABA release are being studied as aids to relapse prevention. Recent research in humans suggests that medications that stimulate the GABA system may even reduce cocaine's overall effect on the dopamine system, which would mean that if you took cocaine with a GABA-enhancing drug, you wouldn't get as high. Clinical trials are ongoing to test these medications, which include the antiepileptic vigabatrin.

NMDA—N-methyl-D-aspartic acid—Receptor Blockers

Another way to get at dopamine indirectly may be to block the substances that block GABA—the excitatory neurotransmitters. It's believed that GABA and these excitatory transmitters have opposite effects, and that these are involved in how memories are stored. Because craving involves drug memory that is too strong or too insistent, it makes sense that this is one place where an anticraving drug would act.

Medications that block the excitatory neurotransmitter NMDA (N-methyl-D-aspartic acid) may work like the GABA-releasing drugs to reduce cocaine's ability to stimulate the release of dopamine. Research and addicts' anecdotes have suggested that an African hallucinogen, ibogaine, has the ability to both reduce withdrawal symptoms from cocaine and heroin and cut desire for them (see also Chapter 19). Until recently, it has been a mystery as to why—or even whether—this drug really works. However, it seems that the drug does inhibit NMDA, which may explain the results. Other medications that block NMDA or its receptors are also being tested, to see whether one such drug can be discovered, which does not have the hallucinatory and disturbing (and possibly harmful) effects of ibogaine. PCP (phencyclidine) and ketamine are also NMDA-receptor antagonists, but it is not likely we will see these frequently abused medications used in treatment.

Interestingly, NMDA blockers hold promise not only as antiwithdrawal drugs, but possibly also as drugs that could prevent the development of physical dependence on opiates. One such drug, dextromethorphan, is currently available as an over-the-counter cough syrup, so it is known to be safe in low doses. The high doses needed both to prevent the development of tolerance and to reduce withdrawal symptoms are not yet known to be safe—so don't try this at home! However, a small safety trial conduced by the National Institute on Drug Abuse did not uncover any difficulties or safety problems so far—and the drug is currently entering trials to see how effective it is.

More research is needed, but if these drugs work, they could help not only addicts but also chronic pain patients who might be able to avoid the problem of needing higher doses and becoming physically dependent on medications. These drugs raise some interesting philosophical questions, as well. If you did have a drug that could totally eliminate craving and withdrawal—basically ending addiction—what would be wrong with recreational drug use?

Antabuse

Oddly, this old drug, which has fallen out of favor for treatment of alcoholics, may have some utility in treating those who abuse both alcohol and cocaine. For those willing to take it, Antabuse significantly reduces both cocaine and alcohol abuse. It probably works because cocaine addicts think that they won't mind being unable to drink—but when they actually try using coke without any drinking, they find heavy use seriously unpleasant, and they stop. The reverse could also be true. Without alcohol to lower their inhibitions, cocaine addicts may be better able to avoid the temptation of using their drug of choice. Also, there is some evidence that Antabuse increases the negative sensations associated with the cocaine high, such as paranoia and edginess.

Naltrexone

Finally, for patients who are both alcohol and cocaine dependent, naltrexone can also reduce use of both drugs—probably for similar reasons to those that make Antabuse useful and with the added benefit that this drug, unlike Antabuse, decreases craving for alcohol. In open-label trials with such patients, early results were promising. A controlled trial is currently underway to try to confirm these results.

We are still at an early stage in our understanding of how best to integrate medications and "talk therapies" in the treatment of addictions. While the recent FDA approval of naltrexone and other medications promises to usher in a new era for addiction treatment, these drugs are not maximally effective without additional support.

For example, it is ludicrous to expect that a pill alone will take a heroin-addicted, chronically unemployed high school dropout from being an addict to becoming a productive citizen. Similarly, someone who is depressed or suffering posttraumatic stress disorder following childhood sexual abuse may not be able to fully recover with Prozac alone. Treatment for mental and emotional troubles works best when care is integrated and combined—involving medication, a social-support network of family members, friends, or self-help groups, and counseling to help keep everything on track.

Craving-Reduction Medications Now Available and Recommended
For alcohol: naltrexone
For cocaine: amantadine (for heavy users), naltrexone

For cocaine and alcohol together: naltrexone, antabuse
For heroin: naltrexone

Maintenance Medications Now Available and Recommended
For heroin: methadone, LAAM (levo-alpha-acetylmethadol, a longer-acting
  form of methadone), buprenorphine (should be approved by publication
  time)

Medications Helpful to Moderate Drinking
Naltrexone

Anticraving Medications in the Pipeline
For alcohol: acamprosate
For cocaine: GABA agonists (example: vigabatrin), NMDA-receptor antagonists (examples: acamprosate, dextromethorphan), anticocaine vaccine
  (unnamed, manufacturer is British firm, Cantab)
For heroin: NMDA-receptor antagonists (examples: acamprosate, dextromethorphan, dextrorphan)

Knowledge Is Power
• Naltrexone, when used as an anticraving medication for alcohol problems,
  can reduce relapse by up to 50%.
• Naltrexone can help those who want to drink moderately to do so.
• Naltrexone is useful for people with both cocaine and alcohol problems,
  and occasionally for those with heroin problems.
• Buprenorphine is very promising as both a maintenance drug and a detox
  medication for opiate addiction.
• There are many other new and promising medications in the pipeline.

CHAPTER 12

Twelve-Step Programs

Twelve-Step Program: A self-help support group based on the 12 steps and other ideology of Alcoholics Anonymous.

Alcoholics Anonymous is a fellowship of men and women who share their experience, strength and hope with each other that they may solve their common problem and help others to recover from alcoholism. The only requirement for membership is a desire to stop drinking. There are no dues or fees for AA membership, we are self-supporting through our own contributions. AA is not allied with any sect, denomination, politics, organization or institution, does not wish to engage in any controversy, neither endorses nor opposes any causes. Our primary purpose is to stop drinking and help other alcoholics to achieve sobriety.

Preamble to Alcoholics Anonymous Meetings

So reads the AA preamble that begins most meetings of the best-known self-help group in the world. As mentioned earlier, AA was founded by two former drunks, one a doctor, the other a stockbroker, who discovered that they could do together what they could not do alone: stay sober. There are now millions of AA members around the globe, and 12-step recovery fellowships have been started to help people with addictions to everything from heroin to messiness.

The opening statement by each speaker, "I'm _____, and I'm an alcoholic," has become a cliché. It is estimated that 13% of the American population has attended at least one 12-step meeting (mostly AA) at some point in their lifetime, either as a potential member or as a guest—and 5% report attending in the past year. Only about 40% of those who start attending AA meetings will continue for more than a year, however.

How valuable is AA to those with drinking problems? What is attending AA like? Are people who recover without it missing something?

In this chapter, we examine these questions and look at both the pros and the cons of 12-step programs. Although the focus here is primarily on AA, because all of the 12-step programs are based on the same steps, the conclusions about their positives and negatives apply to Narcotics Anonymous, Cocaine Anonymous, Marijuana Addicts Anonymous, and other groups aimed at fighting substance addictions.

What Is Twelve-Step Membership Like?

A typical AA meeting opens with a reading of the preamble, and sometimes of the 12 steps. Then, often, the meeting chair will ask whether anyone is celebrating an anniversary or is "counting days." Newcomers typically share how many days it is since they last drank or took other drugs during their first three months in the program, which allows members to know who is new and might need extra support. After the days and anniversaries are applauded, a preselected speaker usually tells her or his story. This is called a "qualification," and it tends to take the form of a chronological tale. Often, child abuse or other early difficulties are discussed, then the joy at finding alcohol or other drugs, and the disaster that resulted. When the speaker has finished, the floor is opened to others who wish to share.

Some meetings are focused on the steps. At these, the speaker tells only a condensed version of his or her story and then describes experiences with the step being discussed. For those who find that "war stories" induce cravings, step meetings are a good alternative.

There are also meetings devoted to particular groups of people, such as women only, men only, gays and lesbians, people with both alcoholism and other mental disorders, and even people over 40, under 20, or with more than 5 years of sobriety.

AA's membership poll found that 42% had problems with another substance in addition to alcohol—and some AA groups are troubled when people discuss this. They read statements in their openings designed to "keep the focus on alcohol." Other groups encourage talking about other drugs. Narcotics Anonymous and Cocaine Anonymous tend to be less fussy about these issues, with some exceptions.

In many cities, AA and NA have very different cultures—with AA attenders tending to be more white and middle class, and NA and CA predominantly working class and minority. This generally follows the race and class divisions of the particular community. People should shop around to find meetings they like; the meeting focused on their drug of choice may not be the best option. It's more important to find people that you like than to match yourself to a program based on which drugs you prefer. The steps are the same in all of them.

It is suggested to newcomers that they go to "90 meetings in 90 days," although there is now a sense that daily meeting attendance after that is also helpful. AA's membership survey found that the average member has about six years of sobriety and attends 2 to 3 meetings a week.

Beginners are typically instructed to get a sponsor (who is a more experienced member who can explain the language to them and who can be called in times of crisis or with questions), and to get involved as early as possible with helping the group.

The Steps

These are the 12 steps of Alcoholics Anonymous:
1. We admitted we were powerless over alcohol—that our lives had become unmanageable.

2. Came to believe that a Power greater than ourselves could restore us to sanity.
3. Made a decision to turn our will and our lives over to the care of God as we understood Him.
4. Made a searching and fearless moral inventory of ourselves.
5. Admitted to God, to ourselves, and to another human being the exact nature of our wrongs.
6. Were entirely ready to have God remove all these defects of character.
7. Humbly asked Him to remove our shortcomings.
8. Made a list of all persons we had harmed, and became willing to make amends to them all.
9. Made direct amends to such people wherever possible, except when to do so would injure them or others.
10. Continued to take personal inventory and when we were wrong, promptly admitted it.
11. Sought through prayer and meditation to improve our conscious contact with God as we understood Him, praying only for knowledge of His will for us and the power to carry that out.
12. Having had a spiritual awakening as the result of these steps, we tried to carry this message to alcoholics and to practice these principles in all our affairs.

It should be noted that immediately after the steps in the *Big Book* is the following passage:

> Many of us exclaimed, "What an order! I can't go through with it." Do not be discouraged. No one among us has been able to maintain anything like perfect adherence to these principles. We are not saints. The point is, we are willing to grow along spiritual lines. The principles we have set down are guides to progress. We claim spiritual progress rather than spiritual perfection.

At one meeting Maia attended, the woman who was reading the passage stressed it like this: "What, an order? I can't go through with it!" to which members responded with almost unanimous recognition laughter. One of the things that often surprises those who join 12-step fellowships is how much humor there is. In fact, you can often spot a newcomer right away because she or he is determinedly serious, while those who have been around a while can laugh at themselves.

The first few steps themselves are devoted to getting people to recognize that drinking is causing problems, not solving them. Once you realize that you are powerless over alcohol, any further experiments with "controlled drinking" make little sense because you know that they will lead only to more trouble. Those not convinced are encouraged to try moderation and to come back if it doesn't work out for them.

In practical terms, "turning our will and our life over to the care of God" (Step 3) means accepting that you need help, don't know everything, and can't control the world. This step often comes as a relief for alcoholics, who frequently turn to drink because things haven't gone according to their plans. Letting a "higher power" take responsibility for the outcomes of one's actions drastically reduces the sphere of things for which one feels responsible when they go wrong.

The fourth step tends to scare the hell out of many people. Members often procrastinate for years before tackling it. Its purpose is not to have people drown in remorse and regret—the idea is to look at where you have gone wrong, in order to avoid repeating it. Many members also stress that an inventory includes both positives and negatives. Seeing the whole picture is crucial to regaining a sense of self-esteem.

Step 5, in which you share your fourth step with someone you trust, is probably more frightening than Step 4. However, most members report a profound sense of relief when they actually do it. Often, they share their darkest secrets with their sponsor—and commonly, the sponsor then shares a darker one. The feeling of shame at being the only one to have ever "been so bad" diminishes. The alienation of feeling undeserving because of your bad behavior starts to ebb.

The sixth and seventh steps are really about working on the problems that drove negative behavior uncovered in Steps 4 and 5. Frequently, people try to become less selfish, less impatient, less angry, less jealous, and less judgmental. After they have practiced this for a while, they become ready to list those to whom they owe amends, and begin making reparations (Steps 8 and 9).

Step 10 is basically a continuing version of Step 4—and the eleventh step involves work on whatever spiritual practice a person finds helpful. The most famous and best-known step—the twelfth—involves telling others about the benefits of 12-step programs and helping people with whatever you can in order to spur their recovery.

The power of the steps is in their ability both to make clear the damage done by addiction and to offer a meaningful new way of life. Because so many alcoholics and other addicts struggle with self-hatred and low self-esteem, the steps provide explicit antidotes. It is very hard to feel like an immoral, useless, evil person when you have made reparations to those you harmed and you work continuously to help others. Although AA believes that alcoholism is a disease rather than a moral failing, the steps allow people to correct for moral weaknesses that cause them to dislike themselves. This decreases the odds that they will wish to drink or take other drugs because people who feel happy and productive have less need of escape than those who are miserable or bored.

The Slogans

Another important part of 12-step programs, often overlooked by researchers and critics, is their body of collective wisdom summarized in what are called "the slogans." These are short, often clichéd statements, which serve as tips on how to stay abstinent. You do not need to like AA to utilize them. In fact, they actually represent techniques similar to those used in cognitive and behavioral therapies.

The best-known of these is probably **"One day at a time."** While it sounds obvious, if you are ruminating on the hell of never being able to drink or use other drugs again, the idea that you are just not doing so "today" can be a great relief, and it can often be the difference between relapsing and maintaining abstinence. Many alcoholics have found themselves with years of recovery after telling themselves, "Well, if it's still this bad tomorrow, I'll drink then," and finding that tomorrow's drink is never actually needed.

"It's the first drink that gets you drunk," is a slogan that often confounds newcomers, who quite rationally assume that it takes a lot more than one drink to get them where they want to go. What it means, however, is that if you don't take the first one, you can't be in the position to need the next one. Although the AA belief that one drink makes alcoholics completely unable to resist more is not supported by research, the core truth of this statement remains, in that craving is enhanced, not diminished, if you "have just one."

"Think it through," a slogan sometimes represented by a sign hung upside down, saying "Think," means that when you crave a drink or drug and imagine it as lovely and soothing, remind yourself of the hangover afterward, the vomiting, the arguments with your family—whatever the negative consequences for you are. This can help you avoid romanticizing your drinking and deter you from returning to it.

"Avoid people, places and things associated with drinking or taking other drugs." This slogan is based on the fact that craving is often linked to environmental cues. Although eventually you need to be able to deal with cues and not relapse, in early recovery, the best way to increase the odds of avoiding drinking is to avoid being around booze and your drinking buddies.

A related slogan, which deals with what cognitive scientists call internal cues, is **"HALT! Don't get too Hungry, Angry, Lonely or Tired."** Most relapse is actually related to seeking emotional relief, not to responding to the sight of a drink or the siren call of drugs or old friends. Many alcoholics and other addicts have lost track of the signals telling them that they need to eat—and instead interpret them as desire for drink or other drugs. When angry, relapse is more easily rationalized, and loneliness and tiredness often spell trouble, as well. AA suggests dealing with hunger by eating, with anger by calling a program friend or sponsor or going to a meeting and talking about it, with loneliness by doing the same, and with tiredness, of course, by sleeping, if possible. If sleep is disturbed, baths and other nonmedical ways of relaxing are encouraged. (If a serious insomnia or oversleeping problem develops, you should be screened for depression—sleep disturbances are often a sign of this illness.)

"Fake it till you make it." This slogan means that even if you don't feel as though you want to be sober or to continue with AA, act as if you do. The more you act as if you want to stay sober, the easier it becomes to do so. This also works with low self-esteem: The more you act as though you like yourself, the more you come to actually do so.

There are many other slogans, some prominent in most regions, others specific to particular places. One key slogan is, **"Keep coming back."** Members often say this to those who are having trouble or have experienced a slip. They know that people often fear being judged if they return to the program and say that they have been drinking or using other drugs again. Twelve-step programs are actually accepting of slips, but there is also a hierarchy of respect in the fellowship, which relates to the length of time one has been clean and sober. Those who have risen often fear the loss of this status (which actually helps keep them abstinent), but if they do slip, they may be too embarrassed to let down the group by returning and admitting it. "Keep coming back" is meant to encourage such people and to let them know that they are welcome and still loved.

Finally, there's **"Take what you like and leave the rest,"** which emphasizes that everything in AA is only a suggestion, and that if there are aspects of the program that you don't believe or like, ignore them and focus on those you find helpful.

A Classic AA Recovery

Fred has been a sober AA member for six years and found the program and its members immeasurably helpful. Although there was no alcohol in the working-class Minneapolis home where he grew up, he learned early on that drinking could ease his pain. The 44-year-old journalist had been abused as a child. "It was brutal, emotionally and physically," he said, "with a lot of ridicule and humiliation and not much encouragement."

"I had my first drink at 14. I got extremely drunk, threw up, and I don't remember much of that night. But I liked the euphoria immediately." For the next few years, he became a daily pot smoker because it was hard for him to get booze. "I didn't have any older brothers, my parents didn't keep it in the house, but I could buy pot at school. " When he started college, however, he found that pot was making him paranoid. "I considered alcohol solid and predictable and I became a heavy drinker."

By his last year in college, he was drinking daily. "I knew vaguely in my mid 20s that I had a problem, but I thought it was related to the emotional abuse I had suffered as a child," he said. At age 38, he found himself living with a woman he didn't love, six months behind on the rent, and unemployable. "I had a sense of quiet and sometimes not so quiet desperation. Once I started drinking, I couldn't stop. I had been a reasonably facile writer and I couldn't get a sentence together. My relationship was based on the fact that I desperately needed a place to stay and she desperately wanted to have a boyfriend."

Just before he entered AA, his girlfriend left for a vacation. "My plan was to have one beer before bed and get up and look for a job," he said. After a four-day binge, he called AA. "I told the woman who answered the phone about my drinking. She was very nice and said, 'I felt just like you did before I got into the program. I know what it's like to wake up hung over and I don't do that anymore.'"

"She suggested that I go to a meeting, and even though I was living in Queens, I asked for one on the Upper West Side. I knew the bars around there and I figured if it was a bust, at least I'd be close to a good place to drink."

"I walked into the meeting and the guy who was speaking had a story which was not at all like mine, but he said things I was feeling. He talked about starting to drink and being unable to stop and feeling like your life is off track but you don't know why. He said, 'I learned I didn't have to drink, and you don't either.'"

"Afterwards, I went to dinner with people from the meeting. They told me not to drink, even just one, tonight and to go to a meeting the next day. And someone called me at 8:30 A.M. the next morning and I went to meet up with him. But he had given me directions to a meeting that wasn't on for that day, and even though I was 15–20 minutes late, he stood out in the rain waiting for me. It was a key event in my recovery. If I'd shown up and there was no one there, it's quite likely that I would have gone to a bar and the good experience of the previous night could have become a nonmemory."

That man became his first sponsor. "I was very blessed. I had the classic stroke of lightning recovery—I never drank again after my first meeting. I had no compulsion to drink. I romanced it once in a while, and occasionally, when I went into a bar for some other reason I could tell you what was in every glass, but I didn't drink."

Fred describes himself as "a fairly committed atheist before I joined AA." He said, "I was pretty sure I was living in a godless world. In *The Sun Also Rises*, one character says to another, 'How did you go bankrupt,' and he responds, 'Gradually, then suddenly,' and that was what it was like for me with spirituality." Today, Fred is a successful journalist. "The best thing was just getting myself back. I have a level of acceptance and contentedness that I never had before."

From Tragedy to Triumph

Some lives are marked by highs and lows of nearly biblical proportions. Many people in 12-step programs speak of miracles—and Laura's story certainly seems to qualify. It is also filled with pain.

The 46-year-old observant Muslim went from being a gifted student to a heroin addict in one straight shot, administered when she was just 11. That day, she'd found her 16-year-old boyfriend and his friends shooting up, and she said, "Oh, I didn't know that you was diabetic"—and everybody laughed. Laura found out that day, as she put it, "[heroin] just made me feel hot on the inside and even as I'm speaking about it now, because the reality of it is that I love dope."

Pregnant at 14 and soon married to the boy who'd given her that first injection, she gave birth to an addicted baby and quickly became involved in selling drugs. By 1987, she had divorced, remarried, and given birth to twins, a boy and a girl. She made a home for her family in suburban Maryland. Coming back from a drug run, however, she found police and fire trucks circling her house, her parents crying outside, and three black bags on her lawn.

> And as I'm driving, I'm [thinking], "Where's my husband?" Of course, I'm fired up. I got coke and angel dust in me. Now I finally look at my house. Where's the front part of my house? The boiler had blown up and it took the lives of my husband and my two-month-old twins. That's what was in those black bags.

Laura immediately left for New York—not even able to bear to attend the funeral:

> I became very violent. I was robbing drug dealers in one building and selling drugs out of the next. I lost faith. I would say to the Lord, "Why didn't you let me burn like them? Why did you take my family and those babies? You're a loving and caring God?" I said, "I'm going for your children now." And that's when I began to rob and hurt human beings. 'Cause they were representative of God's magnificence and His mercy. When I came back to New York, I was homeless by choice. I lived on the A train.

Then, the miracle happened:

> My clean date is May 13th, 1990, because May 13th in 1990 was Mother's Day. I woke up on the train. There were three sisters across from me and they was real clean. And they were wishing each other a happy Mother's Day. I started crying, thinking about my babies. And it was like, "You know what, Laura? You're gonna go to a shelter and sleep in a real bed. You're not gonna use nothing today."
>
> And I got to the shelter and I heard all this clapping and said, "Why are they making noise?" And the other sisters in the dorm was like, "There's a meeting downstairs." I said, "Whoever don't live here got to go. I need some sleep." And the guard reared back in her chair and said, "Well, go ahead down there, Laura, and tell them that."
>
> I went down. When I walked in, I walked right back out. It was full of people. I said, "Well, they got five more minutes." And then a sister came out. I will never forget her; she's since passed away. She said, "Hello, my name is _____ and I'm an addict." I looked at her and I said, "My sister you don't got to think of yourself so lowly. That's why the black man can't elevate in his life because the black women think so poorly of themselves." You know, the militant me. And she was like, "No. It's OK that I'm an addict because I'm getting some help. "
>
> She said, "Do you use drugs?" I said, "Yeah. I get high." And she said, "Well, why don't you just come in and sit down?" . . .
>
> So I went to my first Narcotics Anonymous meeting. There was this lady up in front at this table. She said, "Is there anybody here for the first time, please raise your hand. We can't help you unless we get to know who you are." People were raising their hand and like, "My name is So and So, I'm an addict. This is my first time at a meeting." "Well, girl, yeah! Way to go, keep coming back."
>
> At the end of the meeting, what stuck in my mind was, "We can't help you, unless we know who you are." And there's all these people and now they're in little groups. The meeting is over and I'm like, "How am I gonna let them know who I am? I ain't leaving here without somebody knowing who I am." So I would just bust into the group, no excuse me or nothing, "Hi, my name is Laura. Hi, my name is Laura. Hi, my name is Laura."
>
> The next day, I thought, well I'm going to Harlem to pick up [drugs]. I'm on my way to hop the train, and they gave me this book. It was a meeting list and I said, "Well, I'll just make one of these meetings before I go to Harlem, then go get my package and get high." It was a 12:00 meeting in Brooklyn. People was like, "Oh, how you doing, Laura?" And I said, "Listen, I'll tell you all, if I owe you money, I ain't got no money. I don't know how you know my name . . ." They said, "You just last night introduced yourself to over a hundred recovering addicts." And since then I am truly recovering.

Laura returned to her Islamic roots and finds her faith crucial to her recovery.

Research on AA

Researching AA poses quite a problem to scientists. The organization doesn't keep membership lists and explicitly promises complete anonymity. Most people choose to attend—which means that by randomly assigning people to it, you aren't necessarily studying the real effects of AA because the choice has been made for subjects by someone else. On the other hand, if you only look at those who choose to be there, it could be that these people are the people most committed to recovery and that this commitment, not the program, makes the real difference.

Random assignment studies on people coerced into AA (drunk drivers, coerced employees, etc.) have not found that it performs better than other treatments, and some found that AA did worse. However, those who do affiliate with AA after receiving 12-step oriented treatment or on their own do tend to drink less and have greater life improvements than those who do not. This effect is stronger for men than for women, but quite a few studies show that the more connected a person is with an AA support system, the more likely he or she is to stay sober.

The bottom line is this: Social support for not drinking or taking other drugs can be helpful in maintaining abstinence. If you find that you like 12-step programs and can use them to develop a new network of nondrinking or other non-drug-using friends, becoming involved can be highly positive. Because each meeting is unique, it's often a good idea to try a few different ones before deciding whether it is for you. Some meetings are tolerant of dissent from typical 12-step concepts, others are rigid. If you find 12-step ideas themselves appealing, this may not matter much. If you struggle with them, however, finding a meeting where you are encouraged to "take what you like and leave the rest" may be better. AA and its sisters are the only worldwide substance-disorder support system with members nearly everywhere available almost 24 hours a day. The feeling of knowing that in any city there are strangers ready to help you stay clean and sober can, in itself, be very healing.

FOR FAMILY MEMBERS AND OTHER LOVED ONES: SUPPORT YOUR LOVED ONES' RECOVERY CHOICES

It's important to encourage the use of the method of recovery that appeals most to your loved one who has a substance problem. If this is a 12-step program, he or she may encourage you to attend the 12-step programs for relatives and friends of alcoholics or other addicts: Al-Anon or Nar-Anon. Trying these programs can help you to understand what the person in recovery is going through—and to deal with your own feelings and problems related to your loved one's.

If you have begun to attend these meetings before your loved ones get clean and sober, you may feel that anything other than a 12-step program will fail them. It's a good idea to stress the good points of these fellowships to them, but if they don't like these programs or aren't interested, don't insist. There are other valid routes to recovery, which may help, and if you tell your loved ones that the steps are the only way, they may reject the steps simply out of rebellion. Obviously, if they refuse to take make any attempt to deal with the problem, you may have to distance yourself from them or take other measures to protect yourself. If they are genuinely trying to move forward, however, even if they're not yet totally abstinent, it's probably better to just be as supportive and encouraging as you can, and to praise them when things work and continue to gently remind them of negative consequences linked to drinking and using when they don't seem to make the connection.

If, on the other hand, your loved one is totally gung-ho on AA but Al-Anon leaves you cold, support her or his involvement, but stress that you feel confident about your own ways of dealing with her or his problems and with your own. Many family members and spouses are distressed to find that suddenly, rather than being out drinking all the time, their loved ones are instead away at meetings or with AA friends. Usually this phase passes pretty quickly—and in the first few months, it's probably best to encourage this rather than asking for more time and togetherness. Recovery will ultimately be better for that goal, and it's unlikely to be achieved without at least several months of total attention to it. After your loved one is stabilized, you can raise these issues, and she or he will probably work to address them.

Joe

OTHER TWELVE-STEP PROGRAMS

Sometimes, people in recovery are encouraged to attend additional 12-step programs that focus on particular issues, such as those of "Adult Children of Alcoholics" (ACOA) or "Debtors Anonymous" (for money issues). Two cautions: Some recovering people have found that going to AA on Monday, ACOA on Tuesday, Al-Anon on Wednesday, and Overeaters Anonymous on Thursday can divert their focus from their main problem. By trying to lose weight, deal with relationship issues, deal with childhood abuse memories, and alcoholism all at once, you can put so much pressure on yourself to be "abstinent" in the way each program defines it, that you can actually move toward relapse.

Second, research suggests that putting effort into recalling and excavating memories of childhood trauma may sometimes do more harm than good. If the memories are haunting you and you need to talk about them, that's one thing—but deliberately focusing your energy on remembering them and reliving them may simply make your problems worse. You can find yourself endlessly ruminating on the past and neglecting to deal with your life now. Involvement with ACOA or other abuse- and neglect-focused programs should be assessed based on whether you are having upsetting memories now, rather than on whether you think your childhood is unconsciously affecting your present behavior. If the latter is the case, cognitive and behavioral therapy aimed at dealing with your present problems may be more productive.

Maia

Problems with Twelve-Step Programs

Although these programs do work for some people, there are certain contradictions and paradoxes that prevent others from finding them helpful. The notion that the 12-step way of recovery is superior to others is not backed by research — people can recover without AA, NA, or CA and be just as healthy as those who find them helpful.

Many people are also put off by the religious thinking that dominates 12-step programs. Though these fellowships claim to be spiritual, not religious, and though they can work for people of any faith, there is a definite Christian origin to many of their beliefs. Those who persist in their atheism or agnosticism as long-term members are often thought not to have advanced as much as those who say they have found God.

Some people feel that 12-step programs have a covert theology, as well. They tend to promote the idea that "everything happens for a reason," and "suffering is the touchstone for spiritual growth." Some people find this extremely comforting, as it allows them to feel part of a world imbued with meaning and significance. When a train arrives just when you need it, God is sending a sign; when it comes late, it's a lesson in patience.

Others have said they find this view offensive, however, in light of the Holocaust and other horrors such as slavery and the atrocities in Rwanda. Seeing the way the world is as being ordained by God can promote fatalism. In fact, AA's serenity prayer "God grant me the serenity to accept the things I cannot change, the courage to change the things I can, and the wisdom to know the difference" is often misinterpreted by members to mean that the only thing they can change is themselves. Politics, relationships, injustices — all of these are to be accepted with serenity, without making active attempts to change the actions of others. Obviously, political activists of all stripes find this offensive and dispiriting.

As a result, those who are not religious, those who are poor or disadvantaged, and people who have been traditionally thrust into roles of powerlessness such as women and cultural minorities tend to have difficulties with 12-step programs. Some find ways around it with like-minded people within the fellowship. Others find alternative recovery groups.

If you find the idea of "powerlessness" and "[turning] our will and our lives over to the care of God as we understood him," completely untenable, 12-step programs may not be for you. Because of their ubiquity and usefulness in terms of social support, it can be helpful to get over this (or ignore it while attending meetings), if possible. If not, however, there are other options. There is no need to twist yourself into a knot trying to accept something that doesn't suit you.

The 12-step programs can offer a powerful and compelling way of recovery for some, but for others, they don't make sense. Because upward of 90% of the workers in American drug treatment were trained to believe that 12-step programs are the best form of recovery, it can be hard to find care that doesn't require AA or NA attendance. However, things are changing. Also, if you like 12-step programs, choosing treatment is vastly easier because most treatment incorporates them.

Knowledge Is Power

- Try to give 12-step programs a serious try because they are the most available support group.
- Hearing other people tell their stories and learning how they avoid relapse can hold important lessons. The collective wisdom of thousands of recovering people gets distilled as people listen to each other and repeat what works.
- The steps can help you gain self-esteem and create a meaningful, productive life in recovery, if you find their ideas helpful.
- If you are not religious, you can use AA itself, the "Group of Drunks" or "Good Orderly Direction" as your higher power.
- If you find that the Christian subtext to the program bothers you, there are books about how to apply the 12 steps to other faiths.
- AA's slogans can help people in any type of recovery.
- "Take what you like and leave the rest" is probably the most important slogan for those who have trouble with AA's belief system.
- There are alternatives if you find that AA is just not for you.

CHAPTER 13

Other Self-help Groups

Self-help Groups: Free or low-cost organizations founded by and for people with specific problems, in which they help each other to overcome or handle the problem.

Since the late 1960s, when AA and other 12-step groups became an established part of most mainstream alcoholism and other addiction care, a number of alternative self-help groups have sprung up. Most of these have been started by alcoholics who did not find AA helpful. Some opposed the "God part" of the AA program, others disliked the idea of powerlessness and the requirement of life-long meeting attendance, others found AA sexist, and yet others felt that AA wasn't religious enough for them or didn't comfortably fit their own religious or cultural ideas.

In this chapter, we look at the most popular AA alternatives and discuss their similarities and differences. Although many of these groups remain small and may not be available in some areas, almost all of them have meetings or other support available over the Internet, which is becoming an important new medium for helping people recover. Some of these online meetings are real time, scheduled chats, others are "mailing lists" through which people correspond and help each other via e-mail. If you are not yet online and have trouble with AA, a computer and modem may be a very good investment for your recovery.

All of the programs we discuss here focus on helping people become abstinent—for information on self-help and other support for moderate drinking, see Chapter 16; for information on reducing harm related to heavy drug use, see Chapter 17.

SOS

SOS, which stands alternately for Secular Organizations for Sobriety and Save Our Selves, was the first large-scale AA alternative. There are now 1,200 SOS groups around the world. The organization was founded by Jim Christopher, an alcoholic who quit drinking in 1978. Early in his recovery, he recognized that AA did not suit him: He did not find the spiritual and religious aspects helpful or necessary. Christopher also objected to the idea that recovery came from outside the alcoholic and that without God or some specific "program," alcoholics were powerless to resist drinking again. He did firmly support the AA idea that total, lifelong abstinence from alcohol is necessary and that peer support is useful.

In 1986, after writing and talking about what had helped him overcome his drinking problem, he held the first SOS meeting. SOS members can use the group to deal with alcohol, other drugs, or other compulsive behaviors. Unlike in the 12-step fellowships, no distinction is made by substance of choice.

SOS has no "program," like AA does. On their website, they state, "We don't think the same set of 'steps' is appropriate for everyone and we don't require any-one to complete any particular program; all we ask our members to do is stay sober. We encourage our members to try different methods for staying sober until they find the particular approach that works for them. However, they do it, we respect and support it. Some of our members also attend AA meetings and we have no problem with that."

SOS also calls itself a "secular" rather than an atheist organization. As the website puts it, "We do have atheists and agnostics in our ranks, but we also have members with clearly defined religious beliefs who don't wish to amend or compromise them in order to enjoy the benefits of a recovery support group. . . . We tend to think that alcoholism is fundamentally a health problem and that religion has no more role to play here than it does in the treatment of diabetes, melanoma, schizophrenia, hay fever or psoriasis."

SOS does have a "tool kit," which is available online and which includes numerous cognitive and behavioral relapse-prevention techniques. There is also a book called the *Sobriety Handbook: The SOS Way: An Introduction to Secular Organizations for Sobriety/Save Ourselves*, which offers members techniques for staying sober by using the group. Like AA, SOS is self-supporting through mem-ber contributions.

SOS believes that sobriety must be a priority for its members, and that they must accept that drinking, no matter what the circumstances, is no longer an option for them. In addition, SOS promotes the idea that addiction involves a clash between the survival-oriented and "primitive" lower brain—and the rational and "higher" cortical area. The idea is that your lower regions have been tricked into thinking drugs are needed for survival, while your higher ones become help-less under their power. In order to recover, you need to retrain the lower areas to let go of the short-term pleasure of drugs in favor of the long-term pleasures of recovery. This is an oversimplification: Your brain doesn't really work this way because both areas are integrated with each other, and no thought is entirely "rational" or entirely "emotional." However, it can be useful to recognize that the desire for drugs is often at war with your better intentions—and that you need to be watchful of your thoughts to be sure you aren't setting yourself up to relapse.

Here's a post from the SOS website, which a member addressed to a woman who was just one day sober. It offers a flavor of the positive approach favored by the group:

One day—that's just great. You know . . . we all have just one day—today. The past is history and the future isn't here so now is what we have. It takes great courage to make

the decision to quit drinking. You have made the choice. That's the big one. . . . The
rest will fall into place with honesty and determination.

Really, though, you just have to do it for now. The decision I made to quit drinking
has been the life-saving, most positive action I have ever taken. When I quit, the game
was over for me. The doctor told me that continued drinking would see me dead in
less than 2 years. My mind was a mess, my marriage was nearly done and my employer
was really upset with me. You see, I was a deputy sheriff and a drunk in that business is
bad, bad news. Near the end I remember sitting in a sheriff's vehicle I had driven to
some isolated alley and seriously contemplating using the service revolver— . . .

But I didn't and today I am sober and I tell you it's the greatest feeling to have. My
employer helped me and as I got sober my mental and physical health improved each
day. My marriage stayed and we just had our 27th anniversary. Yes . . . there's lots of
feelings and emotions but, as a great American statesman once said, "there is nothing
to fear but fear itself . . ."

Just stick around and use this list. I just recently discovered it and think it is the best
thing in recovery I have seen for a long time.

Rational Recovery

Rational Recovery (RR), another AA alternative, was founded by Jack Trimpey
in the late 1980s. He, too, was an alcoholic who disliked AA—so much so that a
large proportion of his first book describing RR is devoted to attacking its prede-
cessor. It's even called *The Small Book*—because AA's main text is colloquially
known as "The Big Book." Take sides, he tells professionals and alcoholics—
choose one or the other, not both!

Like SOS, RR does not require belief in a higher power and does support
the idea that total abstinence is required for alcoholics to recover. The main
component of the RR program is called "addictive voice recognition training,"
(AVRT), which is a way to avert relapse. The addictive voice is called the Beast,
because it is believed to be the voice of the lower, or what RR calls the "animal" or "lizard" parts of the brain. What RR sees as the voice of the Beast is
pretty much synonymous with what AA calls the voice of the disease and what
cognitive-behavioral therapists call craving.

The RR program was originally based on a type of cognitive therapy called
rational-emotive behavior therapy (REBT), created by psychologist Albert Ellis.
RR has now rejected both REBT and all of what it calls "psychological"
approaches—AVRT alone is believed to be enough to end addiction without
any other psychological changes. According to Trimpey, reading about AVRT in
the new RR book, *Rational Recovery*, in their online course and possibly attending two to three meetings should be sufficient to learn what you need to know.
RR proponents now believe that "groups" and identifying with other addicts is
part of the problem and not helpful for recovery.

In fact, RR's groups are now devoted almost entirely to political action
aimed at ending the recovery movement and defunding the addiction treatment
industry. As a result, RR may be particularly helpful to those who find AA and
treatment outright offensive, rather than just not for them. Rational Recovery

Systems, which is the official body of RR, is a for-profit corporation owned by Jack Trimpey and his wife, Lois.

Because RR no longer holds meetings for support, its website and newsletter are the centers of its activity. Here's how one member described recovering though the RR website:

> I have to give you a sincere thank you because you didn't save my life. You showed me how to save my own. 12 step groups almost killed me. After 3 inpatient treatments, and countless "relapses" I was in a state of total despair and considering suicide. . . . I waited for this miracle that would remove my compulsions forever. And it never happened. . . .
>
> I examined my childhood for hidden traumas that caused me to use. I began to develop "aberrations" to help explain my use. Each time I went back, I was told my problem was simple. I didn't accept my powerlessness, and was therefore unwilling to turn my life over to the care of GOD as I understand him. (Problem is I don't understand him at all.)
>
> My first treatment was in my 2nd year of college. Since then I have been suspended from school, lost my scholarship, discharged from the military, let go from several jobs, etc. If I had known then what I know now, none of that had to happen.
>
> I was cured one night about a year ago. . . . I was broke, depressed and feeling pretty hopeless. . . . I couldn't bear yet another humiliating meeting and 24 hour chip, so I went on-line and looked up recovery sites.
>
> The Crash Course in AVRT, right here at this website, was all I needed! IMMEDIATELY, all the hopelessness left me. But the Beast reared up quickly, pumping the Program on me, "You're on a pink cloud. You can't quit using. Will power doesn't work!" It was amazing how much ammunition the 12 step program and people had given my Beast to keep me using. But it was easy. I don't use. For years I had been trying to figure out why I got drunk, and had many reasons (excuses). But reading through your site showed me the only real reason I ever got drunk was because I picked up a drink and poured it down my throat. End of story.
>
> Since then I haven't used. I work, I'm about to re-enter school and I have so many things I've never had before. And I did it all myself. But I harbor a hell of a resentment toward AA and the like. (I guess I'm on a dry drunk, ha, ha). I'm happy. RR works where tens of thousands of dollars worth of "medical" treatment failed.

SMART

No, SMART (an acronym for Self Management And Recovery Training) was not founded by another male alcoholic angry at AA! In fact, it developed after a split between Jack Trimpey and some key members of RR. These members felt uncomfortable with Trimpey's plans for the organization—and with the direction he took away from some of the ideas he'd written in *The Small Book*.

SMART recovery is based more broadly on the ideas of cognitive-behavioral and motivational-enhancement therapy. No higher powers are required; like SOS and RR members, SMART members focus on their own competence to recover and change. As the SMART website describes the program's ideas,

> SMART has a scientific foundation, not a spiritual one. SMART teaches increasing self-reliance, rather than powerlessness. SMART views addictive behavior as a maladaptive

habit, rather than a disease. SMART recovery meetings are discussion meetings in which individuals talk with one another, rather than to one another. SMART encourages attendance for months to years, but probably not a lifetime. There are no "sponsors" in SMART. SMART discourages use of labels such as "alcoholic" or "addict." As in RR, SMART meetings can be attended by anyone who wants to deal with a compulsive behavior, whether it's gambling, heroin, or others.

The program doesn't have steps, and it changes its activities to reflect the latest research on what is most helpful. There are four main areas that it focuses on:

1. enhancing and maintaining motivation to abstain;
2. coping with urges;
3. managing thoughts, feelings, and behavior; and
4. balancing momentary and enduring satisfactions.

Unlike RR, SMART does not completely reject moderation as a goal:

> Our services are for those who desire, or think they may desire, to achieve abstinence. Individuals unsure about whether to pursue abstinence may observe in our group discussions how abstinence can be achieved and how it can help. Even those whose ultimate goal is moderated involvement with their substances or activities may benefit from participation in abstinence-oriented discussions. Benefit could occur if the individual aims to engage in selected periods of abstinence or frames the goal as abstaining from over-involvement, as opposed to all involvement.

SMART meetings are run by a coordinator, who can be either a recovering person, or a professional trained in dealing with addictions with methods used by SMART. People discuss their current situations and problems, and they spend time dealing with relapse prevention and motivation to stay clean. The program is still relatively small, but it does have about 250 weekly meetings in the United States, and a mailing list and "live" web meeting at its website.

Choice and Empowerment

Jay, a 51-year-old stained-glass artist and handyperson who participated in one of our naltrexone studies, found SMART to be an important part of his recovery. He'd begun drinking heavily after the end of a 13-year relationship. Jay is gay, and he and his lover had jointly owned a house. The breakup sparked a difficult legal battle, and Jay began bingeing heavily in its aftermath.

Previously, he'd never had a problem with liquor. He'd even keep it in the house for dinner parties but would often go months without so much as a sip. After the breakup, however, he began to drink daily or cycle into binges of heavy use followed by several days of "recovery." He sought help from a local counselor. "He encouraged me to attend some AA meetings," says Jay, "which I did, starting with one a week . . . [but they] were really stressing me out badly to the point where my greatest urges for alcohol were immediately after I got home from the meeting. By the time I got to going to three a week, I was acting on those urges."

Jay's problem with AA was that he didn't relate to the people there. "I just never felt comfortable. The people, while they were nice enough folks, all talked about having a lifelong problem with alcohol, which was not my case, and having had alcoholic parents, which was not my case. I remember sitting there watching the clock wishing the hour away."

Eventually, he stopped going and spent two years trying to deal with his problem on his own. When he saw our ad seeking research subjects and offering free treatment, he decided to give our program a try. Because he was in a study, he did not know whether he was on naltrexone or placebo. He says he's not sure whether it was the medication, the counseling he got here, or the SMART support groups that made the difference, but unlike AA, SMART did not give him urges to drink:

> The difference was that SMART emphasizes individual recovery and discourages the dependence on the group, whereas to me it seems like AA encourages dependence. SMART wouldn't say this but in my own words, I came to realize that AA almost swaps one addiction for another, the alcohol for the group, whereas SMART emphasizes you come as long as you feel it's helpful and then maybe you start coming sometimes, and then you discuss with the group what are your plans to stop coming, and then you stop coming knowing that we are always here and you're welcome back. And I like that approach. It was also just less structured, none of this business, "I'm Jay," and everybody says, "Hi Jay." To me that all seems very rehearsed or not-spontaneous or almost insincere. And there's no pressure to get a sponsor because there aren't any. It's much more an individual thing and they have a workbook of little exercises to do at home. I actually found that to be more helpful than even the meetings themselves.

Jay said he found the cognitive techniques SMART taught helpful, for example, "Stop and look at the situation, whatever is bothering me at the moment, what's the best that could happen, what's the worst that could happen? What's the likelihood that the worst is going to happen? How would a drink affect it?" This idea helped him to think urges through and avoid drinking.

Also, he says, "In the end it's up to me, no one is forcing it down my throat, I am the one who chooses to do it, therefore I'm the one to choose not to do it. Unless I plan to go to AA meetings for the rest of my life, which I don't, at some point, I'm not going to be in a group or a treatment program or whatever, and at that point it is up to me." Jay found SMART empowering in a way that AA was not for him.

Women for Sobriety

Women for Sobriety (WFS) was founded in 1976, when Jean Kirkpatrick (not the former U.N. ambassador) recognized that many of the principles of AA did not meet women's needs. As an alcoholic herself, she struggled with AA's ideology. She noted that the steps particularly focused on encouraging humility and recognition of one's flaws. However, most female alcoholics already spend too much time on these problems—hating themselves because they aren't living up to what they think a woman should be. Their main issue is often not to become less arrogant and more responsive to the needs of others, but to feel better about themselves and to take their own needs into account in their lives. Women for Sobriety's program focuses on building self-esteem and empowering women to make life choices that will sustain their sobriety.

The Women for Sobriety program is laid out in Kirkpatrick's book, *Turnabout: New Help for the Woman Alcoholic*. Meetings are run by a moderator who has been "certified" by the program as being knowledgeable about it. Meetings are open only to women, and the group is self-supporting through member contributions, like AA. The group's website describes the program as follows: "Women for Sobriety is a self help program for women with problems of addiction. It is the first and only self help group program for women only and its precepts take into account the very special problems women have in recovery—the need for feelings of value and self-worth, and the need to expiate feelings of guilt and humiliation." The WFS motto is "We are capable and competent, caring and compassionate, always willing to help another, bonded together in overcoming our addictions." WFS encourages the use of meditation, diet, exercise, and positive-thinking strategies to aid recovery.

Rather than 12 steps, WFS has 13 affirmations (called the New Life Acceptance Program), which it suggests members say daily each morning, then pick one to focus on for each day:

New Life Acceptance Program

1. I have a life-threatening problem that once had me. I now take charge of my life. I accept the responsibility.
2. Negative thoughts destroy only myself. My first conscious act must be to remove negativity from my life.
3. Happiness is a habit I will develop. Happiness is created, not waited for.
4. Problems bother me only to the degree I permit them to. I now better understand my problems and do not permit problems to overwhelm me.
5. I am what I think. I am a capable, competent, caring, compassionate woman.
6. Life can be ordinary, or it can be great. Greatness is mine by a conscious effort.
7. Love can change the course of my world. Caring becomes all important.
8. The fundamental object of life is emotional and spiritual growth. Daily I put my life into a proper order, knowing which are the priorities.
9. The past is gone forever. No longer will I be victimized by the past, I am a new person.
10. All love given returns. I will learn to know that others love me.
11. Enthusiasm is my daily exercise. I treasure all moments of my new life.
12. I am a competent woman and have much to give life. This is what I am and I shall know it always.
13. I am responsible for myself and for my actions. I am in charge of my mind, my thoughts, and my life.

It's Different for Girls

Amy, a 33-year-old journalist whom we will hear more from later, found Women for Sobriety more helpful than AA was to her. Although she ultimately required treatment for another condition before she was able to maintain her recovery, WFS helped her to see that she was not alone in finding that what AA said didn't always apply.

"I had an intuitive sense that I needed more bucking up than squashing down," she says. "And Women for Sobriety sounded feminist and empowering. I was still drinking, I kept trying AA but it just seemed kind of harsh and punitive and it didn't seem at all true to my experience.

"There's so much about learning not to be a 'big shot,' about guys who were so arrogant while drinking that they thought they could easily be the President of the company. As a woman, I never had the slightest bit of confidence that I could even be a middle manager, let alone President.

"My first meeting was very nice. The women were warm, it was very small, I didn't have a sense like I did in AA of having to stick to a script or risk saying the wrong thing and hear it echoing in the air. I felt like I could be honest. And what really struck me was that the women seemed happier. The meeting was held in someone's house—it was cozy and warm and everyone seemed relaxed. I didn't have the sense of that AA "fire in the eyes" to tell someone what to do. These were normal, regular people living happy productive lives and not talking in slogans while they did it.

"I also liked that there wasn't that tremendous emphasis on how much time sober you had—there's a real hierarchy in AA between novices and elders. It's almost against the rules to say that anything is going well if you are a beginner. You're automatically crazy. WFS felt more like, whatever problems I have with alcohol, my strengths as a person were still read and had merit. I didn't have to try to hide them and I felt like I was among equals."

Amy went to the meeting on and off for six months, but because it was located in Westchester and she lived in Manhattan (about an hour away), she eventually stopped going because the commute was so arduous. "I ran a meeting in Manhattan for a while," she says. "That was interesting because I was starting it without that much experience. It was really odd that there wasn't a meeting in Manhattan. But my biggest problem with it was that a lot of the women who came were still drinking and I felt that one of the problems with WFS is that you almost need that intensity and brainwashing of AA in the beginning. WFS was great for maintenance, but not so great for beginners because it doesn't have that 24-hour-a-day, we'll come and cordon off your bed to prevent you drinking system that AA does. Also, in AA, because it has been around longer, there is a lot more group lore—you can always tell someone just to go to a meeting, but I couldn't do that in WFS because there weren't any in the city."

Amy says she did like the affirmations, even though she did sometimes feel silly saying them. She adds, "A woman's experience is genuinely different. I know very few genuinely grandiose women—and many more with confidence problems. WFS says that if you feel like telling yourself you are not such a bad person and might even want to run for President, well, that's not such a bad idea."

Religious Organizations

A large number of churches, mosques, and synagogues have become active in helping members of their faith recover—too many for us to list their individual programs and how they work. (See the appendix.) If you are religious, you may want to ask at your own place of worship whether there is any such support group or program. If you are currently not involved with a particular religious group, you may want to choose one in your faith, which offers help to people dealing with alcoholism and other addictions.

Christian Recovery International and the National Association for Christian Recovery offer information on numerous church-related, mostly 12-step focused groups. Among these are Overcomers Outreach, which is a Christian group using the 12 steps in conjunction with the Bible. (Please note: Some of these groups are not supportive of Christian gays and lesbians—their sites offer links to the "Homosexuals Anonymous" groups that aim to use the steps as a way to become heterosexual.) The programs are very similar to traditional AA—with the exception that Jesus Christ is everyone's higher power, and the religious aspects are heightened, not played down. Also, people with different types of addictions (alcohol, cocaine, gambling, etc.) can meet in the same group.

Jews may want to check out JACS—which stands for Jewish Alcoholics, Chemically dependent people and Significant others. This support group helps Jewish members integrate their religion and the 12 steps.

We have been unable so far to locate a comparable national Islamic resource—although, among African Americans, the Nation of Islam has often been a path to recovery. African-American churches have also been particularly helpful to those with substance problems—and in the resource list in the appendix, you will find several listings that may help you locate a church program near you. Many of these are non-12-step focused, unlike the other Christian programs, because African Americans often find the idea of powerlessness, in the context of the racial inequities of American society, to be politically problematic. African-American church-based recovery tends to be more socially conscious—emphasizing that addiction is not just an individual problem, but a reflection of larger problems in the community.

Research on Other Self-help Groups

Just as there is surprisingly little research on AA, which has over 950,000 groups meeting around the world and is a part of most American addiction treatment, there is even less research on the other self-help groups. SMART tries to use the latest research-based techniques—and the affirmative nature of WFS is sensible, given the research data on female alcoholics. However, no one really knows how successful any of these programs are.

Our advice is, if you don't like AA, try the alternative group that most appeals to you—and if you find you don't like that one, try another one. Developing a network of support can be really helpful in recovery, and most of these groups offer ready-made networks. The Internet has made them available almost everywhere. If you are just starting to get sober, it's best to get as much help and reinforcement for your decision as you can, and AA or other groups can usually provide that. Also, they tend to be far cheaper than continuing professional care and are generally the best type of aftercare there is. We routinely suggest support groups to all the patients in our treatment program. As you become more stable in your recovery, you can decide when and whether to phase them out.

In the next several chapters, we examine the presently available professional help for addiction problems, which many people with serious alcohol or other addiction problems need, in addition to self-help support, to start them on their route to recovery.

Knowledge Is Power

- There are now a good number of alternatives to 12-step programs aimed at dealing with the problems many have with AA and its sisters. All of them are free and subsist on member donations.
- Secular Organizations for Sobriety (SOS) is the oldest, largest, and most established AA alternative, and its program basically consists of members offering support to each other to use whatever methods they feel most helpful in maintaining abstinence.
- Rational Recovery began as an alternative to AA but now is a political organization aimed at attacking AA and eliminating the drug-treatment industry. RR members believe that to quit drinking, just do it.
- SMART (Self Management And Recovery Training) was started by former RR members unhappy with the direction the organization has taken. It uses research-based techniques to help people support each other's recovery from substance problems.
- Women for Sobriety (WFS) is an alternative for women with substance problems, which focuses on building self-esteem and overcoming the shame so often felt by female alcoholics and other addicts.
- Numerous religious organizations support recovery. Ask at your church, temple, or mosque about these; see also our resource listings in the appendix.
- The Internet is an important new tool for recovery and can help those who wish to be involved with some of the smaller programs that may not be available in many areas.
- If you don't like one of these programs, try another—or start your own!

CHAPTER 14

The Minnesota Model

Minnesota Model treatment: Treatment like that provided by Hazelden or the Betty Ford Center, usually requiring a 10- to 28-day inpatient stay. Focuses on teaching the disease model of addiction and on getting alcoholics and other addicts to attend 12-step programs.

When Americans think of alcoholism or other addiction treatment, what typically comes to mind is a monthlong, inpatient stay at a rehab center such as Minnesota's Hazelden or the Betty Ford Center in California. Celebrities such as Carrie Fisher, Elizabeth Taylor, and Darryl Strawberry have praised such programs, and in the late 1980s and early 1990s, most insured people had access to similar, if less famous and cushy, rehabs.

Since the early 1990s, however, more than half of these centers have closed. Insurers and HMOs reduced their coverage of expensive, inpatient care, which could run up to $40,000 for one month and typically now costs between $5,000 and $20,000 per month. People sent to such programs had rarely been screened to determine the severity of their problems and had often not tried less intensive options first. In fact, if people said that they only drank or took cocaine on weekends, they were often believed to be "in denial" about the level of their problem, and counselors would frequently inflate the levels of alcohol or other drug consumption reported because Minnesota Model professionals thought that alcoholics and other addicts always underestimated it. It is easy to see how this could lead to false diagnoses.

For the average person with a drinking or other drug problem, research found that outpatient treatment produced similar results at much lower cost. These studies did not indicate that no one needed inpatient care, but HMOs read them that way and essentially cut off so many people that hundreds of programs were forced to shut down or become outpatient centers. Most insurers now either do not cover inpatient addiction treatment at all or cover it for just 7–14 days maximum.

In this chapter, people with personal experience of treatment describe the typical inpatient experience for those whose problems are severe enough to require it and who can find a way to finance it. We also discuss the research on Minnesota Model treatment and explore what outpatient Minnesota Model care is like. In addition, we offer information about two lower-cost inpatient options.

A Spiritual Awakening

James believes this type of rehab saved his life. "I don't know how people make it without it," he said. The 49-year-old educational consultant is now three months clean. James's father died when James was just 3 years old—and he never got along with the man his mother married when he was 8. He started drinking heavily and smoking pot as a teenager. By 1998, he was smoking crack.

"I was hating my life," he said. "I wasn't enjoying it anymore. Even though I was involved with a gorgeous 27-year-old woman, I think I was moving further from life, closer to tragedy." He also realized he could lose his job. "My boss said to me, 'What is going on? You've never been absent more than 3–4 days a year, but this year you've missed 65.' I told him I needed help, that I had a substance abuse problem." Soon afterward, James entered Arms Acres, a Minnesota Model treatment center in upstate New York. Here's how he describes it:

> July 4th was Independence Day for me. That's my anniversary. I had been on a 4–5 day run. I smoked my last hits and I nearly crashed my car on the way there. For the first three days, I slept and ate, nothing more. After that, it was very scheduled and disciplined. I think structure and discipline are very helpful. We were up at seven, had to clean our rooms, make our beds. Breakfast was from 8 to 8:30, and at 8:45 we had meditation. For most of the time, the men were kept separate from the women.
>
> Relapse prevention class was next. There was a very poor instructor for that, and I would sit there thinking, as an educator, "Well, I would present that lesson this way." But I started to realize that I have to be more disciplined, that I had to really listen, that there might be one or two words I need to hear here. And it enabled me to sit in a seat and pay attention. The focus was on tools you'll need to stay sober: "Easy Does It," meetings, eat properly, ask for help. We'd have lunch and then group therapy. I talked mostly about my girlfriend, and how I wanted to help her. The others would say "be quiet about her. Talk about you!"
>
> Later in the afternoon and in the early evening came the piece that really helped me. It was a group that was just the patients, no counselor. We wouldn't talk about what was the greatest coke we'd ever done, but about how to deal with life, open up to yourself and have real relationships.

For James, a turning point came during what the rehab called "Spiritual Sunday." Strangely, while he was being interviewed, the very song that had played while he had a spiritual awakening came onto the radio just as he was asked about the moments that mattered most.

> There was this staff guy and he would play spiritual songs about love and self-appreciation. I love music and there'd been no music there before this. And this song, this very song, "The Greatest Love of All," by Whitney Houston was what he played. "The greatest love of all is inside of me." And the emotion came flooding out. I cried for hours. I've always had an inclination towards spirituality, so that part wasn't a problem for me. I have a deeper relationship with God now. There have been several things where I feel that maybe God heard my prayers. And that song—I don't think that was a coincidence.

After 19 days in rehab, James went home and began an intensive outpatient program at St. Luke's Hospital in New York City. "I didn't go home by myself," he said. "I was afraid that there would be drugs in the house so I had someone come and help me go through everything."

> I went to three 12-step meetings a day, got a sponsor, and made lots of phone calls to other members, like they suggested. I get up in the morning and pray. I have outpatient treatment twice a week. There's another group therapy meeting and I also see an individual counselor. In AA and NA, people always say "I thought I could do it my way," when they talk about why they relapsed. I haven't picked up doing it the way I'm told. And so I keep asking for help and people thank me for helping them!

Although James didn't find family therapy to be a key part of his recovery, it is a major element in most Minnesota Model treatment. Many Minnesota Model centers have a "Family Week" program, which the people closest to the patient are strongly encouraged to attend. Hazelden, for example, has special groups that family members attend to learn about how to deal with the changes that recovery requires of an alcoholic or other addict. In these groups, family members also discuss issues that may have helped lead to alcoholism and other forms of addiction—and how family members can become overly involved with a patient's addiction and inadvertently encourage it. Because family difficulties can be a major source of stress that can lead to relapse, the addict and his or her family are encouraged to deal with them and attempt to resolve them early on so that they don't pop up later and hinder progress.

My Family Week Story

My rehab experience was very similar to James's. The schedule was virtually the same. I, too, came to believe that I had to start listening to others, rather than relying totally on myself. For me, one of the key parts of treatment was the family program, however.

To start, your family received counseling on the nature of addiction as a disease, and the importance of attendance at 12-step meetings. Then, you attended a large group, which included your family, several other patients and their families, and a family counselor.

I'll never forget one family who underwent the process in my group. The daughter, Stacy, was in treatment. Her older sister had died in a car accident, and their father, who was also an alcoholic, had said to Stacy afterward, "I wish it had been you in that car." She had never really gotten over hearing him say that—and truly believed that he meant it.

The format of the therapy was that each family member had a turn to tell the others about their resentments and, in the case of the people not in treatment, to disclose how the patient's drinking or other drug use affected them. The people in treatment couldn't respond immediately but had a chance to speak later about their own resentments and problems.

When Stacy spoke of how she felt when her father wished her dead, you could see that everyone was paying attention, and many people were weeping in empathy. Her father was a gruff, taciturn man—but he, too, wept and hugged her afterward, apologizing and making it clear that he loved her and truly hadn't meant his devastating words. The family's physical presence literally changed as the therapy progressed. You could almost see the burden of the shame and anger being lifted from their shoulders.

Although my own experience was not as dramatic, it played an important part in my recovery. My parents' discussion of how I'd hurt them during my addiction affected me, but what really gave me pause was when my 10-year-old brother had his say. "I never really got to know you," he said, and for some reason, that got through. I now knew viscerally that getting high wasn't just harming me—it was hurting the people I loved. I could feel their love for me in a way that I hadn't been able to do before, and I knew that only staying clean could allow me to experience the connections with my family and others, which I wanted. I'd thought I could get that safety from drugs—but what I really needed, though I feared it impossible, was the comfort of human connection. Somehow, I got some hope about that in that family group, and in rehab more generally.

Maia

Rehab and Relapse

There are also many patients, quite frequently women, who don't find Minnesota Model treatment particularly helpful.

Amy, the 33-year-old journalist from Chicago whom we heard from regarding Women for Sobriety, had checked herself into a Minnesota Model rehab in 1989 for a drinking problem. The center, now closed, was called Spofford Hall—and she chose it from a guidebook to rehabs, which recommended it. She relapsed soon after she was discharged. She says she found rehab "not abusive or unpleasant, but not very helpful, either."

> I chose inpatient treatment because I wanted a vacation from my whole life—which felt really miserable. And I knew I was not having much luck not drinking on my own. I could quit for maybe two weeks at a time, but I'd always start up again. I'd tried AA meetings a couple of times, but they didn't really do much for me.

Amy says she did find her main counselor at Spofford kind, concerned, and understanding: "She was smart and young and really paid attention to what I was saying. I was so touched that someone was really listening that I just burst into tears. I'd been trying to send all these signals to my friends and my boyfriend over the years, like, 'Hey! I need help!' but, because I was functioning, they hadn't believed it."

Buoyed by that encounter, Amy plunged into the strict routine of rehab determinedly, even though, she says, she found it authoritarian and somewhat confusing. "The worst part," she says, laughing, "was that we had to get up incredibly early, like 6 A.M. I was tired all the time, and I used to sneak naps, even though we weren't supposed to 'isolate' in our rooms. But mostly I tried to do everything the staff told me, be the perfect student, because I really wanted to get well." Despite high motivation, however, Amy found some of the required AA reading upsetting:

> My counselor was a very serious Twelve Stepper and told me that if I was going to recover, I had to read all the literature and do all the Steps, not just the easy things, and especially read the "Twelve Steps and Twelve Traditions." But when I did, I found it horrifying. The hectoring tone it took—"We alcoholics are bad, we've *never* tried to find spiritual meaning, we're self-centered and dishonest"—it felt like someone was shouting at me while stomping on my head with this huge boot: "Bad! Bad!" The fact that it didn't say "you" but was couched in this seemingly equalizing "we," like "We know your secrets," just made it worse. I was viscerally upset.

More fundamentally, she says, "As a journalist, someone who was generally interested in getting at the truth of things, I was also bothered—although then I didn't know how to verbalize it—by the way you were supposed to fit your experience into their paradigm; and if it didn't fit, then you were 'in denial.' I *wasn't* in denial—I'd known I had a problem, which was why I'd checked myself in—and I was aware on some level that I was having to shape my story, you know, play some things up and play other things down, in order to fit the pattern of the spiritually sick alcoholic/addict they were teaching us to repeat back at them. I never felt I could talk about it. After all, they were the experts."

What her counselors at Spofford missed were long-standing problems with depression and anxiety that preceded her drinking problem by years and may have caused it. Even a Spofford psychiatrist, whom she told about her strong family history of depression, failed to make the diagnosis or suggest treatment. Amy has also recently discovered she suffers from a mild case of attention-deficit disorder. "What I really didn't get from treatment was how to avoid having life after drinking feel like life before I started drinking—which was pretty lousy," she says. After rehab, she went to daily AA meetings, "got phone numbers and called people and tried to work the steps," she says. She did everything an AA beginner is told to do.

One day, however, half an hour after a meeting, she drank. "The feeling it gave me, besides guilt, was pure relief," she says. After a long period of getting sober in AA and with the help of another self-help group (at times for stretches of two years or more), only to fall into bouts of depression and relapse, Amy finally realized that her chronic, profoundly bad feelings were not "just normal." "I remember asking my boyfriend, 'About how many times a day do you think about killing yourself?'" she says. "And he said, 'Never,' and that astonished me. I didn't think you could be alive and not think about suicide twice a day or so. I thought, 'Maybe I am depressed.'"

Amy saw a psychiatrist who diagnosed her depression, and she started taking antidepressant medication. She now also takes medication for ADD. Trial and error showed that when she took her medication, she was able to stay sober without difficulty. On two occasions that she tried going off the medication, she relapsed.

Though many Minnesota Model rehabs now do make a thorough effort to diagnose coexisting psychiatric disorders, most still believe that medication should only be used as a last resort. Be sure that any rehab you choose does proper psychiatric evaluation, and if you know you suffer from another disorder, it may be best to choose a program that specializes in dual diagnoses to be sure you get the best care for both.

Minnesota Model on the Cheap: Halfway Houses and Oxford Houses

For those who feel that they need an inpatient stay longer than they can afford at an actual Minnesota Model treatment center, there are two additional, far less expensive options. Ironically, some insurers will pay $10,000 for two weeks in an "inpatient medical rehab," but almost none will cover the $400–$1,000 typically paid per week at a halfway house. Though the active ingredients in both halfway houses and Minnesota Model treatment are AA, group support, and time away from the drinking or drug-using environment, insurers don't see halfway houses as "medical" because they are not run by doctors.

The actual treatment in both places is pretty much the same, although you get somewhat less of it in a halfway house. Residents in halfway houses are expected to work—so you can usually pay for your care while you attend. Days are spent working, and evenings are devoted to group therapy and AA or NA meetings. Residents are also usually required to help clean and maintain the house.

An even less intensive and less expensive inpatient option is the "Oxford house." These are basically group residences for people in 12-step recovery— some have formal groups and house requirements, others just agree to stay clean and sober and attend meetings together. If you are desperate for inpatient treatment, accept the 12-step approach, and cannot afford any of the more formal options, Oxford houses can be helpful.

Intensive Outpatient Treatment

Intensive outpatient Minnesota Model care is similar to the inpatient version, only the patient doesn't stay at the center. Patients attend for two to four hours every weekday, typically—and sleep and live at home. They are usually required to participate in AA or other appropriate 12-step meetings, as well. For those employed during the day, there are evening programs; others operate during normal business hours.

It seems counterintuitive, but there are actually advantages to getting clean and sober in the same environment where you drank or took other drugs. For one, even if you do get inpatient care at first, most people will eventually have to return home in order to resume their lives. In outpatient care, you get supported practice in dealing with temptation, whereas the inpatient situation can be artificially protective.

Increased Self-esteem

Wilson, age 25, an aspiring film director who currently works in new media, began his recovery at the Smithers intensive outpatient program in New York City. The child of a real-estate developer and a boutique owner, he "had a great childhood, great parents, a good education."

Wilson suffered from profound depression, anxiety, and attention deficits beginning early on, however. He began drinking at age 12 or 13, and by 18 he was also smoking pot and taking acid. Soon, he was selling marijuana and "smoking insane amounts—an eighth to a quarter ounce of the best pot a day, with my friends":

> August 25, 1997 was my first day at Smithers. I was terribly uncomfortable in my first group. There were about fifteen people milling about, some drinking coffee. To me it looked like the big dinner scene from the movie "Freaks"—with all these bizarre people looking up at you and you're the new guy.
>
> On a typical day, you'd have first a small group, 5–6 people, with your counselor. Then there were two larger groups, each on a different topic—like relapse triggers, the family in sobriety, money, that sort of thing. Sometimes we would split up into men's and women's groups or to discuss HIV issues or other things like that. The groups were not 12 step oriented, which I'm glad about because at that point, I thought it was weird. If they had pushed it, I would have gotten out. I saw the people in AA as people like those who were in my Temple youth group, smiley happy people, and I just wasn't like that.
>
> I literally see my counselor as a god. He navigated my ship through a storm and the type of steering he had to do for 90 days, five days a week, several hours a day was incredible. It wasn't so much what he said, but sitting in that room, knowing that he cares about you and the harder you work, the more you will get back and the more developed a relationship you will have—a relationship that was giving great things back.
>
> I went five days a week for 10 weeks, and then 3 days a week for one week, 2 days for one week and then once a week for thirteen months. I'm also doing individual therapy and I'm on Zoloft and have just added Wellbutrin because I've just quit smoking.
>
> My self esteem went from 0 to 75 on a scale of 100 because they gave me constant, detailed feedback—support and criticism from people I trusted. The list of what they did for me is huge, monstrous. And I'm 16 months clean now, I go to meetings, I have a sponsor—I think AA is totally cool and I think praying is totally cool and I don't feel like I joined the Temple youth group.

Research on Minnesota Model Treatment

Unfortunately, there has been little controlled research on the Minnesota Model, which makes it difficult to get a real sense of its effectiveness. However, there has been a large evaluation study by an organization called CATOR (Comprehensive Assessment and Treatment Outcome Research), which did examine how 10,000 patients in 38 inpatient and 19 outpatient programs fared following treatment in the late 1980s and early 1990s.

Earlier research by individual rehabs on their own success rates was criticized for relying only on the reports of individuals who responded to surveys mailed to them after treatment. Critics claimed, correctly, that such surveys give a much brighter picture of treatment outcomes than other methods. People who are doing well are far more likely to mail in a survey than are those who have relapsed. In order to control for this response bias, the CATOR study used an estimate of a 30% success rate for those who did not return surveys (which is perhaps a bit generous, given research on other treatments). With this assumption, it found that 44% of inpatients were clean and sober one year after treatment, and 52% of outpatients were. Assuming that all nonresponders had relapsed, the figures were 34% and 42%, respectively. (Discounting nonresponders produced a success rate of 60% for inpatient, 68% for outpatient!)

Note that this doesn't mean that outpatient treatment is better than inpatient. It is far more likely to reflect the fact that those who attend outpatient care have less severe problems in the first place.

Outpatient Minnesota Model treatment was also one of the treatment types included in the major multisite treatment evaluations funded by the National Institute on Drug Abuse, DARP (Drug Abuse Reporting Program), TOPS (Treatment Outcomes Prospective Study), and DATOS (Drug Abuse Treatment Outcome Study). DATOS, the most recent study, found that outpatient drug-free treatment (mainly, but not only, Minnesota Model) typically produced reductions in drug use of 50–60%.

Choosing the Best Minnesota Model Treatment

If you have decided that Minnesota Model treatment is right for you, there are a few things to look for when selecting a center. Hazelden and Betty Ford pioneered this model, so if you have the option to attend either, it makes sense to do so. Don't automatically rule them out if your finances aren't in good shape: Both of these institutions are well-funded and give "scholarships" to some people who couldn't ordinarily afford them. Call each, and see what is possible.

Many patients are lured into inpatient treatment because of its spalike facilities—swimming pools, gyms, massage therapy, and so on. These aren't the best reasons to choose a rehab. However, if you have a family member who is reluctant, you can often sway them with snob appeal when nothing else works. If it's good enough for Elizabeth Taylor, . . .

Other more serious things to look for include a good family program and a daily schedule heavy on therapy and 12-step meetings and light on lectures and films. Also, be aware of how the people at the center respond to questions. If they aren't friendly and helpful when dealing with a potential patient or the patient's family, they probably won't be when they actually have the person signed up.

For Family Members and Other Loved Ones: Participate in Family Week

If someone close to you is attending a Minnesota Model rehab, you will probably be asked to participate in a "Family Day" or "Family Week" program. No matter what you have gone through with your loved one, if at all possible, you should try to participate. Family programs offer everyone the opportunity to air resentments and deal with issues that may have helped maintain the addiction. They are also a good place to learn about how to deal with relationships with people who have substance problems and the particular perils these relationships involve.

In fact, some Minnesota Model rehabs limit contact between patients and the people back home so that the painful emotions that are often evoked can be handled therapeutically in this program. When someone is in treatment, you should be as supportive and "light" as possible on the phone—just as you would be with someone who was facing any other life-threatening illness. Now is not the time to lecture about the past or share scary worries about the future. Of course, if there is something serious like an illness in the family, you should talk about it, but if there are things that can wait, it's probably best to do so.

Though particular family programs vary, typically, families are given information about alcoholism and other forms of addiction similar to that being provided to the patients. Then the families participate in group therapy, usually with multiple families present to offer support to each other. It is up to you how much you wish to participate, but it's generally the case that the more you put into such things, the more you will get out of them. If something is particularly bothering you, try not to be afraid to raise it here. This is your chance to bring things up in a safe place where your loved one has plenty of help to cope with them: If there is something you resent, an unresolved legal issue, an ongoing pattern that is making you nuts, and so on, you can really help by airing it here and now.

Generally, loved ones get the chance to talk about their pain first, but patients are also asked to discuss what bothers them and what kind of support they might need when they get home. The more you can listen, the more you can be open to new ways of dealing with your problems, the more helpful you will be able to be. The process can be painful and uncomfortable, but the healing that results is frequently extremely powerful.

Joe

Knowledge Is Power
- Most insurers will now cover only a week or two of inpatient Minnesota Model treatment, not 30 days, as previously.
- Family therapy is an important part of Minnesota Model treatment.
- Many people find that the AA and NA meetings and patient-led groups are the most "active ingredients" in this treatment.

- If you can't afford Minnesota Model treatment but need inpatient care, you can get the benefit of such peer-led groups while staying in a halfway house or Oxford house program.
- Intensive outpatient treatment is virtually identical to Minnesota Model inpatient treatment, but you sleep at home.
- Many Minnesota Model treatment providers are leery of offering any medication at all to recovering people, so if you know or suspect that you have a coexisting disorder such as anxiety or depression, it may be best to go to either a Minnesota Model provider that specializes in dual diagnoses or a different type of treatment. You can combine treatments—for example, getting a psychiatric evaluation and medication supervision from a psychiatrist, while getting addiction care from an intensive outpatient center.
- Look for a center that has a clearly structured schedule, with lots of therapy and meetings and not too many lectures and films. Try "name brands" such as Hazelden first.
- Be sure that the center's staff seems kind, supportive, and open to questions.

CHAPTER 15

Therapeutic Communities

> **Therapeutic community (TC):** A residential treatment for heroin, cocaine, and marijuana addicts, which can take from 6 to 18 months; has a rigid, hierarchical structure, requiring patients to work their way up to graduate and often uses harsh confrontation to "break down" patients.

Perhaps more than any other treatment, therapeutic communities scare addicts. You may have heard horror stories about being forced to dress as a bum and wear signs saying, "I am an asshole." You may associate the whole idea with brainwashing and with being stripped of your dignity and identity. The idea of living in a group treatment situation for six months or more can in itself be frightening.

The stories are true; however, outcomes research and some addicts' experience suggests that these programs can be extremely helpful in some cases. Also, recognizing the pitfalls of rough confrontation, many of today's TCs have seriously toned down their tactics. In most places, the signs and all-night marathon therapy are a thing of the past. In some, they still persist, however, so consumer awareness is probably more important with this type of treatment than with any other.

In this chapter, we look at the TC experience from the perspectives of both those who were helped by it and those who found it hurtful. We take a look at the research, offer tips on how to find a good TC, and explore who shouldn't attend one.

What Is a TC?

Traditionally, in America, a therapeutic community for the treatment of drug addiction is an inpatient, complete rehabilitation program, which lasts around 18 months. They are modeled after the first program to report success with street addicts—Synanon. Founded by Chuck Dederich in the 1970s, this program later devolved into a violent cult. TCs focus on illicit drugs—in fact, up until the late 1980s, many permitted the use of alcohol in the final phases of treatment, although all TCs now call for complete abstinence.

Since the early 1990s, "modified TCs" which last six to nine months have been started in order to reduce the expense of this type of treatment, which has typically been paid for by state agencies. There are also even some outpatient programs based on TC ideas.

A typical day in a TC is rigidly structured and consists of work activities, group therapy, and "house meetings" to discuss conflicts. Days begin early and end late—free time is rare. Toward the end of treatment, restrictions are gradually lifted, and vocational training or actual job experience is offered. TCs are arranged hierarchically so that you can get the experience of "working your way up."

Most TCs believe that addicts are essentially antisocial—and that confronting them about their deviance is important to remaking them as good citizens. Some have dropped this idea, however, and now believe that focusing on the positive and being gentler is a better way to open people to change. When choosing a TC, it is hard to find out which philosophy is operative because the harsh TCs have typically not revealed exactly what participants can expect, for fear of scaring them off. However, the nonconfrontational TCs are quick to point this out and to discuss how they have become more "user friendly"—so a lack of such discussion may clue you in to an "old school" TC.

Tell It to the Marines

Eric is a former Marine who went to three different therapeutic communities and currently works as an advocate for addicts and ex-addicts. His family—he has 13 brothers and sisters—moved to the United States from the Dominican Republic when he was three. He became involved with selling drugs after he left the service and then started "getting high on his own supply," contrary to the advice for successful dealing. His drugs of choice were alcohol and cocaine. He has now been clean for four years. Eric was living on the streets of New York City by the time he sought help in 1994:

I had been homeless for about a year, away from my family, using crack primarily. I didn't know what to do or how to find a treatment program so I went up to a transit cop. I was very lucky, because most cops don't know but this guy said go to 34th Street, there's an outreach center there. And he let me jump the turnstile and even rode with me to the referral center.

They sent me to a place called Star House. It's one of the oldest therapeutic communities in the country. I stayed for a week. I saw people being verbally assaulted. People were saying things to each other like "Shut the fuck up. Stand over there and look at the wall." There were guys dressed as bums. You couldn't ask a question because you had to talk only to certain people in the chain of command.

I left because I got in trouble for something I didn't know. They told me to write a 500 word essay as punishment and I was punished for asking for a pen and paper to write it. I thought I was being set up. I really wanted to stop using, but how do you function in this type of environment?

When I said I was leaving, they all gathered round and only then did I get support, they all became my buddies and tried to talk me out of it. I left, got high for 2–3 days, a whole weekend and woke up Monday and went back to 34th Street. They sent me to what was then called "Manhattan Bowery Corporation" [now Renewal House] and it was much different.

They put me in bed for two days, let me chill out, relax. Everyone introduced themselves. They were all nice, the staff was nice. I was introduced to my counselor and case manager—they were both good. I was gradually integrated into house procedure.

The daily routine was that we'd have a house meeting, then GI [General Inspection]. You would clean the house and fix stuff. Then, you would have group. They called it "gladiator school," and everyone took their hats off. You could even confront staff. At first, I sat outside the group and watched, so I could learn how to take care of myself.

On Fridays, they would have a confrontation group. You could drop someone's name in a box if you wanted to confront them. People would say things like "You think you are better than us—you're just a crackhead." They would say "Make 'em bleed and then patch 'em up" but there was more bleeding. I became a master at just saying "OK, I'll take a look at that" [instead of responding emotionally and striking out, when I was criticized].

I looked at it like boot camp. They told you there to listen and do, don't ask a lot of questions. I told myself, don't complain, nothing here can hurt you. They just do things to try to create emotions.

MBC got me a job working with the MidTown Community Court doing assessment and referring addicts to treatment. I had about 2 months clean, I worked about five hours a day. I felt like a member of society. But I'd get home and I was at the mercy of the staff.

One month before I had six months [this TC offered a shorter program, which was supposed to last six to nine months], I was put on a contract [punishment] because someone who left the house at the same time as I did got high. I would wake up at 5 A.M. and be on what they called "chain gang" and at the whim of the string master. I couldn't talk to anyone. They kept me off work for 10 days. I had to go in front of the house [everyone] and say, "I'm on contract for condoning deviation and not reporting my brother who got high."

I got a mad resentment because I thought it was unjust. They said "life hands you injustices, that's how life works." But I thought they were doing it deliberately.

I left treatment after 8 months, but I relapsed six months later. I was doing well, had a great job, a great apartment, but I was very arrogant and self involved. In AA, you learn to make amends but I hadn't become involved with AA yet. I had robbed people but now I was making $40,000 a year and I would get mad that [my family and friends] would still be afraid that I would steal from them. I wanted love, but when people were still cautious it hurt my feelings. I thought they should be proud of me.

For about a month before I relapsed, I was walking around saying I wish I would get hit by lightning. I wanted something to snap me out of it. I got my paycheck one Friday, went to the liquor store, bought a bottle of Hennessy and bought an 8 ball of coke. I blew 15 grand in one month.

And then, the money ran out and I didn't have the same heart to hustle that I used to have. I felt bad, I went through all that TC shit just be fucked up again? But I couldn't go back there, I knew they would put me on a contract, hit me hard, tear into my ass.

So, I did my own referral. I pretended I was still working and I called a place that I had sent clients to and I said I was sending someone over. It is now called Samaritan/Forbell. It was a six month modified TC.

When I got there, I cried. Everyone was nice—most of them had been in programs before. Most of the mornings were spent doing work and in the afternoon, the whole house would have group. It was not confrontational, just supportive and encouraging. There were no contracts. And they sent me to AA and NA. In previous programs, you could go but it was such a hassle—you had to go with a group. I went to an AA meeting in Cypress Hills. It was a group of older Latino men. That first year, they really took me under their wing. They would pick me up, take me to meetings, take me fishing. They showed me you could do a lot of things sober. They taught me to accept who I was and the fact that you might not always feel good about yourself. I learned that God works through people—frogs don't come out of the sky to give you a sign. I had to go to a TC—I think it was all part of what had to happen to give me the tools I needed. But I got spirituality from AA.

Recovering from Rape and Incest

Melissa, a New York City antiques dealer, had been in Phoenix House for a year when Maia spoke with her. Melissa had previously tried a Minnesota Model treatment center to deal with her crack cocaine and alcohol problem. While in that treatment, she'd uncovered an incest memory—she had been raped repeatedly by her uncle, starting when she was around seven or eight years old. Her boyfriends had always been abusive. It was a return to one of the men who had hurt her, which precipitated the relapse that led to her admission to Phoenix House:

> My first day here was a year ago. I was really nervous and scared. The first thing they said was, " Welcome to the projects." And I said, " Oh my God!" What was hard was getting over this "better than," attitude that I had when I came in: "Who are these people to make me clean? Don't they know who I am?" Once I realized that maybe I didn't come from the same backgrounds as a lot of people in here but I'm here for the same reason, then I was okay.
>
> What I have gotten out of this program, most importantly is the value of honesty, my own self-worth, that even though I did a lot of bad things out there, I'm not a bad person. I am really beginning to love myself and to realize that all these things that I have been told over the years about how beautiful I am not just outside but inside and how bright I am—I'm starting to feel these things for myself.
>
> It's my personal belief that things that happened to me when I was seven, eight, and nine years old have a lot to do with the drug addiction and the alcoholism, with my relationships with men, and my relationship with my parents and family because I never told them [what happened with my uncle].
>
> [When I was in the first treatment center, and I did tell], my father was shocked and hurt and extremely furious. At that time my uncle was already dead. . . . [They believed me] because [it turned out that] it was the same uncle that raped my mother when she was about that age. And, for that to be your first sexual experience, it's horrible. And Phoenix House has helped me deal with that.
>
> A lot of the women here have similar experiences in their life. . . . It comes out in [women's] groups or sometimes in talking with some of the women here.
>
> When it happened, the reason I didn't tell my parents was this uncle told me, "They'll never believe you." And that stuck with me. And that was a big part of the dishonesty of my whole life was that nobody's ever going to believe what I say. Regardless of how horrible and how true it is, they're never going to believe me.

A lot of things have happened to me during my year. I've had two deaths [in my family,] plus my father went through a heart attack and open heart surgery, so I've learned how to separate from my family and realize that I have to put myself first. 'Cause as badly as I wanted to go home and stay home for those things, I couldn't. I did go to the wake and the funeral and I went to visit in the hospital but I had to come back here and take care of me. 'Cause I wasn't going to be any good to them [if I relapsed]. So I learned how to separate from my family. I've always been trying to please my family my whole life.

And groups are really important as far as that's concerned. They run encounter groups here three times a week. And you have people who are getting to know you or are around you constantly 24 hours a day, 7 days a week, telling you that you are doing this, that, or the other thing wrong, and this is your attitude, and this is your behavior. As defensive as you're going to get, at some point you have to sit down and say, "Well maybe these people do see something in me that I don't see in myself. And maybe this is something I need to work on."

Abusive Treatment

Violet's experience, however, shows what can happen when confrontation goes too far—and does not have its intended effect. The 24-year-old addict had led a tragic life. Her father, an alcoholic, collapsed and died while she looked on in horror when she was six years old. Shortly thereafter, her beloved older brother was killed in an alcohol-related motorcycle accident. From age seven or eight, she, too, had been sexually molested repeatedly by an uncle.

Although she didn't start using crack until she was 19, the drug took her down fast. Soon, she was being pimped by her boyfriend in a minority ghetto area of Queens, New York. Before entering treatment, she'd been anally raped with a stick by a customer and then beaten by her pimp for not bringing him any money. Harsh treatment was not at all what she needed, but it's what she got at the Aurora Concept TC in Queens, New York:

The first week, it was just a lot of cleaning and you're up at like 6 in the morning, you're scrubbing this and you're scrubbing that. And you go to this group, and then you go to that group. They're constantly screaming at you. Every time I turned around I was getting screamed at.

I left there several times. My mother made me come back. They decided to hook me up when I came back the first time, which means you have to wear this cap. You can't wear any makeup. You have to wear a sign and they made me memorize it. It was like, "My name is Violet, and I'm 21 years old, and I'm a useless piece of shit."

I got very upset about it, and I split again. I couldn't handle that. They were constantly saying that I was a junkie, and didn't I give a shit about myself? And I'll tell you at that point, I was in a very angry stage, and I would say, "I don't give a fuck about myself. I hope I do die." Just to say to them that I don't care how much you scream at me, it ain't gonna work, I hate myself anyway. You can't degrade me any more than I already degrade myself. And I split again and my mother made me come back.

And she told me to stay two weeks, and we'll find you another program. And I was like, "I can't take this place." I was still kind of fucked up. I had just been getting high, and they made me sit on this little chair about two feet high.

And I'm sitting there, facing the wall in the corner, and they called a house meeting, which means everybody has to be there. And then they turned me around and so I could pay attention to the meeting. I'm sitting in front of all these people Now the girls are sitting five rows back on the right hand side and the rest is all men. . . . 50 men and maybe 15, 20 women. And I looked horrible. I hadn't slept in three days, five days. . . . I was like 90 pounds and I'm five seven. I'm just sitting there hoping it's over soon.

And the guy who ran the place looked at everybody and he said, "This question is for the fellows. Who in here can tell me how many blow jobs did Violet give when she split here, you can—" I think it was sleep late, or have a day off from treatment or something.

And I was just like. . . . 'Cause I was so out of it. . . . Did he really say that? It took a second. And all the guys just looked at me. And he went on, shouting, "And I better see some hands raised." So they all raised their hands because they knew they were going to get in trouble otherwise.

Another patient in the center at the same time as Violet reported that punishments there included depriving patients of food, keeping them awake for several days at a time, and making them scream until their throats bled. Violet continues,

And I got up off that chair and I ran. Threw the sign while I was running, threw the cap, I was out of there. That was it. How could he do something like that? It's funny. I went to a lot of programs. After I left them, I would try to get sober and go to AA. But every time I left Aurora, which is four times in less than six weeks, I got high. Automatically. It drove me to get high, if anything. Even now—it makes me nauseous when I think about it. I felt worse than I felt before I got there. I do feel that it damaged me.

Violet has now been clean more than three years, thanks to a Minnesota Model program and 12-step support groups, but she believes that her TC experience was harmful and didn't help her at all.

In fact, the TC she attended was investigated by the state substance-abuse agency for a variety of improprieties and afterward refused to take state money so it wouldn't have to meet licensing standards. As of this writing, however, it is still open. Unfortunately, even mainstream TCs that have been praised by celebrities and addiction experts are some times just as abusive.

Who Should and Shouldn't Attend a TC

TCs should be seen as a treatment of last resort, given the length of stay and the intensity of the experience. They are probably best suited to addicts with long criminal histories and few job skills—people whose lives have been chaotic and unstructured for so long that they really need to learn life skills from scratch. Research finds that unemployment is highly correlated with relapse. Those who have not graduated from high school and have no job skills can benefit from the long-term care and vocational training that most TCs offer. People who have a college education and significant employment history usually don't need such long-term and intensive care, but if someone with a college background has been living on the streets or has been in and out of prison for years, a TC might be a good treatment choice.

Because of the confrontational nature of these programs, there are certainly people like Violet who may actually be seriously hurt by them—even if they are in a program that isn't as overtly abusive as the one she attended. As described previously, the negative experiences for some people can be intense—and it's not hard to imagine permanent scars being left by it. Unfortunately, there is little information on the negative effects of treatment because most treatment research is conducted to find benefits, not harm. However, there are enough anecdotes to suggest caution for several groups of people.

Research finds that women are more likely than men to drop out of mixed-sex TCs. Because many female addicts were abused as children (from 40% to 80% report incest or other sexual abuse), women who have had this experience may be particularly sensitive to confrontation. The verbal attacks may be experienced as a repetition of earlier abuse. Because there are more men than women who become addicted, and because most treatment doesn't offer child care, the ratio of men to women in treatment is often as high as 4:1. In such a male-dominated environment, many women feel too uncomfortable to get much benefit and can certainly be harmed by the sexual harassment that often occurs in such situations. Also, as was true for Violet, some TCs even condone sexual humiliation as part of treatment itself, but there is no reason to believe that this helps *anyone* recover from addiction.

Women also are more likely than men to need additional psychiatric treatment, but many TCs refuse to offer medication or special psychiatric care for such patients. They do try to exclude those with obvious psychiatric conditions before admission, but if you suspect that you or a loved one has serious depression, anxiety, or other major problems beyond addiction, most TCs are not a good choice for treatment unless they have specific guidelines or are specifically designed to deal with dual diagnoses. Also, there are a few all-female TCs, and if a woman needs long-term treatment, these are probably a better choice than the mixed-sex centers if you can get a place in one. If you have children, these are the centers that are most likely to offer situations where they can live with you, and to offer child care, as needed, as well.

Gays, lesbians, bisexuals, and transgendered people may also have difficulties with the male heterosexual orientation of most therapeutic communities. Though most no longer use female drag as a punishment for men, some still have a very homophobic environment. Before you enter one, you will probably want to visit and talk to people to see whether this is the case at any center you are considering.

TCs are also not the treatment of choice for most young people. Many parents, desperate to deal with rebellious teens, are attracted by the idea of long-term, "tough love" inpatient care that these programs offer. The programs often promote themselves to parents as the only answer. Don't believe it—anyone who tells you they have the "one" way is, at the very least, misinformed. Start with lower intensity treatment.

FOR FAMILY MEMBERS AND OTHER LOVED ONES:
SOMETIMES, TCs ARE BEST

If someone you care for has been truly ravaged by addiction, a therapeutic community may be the best choice. People who have fallen quite far often need more than rehabilitation—they need what might be called habilitation because they are so unused to working and living by society's rules that for all intents and purposes, they no longer know how. This habilitation process cannot happen in a month or two—at least six months of intensive care are needed to get them back on track.

TCs are scary to addicts, there's no doubt about it, but those who can constructively use what TCs offer can completely turn their lives around. To encourage someone to attend, make sure you have found a center that provides compassionate care—and then have him or her talk to residents and graduates. For someone living on the street, "three hots and a cot" may be all the incentive needed; in other cases, it may take some time before a person is ready to make the commitment. If your loved one has outstanding criminal cases against her or him, you can point out that a person who voluntarily attends treatment has a much better shot of avoiding prison than someone who has not taken any action. Also, if people choose treatment themselves, they can switch centers if they hate one, whereas if they are mandated to it, they may not have such options. The motivational techniques described earlier for getting people into any treatment should be kept in mind, as well.

Once your loved one has decided to go ahead, you should be prepared to participate in family activities related to treatment. Family therapy can often make a real difference in addiction treatment because so frequently, addicts are not aware of how they have affected others or how much people care about them. It can also help resolve issues that may have caused pain and are now used as an excuse to continue taking drugs. Just by showing up for such sessions, you can illustrate to your loved one how important her or his recovery is to you.

As you get involved with treatment, you can also see how the person is doing, and if there are any problems with care. For example, if the staff yells at you or does something you find inappropriate with regard to the patient, you will want to investigate this; or if there is pressure to participate in fundraising activities, you may want to choose another center. If you think something isn't right, don't hesitate to call the state licensing agency or other treatment professionals to determine whether it is a serious problem.

Maintain contact with the person in treatment, as appropriate; phone time may be limited, and letters may be censored, but it is important nonetheless to try to stay in touch. You would be surprised how important and comforting such communication can be to someone who is struggling to make a big change in a strange social setting. Frequently mention how proud you are that your loved one is making this effort, and be positive about the future. Try to keep disturbing news to a minimum, but don't leave out really important things.

As your loved ones progress, they will have greater freedom and privileges, which may be frightening to you because their safety from relapse is less assured. Try not to let this fear show—the more faith you have in them, the more they will have in themselves. Also, the less fuss made about minor setbacks, the less likely it is that they will become major ones. One real advantage of TCs is that they offer a long enough period in care that when people make mistakes as they begin to gain freedom, the mistakes can be corrected without turning into disasters.

Joe

Research on TCs

Unlike the Minnesota Model, the therapeutic community has been the subject of quite a few studies. The big problem with TCs is dropout: The majority of addicts leave treatment in the first month. The strict regimen and intensity of confrontation probably account for this. Only 15–25% will graduate; one national study found that the average completion rate was only 10%. However, TC graduates do very well—one study that compared Phoenix House graduates to dropouts found that while 90% of graduates were not using drugs one year after treatment, only 43% of dropouts were abstinent.

TCs were one of the modalities studied in the large national treatment evaluations—DARP, TOPS, and DATOS. DARP found that abstinence rates three to five years after a TC were 40–50%; the percentage of patients who had improved (decreased drug use and crime) was 70–80%—but these rates were similar to those for methadone and outpatient drug-free treatment. In each of those studies, the longer a person stayed in a TC, the less likely the person was to be unemployed, using drugs, or committing crimes. TCs typically cut drug use at least in half, even for those who did not complete the programs.

How to Choose a TC

Because TCs vary so widely in their philosophies and their harshness, it is important to seriously investigate these programs before committing to them. One key question to ask is about patient complaints. If the center staff can tell you the procedure by which patient complaints are handled, if there's either a particular staff member who handles them or a written policy for complaints, you are probably dealing with a reputable organization. The idea that someone cannot "violate chain of command" or talk to anyone but one staff member is a recipe for abuse.

Also, be sure to check out the history of the center with the state licensing agencies and in the media. Most states have an alcohol and other drug abuse treatment agency; sometimes this agency is listed under "Mental Health." Often, they have a hotline for patient complaints. You should at least be able to learn whether a center is licensed, and unlicensed facilities are definitely to be avoided.

A world wide web (Internet) search can also yield helpful information—as can a call to the local newspaper. Local news coverage can sometimes turn up information on such troubles, as well. Check back issues at the library or online.

If there is a need for vocational training, be sure to ask about how the program handles that. Some TCs have real contacts with employers and focus on marketable skills; others have residents spend their days cleaning and doing kitchen work. The best programs make sure that graduates already have a job lined up when they leave.

Talking to graduates is, of course, another great way to get a sense of whether a TC is for you. Make sure you can speak with them alone, outside the center. If this is not permitted, do not consider the facility. Ask graduates about contracts, punishment, contact with parents or other relatives, and how they were treated in general. If there are times when contact with the outside world is limited, find out what the exceptions to this are and how long it lasts. You don't want yourself or your loved one to attend a center that won't tell you if your parents have died, for example, which has happened to some people in these centers. If the graduate seems unwilling to discuss details or overly uses jargon, which he or she is unwilling to explain, the center may be a bad bet.

Many therapeutic communities, like Minnesota Model centers, encourage family participation and integrate family therapy into their treatment. This can be extremely helpful—so ask about it. Another thing to look for is aftercare. If you have been in treatment for months, you probably have had little chance to be exposed to temptation or to stimuli such as your old haunts, which can induce craving. Though TCs do gradually increase the amount of freedom residents have as they get closer to graduation, it's important that you have a way to get connected to a support network when you return home. Two signs of a good program are the provision of nearby aftercare groups or continuing counseling after you leave. If these are not available, be sure that you have some plan for continuing support, whether it be 12-step or other self-help groups or counseling.

Phoenix House and Daytop Village are the nation's largest therapeutic communities, and both have good reputations within the TC field. However, both still do use "contracts" and confrontation extensively, and their policies on medication vary from center to center. With both, you can be assured that they are not fly-by-night operations, but you will probably want to speak to local graduates and discuss the programs in question and their complaint policies to see whether you are comfortable with them if you are considering one or the other.

Samaritan Village in New York is a TC that no longer stresses confrontation and is built on a model that is more "user-friendly" than other TCs. Again, however, even if you've heard a center is good, it's important to check it out yourself. Financing is often shaky, and a place that has a fine reputation one year can be horrible the next. Caveat emptor is unfortunately the rule for choosing addiction care.

TC TIPS

To minimize fear and friction in a TC, simply follow instructions. Most TCs are pretty clear about what they want residents to do and not to do. If you aren't sure, ask. You will have far less trouble if you just do what they want, rather than try to avoid it.

Another key: Try to do things cheerfully and without indication of resentment. TCs are big on "attitude" infractions—and the less you resist or show signs that you think what they want you to do is silly or beneath you, the less likely you are to be punished for "attitude."

If something is upsetting you, talk about it. If you use the appropriate channels—therapy groups, house meetings, and the like—to discuss what is making you unhappy, you won't get in trouble. Also, the more you participate in such things, the easier it will be to progress. There's little point in attending a TC if you aren't going to open up and go for it—and the less resistance you have to doing this, the easier it will be for you.

However, if there is a major issue such as sexual abuse or some other type of "dark secret" that you fear people will use against you in some way, share it only with those you trust. For example, you might talk about having been raped in a women's group, but you needn't feel obligated to tell the whole community about it. Keep in mind, too, that no one can use anything against you in a harmful way unless you let them—the less you judge yourself, the less any put-downs someone can devise will bother you. The best way to defuse such things, as Eric pointed out in his story, is simply to say "Yeah, I'll take a look at that."

If you really feel that you are being treated unfairly or that you are miserable, and it is not having any therapeutic effect, you should talk to the person in charge of dealing with patient complaints and to your outside friends and family. You may need something different—or you may just be in the darkness before the dawn.

Maia

Knowledge Is Power

- Graduates of therapeutic communities do very well—with at least 40% drug-free three to five years later. However, only 10–25% of those who enter TCs will graduate.
- TCs are best for people with little history of employment or long criminal records because of the intensive orientation toward work.
- Family therapy and arrangements for aftercare are important parts of therapeutic community treatment.
- Women, people with psychiatric disorders, young people, gays, lesbians, and transgendered people should be wary of confrontational TCs, as should anyone who has been sexually or physically abused.
- Family members should be in contact with their loved ones in treatment as much as possible. If something doesn't feel right, don't be cowed by "the professionals"—get a second opinion.
- Speaking to graduates, reading local newspaper stories, and calling the government agency that licenses drug treatment in your area can help you find the right therapeutic community.

CHAPTER 16

Moderate-Drinking Approaches

To many, the idea of teaching an alcoholic to drink moderately is as absurd as the idea of toilet training a newborn. While it might be technically possible in a rare few instances, it seems highly unlikely to succeed without causing a great deal of trauma and pain to everyone around. The vehemence with which proponents of abstinence-focused treatment have opposed even discussing the question has made unbiased information about such treatment very difficult to find. Even though AA recommends that people who are not convinced that they are alcoholics try controlled drinking, Minnesota Model treatment providers tend to think that helping people do so is "enabling." The fear is that offering the hope of control will simply make alcoholics unwilling ever to put down the booze.

In this chapter, we look at the research on moderate-drinking programs, people's experiences in them, and the options available in this approach. Despite how it has been demonized, many benefit from it, and you may be surprised at how straightforward and sensible the techniques are.

Who Can Be Helped by Moderate-Drinking Programs?

Part of the debate about moderate drinking has resulted from difficulties in classifying drinking problems. Because many people define alcoholics as people who can never control their drinking, tautologically, moderation is impossible for such people. However, if you define alcoholism by a certain level of drinking and a certain number of negative events related to drinking, as the psychiatric (Diagnostic and Statistical Manual—DSM) definition does, return to nondestructive drinking becomes at least a possibility. Many opponents of controlled drinking have claimed, however, that if someone manages to moderate, "he or she wasn't *really* an alcoholic," even if he or she drank just as much for just as long as someone who couldn't learn control.

Research on whether those who have had drinking problems can return to normal drinking patterns shows several things. For one, the longer and more problematic the drinking is, the less likely moderation becomes, though even here, there is a tiny minority who do attain it. Second, moderation among long-term heavy drinkers is more difficult to achieve and maintain than abstinence is. For those whose drinking problems are not the most severe and long-standing, moderate drinking is achieved about as often as complete and lasting abstinence is—that is, among around 15–20% of those who try it at any given time. In the population of heavy drinkers, those on the less severe end of the spectrum outnumber the extremely dependent alcoholics by about 3:1.

How can you determine whether to try for moderation or abstinence for yourself? The worse your drinking is, the less likely it is that you will be able to successfully moderate it, so that is one factor to consider. Also, abstinence is without question the least risky option: If you don't drink, you can't have alcohol-related problems, period. If you are already comfortably abstinent, why take the risk? However, if you are like most people who are currently experiencing serious drinking problems, abstinence may seem like the least appealing choice. If you can't imagine totally quitting drinking and believe that you will be able to achieve and maintain control, a moderate-drinking program may be a good place to start. If you do get a handle on your drinking, the problem is solved—if not, the motivation to become abstinent becomes more compelling. Many alcoholics do not believe that their drinking is harmful and think that they have total control over it. An attempt at moderation with guidance can be the decisive evidence you need to determine for yourself whether drinking is a problem: If you are honest, and you work hard at the program, you will learn whether moderation is possible for you. If not, you will certainly be more aware of your drinking problem and its effects on you and those around you, which is likely to lead you to take further action to deal with it.

FOR FAMILY MEMBERS AND OTHER LOVED ONES: SUPPORT HIS OR HER SUCCESSES

When people you love drink heavily, you often come to hate the way they are while drunk, and just the smell of alcohol may become repellent. If your loved ones decide not to quit, but just to moderate, you may feel betrayed or that they aren't really trying. If possible, try not to see it this way—try to see these efforts as a first step. If your loved ones have started treatment because you have been showing them how drinking is harming their relationships, try reaching an agreement that if they don't succeed at moderation after a set period of time, they will enter abstinence-oriented treatment. Three to six months is typically long enough to tell.

You should see improvements if your loved ones are actually moderating—and if not, you should try to gently foster recognition that things aren't getting better. Their therapist or support group will challenge them if there's no significant progress during the trial period, and this itself should help prepare them to try for abstinence without constantly thinking, "I know I could control it, I never even tried to cut back. I don't really have a problem."

While your loved ones work on moderation, you should try to support them in their successes and to recognize how hard this type of change can be. During their 30 days of abstinence, remember how irritable people can feel when changing major habits, and try to be easy on them. If problems in your relationship have become tied up with their drinking, you may want to have some joint counseling to deal with this.

There are currently no support programs that help family members of those who are trying to moderate. Al-Anon doesn't recognize such efforts as valid, and attending it may make you feel worse as a result—though some family members of people who have moderated have reported that they find it helpful.

You may be asked to help your loved ones remember to take their naltrexone or other medications. To do so, try to make it a part of your morning or evening routine. Don't ask about it more than once, but if you have agreed to contact their counselor if they don't take it, be sure you do so, and don't let them talk you out of it. Setting up a definite system can help keep everything on track if you both are consistent about it.

Joe

How Do Moderate-Drinking Programs Work?

Currently, there are several moderate-drinking programs available in the United States. Some counselors offer a program called "Drinkwise," developed by Canadian researcher Martha Sanchez-Craig. Others offer other cognitive and behavioral therapies aimed at helping people cut down. There is also a small self-help group called "Moderation Management," which has adopted some of Sanchez-Craig's approach, as well as other techniques that research-based programs found to be helpful. Additionally, there are several self-help books aimed at achieving this outcome. Also, many alcoholism research centers, such as ours at U Penn, will support someone who chooses moderation as a valid treatment option, although abstinence is our primary recommendation.

We know of no inpatient programs aimed at moderate drinking because there would be little sense to them. If a person's problem is severe enough to require inpatient treatment, moderation is an unlikely outcome. Also, how would you practice and monitor your drinking in a hospital? The artificial environment wouldn't teach you much about dealing with your problem in your real life.

Most moderate-drinking programs start with a month-long period of abstinence, to create a transition between the problematic drinking and moderate drinking as well as to break the "habit" aspect of the previous drinking. This allows a fresh start when drinking is resumed. Also, if you cannot successfully abstain for 30 days, you are extremely unlikely to be able to control your drinking.

After this, drinking is permitted, but only within guidelines that are healthy. For women, they are generally not to exceed 3 standard drinks per day or 9 drinks per week and not to drink on more than 4 days a week. For men, the limits tend to be 4 drinks a day, 14 a week and not to drink on more than 4 days a week. These are maximums—many members actually drink much less. Guidelines also include such things as never drinking and driving and not drinking to get drunk. Moderation Management's guidelines state, "A moderate drinker considers an occasional drink to be a small, though enjoyable part of life."

Participants are expected to count their drinks and report to the group (or therapist, if they are doing it through individual counseling) about whether they managed to moderate, and if not, what they believe led to the failure. Over time, a lighter drinking pattern becomes established, or if not, people are encouraged to enter abstinence-oriented treatment.

The Moderation Management (MM) program was created in 1995 by Audrey Kishline, a heavy drinker who had been unable to find a program she thought suitable to deal with her own problem. Kishline read the research showing that moderate drinking is as likely an outcome for many problem drinkers as is abstinence. Her book *Moderate Drinking: The Moderation Management Guide* was published by Crown and is a good place to start if you are considering trying the program.

The MM program has nine steps:

1. Attend meetings and learn about the program of Moderation Management.
2. Abstain from alcoholic beverages for 30 days, and complete Steps 3 through 6 during this time.
3. Examine how drinking has affected your life.
4. Write down your life priorities.
5. Take a look at how much, how often, and under what circumstances you used to drink.
6. Learn the MM guidelines and limits for moderate drinking.
7. Set moderate drinking limits, and start weekly "small steps" toward balance in other areas of your life.
8. Review your progress, and update your goals.
9. Continue to make positive lifestyle changes and attend meetings for ongoing support and to help newcomers.

A Return to Social Drinking

Alicia, a 38-year-old actress, successfully moderated her drinking though the Moderation Management program in New York. "In show biz, there's lots of drugs and alcohol," she said. "I was drinking daily. I felt like crap most of the time. A few times a week, I would drink enough that I would feel lousy the next day."

She tried quitting by herself, but, "It was like dieting," she said. Alicia is overweight and still fighting the battle of the bulge. "I just vowed to cut down over and over but never did."

Alicia tried AA, but "detested it," she said. "I didn't feel that my experience matched the stories I was hearing. I am an atheist and didn't agree with the concept of powerlessness." She saw an article in the *New York Times* about Moderation Management and decided to try it.

Alicia began with a month of total abstinence. "The 30 [days] separates the men from the boys," she said. "If someone repeatedly tries but cannot put 30 days together or is consistently drunk, then they urge them to check out absti- nence treatment." She herself was able to do it, and then she began keeping a chart of her drinking and reporting on herself at weekly MM meetings.

"The steps are about examining the role of alcohol in your life," said Alicia, who found that for her, alcohol was tied up with her family. "There's alcoholism in my family," she said. "I didn't want to be like that.

"The first year was very tough, but it got progressively easier. When I was hav- ing lunch before we met for this interview, I thought, 'Gee, I'd like a glass of wine.' But because I was going to be interviewed, I thought I wouldn't. It's not a huge deal now—it's like not eating dessert. And though I've had a weight prob- lem for years, the alcohol problem was more urgent if less unsightly.

"I'm much happier now. I've not had a drinking problem for two years. I feel like a normal person."

Alicia has, however, lost friends because of her affiliation with MM. "My friends who are in AA cut off contact. They think we give people permission to drink and be in denial."

She has also seen some people in the program fail. "One member came for months and showed no signs of change. I sat down with the group leader to talk about it, and the following week, [the guy's] chart showed that he was triple the weekly limit. But he insisted that that was progress and he was happy—it was half of what he had been drinking before."

Other members said to him, "Normal people can stop drinking for 30 days and can drink within the guidelines." Though he got angry, however, he con- tinued to attend and now is closer to the limits. Some would consider this a suc- cessful outcome, but those who believe in the Minnesota Model might be dubious.

"It's easier to be abstinent—we talk about that a lot," said Alicia. "But our basis is individual choice. And for me, once I acknowledged how important drinking was to me, it became progressively less important."

Moderation Management literature says explicitly that it is not for "former dependent drinkers who are now abstaining and want to try drinking again." Nonetheless, Alicia reports that some former AA members have tried MM— some successfully, some not. "They have a lot of guilt," she said.

MM is also exclusively for dealing with alcohol problems—members didn't want the added controversy of trying to help people moderate an illegal habit, and they also wanted to keep the focus on drinking. They have not addressed the question of someone who had a drug problem once and now wants to see whether they can drink safely, although anyone who wants to work on moderate drinking is welcome.

An Unlikely Success

Gordon's drinking was dramatically reduced at our research program here at U Penn. Many would think him a poor candidate for moderation because his drinking problem was much more serious than that of Alicia, but naltrexone seems to have made the difference for him. He's a 46-year-old loan officer who had applied to take part in a study of this drug and other medication for depression and alcoholism. His marriage was "falling apart," he said. He had been drinking daily for more than 20 years—and had been arrested for DWIs and had caused drunk-driving accidents. He says, "My father drank. I would say there was a good chance he was an alcoholic."

When he didn't qualify for the study he had come in for, I took him on as a patient in my private practice. I told him that the medication we would have used in the study might help him with his goal of regaining control over his drinking.

"I have two kids. I was trying to hold my family together. I was drinking anywhere between 15 and 18 cans of beer a night, 12-ounce cans. The way I used to drink was, once I started, I didn't stop. Now I can have a couple of drinks and I'm fine," he said.

Gordon had never tried treatment previously because he thought it meant going to the hospital or a treatment center, and "I didn't think that those were really pleasant places to be. I didn't think I needed to be there, it's not like I was down and out and laying in the gutter somewhere, or I couldn't function to the point where I was losing my job. I used to see my father-in-law at 5:00 A.M. before he'd go to work wacking down beers or vodka, and he would continue to do that all day long. I never did that. I would work; when I was done working, I would have my few beers and it just got out of control."

He was mandated into counseling after a drunk-driving arrest, but, "It didn't help. You went there and you were in there with a bunch of other people in the same situation, and you were forced to do that, but as far as counseling, the counselor was there collecting his money and you showed up you got credit for your time and you're out the door and that was it."

When he saw our ad in the paper, he told his wife that he was going to try to take part in the study, and that he wanted to deal with his drinking problem. He hadn't known that there was any alternative to complete abstinence. We gave him a medication to help him detoxify from the heavy drinking, and after about 10 days of abstinence, he began taking naltrexone.

Now I can have a couple of drinks and stop and I'm fine. You don't have the euphoric high, you feel more in control, you feel more clear-headed, you don't get drunk. When you drink and you're taking this stuff, I don't know how it works, but my impression is it does something to your brain, and you just don't get that sloppy, you don't want to just keep drinking.

My consumption has decreased by at least two thirds. Now sometimes I'll have four or five drinks in the evening, after work or whatever—and I can stop in the middle of that, it's more controlled. I don't think over the last six months, there's been a time when I've binged on it—and I used to do that every day.

My wife and I are separated now—I wish we weren't, but what are you going to do, you can't twist someone's arm to love you. She gave me no support in treatment—she was, this is it, it's over. I'm content with where my drinking is at now, and I'm prepared to take this medication for the rest of my life if that's what it takes.

From "Moderation" to Abstinence

Tim, a 59-year-old lawyer, entered treatment at the request of his new, young wife, who complained that when Tim was at social functions, he made a complete fool of himself. Tim himself admitted that occasionally his drinking might embarrass him but pointed out that, "I drink at least a six-pack every day, and only rarely does drinking get out of hand." Tim was in remarkably good health for someone his age, and he exercised regularly and was successful in his law practice.

It is true that his first wife had been upset about his drinking constantly, but he said, "she complained about everything I did." On further evaluation, Tim also admitted that he was having some difficulty getting and maintaining erections. When it was pointed out that excessive drinking could have this "side effect," he decided to moderate. Although Tim was advised that complete abstinence was probably a better option in his case, he resisted this suggestion. He agreed to not have more than four drinks a day and to maintain a drinking diary. Tim was also given the option of taking naltrexone and attending Moderation-Management meetings, but he said, "I'll do it on my own, Doc."

The first month, Tim showed some improvement. He did have fewer than five drinks per day on 15 days that month. Unfortunately, he also had 15 days in which his drinking exceeded four drinks, often by a great deal. After three months of similar results, Tim decided to change tactics. It probably helped that at this time, his new wife was increasingly concerned that things were not improving in the bedroom.

When a month of abstinence was suggested as a start, Tim now agreed to try it. His wife rolled her eyes in disbelief. Antabuse was recommended, with his wife to monitor him in taking it. When she heard about the bad consequences of drinking on top of Antabuse, she began to smile. "You mean on this pill, he will get violently ill, throw up, and could die if he drinks? I'll be sure to see that he takes it." If Tim refused, she was to call her doctor, but not nag Tim about taking the medication. During the next month, Tim did abstain completely from alcohol, and he remained on Antabuse for the next six months. At that time, Tim reported that he had no desire to drink. His relationship with his wife had never been better, and he smiled, "Doc, things are much better in the bedroom, in fact they are better in the den, the sofa in the living room, and on the chaise lounge on the patio, too. This abstinence is better—and cheaper—than Viagra, and I'm going to keep doing it, a day at a time."

Research on Moderate-Drinking Programs

The research on moderate drinking is among the most hotly contested in the field. One study, by Mark and Linda Sobell, has been used by both sides of the debate: The authors say it shows that moderate drinking can be achieved even by severe alcoholics; others, who followed up the patients later, say that it demonstrates that moderation is rarely achieved. The controversy over this one study from 1973 continues to this day.

In this book, we choose to ignore it and to focus instead on the rest of the literature. Basically, the research finds that people with alcohol problems on the less severe end of the spectrum (with drinking patterns more like Alicia than like Gordon) do as well with moderate-drinking attempts as they do with trying to abstain. One study by Martha Sanchez-Craig randomly assigned such drinkers to either an abstinence-focused program or a controlled-drinking one. After two years follow-up, both groups were doing equally well. Several other researchers replicated these results.

One interesting finding that shows up in many studies is that women are more likely than men to succeed at drinking moderately. This may be due to the fact that cultural notions of masculinity are often tied up with "drinking like a man" and that moderation may be seen as wimpish. For women, excess is more often viewed as taboo—and a drunk woman is seen as immoral. Moderation fits society's female role better than it does the male role, basically.

William Miller has also done numerous studies of moderate drinking, and his research finds that over time, many drinkers who initially choose moderation, decide to abstain. In fact, the research shows that over time, more drinkers who start with a moderation goal wind up abstinent than continue moderation. The success rates are comparable to those for abstinence treatment—so it is not as though moderation treatment convinces people who would have otherwise abstained to keep drinking for longer. It simply helps those who planned on continuing to drink (whether their treatment program offered them a goal of moderation or not) to reduce harmful consequences associated with alcohol use.

How to Choose a Moderate-Drinking Program

Unfortunately, because moderate drinking is so controversial in the United States, in many regions, you may not have much of a choice if you are interested in moderation. In fact, in some places, there may be no counselors or treatment programs that offer moderate-drinking goals at all. Moderation Management (MM) is still a small program—and even in many cities, there are only one or two groups. Contacting MM is a good place to start. Their website offers online meetings and complete information about the program. Often, local therapists who help patients with moderation refer them to MM, as well—so people at MM can frequently refer you to a supportive therapist.

Another place to check is any nearby university with a center focused on alcohol and other drug problems. Many—such as the University of Pennsylvania, the University of New Mexico, the University of Washington—Seattle, and Rutgers University (New Jersey)—have long researched this area and may offer help with moderate drinking as part of ongoing studies. You may want to call the treatment research center at the closest of these universities to you, even if you don't live near enough to attend treatment there, to see whether they can refer you to someone locally.

Also, if there is no local moderation program, you may want to start your own MM group. While this sounds like a challenging process, it is the people who work hardest at their recovery who tend to do the best. MM's website has information on how to do this and whom to contact.

If you are not this ambitious, however, you may simply want to read the books listed on this subject in the appendix. Interestingly, those who used "bibliotherapy," in the form of a guide produced by William Miller, have been studied extensively. The research found that even with almost no counseling, many patients who used the guide did as well as those who received more intensive treatment. There was one important difference, however: Those who received empathetic and supportive counseling did better than those who tried to moderate with minimal support. Also, those whose counselors were not seen as understanding actually did worse than those who had no or little contact with professionals at all! Once again, this confirmed the research showing that people who see counselors who are confrontational and abrasive drink more than those whose counselors are supportive—and they drink even more than those who get no counseling!

Please note: This doesn't mean that an empathetic counselor will avoid issues such as whether you are actually succeeding at moderation and will only say "nice" things. It just means that they will present difficult information when necessary in a sensitive and understanding fashion, rather than trying to pound it into your head.

Knowledge Is Power

- Because those who do not wish to become abstinent will attempt to control their drinking after abstinence-oriented treatment anyway, research finds that moderate-drinking programs do not make it more likely that someone who should be abstinent will drink longer.
- Those whose drinking problems are on the less severe end of the spectrum—who drink less often, who drink fewer drinks, and who have been having a problem for the shortest periods of time—are most likely to succeed at moderation.
- Women are more likely than men to succeed at controlling their drinking.
- Most moderate-drinking programs begin with at least 30 days of complete abstinence—if you cannot achieve this, moderation is unlikely to be successful for you.
- Naltrexone can be a useful aid for those who wish to moderate their drinking because it cuts craving for the second drink dramatically. However, if you wish to use it this way, you will probably have to continue taking it, so long as you continue to drink moderately because the "anti–second drink" effect works only while you are taking it.
- Empathetic and supportive counselors are very important for those working on moderate drinking; confrontational counselors can actually be worse than no counselor at all.

CHAPTER 17

Harm Reduction

Harm reduction: A way of dealing with addicts, which helps minimize harm related to drug use and often hooks them up with additional services such as abstinence-oriented treatment; similar to MET for alcoholics; also, a drug-policy philosophy recognizing that drugs will always be with us, but the harm they do can be minimized.

On Manhattan's Lower East Side, in a small, unlabeled storefront, is a program that doesn't look as though it provides drug treatment. Addicts come in carrying large numbers of used needles and leave carrying a similar number of clean ones. No one is told to stop taking drugs. In fact, some people have argued that by providing the means for safe injection, needle-exchange workers are actually encouraging drug use.

Why should we focus on needle exchange in a book about drug treatment? Because needle exchange—and other so-called harm-reduction programs—are crucial in helping some people survive and recover from drug problems. Just as controlled-drinking programs don't extend the time people spend drinking, but rather help those who wouldn't have quit anyway, needle exchanges help intravenous (IV) drug users who aren't ready to stop injecting to reduce the risks they are taking.

What Is Harm Reduction?

The idea of harm reduction is simple. Keep people alive during their drug use, keep them as healthy as possible, and they will be more likely to recover. In fact, some see methadone maintenance (see Chapter 18) as one of the earliest types of harm-reduction treatment. Some people continue to use other drugs, but the medical care and the methadone itself allows them to do so less dangerously than if they hadn't had access to methadone. It buys time to consider quitting entirely—and even when it doesn't eliminate additional drug use, it almost always reduces it. This means that it cuts HIV risk. The fewer injections you do, the less the risk of catching something. The less urgent the need for drugs, the less likely you are to commit crimes to get them.

The real beauty of harm reduction isn't immediately obvious, however. Unlike other programs, harm-reduction programs can reach addicts in the early stages of change—such as precontemplation, contemplation, and relapse, when they haven't yet considered quitting or are ambivalent about their ability to stop. By providing care during this time, by being nonjudgmental, and by not requiring abstinence, health-care providers can help addicts build their own desire to quit or, barring that, to use drugs in a healthier manner. All of these outcomes can save their lives and, by preventing HIV infection and other blood-borne illnesses, they can save the lives of those whom the users may contact sexually.

Also, the more health is improved, the better people feel about themselves, the less attached they are to destructive drug use. Many people who work at needle-exchange programs are ex-addicts themselves. The people coming in to get needles often ask, "Well, how did you stop?" This is a priceless opportunity to offer help to someone who isn't necessarily yet aware of seeking it. Also, though most users will not stop immediately, when they see that there is hope and that recovery doesn't have to be the hell they fear it is, they slowly become ready to change.

This outcome directly contradicts many traditional ideas about treatment, which see "rock bottom" as a requirement, and any relief from consequences for addicts as "enabling." However, as William White, who works with poor women who have traditionally not been well-served by drug treatment, put it in an interview with Bill Moyers, "I kept going back and interviewing clients and interviewing outreach workers and what they told me was not at all what I thought I would hear. I had outreach workers saying, "You don't understand, my clients don't hit bottom, they live on the bottom. Bottom is not new for them." What they said is—think in terms of histories of victimization—these women's capacity for physical and psychological pain is almost limitless. If we wait for them to hit bottom they will die. The issue is not an absence of pain in their lives. They've got more pain than most of us can even comprehend. The issue is an absence of hope."

Rather than making drug life more punishing, harm reduction tries to offer hope. By showing addicts that they deserve to live and be healthy, it allows them to see that there might be alternatives, and that they have choices about what they do.

This chapter explores what harm-reduction programs can do for those who are not ready to give up drugs. In it, people who have used these programs discuss their experiences. If you are not interested in drug-free treatment, these programs may be the place to start. Give up on no one, and help people choose themselves what's best for them—that's the motto for this type of care—and the results are promising.

Hard-core Addiction

Harris was born in Fleming, Kentucky, but spent most of his life in Milwaukee. The 49-year-old heroin addict has 10 brothers and sisters. He started using alcohol at age 12 or 13, then moved to pills, marijuana, heroin, and cocaine. He says he was always a troublemaker and was sent to reform school at age 14. His mother was a nurse's aide; his father worked for Harley Davidson. "My parents never approved of what I did, and my father could never understand why I kept doing it. The people I looked up to were hustlers, dealers, pimps, and users. It's hard to believe but that's how it was."

Harris didn't finish high school and started injecting drugs when he was 21. During his addiction, he fathered five children by four different women, stole cars, and cycled in and out of jail. He had tried treatment twice but relapsed shortly after each attempt before coming in contact with Milwaukee's Life Point Needle Exchange program in 1995:

> A neighbor told me about this van that gave out new needles, bleach, and condoms. And when I got on the van, I saw people I used to know. They were clean, they had money, they looked good. They said to me, 'Aren't you tired? Are you ready for something else?' I would hear them, and I would think about what they were saying when I got high, but I didn't stop.
>
> Once I realized I could get clean needles, I didn't share any more. I have a few friends who are HIV positive that I used to get high with. One died, the others are still here. I think that the needle exchange allowed me to avoid that disease and to avoid getting anything sexually because they give out condoms.

Harris says needle exchange was also important in the process that led to his recovery. "When you are using, when other people stop, they sort of drop off the face of the earth, you don't see them any more. But you see these people on the van, and they're shining. Marcus [one of the needle exchange workers] and I used to get high, and I see him there looking fat and shiny. I think everyone wants to stop using, but it's just a question of how. They are afraid of the element of the unknown. I was afraid of the unknown, and when you are using heroin, you have that fear of being sick."

After almost a year of visiting the needle exchange, Harris decided to try recovery. "They'd taken my son," he says, "and I was talking to a social worker about treatment. I said I had no insurance, but she said she could find me something that they would pay for. I felt like I couldn't say no because it was free."

The program he attended, Genesis Residential Treatment Center, was a modified TC, which introduced him to 12-step fellowships. He works there now and has three years clean. He also volunteers at the exchange. "I say, just try it [being clean] for a minute, give it a chance, you might like it. Most of the people that use heroin and cocaine here, I know. They say, 'Man, [Harris], if you can stop, I can stop.' I want people to know that it does work. I was hard-core—if I can stop, anyone can."

FOR FAMILY MEMBERS AND OTHER LOVED ONES: LESS HARM IS BETTER

Just as the idea of long-term residential treatment terrifies addicts but may soothe families, the idea of harm reduction is often readily accepted by addicts but not so much by those who love them. Quite sensibly, they feel that abstinence is a much safer and better goal than moderating the use of something that is, after all, still illegal.

However, if your loved ones simply refuse to stop or relapse so often that they are still at serious risk for overdose, HIV, or other infections, harm reduction becomes more understandable. After all, you don't want to see the people you care about die or get fatally ill if it can be prevented. Most people would rather have slightly impaired, living friends and relatives than dead ones—even though they wish the choice was just between abstinent and impaired. People who work at harm reduction often see addicts whose recovery just wouldn't start until they had found a place where they felt accepted as they were using and didn't feel hated or judged.

There is some conflict between the ideology of harm reduction and that of 12-step programs. The steps emphasize that people who are using are powerless and out of control, while harm reduction says that addicts can and do make choices while they take drugs. The truth lies in between: Addicts certainly have some control over what they do while using, but they are often more impaired than others in exercising that control. Harm reduction can ready people for abstinence by teaching them to examine the choices they make. If they find that no matter what, if they are still using, they continue to have troubled, chaotic lives, abstinence becomes more necessary. If they can reintegrate their lives while still getting high occasionally, then that's a great improvement, as well.

It's important for family and friends to recognize the importance of small steps. It may not seem like much that someone now uses twice a week rather than daily, but that can make the difference between an ability to work and be present for relationships and being totally incapacitated. Keep in mind that you can't let the best be the enemy of the good—change is not necessarily all or nothing. Some reduction is better than none—even though elimination of the problem is ideal.

So, if the people close to you with a substance problem refuse to become abstinent or just seem unable to avoid repeated relapses, be sure they are familiar with harm-reduction ideas related to the drug(s) used. Support them in their efforts to protect themselves—and to attempt to cut down or reduce harm in other ways. If you see a real improvement, say so. If you don't, you should try to let them know in as kind a way as possible that it may be time to try abstinence, even just as an experiment. The more you ally yourself with your loved ones, and the more you let them see that you are on their side, the more likely it is that you will be able to help them move along the road to recovery.

Joe

Attracted into Recovery

Anita's recovery began at a unique program in New York called "ARRIVE," run by an organization called Exponents, Inc. It is not actually a drug-treatment program—its focus is to teach drug users and former users about HIV and AIDS.

After completing the eight-week course, graduates are qualified to become peer educators and counselors in HIV-outreach programs. They are taught public-speaking skills and given advice on résumés and interviews. They also learn the latest information about HIV testing, prevention, and treatment. Some continue in the program as volunteers, many move on from there to get paid a small stipend for their work, and a good number are eventually hired by the program itself in full-time positions. Many of those who begin ARRIVE as drug users leave it as ex-users.

That was Anita's story. Anita, age 42, describes her childhood as having been "somewhere between neglectful and serene." Her mother divorced her alcoholic father when she was born—only to marry another alcoholic. They lived in rural Pennsylvania. "My mother and stepfather were both alcoholics," she said. "I had to care for my two stepbrothers, but I grew up in the country, and school was fine," she says.

At 17, she began drinking and smoking pot, then moved on to psychedelics and all sorts of pills. Anita learned at age 22 that she was manic depressive (also called "bipolar"), and when she was experiencing manic episodes, she would often drink and do impulsive things: Once, she stole a police car. When she was in her late 30s or early 40s, a close friend was stricken with AIDS. She cared for him until he died, and "it was very emotionally painful." Other friends had also become ill or died, so Anita began attending a support group at Gay Men's Health Crisis. It was GMHC that referred her to ARRIVE. "If you want your life to turn around, ARRIVE is the place to go," she says. "It's like no program I've ever heard of.

"I was still drinking and smoking pot when I came to ARRIVE," says Anita, "but my one goal was to stay off alcohol and pot for the eight weeks of the class. I pretty much did, I had one glass of liquor and one puff on a joint. People at ARRIVE are very motivated to change their lives—I saw that they were in recovery and I said, 'I want to do that.' I told them about my relapses, and the group didn't beat me up for it.

"In ARRIVE, I learned to be more assertive, to face my fears, to communicate, and also about HIV and how to stay [HIV] negative," she says. "I like the trainers, they are very energetic, very positive. I felt very relaxed and I could always find someone to talk to."

After graduation, however, the first week Anita started as a volunteer, she had a serious relapse. "I was hanging out with street people, and they were smoking crack, and so I did. I got drunk and high on crack—I don't know why. But it motivated me." In addition to continuing to volunteer, she entered an outpatient treatment program, which provided group support and helped her to attend AA. After her relapse, Anita also received weekly acupressure sessions (done with beads placed on acupuncture points on the ears) at ARRIVE. "It really reduces the craving," she says. "And right after the ARRIVE graduation, I said, 'I feel like I could do anything.' I saw an ad for an income tax preparation class. I took it and passed—ARRIVE gave me the self-esteem to do that."

Anita, who has been on disability for years due to her manic depression, is now reentering the world of work. "ARRIVE offered me hope," she says. She is now six months clean.

TO THE ADDICT: CONTROL

Some addicts believe that they always have control over their drug use, even when they act as though they can't stop. Others feel powerless and say they want to stop but still continue using. The issue of willpower is complicated and veers to the philosophical, but you can avoid these debates about human nature and addict nature generally by focusing on yourself and your goals.

How is your drug use affecting you? Do you find yourself using at times when you know you shouldn't? Do you feel guilty about it, and is it getting in the way of what you want to do? What happens when you try to cut back—do you break promises to yourself or find yourself excusing using that you said you wouldn't do?

Answering these questions and watching yourself should let you know how much control you have—if you are honest with yourself. Some people recognize that they are making bad choices but want to make them anyway because they feel that these choices are nonetheless better than the alternatives. As you try to work on harm reduction, you should continue to look at your behavior and whether your feelings about your drug use are biasing you to make decisions that aren't as good as they could be. Are there options you are leaving out because you don't think them possible for you? Have you looked at your whole range of choices, or are you looking only at those you see immediately? What about your plans for the future?

If you find that you can manage to cut back on your use and reduce the chaos in your life related to drugs to a point where it is manageable, you are making good use of harm reduction. Almost everyone should be able to practice safer injection and overdose treatment, but cutting back on drug use and taking futher steps is more difficult. You should always ask yourself, "Is this the best I can do with regard to my using?" to avoid accepting a limited life when you could have a fuller one. Giving abstinence a serious try can give you a sense of what it's like—but remember that if you don't try it for at least several months, you won't get the full benefit because your body will not have readjusted totally.

If you find that you cannot control or cut down your use and that your life remains chaotic and unhappy, you should consider abstinence-focused treatment and give it a real chance. There is nothing wrong with not being able to learn moderate use—most addicts can't, otherwise they would no longer be addicts!

Maia

Harm Reduction without Abstinence

Harm reduction's results, like those of other treatments, aren't always unequivocal, however. Victor is a 45-year-old homeless man whom Maia met at a conference, where he gave a moving speech about helping addicts get a voice in drug policy. He still drinks, sometimes heavily, and uses drugs besides his methadone, but he has managed to avoid HIV and is gradually reducing his use.

Victor hails from South Carolina. He spent much of his youth in New York City. His mother, although she was poor, refused to accept welfare after she and his father divorced. She went on to become a neuroscience researcher. Nonetheless, her son got involved with gangs early on, and by age 16, he was drinking regularly. At 18, he started using marijuana, then moved on to amphetamine and finally heroin. Victor's story and his thinking illustrate the complexity of drug problems and how harm reduction differs from other strategies. In the early 1990s, he tried AA:

> I sincerely gave it a try, that I have to say. I made a sincere effort to embrace the 12 steps, to stay completely abstinent. I went through six months of hell working with a psychiatrist. There were days where it was so tough for me, I felt like I was going insane. I would drink herbal teas, and I would jog. I did everything I could. I just didn't get better. I felt worse and worse. That isn't to say that if I hadn't kept my nose to the grindstone that I wouldn't have reached the point where it would start to get better. But what I came to in a meandering way was that I did not want to live that life. Even though if I were to weigh it, and the benefits that would accrue to me from being sober infinitely outweighed those of using, I still was not prepared to go that route.
>
> I felt that the 12-step AA model was irrational. I felt that I would be living a lie. I think that it's a religiously oriented model, that it wants you to become an evangelist for abstinence. It doesn't give people the chance to recover on the basis of their own individual needs.
>
> My first time at the needle exchange [storefront] was a tremendous experience. Here, for the first time, was a place where I was treated unconditionally fairly with no regard for my status as a drug user. In fact, my status as a drug user probably gave me some perks because that is who the place is set up for. It was so different from most of the social agencies in New York. Here was a place where I could crash out, and nobody was yelling, "Yo, you've got to get up!"
>
> But I still ask myself sometimes, "How would you feel if you were to live five years totally abstinent?" We have one life to live, and I don't know if I'm prepared to experiment. I can't but say that I'm troubled by that. Who's to say I wouldn't develop a natural rhythm that I probably can't remember from childhood of being happy and complete?

Victor's drug use has been declining since he's been involved with the needle exchange. "I don't drink nearly as much as I used to," he says. "At one point I was a true alcoholic but now I drink much less. I don't drink every day. I do less drugs." And that is harm reduction.

Research on Harm Reduction

Because harm reduction focuses on reducing drug-related problems, rather than eliminating drug use, success or failure must be measured differently in these programs than in abstinence-focused treatment. Needle exchange, for example, clearly reduces HIV risk. Almost every study ever done shows that if you give addicts access to clean needles, they will share needles less, and less HIV will be spread. An international survey found that in cities with needle exchanges, HIV prevalence declined 5.8% per year in IV drug users, while in cities without them, it rose 5.9%. In San Francisco, which has a large IV-drug-using population, needle exchange and education about safer syringe use began as early as 1988. The campaign included widespread access to syringes and even television commercials. The HIV infection rate among addicts there never rose above 15%; in New York City, which still has only small needle-exchange programs, the rate climbed to 50% (and in some neighborhoods, 80%) before beginning to drop. Most AIDS babies have at least one parent who was directly infected by IV drug use—and in San Francisco, thanks to needle exchange (and the use of AZT, which cuts infection in children by two thirds when used by HIV-positive pregnant women), there have been *no* AIDS babies born since 1994.

There is also no evidence that needle availability increases the number of IV drug users. Syringes are available without a prescription in 38 states; these states have fewer IV drug users per capita than the states that ban them. As one public health expert put it, banning syringes doesn't reduce IV drug use; it just increases disease. Research on addicts who attend needle exchanges find that those who attend most regularly often cut their drug use over time. It also finds that needle-exchange attenders don't stay addicted longer than those who don't use needle exchange: Basically, people stop when they are ready to stop. In some cities—New Haven, Connecticut, and Tacoma, Washington, are both pioneers of needle exchange—the exchange programs have become the major source of referrals to other treatment.

The ARRIVE program attended by Anita began its life as a research project funded by the National Institute on Drug Abuse. An evaluation of the program found that it increased condom use; decreased arrests, cocaine sniffing, IV drug use, and marijuana use; and increased testing for HIV, employment, and participation in other drug treatment.

Choosing a Harm-Reduction Program

As with moderate-drinking programs, options for harm reduction are limited. There may be only one local needle exchange—or perhaps none. Most acupuncture treatment works with addicts on a harm-reduction basis. This treatment may be available where other services are not.

While harm reduction may not satisfy the desire for a picture-perfect shift to abstinence, it can lead the way to one and can also help those who are slow in getting there to have a better life in the meantime. Life situations where one must choose the lesser of two evils, rather than selecting the "good" choice over the "bad" one, are unfortunately quite common—and addiction sadly often presents such a dilemma. Harm reduction offers a number of strategies that can save lives, however, and where there is life, there is always hope.

Harm-Reduction Strategies

This section offers some harm-reduction tips and techniques.

- Never mix downs

    The vast majority of heroin overdoses are actually heroin and alcohol overdoses or heroin and benzodiazepine or barbiturate mixes. Alcohol mixed with benzos or other downs is also extremely dangerous. All of these are recipes for coma or even death. They tend to cause unconsciousness rather than a high, anyway.

- Treat overdoses *immediately!*

    If you think someone has OD'd, call 911 pronto. Most heroin overdoses are not fatal if treated quickly. Your timing can be the difference between life and death. Do not hesitate—if you fear the police, you can flush your drugs after you make the call. However, if there is any left of what the OD'd person has taken, place it in the person's clothes or near her or him—his or her life is more likely to be saved if the doctors know exactly what he or she took, particularly if it turns out to be some odd synthetic. Do not leave someone who has overdosed alone. Tell the emergency medical services (EMS) technicians as much as you know—they are interested in saving lives, not busting you. If the person has stopped breathing, try mouth-to-mouth resuscitation while you are waiting for help. If the person's heart has stopped, CPR may be necessary.

    Don't try putting him or her in the shower or injecting him or her with salt or any other techniques you've seen in movies. There is a drug called naloxone (Narcan), which can instantly reverse opiate overdose and is used by doctors and emergency medical technicians for this purpose. Harm-reduction activists are calling for it to be distributed at needle exchanges because it is a safe drug (the only side effects are opiate withdrawal in those who are dependent) and because seconds count in OD treatment. If you have access to this drug, which is administered by injection, use it. Naltrexone could potentially be used to reverse overdose, as well, but because the current formula of the drug is not injectable and because oral administration to unconscious people is usually impossible, you can't currently use it. Again, don't try anything before calling for help—call first.

- Try to switch to less harmful drugs and routes of administration

    Injection is much, much more dangerous than most addicts think. You can lose limbs. Blood clots can travel to your heart or lungs and kill you or to your brain and cause a stroke, which could leave you paralyzed or speechless, if not dead. You can catch deadly or highly unpleasant diseases, not to mention potentially killing yourself by OD. If at all possible, don't even start—if you have already, try to switch back to smoking or sniffing, if at all possible.

    Marijuana and very moderate alcohol use (one glass of wine a day for women or two for men) are the least harmful psychoactive substances aside from caffeine. Low-level alcohol consumption actually has health benefits—decreased heart-disease risk and decreased stroke risk. If you can switch from heroin or cocaine to *moderate* use of these drugs (or even heavy use of marijuana), you will drastically reduce your risk of a drug-related death. Of course, if your problem is marijuana, the only way to reduce drug-related harm in your life is to cut down or quit.

• Get a source of clean needles if you are injecting. If you have none and feel that you must share, clean the ones you do have with bleach.

First, try to get clean needles: Check out whether there are needle exchanges near you, and if not, ask a physician to prescribe for you if they are not available over-the-counter where you live. Though doctors often disapprove of addicts, most recognize the public-health implications of not preventing the spread of diseases, and many will prescribe or give you works if you are honest with them, keep it quiet, and show that you are already injecting anyway.

If you can't get needles legally, always clean any needle that may possibly have been used by anyone else (this means any bought on the street—sellers do repackage used ones) with 100% bleach. Run bleach through the syringe twice or more, run it all over the outside and the point—try to get it into every nook and cranny. To kill HIV, you must expose the works to bleach for at least two minutes. After very, very thoroughly bleaching the syringe, rinse it with water—at least four to five times. Shooting bleach is very unpleasant, though not deadly—you will taste it and breathe it out for hours. Also be aware: The hepatitis C virus is much hardier than HIV—bleach may not kill it, and it can live for months, even in dried blood. If someone else's blood is visible on anything—do not touch! If you make a mess, be polite and clean it up! Also, never share cotton, cookers, spoons—these are easily available, so why take the risk?

• Use alcohol pads to clean the injection site before you shoot drugs.

There are microorganisms on your skin, which can kill you if they get into your blood. Endocarditis, a potentially deadly heart disease, is one. It's easy to prevent exposure: Use clean works for each shot, and clean the injection site with alcohol before you shoot. If you have to reuse your own works, you should clean them even if no one else has used them, to prevent any bugs that may have grown in the needle or the barrel from getting into your bloodstream.

• Seek help immediately if you think you have been exposed to HIV.

If you suspect you have been exposed to HIV, see a doctor right away. There is evidence that a course of antiviral drugs can reduce the odds of infection if taken immediately after exposure. You cannot (and probably will not want to) do this repeatedly, however—the drugs have serious side effects and are hard on your body. If you find yourself this close to getting infected, it may be time to seriously reevaluate your drug use.

• If you are injecting heroin and don't feel ready to stop using drugs entirely but want a break, try methadone.

Methadone treatment can help you cut down heroin use—and other drug use, as well. If you are on a decent dose, the urge to use heroin will be dramatically reduced, you won't be sick, and you will tend, over time, to use less of other drugs, as well. Of course, if you continue to have dirty urines, many programs will make you visit every day, but at least your risk of blood-borne illness will be reduced, and you will have a choice not to use without undergoing withdrawal. Note: Methadone does not fight cocaine craving, and cocaine makes your body metabolize methadone faster, so the methadone lasts for a shorter period of time, and withdrawal can set in before you are due for your next dose. As a result, continued cocaine use will become increasingly uncomfortable, and heroin craving may return.

- Use less in each hit, and use less frequently.

    This sounds ludicrous to most addicts, but if you want to get control over your habit and want to be able to experience a good high from the drugs you do take, it's the best way to go. The less you use, the less tolerance you will have, and the greater the effect any particular drug will have. Try not to use daily. If you find it impossible to cut back at all, it may be time to consider abstinence.

- Take a month off.

    As with trying to moderate alcohol use, it's a good idea to take 30 days off from *everything* before attempting to switch drugs or cut down. This helps break the habit aspect of use. If you find that you feel better while not using, you may want to extend your time off.

- Work more.

    If you are employed in a job you like, try to improve your productivity and become more engaged in your job. The more you work, the less time you have to get high. (Getting high on the job is seriously unlikely to improve your prospects and rarely improves your productivity in the long run.) If your job isn't challenging or you aren't working, think about what you would like to do. Will drugs get in the way of this? What is most important? Can you find something that will structure your time and help you pull yourself away from destructive drug use? The relationship between unemployment and drug use is quite strong, and not just because people get fired for using. More often, people without work have little to occupy their time and attention.

- Play More.

    The more you have to do, the less time you will have for using or obsessing about using. Try sports, local theater groups, writing, reading, computer activities, political activism, artwork, movies, yoga, meditation, church, or music events (yes, you can go to a concert and not get high; some concerts even have support groups for people who don't want to get high there—look for the yellow balloons of the Wharf Rats!)— the list is endless. Even spending more time with friends who don't use can help you begin to develop a life that doesn't revolve around drugs.

- Learn to recognize cues that lead to heavy drug use.

    Many addicts have binge patterns of using, or times when they get particularly crazy. Usually, there is an emotional or psychological event that precedes these—or sometimes, the sight of a drug buddy, a drug-dealing location, the smell of drugs, or a look at drug paraphernalia can prompt intense craving. If you know what grabs you, you can try to avoid using at these times. You may be able to recognize these patterns by keeping a chart of what is happening daily, how you feel about it, and when, how much, and with whom you are using. If emotional stress precedes binges, you will probably need to develop other techniques for dealing with it—which will also help you if you decide to get clean.

- Take care of yourself.

  Try to eat a healthful diet, get exercise, and so on. Drug urges are often reduced when you are well-fed, rather than malnourished. This will also help increase your resistance to disease—though, of course, you shouldn't count on it for protection if you are crazy enough to share unclean works. If you are drinking heavily, be sure to take thiamine and folate supplements, which can reduce the chances of alcoholic brain damage.

- Get a psychiatric evaluation.

  Yes, we keep mentioning this, but legal drugs might actually solve your problems in a safer and more comfortable way.

- Also, if cutting back or reducing harm just isn't happening, try abstinence-focused treatment.

CHAPTER 18

Methadone

> **Methadone maintenance:** An outpatient treatment for heroin addiction involving the provision of the opiate substitute drug methadone, sometimes for a lifetime.

You've probably heard horrible things about methadone maintenance—it is perhaps the addiction treatment with the worst reputation. Because heroin addicts tend to be seen as the lowest of the low, treatment for them is a magnet for controversy and abuse. The American methadone system is yet another example of treatment using repressive tactics that wouldn't be acceptable for use on any other type of patients. On the street, methadone is known as "the orange handcuffs" (orange because it is often consumed with orange drink). It's seen as enslaving addicts, chaining them to seedy clinics for decades. Even the recovery community joins in to bash methadone—some experts and ex-addicts say it's "not real recovery."

In reality, methadone maintenance is the most successful treatment known for heroin addiction. Heroin addiction is a particularly deadly condition—with 1–3% of all active addicts dying every year. One study found that methadone was 100 times more effective at cutting the death rate among heroin addicts than abstinence-based treatment. This study followed 3,000 addicts for 10 years but ended in 1977—before AIDS was discovered. Methadone has been found to dramatically decrease the risk of HIV infection, so a more recent study of mortality would probably find methadone even better.

The National Institute on Drug Abuse, the Institute of Medicine, and the American Medical Association have each explored the research on methadone maintenance, and all concluded, as the Institute of Medicine put it in 1995, that "methadone maintenance has been the most rigorously studied modality and has yielded the most incontrovertibly positive results." This chapter looks at the methadone controversy, offers an inside view of methadone treatment, and provides suggestions on how to find the best programs.

How Methadone Works

So why does methadone have such a bad name? There are numerous reasons. First, some proponents of methadone say that it "blocks" the heroin high without creating a high of its own. This is not the whole story. What methadone does is

198

act on the same brain receptors that heroin does—so in proper doses, it will prevent heroin from working by gumming up the receptors. It works on the receptors in the same way that heroin does, however, so a person who has never taken opiates and who takes methadone for the first time, will indeed feel a high.

There are drugs (such as naltrexone) that block opiate receptors without activating them, but they have not proven anywhere near as successful as methadone for opiate addiction. Unlike alcoholics who have few side effects from naltrexone, many heroin addicts find that naltrexone makes them uncomfortable. However, about 20% do benefit. It may be particularly helpful for younger, less chronic opiate addicts. Because naltrexone doesn't cause physical dependence, it is not a controlled substance like methadone.

Opponents of methadone take this to mean that methadone patients are always high. This is not, in fact, the case. After a steady methadone dose is administered, tolerance builds rapidly, and after about a week or so, the patient no longer feels much effect except for a lack of opiate craving. Unlike heroin, which needs to be administered several times a day—resulting in highs and lows—methadone's effects last 24 hours, so the person doesn't experience a roller coaster effect.

In fact, research has found that many heroin addicts have an abnormal stress response. This could have led to their addiction or could have been caused by it, but methadone normalizes this response, whereas for some people, abstinence does not. This could be one reason why the relapse rates for heroin are so high. If the slightest stress makes you go into overdrive, it's very hard to function and be comfortable.

Methadone patients on stable doses are not in any way impaired—they can drive safely, take care of their children, even teach college if that's what they are trained to do. One college professor in the Midwest is on a steady dose of over 1,000 milligrams (a typical dose is between 40 and 120 mg per day)—and is able to teach and do research without his colleagues or students being aware of his treatment.

The confusion over whether methadone is "just a substitute" is really confusion over the definition of addiction. Methadone maintenance takes addiction— where a person is having negative consequences from the use of heroin—and replaces it with physical dependence, which is just reliance on a substance (like we all do with food) to function. Because the results of effective methadone maintenance are positive—increased employment, better relationships, reduced drug use, and so on—it cannot be considered "a substitute addiction." A substitute addiction would have negative effects that outweighed the positive ones.

The American Methadone-Clinic System

Another reason methadone maintenance has such a bad reputation is because the American methadone-clinic system is overregulated, and many programs are poorly run. Methadone is the most restricted drug in the American pharmacopoeia. Addicts beginning maintenance have to visit the clinic every day and give supervised urine samples at least once a week. They are often watched while they swallow the drug and not permitted to take any home for several months. This means that vacations, business trips, or even going to work early or late and missing clinic hours are out of the question if the person doesn't want to start feeling withdrawal symptoms.

The whole system is demeaning and controlling—and few methadone patients have nice things to say about it. Counselors' salaries are low, and educational requirements for counselors are unstandardized—some don't even have a high school degree. The clinics are also often located in the worst neighborhoods because wealthy communities refuse to allow them.

Also, because the dilapidated clinics and the "it's just another drug" people give methadone a bad rap, people who are doing well on it are afraid to go public—while those who are doing poorly happily denounce the clinics in the media. A good treatment has been nearly wrecked by a combination of regulation, prejudice, and misinformation.

FOR FAMILY MEMBERS AND OTHER LOVED ONES: THE STIGMA OF METHADONE

Even among physicians, methadone has a bad reputation. The problem is not in the medication, but in America's puritanical attitude toward drugs, particularly opiates. As a result, the most successful treatment for heroin addiction is only used as a last resort.

If your loved one decides on methadone treatment, you may have to fight your own prejudice against it—and that of society. It may be advisable not to tell friends, relatives, neighbors, and employers about it until you are sure that it won't result in negative consequences. Discuss this with the recovering person, and respect his or her wishes.

Keep in mind how deadly heroin addiction is—and how dramatically methadone can reduce the death rate. Support the person's efforts to recover in her or his treatment of choice. Don't push detoxification from methadone unless that is your loved one's goal. If someone is stable and comfortable on methadone, why mess with success?

Family therapy is not often offered to methadone patients by their clinics, but if it is, try to participate. Your loved one probably feels a great deal of shame about addiction and recovery via methadone, so this type of support is particularly helpful. Do not imply that he or she is not "really" in recovery yet or that methadone is an inferior treatment option. Learn about the medication and about the myths about it so that you can debunk them when necessary.

Also, if the person in treatment has other medical problems, you may have to advocate for her or him with medical professionals. Health-care professionals often have an adversarial relationship with addicts and deny them proper pain control and neglect their other complaints. Make sure that this prejudice is not affecting the quality of care your loved one is receiving. Don't be afraid to speak up.

Joe

Common Myths about Methadone

There are many common myths about methadone, which make people reluctant to consider using it. On the streets, addicts say that methadone "gets in your bones" and causes long-term physical damage. There is no evidence that methadone maintenance causes any physical problems aside from constipation, which can be treated. It does not rot your teeth: What makes junkies notorious for bad teeth is a combination of unsterile injections and a high-sugar diet.

Another myth is that "methadone is harder to kick than heroin." Some people do suffer a more protracted withdrawal from methadone than they do with heroin, but another reason methadone withdrawal often seems worse is that the longer you have used opiates, the harder the withdrawal is. Because people on methadone have generally been using opiates longer than people on heroin, this gives the impression that methadone withdrawal is more uncomfortable. Methadone also has a longer half-life than heroin, so it slowly leaves the body over the course of a couple of days, not the few hours of heroin.

Whatever the real reason for the perception, withdrawal is not the major obstacle to recovery: In the long run, staying away from street drugs is the real challenge. That obstacle can be surmounted either by continuing methadone maintenance or through other recovery programs. One study found that six years after detoxification following methadone maintenance, 83% of those who had been seen by themselves and by their counselors as ready to end treatment were heroin free. Methadone maintenance does not have to last forever, although for some people, this might be advisable. When used properly either way, it can be a true aid to recovery.

Also, there is other good news for those considering methadone. Clinics are recognizing that becoming more user friendly not only helps reduce conflict, but also improves outcomes. Drug Czar Barry McCaffrey is pushing to allow regular physicians to prescribe the medication so that people can pick it up at normal pharmacies, like they would get Prozac. Legislation has been introduced into Congress to permit this. If it is passed, it could dramatically improve access to methadone and could thereby enhance recovery rates, as well as making this treatment more attractive to middle- and upper-class heroin addicts. Currently, several experimental "medical maintenance" programs for long-term methadone patients exist, where people can pick up medications just once a month, like other prescription drugs. One such program is operated by New York's pioneer methadone prescriber, Beth Israel Medical Center.

Also, a longer-acting type of methadone—called LAAM—is available at some clinics. This medication is taken every other day, reducing the number of trips to the clinic. However, some people find that they don't feel as comfortable on this medication, while others prefer it—so once again, it's important for treatment to be tailored to individual needs. Those considering maintenance may also want to check out a drug called buprenorphine, which is expected to be approved soon by the FDA. It may be available from regular doctors, and many patients find it to be indistinguishable from or even preferable to methadone.

Inside Methadone Treatment

Alejandra is 37—and was an early methadone success story, though it took her years to accept the role of the drug in her life. She had been troubled since childhood, extremely bright but extremely oversensitive. Half Puerto Rican and half Irish, she grew up in a wealthy family in New York's Westchester County. As she tells it, "My mother used to say that I was more finely tuned than anyone, I heard noises louder or saw colors more vividly. I walked through the world differently."

At age 13, when her parents divorced, she picked up drugs, and by 14 was injecting heroin. She got arrested, and her parents picked her up after a night in jail. "With heroin," she said, "I felt normal, it made me feel safe. And in a state that I could communicate with other people. I didn't feel these raging hormones or these raging emotions, everything was tuned down. I felt naked and vulnerable and desperate without it."

Because of her family's status, she was allowed to enter a methadone program for treatment at that time, though she was only 15 and technically under age. Her first experience with methadone was tremendously positive—she stopped using heroin, graduated from high school, and went off to Boston University. Gradually, she cut her methadone dose to zero and graduated from college with honors. However, while attending NYU Law School, she became deeply depressed and disillusioned. She started using cocaine, and when a long-term relationship ended, she became readdicted to heroin:

> Now, I was using alone which I had never done. I felt sleazy. It was always worst to me after the sun was coming up in the morning. You've exhausted your resources. You feel dirty and disgusting and the rest of the world is just waking up to a brand new day.

She didn't want to return to methadone, however, seeing it as a defeat. When things got really bad, however, she did:

> I finally got on the methadone program. It took a while for the cocaine to stop. I didn't have any lifestyle changes. It was the same life, I just wasn't sick physically.
>
> And I was working on and off. I remember not having a network of friends. I really burned bridges all over the place, just not knowing what else to do with myself. There was a groove right down to the cocaine, and it was so familiar. It took me a long time. In the beginning, when I got on methadone, I used cocaine regularly.
>
> Then, the periods in between [cocaine use] became longer. It tapered off, but [whenever] I would still use, it would get worse and worse. I would go through more and more money. The last time I used was absolutely repulsively disgusting.

Methadone gradually allowed her to stabilize her life. Though the counseling at the program she attended was a mixed bag (one counselor had an affair with her, others were abusive, but some were helpful), the drug itself helped her to distance herself from the street scene. She met a man who was not a drug user and got married. She still kept believing that she couldn't get on with her life unless she got off methadone, though:

I always qualified it as, " When I get off methadone. . . I still believed that this was a temporary thing. I resented it, I felt like crap for being on it. I wouldn't go back to law school until I got off of it because I didn't trust my mental faculties. You name it, anything that was wrong with me I blamed on the methadone. If I was too hyper, if I was obnoxious, if I drank too much, anything. . . I would blame it on the methadone.

Finally, carefully, she detoxed after several years and went into a 28-day rehab. Shortly before she would have had her first year drug-free, however, she relapsed and fell into despair. Returning to the methadone program, she resolved not to let it be an excuse. She began to see methadone as a medication that could help an imbalance in her neurochemistry, rather than a recreational drug that she was bad for wanting. She read the research and found that her beliefs about methadone impairing her abilities were false. She returned to law school, got her degree, and is now practicing. "I do believe that methadone saved my life," she said.

Methadone Gives You a Choice

Moishe, age 49, also found methadone helpful, though he has now been drug free for 14 years. He was born and raised in an observant Jewish household in Brooklyn. Moishe was 14 when he drank his first alcohol outside of religious rituals. At 16, he had his first blackout. He soon became a frequent pot smoker and then moved on to LSD, barbiturates, and, finally, heroin. "I fell wonderfully in love," he says of the experience. Although he kept trying to stop, every time he detoxed, he would relapse. In 1973, he tried his first methadone program.

> A lot of people don't look at methadone as a step forwards, they see it as a step sideways, but for me, it took away the urgency. That sense where your whole life is concerned with "how do I get money?" "when can I cop?" "Am I going to OD?". I got stabilized. I enjoyed eating again, I went back to college, I found a better job. I went to different programs because I kept trying to get off.
>
> Finally, I went to a program in Queens called Bridge Plaza. I remember this one counselor. He had tattoos all over his body, he was an ex-biker, and he explained his journey on and off methadone to me. This guy really counseled me. He started me going to AA, and I had 10 years of clean urines in that program.

Moishe left there, however, because of an injustice, one that is unfortunately all too common at methadone programs: "They told me that two of my urines came back pregnant," he said, (as though he'd substituted a woman's urine for his own). "They made me give a supervised urine."

This also came back pregnant, and rather than believe that their test was off or consider other possibilities, they punished Moishe. What they should have done was send him to a doctor—a man's urine that shows up pregnant can be a sign of a serious hormonal disorder. Moishe had previously been picking up his dose once a week—now, he was to pick up six days a week. This routine would jeopardize his employment, though, so instead, he went into a hospital to detox.

"I fully expected to stay on methadone for the rest of my life," he said. "I was functioning at a better level than most human beings. I'd completed my BA, I had fallen in love and started to raise a stepfamily. My mother had passed away, and I didn't pick up [drugs] behind that. It was like a vitamin to me."

MY METHADONE NIGHTMARE

My experience on methadone was a disaster—even though I attended the same clinic that Moishe had mainly found helpful. I started in the 21-day detox program, planning to come off both heroin and methadone. I was still using cocaine.

The clinic I attended was located in an industrial area of Queens. The building was grungy and built like a fortress. There were security cameras everywhere, and the front door was armored. My first day, I buzzed the doorbell and was let into a small antechamber, with another videocamera and another thick, vaultlike door.

Once inside, I was interviewed and made to take a urine test to prove I was addicted to heroin. I was given an appointment to see a physician the next day—if everything checked out, I would then get my first dose. The clinic hours were from 6 to 10 A.M. every morning and from 5 to 7 P.M. every evening. If you didn't show up then, you were out of luck.

Early the next morning I spent my first day on the methadone line. There were about 30 people waiting for the door to open—many looking thin and unhealthy, others normal. After being examined, I got on the medication line. I was to be given 20 mg, and I watched as the nurse pressed a button and a splotch of clear liquid squirted into a plastic cup. She then added some orange drink, and I swallowed the whole thing down. Although the drink was sickly sweet, I could still taste the bitterness of the drug.

I didn't feel anything right away, but after about an hour, I felt a calm and a heroin-like euphoria. I even nodded for a bit—and I thought, "This isn't so bad." Of course, after about a week, I had a tolerance to that dose and didn't feel any effects at all. Because I was still using cocaine, when I went to the clinic in the morning, I would be in withdrawal because cocaine speeds up the metabolism of methadone.

Counseling sessions were required, I think once or twice a week. They didn't do much for me. The counselor would say, "You've had a dirty urine, you should stop using cocaine." I would say, "Yeah, I'll try." He would say, "You should go to Narcotics Anonymous," and I would say, "I haven't seen it do anything for my friends." He would try to talk me into it, but I wasn't having it. I didn't think he had any insight—why wasn't he helping me rather than telling me to go somewhere else?

As they started to lower my dose, I began to feel worse. I asked to be switched to the six-month detox program because I knew that I would return to heroin otherwise. They raised my dose to 30 mg, and after a week of comfort, began lowering it again. I continued to use cocaine, and as they decreased the methadone, I started using heroin to make up for it. I felt miserable—every day I would swear to myself that I wouldn't shoot cocaine, and every evening I'd wind up wired to the gills, desperate for heroin to take the edge off. I was urine tested twice a week at the program, and I'll never forget that humiliation.

I would be so dehydrated from a night of cocaine use that I wouldn't be able to produce enough urine for the sample. This was particularly awful when it was a supervised urine—a female counselor would have to come in several times to watch me before I eked out enough. No wonder the counselors weren't very pleasant. Only someone with a same-sex urine fetish could enjoy such work.

When the six-month "detox" ended, I had as big a heroin habit as I did when I started. I begged them to transfer me to methadone maintenance, but because of my cocaine use and the fact that my heroin habit hadn't lasted for very long, they refused. I was on my own again to seek treatment—and for years I opposed methadone because I thought all methadone treatment was like the hell I'd been through.

Maia

Who Should Try Methadone? Who Shouldn't?

Going on methadone maintenance is like marrying an extremely possessive partner—it's a long-term commitment, and it can really cramp your style. At first, most clinics require daily attendance for several months—even on holidays and weekends. Unless you are completely drug free for this period, you cannot "earn" the privilege of getting medication to take home. Clinic hours are limited, and this can impose serious constraints on your work options. Attendance at counseling sessions is mandatory, as well. If you have to pick up medication daily, you cannot travel far from your clinic unless you make arrangements in advance to get medicated at a clinic in the area you are visiting.

After a certain number of consecutive clean urines, most clinics relax these restrictions. You can arrange to visit the clinic just twice a week—and can get up to a two-week supply for travel or vacations. However, this is still a serious limitation on your freedom, and it should be taken into account when considering this form of care.

We hope that in the next few years, these restrictions and constraints will be eased, and methadone will be allowed to be prescribed by doctors just like any other drug for most patients. Right now, however, this is not the case, so even though methadone maintenance offers the best chance for recovery from heroin addiction, it's best to exhaust other options first before tying this particular knot.

If you have tried three drug-free programs, and there are no alternative maintenance programs available and you have been unable to stay away from heroin, you should seriously consider methadone, however. If you are HIV-positive, methadone is a good option because it reduces the odds of relapse, and relapse can be particularly deadly for people with HIV. Studies have found that HIV sufferers who are on methadone progress to AIDS more slowly than those who don't get treatment. If you are injecting drugs and find yourself unable to consistently use clean needles, again, seriously consider methadone because it is better to reduce the HIV and hepatitis C risk as quickly as possible.

The longer you have been physically dependent on opiates, the more likely it is that methadone will be the best treatment for you. It's possible that after years of opiate use, the brain's natural opioid systems decline and may take years to recover. This means that you may have to make it through several years of mood swings, anxiety, and discomfort without relapse before achieving a normal balance. Methadone can create that balance without the wait.

Methadone does not make sense for most young people, who haven't had time to develop the long-term habits that make it necessary. When Alejandra was placed into treatment, this wasn't yet known. Also, methadone cannot be used for people who are not addicted to opiates. If a person uses both cocaine or other drugs and heroin, successful methadone treatment may take longer—as in Alejandra's case, where she slowly stopped the cocaine as methadone helped her feel more stable. However, some people may need additional counseling to stop cocaine or other drug use, and if these drugs are the primary addiction, methadone maintenance is not useful. The more substances involved, the less likely methadone is to solve the whole problem.

Research on Methadone Maintenance

Over 300 published studies have examined the effectiveness of methadone maintenance—making it the most thoroughly studied drug-treatment modality. All of them have found that methadone itself, when given in proper doses, reduces drug use and crime. People who stay on methadone for one year tend to reduce their drug use by 60%—so they are using only 40% as much or as often as they were before entering care, and many are not using at all. Those who continue treatment for two or more years reduce their drug use by 85%.

Every city that has increased methadone access has found that crime drops. In 1973, when New York City added 20,000 methadone slots, drug arrests fell by 40,000, and arrests for robbery, burglary, and larceny decreased from 350,000 to 273,000. In California, when methadone-maintenance patients were forced into abstinence, overdose deaths rose.

Research has also found that methadone dramatically cuts HIV infection rates. One study compared methadone patients in Philadelphia to their addicted friends and neighbors who were not in treatment. Over time, the HIV infection rate was more than five times greater for the addicts who were not in methadone programs. Studies have also shown that adding auxiliary services—such as job-preparation programs, family therapy, and psychiatric care—greatly improves methadone success rates.

How to Choose Methadone Treatment

In many locations, there may be no choice about methadone treatment: Some areas have no clinics, some have only one. In larger cities, such as New York, however, there are quite a few. Location is important because you will be visiting the clinic every day for at least a few months, so it's a good idea to check out several if you have options. Many people find it worthwhile to go out of their way if the more distant clinic has more compassion and more flexibility. Also, if a clinic is in a really bad neighborhood where you have to walk through a drug market to get there, it might be better to select another.

With most kinds of care, private facilities tend to be more responsive to people's needs than public centers. However, this is not necessarily true for methadone, where many of the clinics with the worst reputations have been private, for-profit clinics.

The first thing you want to ask about is dosing policies. Doses should be individualized to meet people's needs, but research finds that most people do best somewhere between 60 and 120 mg. Because the average dose at American clinics is 50 mg, many people are getting much less than necessary. *"Blind" dosing*, where a patient is kept unaware of the dose, is not considered a good practice. If a program is rigid about doses, you may want to avoid it.

Second, as always, you want to ask about patient complaint procedures. These are crucial at methadone programs because counselors have so much control over patients' lives. They can deny a vacation or business trip if they so choose by refusing to authorize take-home medication. Therefore, you want to know what the procedure is for dealing with conflict and whether there is a patient ombudsman or advocate. The best clinics have a full-time employee whose sole job is to deal with patient complaints.

Finally, you want to know all the rules in advance. How long does it take to get medication to take home? How often do counselors have to watch patients urinate? What is the procedure if urine shows heroin or cocaine use? What if your urine tests dirty when you haven't used drugs—who mediates such disputes?

Some clinics will raise dosage levels if urines are dirty, whereas others may threaten to drop people from treatment. Some private centers even "administratively detox" [cut dose over time] people who don't pay their bills on time. It is against federal regulations to cut people from treatment for dirty urines or to detox them just for not paying a bill when they do not choose detox or when a physician does not advise it. Unfortunately, this happens anyway from time to time, and people need to become aware of their rights and to fight for them before these practices will be eliminated.

A good resource for choosing clinics and handling clinic problems is an organization called the National Association of Methadone Advocates. Made up of patients and people who work at methadone clinics, this group tries to help people with problems at their clinics and is a good source of inside information on the best care. Some of their local affiliates have newsletters and active memberships, which work to improve the lives of people on methadone. There is also a new methadone advocates group called ARM (Advocates for Recovery through Medicine).

Another consideration when choosing methadone is counseling. Many programs provide minimal counseling and don't offer support groups or job training the way they did in the past. If your local clinic lacks a service you think is important (e.g., if you know you need job training or psychiatric care), it may be a good idea to seek additional help from outside or choose another clinic. Flexibility in the provision of services—such as a counselor recognizing that not everyone needs the same types and amount of care—is a sign of good treatment.

One caution for those seeking additional support: While 12-step groups are usually a good source of help for alcoholics and other addicts, Narcotics Anonymous is not usually the best place to go for people who plan to stay on methadone. NA considers people on methadone to be just as drug involved as people on heroin—it does not allow them to speak during meetings or fully participate in the program. Some meetings may be better about this than others, but many people on methadone find NA unhelpful because of this attitude. Because AA is open to anyone with a desire to stop drinking, some addicts have sought support in AA to avoid this problem. AA believes that any medication that is prescribed by a doctor who has full knowledge of the patient's addictive history is OK if used as directed. If alcohol was among the drugs you abused, AA can be a good source of support.

In addition, some methadone clinics offer a program called "Methadone Anonymous," in which you can get 12-step support while detoxing or being maintained. These meetings can be a good place to find out about how other people at the clinic are doing, and what to expect as a patient there.

Methadone treatment sounds scary, but it can keep people alive who would otherwise have died of HIV, hepatitis C, or overdoses. Do not rule it out for fear of later difficulties ending it if someone is in serious danger on the street right now. Many people live full and productive lives on methadone, and many maintenance patients do withdraw from it successfully. Dead addicts, however, don't recover.

Knowledge Is Power
- Methadone maintenance is the best-researched and most successful treatment now available for heroin addiction.
- Methadone doesn't "get in your bones," necessarily result in more severe withdrawal than heroin, or cause tooth decay or other health problems.
- Methadone maintenance is the long-term use of the drug on an outpatient basis; methadone can also be used for detoxification in shorter programs, which are rarely successful without further care.
- Because the American clinic system is so restrictive, methadone should only be tried in the following situations: (a) failure at drug-free treatment three or more times; (b) HIV positive, hepatitis C positive, or at high risk of either; (c) history of opiate addiction for more than five years and either failure at drug-free treatment or preference for methadone.
- Buprenorphine maintenance should soon be available and may be a better choice because it will be available by ordinary prescription.
- When choosing a methadone clinic, look for compassion and flexibility, but also consider location because you will have to visit daily for at least your first few months.
- People under age 18 are not appropriate for methadone treatment except in extreme circumstances, such as frequent needle sharing.

CHAPTER 19

Alternative Treatments

Substance-abuse treatment is one of the few areas of medicine where a treatment that would be considered alternative for most conditions—meeting in groups and praying for help—is mainstream and recommended by physicians, and where research-based treatments are the exception rather than the rule! Because of this, it's often hard for a consumer to determine which treatment recommendations fall within ordinary medicine for addictions, and which are based on the flimsiest of scientific research and evidence. The growing popularity of alternative medicine in general—from acupuncture to zinc—has made the field even more confusing. Most alternative addiction treatments are unproven, but most are at least known not to be harmful, with occasional unfortunate exceptions.

In this chapter, we look at some commonly used alternative treatments for alcoholism and other addictions and explore what evidence there is for their safety and effectiveness. Where possible, we offer patients' experiences of such treatment. We've chosen to focus on three of the most commonly touted addiction alternatives: acupuncture, herbal and nutritional programs, and a drug called ibogaine, which is currently being promoted as a cure for cocaine, alcohol, and heroin habits.

Acupuncture

In Chinese medicine, the insertion of needles into certain "points" or "meridians" on the body has been used for centuries to relieve pain and other symptoms of illness. American interest in the technique was sparked in the 1970s, when *New York Times* reporter James Reston required emergency surgery for appendicitis while in China. He was treated successfully for postoperative pain with acupuncture. His reporting on his experience and his coverage of Chinese surgeries using acupuncture for anesthesia caused a great stir.

Researchers soon discovered that acupuncture was linked with the release of our good friends the endorphins; also, if someone was given the opiate-blocking drug naloxone before acupuncture, the acupuncture was not effective in killing pain. This finding suggested that acupuncture works by causing the body to release its own painkilling substances. When this was discovered, researchers in the addiction field wondered whether acupuncture might also help patients undergoing withdrawal from opiate drugs by helping to get their natural opioid system back on line.

Serendipitously, a Hong Kong neurosurgeon operating on an opium addict noted that the acupuncture used during surgery also relieved his withdrawal symptoms. Michael Smith, of Lincoln Hospital Center in the Bronx, pioneered acupuncture treatment for addiction in America and has treated thousands of addicts; he has also trained most of the hundreds of acupuncturists working in the addiction field in the United States today. He began working with acupuncture two decades ago. His center currently treats 250 addicts each day, primarily inner-city crack and heroin users, with acupuncture and counseling. Treatment is conducted entirely on an outpatient basis. Numerous drug courts and needle exchanges swear by his techniques—and Smith claims that between 50% and 75% of his patients continue treatment for three months and are clean at the end of the program, a rate comparable to that seen for other treatments, but high for a poor population with high unemployment rates.

Although acupuncture treatment for heroin, alcohol, and cocaine craving is now used in many places, the evidence about its utility is still very sketchy. The National Institutes on Health (NIH) recently organized a "consensus statement" on acupuncture to guide doctors and patients in their choice of treatments. They found that while acupuncture has shown "promising" results in the treatment of postoperative dental pain and for nausea, the results on addiction are more equivocal. Acupuncture does not seem to help in nicotine withdrawal at all—but, according to the NIH, it "may be useful as an adjunct treatment or an acceptable alternative or be included in a comprehensive management program" for other addictions.

Most of the controlled studies that have been conducted (using "fake" acupuncture points rather than the real ones) either have shown no positive result, have found that the fake points worked better than the real ones, or were unable to yield any conclusions because the dropout rates for both groups were so high. A study of Smith's patients was unable to support his claims because of high dropout rates. However, this study looked at acupuncture in isolation, with no counseling or support, which are part of all effective addiction treatment, so it's unfair to judge Smith's program—which includes comprehensive support—on this basis alone.

One study done with alcoholics, however, found that acupuncture helped people stay in treatment longer and helped them drink less and crave alcohol less. Among the acupuncture group, 52.5% completed treatment, while only 2.5% of the controls did. An attempt to directly replicate this study failed, however.

As with so much in addiction treatment, we don't really yet know whether acupuncture works. If it appeals to you, it certainly can't hurt to try it, but the evidence suggests that you shouldn't count on it as the only support for your recovery. If you don't find it helpful—one study found increased craving in the "active treatment" group, as compared to the "fake acupuncture" group—don't hesitate to try something else.

Relaxing with Acupuncture

Sherry, a 31-year-old former crack addict, says unhesitatingly that the acupuncture at the Lincoln Hospital acupuncture program was what made the difference for her. "It helped me relax, it took away the craving," she said—"not the thought of crack, but the desire to use it."

Sherry was 14 when she began smoking pot, and at 20, she started smoking crack. Her parents divorced when she was 9, and she remembers crying every day for a week at the time. She graduated from high school but "followed my cousin into crack."

"I liked the taste," she said. "It was sweet and smelled so good. I was going through a lot at the time. My daughter was seven months old and I was living with my mom. I had married [my daughter's] father, but he was in jail. He came home when she was one, and I stopped getting high and moved to Brooklyn with him, but we broke up."

Soon, she was using again and "selling all my stuff" in the street. Her father insisted that she get help, and she stayed 25 months in a residential program called ARC, which is in Harlem. "I did it, but I knew I wasn't going to stop," she says. "It was all right—it wasn't like a TC, which I also tried. I went to Project Return. I hated that place. All they did was yell in my face and I didn't like that. It did nothing but piss me off, and I used three to four months after I left there."

Then, "I really got tired. I was sleeping in the park and sleeping with all kinds of men. I wasn't able to wash or eat, and I did things I didn't want to do—having sex for money or sex for drugs. I didn't want them touching me but I needed the money to get high. My sister had my oldest daughter, and my baby was with his dad. I sat in the park one Friday, and this guy I met said that I could come to his house. We got high, had sex, and I went out to the store, and I ran into a woman I knew named Sara. I got high all night with her. She [had attended the acupuncture program] but was relapsing. She wanted to talk, but I wanted to sleep. But when we got up, I was sitting in her living room and I started crying. I said, 'Sara, I'm tired, this is not how I want to be.' And she said stay at my house, and I'll talk to the program and see if we can get you in. I've been here ever since."

Sadly, "Sara isn't here no more," says Sherry. "I don't know what happened to her, but I'm never going to leave. The acupuncture really helps me—and it took a lot for me to let them do it because I'm terrified of needles. But it relaxes me and takes away the cravings, it really does."

Sherry also finds the NA meetings helpful. "It shows me that I'm not by myself, and that everything that I did, someone else did it if not more than me, then less. It's good to be around people that understand." She says that the other groups are "OK. The women's rap is not one of my favorites because I feel that some of the women there are not sincere."

Sherry currently has over three months clean and is living in a sober shelter. She hopes to get her kids back as soon as she gets permanent housing.

Nutrition

It has long been known that many severe alcoholics suffer from malnutrition. In fact, the brain-damage syndrome known colloquially as "wet brain," is actually caused by a deficiency in the nutrient thiamine. Drinking large quantities of alcohol depletes the body of this nutrient, as well as many others, particularly folic acid, vitamin B12, and the omega DHA (docosahexaenoic acid). Alcohol itself can cause *hypoglycemia* (low blood sugar) 3–36 hours after drinking—and this may be interpreted by alcoholics as craving for alcohol, rather than hunger. Also, because alcoholics and other addicts tend to be more concerned with getting psychoactive substances than with eating, good dietary habits are rare, and some enter treatment suffering starvation and major nutrient deficits.

As a result, the idea of using diet to help people recover from addictions is a good one. Unfortunately, many of the ideas used to design nutritional treatments for substance abuse are based on junk science—most notably the idea that alcoholics' metabolism of alcohol produces a chemical called "THIQ" (tetra-hydro-isoquinoline), not found in normal drinkers. This chemical is alleged to interact with the brain's opiate receptors, explaining why alcohol is addictive to alcoholics, but not to others.

It's a nice idea and sounds great. Many treatment centers still teach alcoholics about it as a way of demonstrating that, yes, scientifically, alcoholism is a disease. Unfortunately, it's based on decades-old research done on the autopsied brains of street drunks. It has not been replicated, and few mainstream alcohol researchers buy into it anymore. Nonetheless, many of the books on alcoholism and nutrition (even including a 1997 book on nutrition and alcohol problems by Susan Powter) use the idea as a way to individualize diet programs. These all seem to be variations on one theme, however.

The basic diet—from the *Seven Weeks to Sobriety* program to Food for Recovery—is pretty simple. Eliminate caffeine, nicotine, sugar, and white flour. Supplement your diet with antioxidants (vitamins C and E and selenium), amino acids (particularly 5HTP (5-hydroxy-tryptophan) and DL-phenylalanine, which are precursors to the neurotransmitters serotonin and dopamine, respectively), calcium, magnesium, essential fatty acids, pancreatic enzymes, and L-glutamine.

When we looked for research to support this diet, we found that the one published study most often cited actually does not show anything near what the book authors claim it does. A 1991 article published in the *Journal of the American Dietetic Association* studied the effects of limiting sugar intake, eliminating caffeine use, and providing nutritional counseling to patients undergoing a traditional Minnesota Model treatment. The patients who got these services were compared with those who received the standard treatment, and in the abstract of the study, the authors claim that the patients in the nutritional group suffered fewer alcohol cravings, ate better, and drank less.

If you read the whole paper, however, the conclusion admits that the results were *not* statistically significant, due to a large number of patients who were lost to follow-up, so no conclusions at all can be drawn from this study regarding whether the diet helped.

Nonetheless, the proponents of the "no sugar/no refined flour" regimes (like the Health Recovery Center of Minnesota, which is run by the author of *Seven Weeks to Sobriety*) cite this study to back their claims. They also rely on anecdotal evidence. Health Recovery Center claims 75% success rates, but these claims have never been properly documented.

Supporters of nutritional approaches to alcoholism and other forms of addiction also tend to believe that *Candida* yeast infections are a common and widespread source of ill health, particularly among alcoholics and other addicts. There is little conclusive evidence on this either, but it is one of the reasons given for opposing the use of refined sugar and flour. Both *Candida* infection and hypoglycemia are believed to create mood swings related to blood-sugar levels, and *Candida* is believed to thrive in sugar-filled environments. Unfortunately, the symptoms used to diagnose these ills can easily be found in anyone. The medical tests recommended to diagnose these conditions are also difficult to interpret because proponents of the diets sometimes identify as "abnormal" levels that most physicians consider normal.

As for the particular elements of the diet, at least one has been subjected to some research. There is some evidence that L-glutamine, an amino acid available at health-food stores, may help reduce cravings for alcohol. Studies done as far back as the 1950s reported positive effects—one rat study found that L-glutamine decreased the animals' alcohol intake by 34%. Case reports from the 1950s, observing alcoholics who took L-glutamine, report decreased cravings, increased ability to sleep normally, and even, for some, a return to control over alcohol intake. Anecdotes from the promoters of nutritional programs report similar effects from L-glutamine today, but there still hasn't been a good study that would clarify whether these effects are better than placebo. Note: If you wish to take L-glutamine and you have liver disease, consult your doctor first. Those with the most serious types of disease can be harmed by it.

Are these diets or any of their elements generally harmful? There is no evidence that they are, but some alcoholics and other addicts may find it frustrating and intolerable to introduce such a restricted diet soon after quitting drinking and other drugs. When you have just given up your main source of comfort, it's a good idea to be easy on yourself about others—such as fatty, sugary foods. Proponents of these regimes suggest cutting back gradually to avoid this problem. If you want to experiment with diets to aid your recovery, there is little reason not to, but like many treatments, they are unlikely to be a miracle cure and may offer no help at all. It certainly can help your overall health and sense of well-being to eat a balanced, sensible diet and to exercise often. If you were malnourished during your drinking or other drug taking (or if you are significantly under- or overweight), a good nutritional workup makes sense, to handle any deficiencies and to begin to explore weight-control issues.

A healthful diet, a good multivitamin, and an exercise plan can make anyone feel better—and you probably know the drill here. Eat your fruits and veggies, and cut back on fats and excessive carbohydrates. Replace refined flour with whole wheat as much as possible. Cut down on salty or sugary snacks. Reduce caffeine. If you find that you get extremely irritable or weak and suddenly hungry when you haven't eaten for a while, you may be at least mildly hypoglycemic, and it may feel better to you if you eat meals that combine protein with complex carbohydrates, rather than something sugary, to combat this problem. This may help reduce craving for both sugar and alcohol, but again, no one really knows. Exercise is also important—get to the gym or walk or dance or do some other physical activity that you enjoy and can do regularly. We're sure little of this is news to you, but you may be surprised by how good exercise and a balanced diet can make you feel once you get into it.

On the other hand, we are much less sure as to whether the effort and expense required to drop sugar and refined flour entirely and to add supplements based on specialized advice to alcoholics and other addicts is warranted. We contacted the Health Recovery Center to see whether they had any graduates who were willing to speak with us about their experiences. They refused, citing confidentiality concerns—despite our willingness to keep names and identifying details out of the book. They were the only treatment provider we found who had this policy—even AA and Hazelden offer the press a chance to speak with those who have succeeded, so long as you use first names only. We were also unable to locate anyone who believed that using one of these recovery diets had been harmful to them.

Ibogaine

In the 1960s, psychologists studying LSD began to research whether a psychedelic experience could serve as the "spiritual awakening" AA believed necessary to free alcoholics from drink. Bill Wilson, AA's founder, even tried a few trips. The early work was promising, but it was never replicated because the government made the drug illegal.

At about the same time, a heroin addict made a surprising discovery about an African psychedelic called *ibogaine:* It seemed to eliminate heroin withdrawal symptoms and craving. Animal research has now confirmed this effect of the drug, but no human safety studies have been completed. The man who discovered ibogaine's impact on heroin addiction, Howard Lotsof, has patented the drug. His organization takes those willing to pay $10,000 to be treated with it out of the United States for care. At least one death has occurred during the treatment process, and early claims about ibogaine as "the cure" have not held up. A medical researcher who has been funded by NIDA to study the drug has now begun offering treatment with it at a for-profit center in the Bahamas while she conducts further research. Again, however, safety questions have not been resolved, and the drug is not FDA approved. Some addicts in New York report that there have been other deaths and numerous relapses, which ibogaine's promoters have ignored.

Animal research indicates that the drug may act by working on the NMDA-receptor in the brain, and currently, clinical trials are being conducted on other drugs, which seem to have similar brain effects, but which have already been FDA approved. Within the next few years, research should discover whether a true painless detox is possible—but given the success of past efforts, we wouldn't suggest holding your breath while waiting for it.

Given the sketchy research and the uncertainty over what has caused the ibogaine-linked deaths, it's probably better to wait until the safety studies are completed before trying to detox with ibogaine or other NMDA-receptor antagonist drugs. Addicts tend to like home chemistry and underground ways of kicking. Because detox isn't what ultimately makes the difference about who stays clean and who doesn't, however, if you really want to quit, it's best to do so in a way that won't further endanger your life.

Knowledge Is Power

- Research on acupuncture is equivocal, but some report that it helps reduce cravings and anxiety.
- While there is no evidence that specialized alcohol-recovery diets are effective, good nutrition and exercise can help improve mood and health, and the better you feel, the less likely you are to relapse.
- There is some evidence that the supplement L-glutamine may help reduce craving for alcohol. Unless you have serious liver problems, this substance is unlikely to be harmful.
- Brain damage related to alcohol is generally caused by a thiamine deficiency, so it is important to supplement this nutrient if you have been drinking heavily.
- Ibogaine shows some promise as a treatment for opiate addiction, but because there have been deaths related to it, and it is not FDA approved, it is best to wait for more research before trying it.

CHAPTER 20

Teen Treatment

James Nelson came home from work and detected a familiar sweet smell wafting from his 16-year-old son Brandon's bedroom. It took him back to his own teenage years—but then he panicked, "My God! It's my kid. Today's pot is stronger. What do I do?" He pounded on the door, and while Brandon managed to hide the evidence, his dad could see from his spacey stare and red eyes that he was indeed stoned.

Susan Garner's son Sean came home in a police car, looking at her fearfully and seeming incredibly young as the burly officer brought him to the door. "We found him drinking with some kids in the park," the officer said. "Next time, we'll have to arrest him." She had feared far worse, but she screamed at her 17-year-old, "You're grounded for life."

It was a school day, and Joanne Kopple hadn't heard her daughter Emily stirring, so she pounded on her door. Nothing. She knocked again, and then, terrified, she burst in. Emily was lying in bed, very pale, and hardly breathing. Just then, Joanne noticed a piece of tin foil with brown stains on it next to her bed. She dialed 911. The emergency medical technician (EMT) said it was probably a heroin overdose. She shrieked, she couldn't comprehend it. "She's an honor student, for goodness sake." The technician stabilized Emily's breathing and gave her a shot of Narcan, and Emily came to.

Recognizing the Problem

Most parents can't believe it's happening to them. "Not my kid," they say, when asked whether their son or daughter drinks heavily or uses other drugs. When presented with incontrovertible evidence that their child is indeed getting high, however, for many parents, utter panic sets in.

Because of America's "War on Drugs," it's very difficult to get clear, unbiased information about what to do if you discover your kid taking drugs. Even if it's marijuana, which is the most commonly used illicit drug, and which most Americans with teenage children have taken themselves, parents have become convinced that "it's different now." Though they themselves turned out OK despite smoking pot, they fear for their kids' lives. Billions of dollars worth of propaganda have been aimed at convincing parents that marijuana is as dangerous as any other drug and that it leads inevitably to cocaine or heroin.

However, half of our youths at least try pot, and the vast majority don't become marijuana addicts, let alone move on to heroin or cocaine. With marijuana use this common experimentation cannot be seen as "abnormal" behavior. In fact, one long-term study found that the kids who experimented with marijuana and alcohol were more healthy psychologically than those who didn't try anything—though those who didn't try any drugs were slightly more well-adjusted than those who used heavily. This study also found that social and psychological difficulties in preschool predicted which kids would fall into either the heavy use or the nonuse groups. Such research has obvious implications about who is most likely to have drug problems and the treatment needs of those who do get in trouble. It also tells us one of the most important things a parent needs to know about heavy drug use by teenagers—it is most often a symptom of some other problem, and if you can deal with that problem before addiction has taken hold, the drug use itself will probably diminish over time.

In a country that is trying to teach its youths that drug use is wrong, despite 50% of its population engaging in it, it can be hard to know when a kid has a real problem, and when he or she is just experimenting or "going through a phase." Obviously, in the preceding examples, Emily has a serious drug problem—but the cases of Sean and Brandon aren't so clear cut.

To further complicate your decision making about treatment, recent research by the National Institute on Drug Abuse (NIDA) has found that there are substantial negative effects of addiction treatment for some teens. You can put a pot-smoking binge drinker in, and get someone determined to try heroin and cocaine out. The data shows that kids leaving treatment use 200% more crack (many hadn't tried it when they went in), and 13% more alcohol after they leave care. The study, which was conducted at 120 treatment centers around the country, found that there was no decrease at all in adolescent drug use after traditional treatment in the current system—either in outpatient, Minnesota Model, or TC treatment.

The problem is that traditional teen treatment is based on care aimed at adults—some of which can be quite brutal, as we've seen—without much consideration of the special needs of teens. For example, most teenagers haven't yet settled on an identity. They really don't know whom they want to be. Many treatments focus on making them admit that they are addicts. They talk about the negative qualities they believe that addicts have: such as being liars, manipulators, and con artists.

Because research finds that even teens who use heavily aren't necessarily addicts, and not all addicts share these negative qualities, suggesting that someone adopt such ideas about themselves can be dangerous. If you convince teenagers that they are manipulative thieves, they may just try to prove you right. Also, if you convince teens that they have the disease of addiction, which will take control of them if they ever take a drink or another drug, you may create a self-fulfilling prophecy. Among teens leaving treatment, 90% will relapse at least once, and if they believe that they have no control over themselves once they get a drink or another drug in their system, using drugs can become an excuse for all sorts of negative behavior. Teens who actually could have learned to stop even if they slip up can come to believe that once they take anything, they must binge. Teens who would have outgrown the view of themselves as "druggies" and would have moved on to less destructive recreational activity may become trapped in drug use if told that they will be addicts forever.

So, what's a concerned parent to do? If it's an emergency—a situation where a child has overdosed, has run away repeatedly, has lost weight or otherwise become debilitated, is using drugs intravenously, or has harmed him or herself or others or is threatening to do so—hospitalization and other inpatient care is required, at least for a few days, to ensure safety. As with adults, don't worry too much about where the initial stabilization takes place, but while the child is hospitalized or is in a home for runaways, check out further options. First, to get a flavor of what teen treatment is like, we look at some experiences of it. Later in this chapter, we discuss how to choose the best—and avoid the worst.

Tired of Making Trouble

Ari is a 16-year-old who was adopted by a high-level church official in Minnesota and a social worker. Ari reports a happy early childhood but doesn't know whether his birth parents had a history of addiction. Ari himself suffers from attention-deficit disorder (ADD) and conduct disorder, and from a very early age, he was stealing and using and dealing drugs.

"I first tried marijuana when I was 9," he says matter-of-factly. "It was curiosity, but not many of my friends were using at that age. I saw my older brother doing it, and I stole some of his. I did it on my own." By age 13, Ari was smoking daily, selling pot at school, and drinking.

"I liked the sense of power it gave me," he says of dealing; "and it was easy money. Pot boosted my fun. Later, I used it when I was sad or mad—it was my cure to get away from everything. I was depressed, but that was not the main reason I did it. I did it for fun." Ari started treatment for his ADD with Ritalin and other medications when he was in fourth grade, but in his case, it did not keep him from acting out or using other drugs.

Ari has been suspended and expelled from six different schools. Most of these suspensions resulted from his drug dealing at school—others followed when he was caught reeking of marijuana. He first entered drug treatment when he was 13 or 14. "I came home high, I started yelling and breaking stuff," he says of the incident that prompted his parents to seek help. "I went to the Fairview STOP Program in Minneapolis. But I didn't take it seriously. You were locked in, you shared a room with another guy. The days were structured—you would get up and have breakfast, have classes, then free time and a drug group and after lunch, more classes and more groups. I went because I knew I would be court-ordered to go if I didn't agree. And a few weeks after I came out, I started using again."

While attending outpatient aftercare at Fairview, he got new customers for his drug-dealing enterprise. "I was selling to kids at the center," he says. He was sent to a longer-term inpatient facility called Woodbury, as a result. "It was really laid back," he says. "There were groups, steps to do [it was a 12-step-oriented program], and also a lot of free time on the weekends. I watched TV, played pool. It didn't give me much—but I didn't want to take anything either. I always knew I would use when I got out. I was there for 3 ¹/₂ months.

"I heard others in treatment talking about mushrooms, and that sounded interesting," he says. He tried them and continued to smoke and sell pot. He was then thrown out of three more schools—and sent to a juvenile corrections facility for stealing cars. After two other failed treatment attempts, he was court-mandated to Bar None, a therapeutic community for teens, for two years.

"They analyzed everything you did," he said, "and made you feel bad if you did something wrong. I had my own room, it was a locked facility and they counted all the forks, they wouldn't let you carry even a pen, it was very structured and they just nailed you for everything.

"It really helped me," he said. "It made me look at a lot of things. The first six months, I was in a lot of trouble, but I realized I'd been wrong. I came to want to learn from them. I needed that tough stuff in order to take advantage of treatment, I think. I basically realized I couldn't live that life anymore. I was getting locked up, I couldn't see my family or friends, I was sick and tired of being in trouble all the time." At Bar None, he also had family therapy, which helped reconcile him with both of his parents, whom he says, "had given up on me." Ari has also continued to take medication for his ADD and depression. He currently is prescribed Wellbutrin (an antidepressant) and dexedrine (a stimulant).

His counselors recommended that he attend Sobriety High, a Minnesota public school for teenage recovering alcoholics and other addicts, after treatment. Although he had one relapse, he is now four months clean. He describes a typical school day: "Most people get here a little early, I play Ping-Pong before my first class at 9:00 A.M." Between classes, the school allows the kids to smoke cigarettes rather than constantly having to police smoking and possibly precipitate relapses into other drug use. Other than that, it's a typical high school—including gym class, drama, health—but one class a day is a group, devoted to recovery.

"It makes you feel loved," he says of Sobriety High. "Everyone is nice and willing to help. It's different from other schools. I want to learn more. It's easier in some ways, but harder in others to be sober. You feel much better about yourself."

Increased Curiosity about Drugs

Suzy, a 19-year-old art student from Miami, is currently attending college. She is the oldest of two daughters—her parents are solidly middle class. When she was 9 years old, her parents divorced, and her father remarried when she was 13. "I had a feeling of being left out and unloved," she said. "I adopted an 'I don't care' attitude. I dressed in black, and my father refused to be seen with me and insulted the way I dressed. All I wanted was support, but I felt really neglected."

She became so depressed that her parents took her to a psychiatrist. She was prescribed Zoloft. "That helped immensely," she said, "but I still felt something was missing. I wanted an escape, a way of forgetting, having fun, being happy."

"People are just curious, I think," she added, and at age 15, she tried marijuana. "It was OK. But I never liked downers. I'm naturally mellow." She started skipping school and got caught with friends, using alcohol and marijuana. "I was suspended from school for two weeks. I thought it was a joke—I cut school, so you throw me out? At that point, I'd been using pot and acid. My parents sent me to rehab."

Suzy spent only a week in an inpatient treatment center, but she made new friends there who were into harder drugs. "It was OK," she says, "but I wouldn't want to be there again. Certain aspects I hated—like waking up at 6 A.M., no music, no shoelaces. There were three or four counseling sessions a day, school, and gym. I went to Narcotics Anonymous a few times, but I didn't like it. I did get very close to the people I was in treatment with, and I made some good friends. But treatment made me more curious about drugs. It taught me how to manipulate my parents because I heard others talking about how they had gotten away with things."

After she left rehab, Suzy started using cocaine with a friend from rehab. "I tried a little tiny line. I thought 'that doesn't do much,' and I progressed from there. All summer, I did it every day. I would get up, eat breakfast, my friends would pick me up, we'd snort and then hang out and drink beers and do more."

When she returned to school in the fall, a friend introduced her to the TRUST ("To Reach the Ultimate Success Together") program, based in the Miami public school system. It offers counseling and groups for teens who are worried about their drug use. Suzy describes an incident that committed her to cutting down:

> I came home very late. My little sister was watching TV and she wanted to talk. She had always put me on a pedestal, and she wanted my advice about some guy she liked or something, but all I could think of was, "Am I acting normal?" And it hit me, and it hurt me that all I cared about was how I seemed, and I couldn't really be there for her.
>
> I met Ms. [Robin] Tassler [who runs the TRUST program in her school], and I had group and private sessions. And gradually, I just stopped. I started telling people, "No, thanks." I stopped hanging out with people who used, we just grew apart.

Suzy says she enjoyed the TRUST groups, "It was that, and mostly learning that others have the same temptations and desire that you do, so you don't have to think of yourself as an awful person. And I got advice on things like how to deal with my mother [who was understandably reluctant to trust Suzy again after the lies she told when she was using]. Ms. Tassler is really a saint," she adds. Suzy now does not use illicit drugs but does drink moderately and occasionally.

Rehab Hell

Joanne, now 24 years old, spent 4½ years in a profoundly abusive treatment center—which was nonetheless praised by the *New York Times* magazine, Nancy Reagan, Princess Diana, and the man who headed the National Institute on

Drug Abuse when the treatment center was founded. Her story may seem so extreme as to be aberrant, but we include it because the center she attended got long-term mainstream support and was permitted to move from state to state under different names, after lawsuits in the previous states forced closure.

The program began life as Straight, Inc., in Florida in the late 1970s. It was founded by two Republican Party contributors. Both gave so much to the Bush campaign that they were rewarded with ambassadorships, including one to Spain, though he didn't speak Spanish. By the early 1980s, there were already newspaper reports of the abuse the center seemed to specialize in: assault, kidnapping, denial of food and sleep, force feeding, and isolation from outside contact. By the mid 1980s, the Florida centers had been forced to pay out over a million dollars in court settlements to abused patients and their families.

The heat in Florida eventually proved too hot for the center's director, Virgil Miller Newton (who has a mail-order Ph.D.), so he moved to New Jersey and reopened the program under a new name, KIDS. In 1986, the *New York Times* gushingly praised its success—clearly unaware of the lawsuits in Florida. The center is still operating in New Jersey and, until late 1998, was receiving Medicaid funds for its "care."

Joanne, who is from Canada, had started using drugs at age 14. Like many other kids her age, she drank and smoked hash and pot. "I was basically using on weekends," she says. "I was trying to stop because I wasn't doing well in school. I got free counseling from the Alberta Adolescent Drug Abuse Center, and it did help, and I loved my counselor there. She discouraged my mom from putting me into KIDS, though, and after that, my mom wouldn't let me go back."

Her mother had heard about the program from friends and had become convinced that it was the only answer. Newton tells parents that any drug use at all is dangerous and abnormal and requires inpatient treatment. He says that your child will probably die if he or she doesn't attend Newton's rehab. A reputable drug-treatment professional knows that this is completely false (as you can see from the data cited previously), but a worried parent is unlikely to think a professional would lie.

Joanne entered the KIDS program in September 1989. A typical day was spent seated on hard-backed chairs, taking a "moral inventory" of your sins and shortcomings, and yelling at other patients for not being honest about theirs. "You had to sit with your hands on your knees and your feet on the floor. If you were slouching, you would be 'restrained.' " This technique involves throwing the offender to the floor and having several people pull on and hold down her hands and feet, while others cover her mouth and nose so that she cannot breathe. This technique was used, with the same name, at Straight, Inc.

Any minor infraction—such as looking at a member of the opposite sex or even speaking to a staff member who wasn't your counselor—would be punished in this way. Also, once punishment was administered, you lost the day as part of your treatment, and you got further and further away from being allowed to go home. Joanne did not comply at first—and was constantly punished.

One of the ways that KIDS managed to avoid losing its licensing in New Jersey was to claim that it was outpatient treatment. This was true in that the children didn't sleep at the center, but they didn't sleep at home, either. They were made to stay at specially prepared "host homes," which were owned by staff members or parents of other children in the program. At this "home," there would be alarms on the doors and windows to prevent escape, and the teens would be locked in at night.

Even more psychologically disturbing was a total lack of privacy. At all times, teens had to be accompanied by someone else in the program, who kept his or her fingers in the belt loops of the teens pants, from behind. If the person monitoring the host home wanted to take a shower, the teens staying there had to sing outside the shower and had to keep their hands visible above the curtain so that the monitor would know that they weren't talking privately or using drugs. Conversations with outsiders—even parents, during the very short and occasional visits that were permitted—had to be scripted ahead of time, and any deviation would be reported by a monitor and punished later.

"I was on day negative 300," said Joanne. "I didn't know where to go or what to do. I found a screw on the floor and started cutting my wrists. I thought that maybe someone from outside would see [and rescue me]. It was a release. I wasn't allowed to talk at that point.

"Eventually, I got caught. I was strip-searched. They made you squat and spread your bum and lift your boobs. They restrained me—and they used so much force on my joints that my shoulder was dislocated. I gave in—I cried, and when they said, 'Are you willing to let us help you?' I said 'yes.' Then I had to relate 'my past' in group and make amends to every staff member and host parent for 'being a shithead.' "

For girls, these confessions included relating in detail, to mixed-sex groups, the story of how they lost their virginity. Says Joanne, "I had to relive that incident, while they tried to make me feel ashamed, dirty, disgusted, in front of 150 people. The guys said 'You know how I used to feel about girls like you, you were sick and disgusting sluts.' " At KIDS, sexual desire itself was considered sick—anyone caught masturbating would be severely punished.

"My shoulder was in pain for a few months—it still gives me trouble," says Joanne. "They had a nurse look at it who worked there, but they didn't take me to a doctor at first. Then, they took me for X-rays and two big staff members threatened me that if I said anything to the doctor, they would tell Dr. Newton."

Eventually, Joanne totally complied and worked her way up within the program to become a "junior staff member." At this point, instead of her mother spending several thousand dollars a month for her "treatment," she was paid "$144.12 for each two weeks. The hours were from 6 A.M., to sometimes 2 A.M. in the morning and you were on call 24 hours. I was down to a size 3, weighing 105 pounds, and I should be 127–130—I'm 5'5".

Then, her father became fatally ill. "My brothers called, but they wouldn't let me talk to them, because 'they're sick.' [Staff members] told me, 'You can see him on his deathbed, or go to the funeral, but not both.' "

Joanne began plotting a way out. She became romantically involved with a fellow staff member, even though both could be returned to patient status if they had been caught so much as talking to each other. They ran away together—and the treatment center notified the Canadian border patrol to look out for them, saying that they were criminals and were using drugs. They stayed in the United States, and though they became engaged, Joanne broke it off. "I hid for a long time," says Joanne. "My mother refused to talk to me, she thought I'd become a prostitute [because of what the people at the program had told her]."

Gradually, she returned to normal life. At first, she was afraid even to go to stores. She tried drinking again and experimented with mushrooms and acid—substances she hadn't taken before treatment. "I liked them at the time, but it's not something I do now," she says. "I drink occasionally, but it's not something I'm really into."

Now, she has graduated from college and become a massage therapist. "I love it," she says of her work. She has reconciled with her mother, who now feels guilty about what Joanne went through. "They treat you inhumanely and unethically and teach you how to hate yourself and depend on them," says Joanne. "I'm not [speaking out] for revenge, but there are a lot of people who are hurt by it. I still haven't talked to my boyfriend about it all—he cringes just to hear about it, he cries. How do you talk to someone about something like that?"

How to Choose Treatment for Teenagers

Obviously, given the potential pitfalls, parents should choose treatment for teens very cautiously. If someone talks about "the cure" or a particular treatment that "is the only thing that works" and it involves the type of total control that KIDS does, run the other way. As with adult treatment, the best way to smoke out abusive care is to ask about an ombudsman for patients and to get a detailed description of complaint procedures. [Joanne laughed and said, "Are you kidding?" when I asked her about such systems at KIDS.] Ask about privacy, about rules, and about a typical day in treatment. Trust your instincts: If it doesn't seem like a kind and supportive environment, don't trust a treatment center with your child. Never choose a center in which teens stay at "host homes." Also, never choose a provider that mixes adults and teens in therapy groups—this can lead to sexual abuse and to the teens emulating the more seriously addicted adults.

Also, don't send your child out of the country for treatment that is advertised in the United States: Most centers that solicit people outside the country where they are located do so because they have bad reputations at home or are located outside of the United States to avoid regulations.

Except for the emergencies discussed previously, the place to start is with one-on-one outpatient counseling. Before choosing a counselor, your child should have a thorough evaluation by a psychiatrist to determine the severity of the drug problem and to look for other conditions. At least half of teens with drug problems have a coexisting psychiatric disorder. Even those who don't have an overt disorder may be using drugs to escape a particular emotional or social problem. Quite often, it is the discomfort of these conditions that leads to heavy drug use. If they are properly treated or dealt with, the insistence of the urge for drugs can decline greatly. Even if a condition is found, however, treatment to deal with the drug use itself may be necessary because once the habit has been set in motion, it can take on a life of its own.

Assessment can determine how best to proceed. Counseling or therapy should be done by a credentialed substance-abuse counselor, social worker, or psychologist. If medications are used as part of treatment, a psychiatrist who specializes in young adults can be helpful. If needed, treatment for both the drug problem and the psychiatric condition should occur simultaneously.

Attention-deficit disorder, particularly in combination with conduct disorder, is extremely common in teens with drug problems. Several studies found that between 40% and 80% of teen substance abusers suffered from one or both of these problems. *Conduct disorder*—which involves disobedience, extremely rebellious behavior, and often even criminal forms of "acting out"—can be particularly tricky and is often associated with the most high-risk drug use. Medication for these conditions with Ritalin or other appropriate drugs should not be avoided: Research has found that proper treatment of ADD and conduct disorder among teens reduces, rather than increases, drug problems. The reason these kids seek illicit substances is often because they don't have access to the licit ones that would help them focus and behave—however, treatment for ADD, as you can see from Ari's case, is not always a panacea.

Although you may yearn to send your kid away to long-term treatment at the slightest sign of trouble, this really can be more dangerous and less helpful than having your child treated while at home. Outpatient one-on-one counseling has the least potential to cause harm (it's not going to put your kid in with kids who use more and seem "cooler," for one), and it can help your child discover what's behind his or her drug use. If the less restrictive environment is not working, then one can always move up to a day treatment or residential program.

WHAT ARE THE SIGNS OF A CHILD'S DRUG PROBLEM?

You've probably seen checklists about the signs of drug use—poor school performance, mood swings, staying up late, sleeping at weird hours, hostility to parents, and some even list new weird friends, tattoos, and support for civil rights. Most such lists offer little help because they don't tell you how to distinguish normal teenage angst from problematic drug use.

Here's how to recognize intoxicated states: Drunk children are certainly easy to detect by the smell of their breath and by general clumsiness; marijuana tends to give itself away because of its smell and because users often have reddish eyes and giggle a lot. A child high on cocaine or amphetamine can be spotted by looking for extremely dilated pupils, jitteriness, and a hyperkinetic, edgy energy. Dilated pupils are also characteristic of LSD and other psychedelic drugs, but the difference here is that there is usually less twitchiness and more weird behavior and laughter. Heroin use is distinguished by pinpoint pupils and sudden "nodding"— that is, falling asleep in moments with a characteristic head droop and overall muscular relaxation.

Heroin withdrawal looks like the flu but with insomnia, dilated pupils, anxiety, and depression. Track marks from IV use look like small cuts at the sites of veins—there may also be bruising. Sudden, severe weight loss could be symptomatic of either a drug problem, an eating disorder, or other serious illness, and it should be given immediate medical attention.

It's not too hard to tell whether someone is high or drunk, but with psychedelics, pot, and alcohol, it's not so easy to determine the real extent of the problem. A straight-A student whom you caught drunk at a party is probably fine—but how do you know whether this is the one time you caught him or her or is part of a regular pattern?

Obviously, if you have discovered heroin withdrawal or tracks, immediate action is needed. Heroin overdose can be fatal, and IV drug use can transmit deadly diseases. If you have just found a kid smoking pot or drunk, and the rest of his or her life seems OK, though, it's much harder to know what to do. The first time, you can probably let your kid off with a lecture, but if it recurs or you notice any type of decline in grades or other problematic situations, a professional evaluation may be needed. Also, if you have no evidence that your kid with a tattoo, concerned with world peace, is using drugs, let her or him be!

Maia

Dealing with Suspected Drug Use

If nothing as dramatic as Emily's situation has taken place—and you've discovered pot smoking or binge drinking like the parents of Sean and Brandon, you have more time and more options. First, try to relax—the problem may not be as bad as you think. Most kids experiment a few times and then stop. The vast majority of kids who try drugs do not become addicted. If your teen's grades are good and her or his friendships and family relationships are strong, and there has been just one marijuana incident, you may want to stress that no matter what he or she feels (or you, for that matter) about marijuana's relative harms and whether it should be legal, the law now is the law, and a criminal record can really mess up your life.

Tell your children that you do not want marijuana in your house, and that when they are adults, they can decide for themselves what to do, but while they live with you, they need to follow your rules. If you smoked pot yourself as a teenager, admit it—and try to talk about why you are worried about them smoking it now. Discuss particularly such ideas as you "knew it all" and "could take care of yourself" when you were their age—and how that can lead to overconfidence, which can be risky. If you experienced negative consequences related to your drug use, detail them.

If your kids still insist that it is unfair that pot is illegal, you might suggest that if they want to take a principled position in objection to the current laws, they should write letters to the editor and to politicians. Sitting around smoking pot won't help the cause, however. Instead, it will simply subject them to increasing penalties. If your children's problems are more serious than experimentation and they are having other difficulties—such as lower grades or truancy, you will probably need to take more direct action.

SHOULD YOU DRUG TEST CHILDREN
WITHOUT ANY SUSPICION OF A PROBLEM?

Some antidrug activists have suggested that parents drug test their children starting from puberty, as a form of prevention. This is unnecessary and may harm your relationship with them. Think about how you would react if your parents had wanted to do it to you when you were their age. Even if you are going to use a hair or saliva test, rather than a urine test, any test still feels invasive to most people. Also, the message it sends is not a nice one: I don't trust you to do the right thing without being threatened, I don't believe what you say to me, and I won't allow you to learn for yourself.

A better way of "testing" your kids is to know what's going on with them. Are they happy in school? Do they have friends? What are their fears? What are their goals and interests? Truly happy, well-adjusted kids are far less likely to run into trouble with any drugs they try than are children who are miserable and friendless.

Social skills are crucial. If your child is either a bully, an outcast (no friends—not a "low-status clique" or group that dresses funny), or a scape-goat, get help early. A counselor or program that can teach a child to read social signals and to identify difficult emotions and deal with them will help these high-risk kids more than any chemical test for a substance possibly could.

Also, you should look at your own substance use. Are you drinking heavily? Have you had negative consequences related to any present illicit drug use or alcohol use? Is there alcoholism or other addiction in your family? If there is genetic risk, you should tell your kids about it early and teach them from a young age what addiction is (i.e., use despite negative consequences), how people avoid recognizing it, and that they should come to you if they feel they are having trouble either because they've tried something and feel out of control or because they are in pain and need relief. Another thing to stress to your child: "I don't want you to try drugs, but if you do and something feels better than you've ever felt before, stop right there. That's a sign that you are at great risk of becoming addicted—and I want you to tell me so we can find other ways for you to feel good."

Joe

The first step is to talk to your teenagers and keep open the lines of communication. If you have said things in the past such as "If I ever catch you using drugs, I'll kill you," it may be hard to get them to open up, so try to start the discussion in the safest conditions possible. Tell them that if they tell the truth, you won't punish them—but that if there is a problem, you will want to get help.

The best way to proceed is to be nonconfrontational and gentle—and to bring up the subject at a time when you are not in the middle of a fight over something else. Express concern, and tell your children how much you love and care for them and ask them to tell you what is going on in school, or with their grades and with their friends or sweethearts. Ask directly whether they are using drugs regularly.

If they still deny it and you feel that you still have reason to be suspicious, ask whether they would be willing to take a drug test on a random day once a week for the next month. Tell them that you are not trying to punish them, but that you are concerned that there might be trouble, and you want to rule out drugs. Stress that you do trust them, but that sometimes people with alcohol and other drug problems can't see them, and so you want to avoid that problem. Also, tell them that you would like them to see a psychiatrist, so that you can be sure of the real nature of the problem. In fact, it may help to say, "I don't know whether you have a drug problem—why don't we let a professional help us determine that?"

Be sure that they don't fear that you think they are "crazy," but tell them that you want to be sure that they feel as good as they possibly can, without harming themselves, and that treatment of psychological conditions can often assure this. Teens often worry that treatment of any sort is designed to take away their fun and pleasure. Reassure them that this is not the case, and that what happens with drug problems is that the drugs wind up causing more pain than joy. Emphasize, as well, that the proper medication for most psychological disorders improves mood and functioning better than self-medication ultimately does.

Choosing a Counselor

If you determine that counseling is needed, look for someone who is empathetic and supportive, who relates well to teenagers. If your teens can't stand their counselor, not much is likely to come of the treatment. Also, try to choose someone familiar with MET and CBT. Supportive counseling alone, without the use of behavioral techniques, is not as effective. One study found that only 9% of teens given six months of supportive counseling were abstinent at the end of the study—but 73% of youths receiving an empathetic behavioral therapy, which involved helping change poor family and peer relationships, were abstinent at six months. Other evidence shows that cognitive and behavioral treatments are the most effective talk therapies for teens with other mental disorders, including depression, obsessive-compulsive disorder, and posttraumatic stress disorder, and these techniques are now beginning to be studied with teen substance problems.

One place to start seeking referrals is from your child's school guidance counselor or school psychologist. They will often know who has done well with local kids. Another excellent source of referrals may be the nearest research university. The National Institute on Drug Abuse is starting to set up a series of research centers aimed at dealing with the current lack of knowledge about what works best in treatment for both adolescents and adults. These centers will be similar to the system now in place to study cancer treatment—which involves care in some of the best hospitals in the country. The treatment research centers will eventually be within reach of people in most states and will offer state-of-the-art care in their programs, usually at low or no cost.

Once you have located several counselors whom you feel are appropriate, let your teen make the final choice. People do best in treatment they have chosen themselves—and this is probably even more important for adolescents, who feel that they have little choice about many of their life activities. Even if your kid isn't thrilled with the idea of counseling, having a choice in the matter can help mitigate resistance.

If your children refuse to attend counseling, and the psychiatric evaluation has shown evidence of a drug problem, you may want to insist on drug-testing them at random. That way, if there is no problem, as they will probably claim, they can prove it to you. If there is one, however, you will be helping to establish a relationship between drug use and trouble, which can help your children move forward through the stages of change in dealing with the problem. Explain that addiction is defined as compulsive use despite negative consequences and that if they really are casual users, they should be able to avoid taking drugs until they live on their own and are not doing so in your house. Be clear that there will be consequences if they test positive or are caught using, and establish these in advance. However, do not make the consequences overly punitive—grounding your child for weeks or days, not for a year, for example—because otherwise you do not give them a chance to learn from their mistakes. Keep your rules consistent.

Many teens say that being drug-tested offers them a reason to refuse drugs, which keeps them from feeling socially excluded. Testing itself can often resolve the problem, but if your child has a series of positive tests, you should insist on treatment. Most teens will agree to it at this point because it's hard to deny use after a series of positive tests. Counseling once or twice a week doesn't seem too threatening when you point out that the alternative is continual loss of privileges or going away for treatment if addiction becomes severe. Don't use the idea of inpatient treatment as an explicit threat, however, just say that those who develop the most serious drug problems—such as those who run away or quit school—often need it.

Once your teens have agreed to treatment, you will probably want to discuss with their counselor how things should proceed with regard to house rules. For example, if kids are really trying but have a slip and admit it, you will probably not want to punish them, but rather to support them in their efforts to stay clean. Ending a drug problem is difficult for most people—and punishment can discourage someone who is making a sincere effort from continuing to try. Instead, it may make them seek to hide the problem. Lack of consequences and few rules are not good for teens with drug problems—but neither is overly rigid insistence on them.

It can also be extremely helpful to include some family therapy in your child's treatment—in fact, family therapy is one of the few areas that has been studied and found successful for teen treatment. Motivational and cognitive family therapy is the type most supported by research. If you are in the midst of an obvious crisis, such as a divorce or the aftermath of a death or illness, this can be particularly important. Your teenagers may be more able to discuss what they resent and what they find harmful in a family therapy setting than at home. Also, patterns of poor communication or repeated fights over particular issues can be resolved, helping reduce the risk of relapse for your child and making family life easier for everyone. Don't blame yourself for your child's problems—family dynamics can take on a life of their own.

Intensive Outpatient Treatment

If counseling doesn't work (you should give it at least six months to a year unless things are getting visibly worse), you may want to try intensive outpatient treatment. Ideally, group therapy in this treatment will be done with kids whose problems are equally severe. Unfortunately, however, many treatment centers don't construct their groups in this manner. If they do, you have probably found a good program. Also, if your child has gotten to the point where counseling hasn't worked and drug use is ongoing, the danger of being exposed to kids with "cooler" and worse drug problems has probably passed anyway.

Only after a child has failed intensive outpatient treatment (or in the emergency situations described previously) should you consider inpatient care. Once again, you should start with the shortest length of treatment at first. Your teens are going to have to deal with the real world eventually—and keeping them out of circulation in a protected environment for years isn't going to make the temptation much easier to handle. Educational opportunities in inpatient long-term treatment often aren't as good as those provided by a regular school, and a decent education is probably your child's best ticket out of the drug world and into a good career. So, unless your children are among the most profoundly addicted—if, say, they're running away, prostituting themselves, smoking crack, injecting heroin daily, or involved in serious criminal activity—your best bet is to avoid inpatient treatment longer than a month.

For the most seriously addicted, special schools such as Minnesota's Sobriety High or long-term outpatient treatment with education provided by a local school can also be a good choice. At Sobriety High, one of the very few high schools in the country aimed at dealing with the special problems of kids recovering from alcohol and other drug problems, teens get support and counseling, as well as a full education. It is a public school, so kids who wish to attend need to live in the area or have relatives there with whom they can stay during the school year.

The tips for selecting the best inpatient care, noted in Chapter 8, are applicable to teen treatment once you keep in mind the caveats added here. As with adults, the importance of aftercare cannot be stressed enough. When people leave the protected shell of the treatment center, they are at the most risk of slipping and of not recovering quickly from it. Aftercare can help reduce the odds.

Another important factor—probably a key factor and even more important to teens than to adults—is structure. Teens often try to test the rules to see what they can get away with. They may actually violate rules or just slack off and do the minimum in classes and groups. There need to be consequences for doing these things—not consequences as harsh as physical assault or verbal abuse, but things such as loss of privileges and other unpleasant but not emotionally devastating demotions. Also, too much free, unscheduled time in a teen treatment center can lead to situations where kids spend hours reminiscing about the good times of using drugs, sharing tips on getting drugs, and plotting to get high together. When looking for either inpatient or intensive outpatient treatment, be sure that most time is spent in structured, therapeutic activity.

A Note on Self-help Groups

Many teen treatment centers, like their adult counterparts, recommend that patients attend and participate in the appropriate 12-step fellowship. If you live in a large community where there are special AA or NA groups for teens, your child may be able to find a new source of friends and social support there. However, in many small towns, only regular meetings are available—and there may be only one other person under age 20 in the room. As a result, many teens will feel that they don't fit in and can't relate to the stories about broken marriages, jobs, and children. Some may enjoy being adopted as a sort of "mascot" and getting special treatment as the young one in the group, but many will feel that hanging around with adults is boring and uncool.

Another problem that teens may have with 12-step groups is identifying themselves as alcoholics or other addicts. As mentioned earlier, teens don't really know who they are, so pushing them to adopt an addict identity may not be healthy. Unless they have clearly had a disastrous relationship with drink and other drugs from day one, they may genuinely be telling the truth when they say that they don't know whether they are alcoholics or other addicts, rather than being "in denial."

Our advice is this: If your children take to AA or NA like fish to water, encourage it. If they can't stand it, don't push it, but do insist that they get some kind of support for avoiding alcohol and other drugs—such as continued, if less frequent, counseling or participation in an alternative self-help group. This should continue until they have at least a year of reduced drug use—if not complete abstinence, at least a return to proper functioning in school and with family and friends, even if there is the odd slip or two.

Harm Reduction for Teens

What if the worst happens: Your child refuses to stop taking drugs, keeps running away and checking back in only now and then, looking haggard and worn, but not accepting any kind of help? In this case, you want to be sure most of all that your child stays alive—which means making sure that she or he at least knows how to avoid being infected with HIV or hepatitis, as well as to prevent overdose. Harm-reduction advice may not always be followed, but the more it is followed, the less likely it is that your child will die and not make it to recovery.

See Chapter 17 for advice on reducing drug-related harm. Also review Chapter 6 for information on how to help move someone through the stages of change.

Parents whose children continually relapse or won't accept help need particular support. CRAFT (detailed in Chapter 6 and Chapter 16) can be helpful both for family members and as a way to try to speed the teen's recovery process. Also useful for family members are 12-step support groups such as Al-Anon and Nar-Anon, which help people care for themselves, as well as for their loved ones.

Dealing with the Police

Many parents believe, mistakenly, that if they involve the police in their kids' drug problems—by say, calling the police when their children have drugs in their possession, the seriousness of the situation will sink in, and they will shape up. Unfortunately, more often than not, what happens is that the kid winds up with a criminal record and a big resentment of his or her parents. These days, a drug conviction can also mean ineligibility for student loans. As one counselor described an attempt by parents to scare sense into their daughter by staging a "home invasion" by actors paid to threaten her, which ended in a real police raid, "These interventions backfire because it reinforces the idea that their parents are assholes." Also, terrible things can happen to teens in juvenile prisons. Many do not provide any treatment at all—and those that do offer some, often don't provide the best.

If the police are already involved, as in Sean's situation described at the beginning of the chapter, you may have to deal with the courts and the justice system, but if you can keep your child out of courts, jails, and prisons, the situation will probably be better all around. The justice system's primary focus is to stop criminals and punish them—not to help or rehabilitate them. This doesn't mean you should get your kid off and leave her or him alone, of course. It means that you should, if at all possible, aim for a noncustodial sentence, probation, or a treatment center that you have selected, rather than "letting him or her experience consequences" by not intervening with legal help and bail. Research shows that young people sentenced to treatment do much better than those who are incarcerated, and the longer someone is incarcerated, the *more* likely he or she is to reoffend.

Also, America's drug laws are harsher than you may think—a 17-year-old can wind up in prison for decades on many non-violent, first drug-dealing/large-possession offenses. No one wants this for their kid, and it doesn't teach those who are sentenced much more than bitterness. Get a good lawyer, and put your child into treatment.

Research on Teen Treatment

Unfortunately, aside from the scant information presented here, there is very little information on success rates for teen treatment or on what is most effective. One extensive review of the literature on adolescent treatment tentatively concluded that some treatment is probably better than none, but the NIDA study directly contradicts that. A few studies support CBT and family therapy, however.

Dealing with a teenager with a drug problem can be one of the most trying and terrifying experiences a parent can have—and the media, politicians, and treatment professionals haven't made it much better by using scare tactics to get parents to try to "confront" or "tough love" their kids out of drugs. School policies of "zero tolerance" continue to backfire by taking those who get caught using drugs out of the structured schedule of school and leaving them to fend for themselves (and probably to do more drugs) while suspended. Expulsions make it even worse—they may rid particular schools of problem children, but they decrease the odds that the kids who are put out will recover, by increasing the barriers to education. The more education kids have, the more likely they are to outgrow drug problems. Unemployment, lack of structure, and lack of a high school degree all make recovery harder and relapse more likely. For kids, challenging schools and exciting extracurricular activities are some of our best weapons against drugs—and often, the first thing we do when kids use drugs is to deny them these and give them more free time to get high!

If your kid is taking drugs or drinking heavily, do your best to help him or her stop, but also keep reminding yourself that heavy substance use in teens does not necessarily predict heavy drug use in adults. The vast majority will outgrow the problem in a few years. It is the teens and early 20s when pressures to "party hearty" are the heaviest. At least half of all college students report serious binge drinking, but only about 5% of those ages 25–34 can be defined as "alcohol dependent" or "alcoholic." Among twelfth graders, 22% report having spent at least a month smoking marijuana daily in their lifetimes—but only 5% report that they are still doing so, and the vast majority of the kids who quit received no treatment. Just 1.6% of those ages 26 to 35 smoke pot daily.

Above all, never give up!

Knowledge Is Power
- Don't panic! If you catch your child with drugs, it doesn't automatically mean that he or she has a problem or needs treatment.
- In an emergency, most hospitals or other programs aimed at stabilizing and keeping your child safe will do in the short run. While your teen is there, you can select and plan for longer-term care.
- Make sure that your child gets a complete psychiatric evaluation and that any coexisting problems are treated appropriately.
- Because teen treatment can make kids more curious about drugs they haven't tried, don't use it as a first resort—particularly if your child is smoking pot or drinking but is not involved with other drugs.
- Start with outpatient one-on-one counseling, which can avoid the problem of exposing your child to kids with more serious problems.
- Make sure your teen likes his or her counselor—give him or her a choice if you can.
- Never send your child to a treatment center where patients live with "host families," where you are not permitted to have unsupervised contact with

them, where adults mix with teens, or which is located outside of the country where you live.

- Cognitive-behavioral and motivational treatment for teens has the most research support, and there is no evidence that it can do harm.
- Use the tips mentioned in Chapter 8 to select inpatient care if needed, and make sure that any center you choose has a patient complaint procedure.
- Look for structure and compassion in any treatment.
- If you are going to use drug testing, do so consistently, and make consequences consistent and not overly harsh. Don't punish a child who admits relapse and is already upset about it.
- Family therapy is an important part of teen treatment.
- Though it is scary to catch your child drinking alcohol or taking other drugs, keep in mind that the majority of those who experiment will not become addicts, and even most of those who use heavily as teens will outgrow it.
- A good education followed by enjoyable employment is the best antidote to long-term addiction. Make sure that any treatment you choose does not neglect this area.

PART THREE

Life after Treatment

CHAPTER 21

Relapse and Relapse Prevention

These days, most treatment of alcoholism and other forms of addiction focuses heavily on preventing relapse. This is, as Martha Stewart might put it, a good thing. However, the majority of American treatment centers use relapse-prevention materials based on a system (the CENAPS model, promoted by Terry Gorski) that has never been subjected to controlled study. This chapter summarizes the scientific research on relapse prevention and the best techniques to accomplish it.

G. Alan Marlatt of the University of Washington—Seattle is the leading scientific expert on relapse. He found that one of the biggest contributors to serious relapse is a view of it as the end of recovery—as an insurmountable hurdle, rather than a bump on the road. When alcoholics and other addicts are asked to discuss relapse, they often say things like "It's over. I'm not recovering any more," or "I've blown it again." Relapse is seen not only as a shift out of recovery, but as a sign of personal failure and an indication that staying drug free is impossible.

Marlatt's work suggests that it is this perception, not the "first drink" or "first drug" itself, that often allows a small lapse in vigilance to develop into a full-blown relapse. While it is obviously better to avoid the first drink or other drug, if you have already taken the first sip, you are not obligated to drink the rest of the glass. Studies have found that alcoholics (not in recovery!) who are given what they believe to be alcohol-containing drinks, but which are actually alcohol free, they request just as many more drinks as those who have been given drinks that actually do contain booze. There is no irresistible pharmacological power of the first drink— although taking it may certainly increase craving. The most important factor in making a small slip into big trouble is the belief that one drink inevitably causes total loss of control. This suggests that it is best to distinguish between slips such as drinking half a glass of wine or having one puff on a joint and full-blown binges lasting hours or more.

If you do not make this distinction, the "might as well be hung for a sheep as a lamb" syndrome can develop (or less politely, the "screw it, I've already blown it" attitude). If it's just as bad to have a little as a lot, why take the complete punishment later but not enjoy the full monty now?

Although 12-step programs don't distinguish between a small lapse such as a sip and an all-out relapse, it's probably a good idea for you to do so. The advice that you cannot get drunk without the first drink still holds—but it's best to stop yourself as quickly as possible if you do lapse. Marlatt and his colleagues have shown that people who don't view relapse in an "on/off" way are less likely to be sidetracked and less likely to let a slip take them back to active addiction. It's easier to self-correct early on, basically. This is one of the foundations of relapse prevention.

Marlatt uses several analogies that help reinforce this idea. One is also commonly used in AA: the notion of having a set of tools in a tool kit, and acting as a "maintenance person" for your own recovery. Maintenance people cannot prevent all breakdowns—but if something goes wrong, they are prepared with the right equipment. Marlatt also compares recovery to flying. He quotes a pilot who says of the safety procedures, "It's better to know them and not need them than to need them and not know them." These ideas can help reduce the shame and pain of relapse—which is important because those feelings can often drive continued use. Relapse is not a requirement, but because a vast majority of those who try quitting alcohol or other drugs will experience it at least once, it's best to be prepared and try to minimize any damage.

If you do slip, use it as a learning experience, and stop consuming psychoactive substances as soon as possible. Try to work out the sequence of events that lead up to the slip—and what you could have done differently in order to avoid it. Don't allow yourself excuses. The sooner you put the stuff down, the more quickly you will return to stable recovery. And don't beat yourself up. The most important thing is that you have recognized that you have slipped (rather than telling yourself "I can use now. I'm cured!"), and that you are now trying to get back on track. Compliment yourself for your efforts to stay clean now, rather than punishing yourself for the mistake that led to the slip. Particularly with a drug such as heroin, where physical dependence is quite easily reestablished, stopping sooner means far less physical and mental angst.

A lapse or a slip does not have to become a relapse, and a relapse does not have to mean a return to years of active addiction. If you use or drink again, get right back on that horse (No, not *that* horse!) before the fear or a sense of failure paralyzes you.

Dealing with Stress

Because stress is probably the most important factor that drives people to heavy drinking and other drug taking in the first place, you probably won't be surprised to learn that stress and the negative emotions that often accompany it— anger, depression, anxiety—are also the most common cause of relapse. Over one third of relapses begin with these negative emotions.

Richard, a 41-year-old heroin addict who has suffered numerous relapses, describes two relapses that began with stress: "I was uncomfortable. My wife is straight, and I'd be stressed out and she'd be watching me like a hawk. I'd want to grab something and get high, so I would deliberately start fights with her in order to have an excuse to jump up and go out and cop."

More recently, he was in a detox, and another patient described a street corner where "really good" drugs were being sold. "I'd been miserable and unhappy and so the day after I got out, Thursday, I went there and did one bag and Friday, Saturday, and Sunday, I did five more and by 2 A.M. Sunday I was so sick [with withdrawal] that I was puking and my wife was all upset."

In order to prevent such relapses, you need to develop alternative ways of dealing with stress. The first step is to recognize when you are stressed—often the feeling won't manifest itself explicitly. Feelings of boredom, edginess, listlessness, fear, dread, and apprehension are all good indicators. Physical signs such as jitteriness, increased heart rate, and muscle tension are also clues. If stress becomes more acute, it can develop into sadness, anger, and even depression. If you feel at all lousy or out of sorts, pay attention!

When you give up addiction, you often feel at a loss for other ways of dealing with stress. For you, such things as calling a friend, reading, going to a support-group meeting, listening to music, meditating, having a massage, watching movies, having sex, or exercising pale in comparison with what you may believe to be the supreme healing power of your favorite drug. This comparison is an illusion—caused by the fact that the addiction has pushed aside most other ways of stress reduction and has allowed you to forget that they, too, can help. During your addiction, you will probably have stopped using these strategies because they were unavailable (friends tire of drunken wailing, for example) or because seeking the drug took up most of your time. This doesn't mean that these alternatives can't work now. Also, the more you practice them, the more you expand your repertoire of nondrug enjoyable experiences, the better you will become at coping with stress and the less likely relapse will become. Classes on relaxation and meditation are often helpful—because otherwise, these can remain in your head as a nice idea, rather than a practice. Exercise that you like—even just taking a walk—is also a good choice.

Of course, if you are living in a situation that is unbearably stressful, or if you have an untreated mental illness, these techniques may not be enough. The key here is to keep seeking help until you have found something that works for you.

Family or Marital Conflict

As in Richard's situation, conflict between spouses is often part of the addictive cycle. Most treatment centers offer family workshops and therapy in order to minimize these conflicts, but because living with people is difficult, these conflicts can flare up at any time. About 16% of relapses occur after a fight with a spouse, partner, family member, or close friend. The best way to avoid such relapses is to be aware that arguments and disagreements present the danger of relapse, and to set up other ways of coping with disagreement.

It often helps to change the way you argue. If both parties stick to how they feel about situations in the present, rather than attacking each other about how "you always" or "you are. . . ," fights can become less vicious, and solutions to problems can become more obvious. However, the emotions around conflict are frequently potent, and this alone can trigger a strong urge to use drugs in order to escape or minimize them.

Again, relaxation techniques, meditation, and exercise can be helpful—and certainly calling someone from a support group is also a good idea. Some people find it helpful to resolve that "I won't let her make me drink," "I won't let some man spoil my recovery," or "I won't use on impulse." AA's notion of "one day at a time" can work here. If you have decided not to drink today, the urge to do so tomorrow, when emotions are less raw will almost certainly be diminished.

Avoiding conflict when you are angry or stressed about issues that have nothing to do with your relationships is generally a good plan. This way, your fights will be more likely to be about the issues you want to deal with, rather than about "I'm in a bad mood, so let me take it out on him," or "I'm really resentful that she does X, but I can't tell her, so I'll yell at her about Y."

Deciding on a specific time to discuss issues that are bothering you—when both of you are less upset—can be very useful. Then, both parties can be prepared to say what they have to, and to listen to the other. If there is constant conflict, however, couples or family therapy may be needed.

Peer Pressures

Another big cause of relapse is also a cause of drug-use initiation: good old peer pressure. This can be overt—as in someone saying, "Hey, you can have just one for old time's sake," or covert. Sometimes, as in one of Richard's relapses, just seeing an old drug buddy (even if that person is now in recovery) can trigger an urge to use drugs. Because of this, it's important, especially in early recovery to avoid the "people, places, and things" you most associate with your addiction. Direct or indirect peer pressure initiates 20% of relapses.

Cues, Urges, Cravings

Just because you have an urge, you don't necessarily have to have a relapse. One of the most pernicious myths about addiction is that urges are somehow immune to the exercise of will, and that once you have an urge, you are doomed to failure. In fact, early recovery—even among those who quit successfully—is filled with urges and desires to use. Maia spent most of her first six months of recovery talking about and fantasizing about drugs—but this didn't mean that she took any. The obsession is not surprising. Both your conscious and your unconscious mind are pulled toward returning to the pattern that has recently framed all your activities. This also means that when you see a spoon, you'll think about shooting up; when you see a glass, you'll want a drink; when you watch TV, you'll want to smoke pot—even if you just experience a nice feeling, you'll probably want to "top it up" with your favorite substance(s).

This is completely normal, but the key here is another 12-step slogan: This, too, shall pass. A little-known fact about compulsive behavior is that if you give in to an urge, you actually make it stronger, rather than decreasing it. This is completely counterintuitive: It should be that if you yield, you feel satisfied and don't want more. Even if you are satisfied by the drug now, however, the fact of giving in to your desire for it automatically increases your wish to do it again later. It only teaches you that yielding to urges provides relief.

In order to get rid of urges, you have to learn to ignore them, or if you can't, at least to avoid giving in to them. The more you refuse to yield, the weaker they will become because the automatic aspect of the behavior will be reduced. The stimulus-response connection will be broken, and over time, you will find that you can see a spoon and say, "Hey, where's the ice cream," without even thinking of injections.

If you have been using drugs for many years, however, this may take a good long while. Also, at first, it's best to avoid situations that provoke strong urges. However, if you are to live a full life (and to eat soup or ice cream again!), you are going to have to deal with spoons, and the more you use spoons for their intended purpose, the less they will be connected with your drug habit.

One important technique for handling urges is to disconnect yourself from them. Rather than saying, "I feel like getting high now," reframe the feeling by saying, "I'm experiencing an urge to get high now," and ask yourself about what might have prompted it. If it is a situation that you can leave, do so. (In fact, it helps to prepare ahead of time for such eventualities by telling people in advance that, for example, you may have to leave a party early because your baby-sitter might not be able to stay late or by claiming not to feel well or having forgotten to make an important phone call. The embarrassment of relapsing because you couldn't get out of a situation that made you uncomfortable will be far greater than having to explain why you left suddenly.)

If the desire to use drugs comes from being hungry or tired, eat or sleep. Often, people in early recovery confuse natural hunger with drug hunger. Also, if the urge is related to an emotional situation that is upsetting you, try to calm yourself, and reassure yourself that you will be able to get through it. If you have to cry, cry. Most often, resisting emotions is worse than simply allowing yourself to feel them and get it over with. They pass much faster if you just accept them and move on. Feelings may be uncomfortable, but they won't kill you.

Another common source of urges to use drugs is disappointment. Alcoholics and other addicts often believe that they shouldn't feel disappointed because they shouldn't have expected things to work out, or because they should be "more mature." Again, allow yourself to feel whatever you are feeling—and don't judge yourself for it. Often, the voice of judgment increases your pain to the level where it becomes so unbearable that you feel as though you have to get blitzed. It's bad enough to feel bad, but you make matters worse if you are angry with yourself on top of that for feeling that way. If you can get rid of this extra source of pain, the situation is much easier to take.

Marlatt's research has also confirmed what many people in recovery find to be common sense: The more you deprive yourself, the more likely you are to eventually erupt into excess. If you fill your life with pleasurable things as much as possible (as he puts it, increase the ratio of things you *want* to do, compared with things you *should* do), you will be far less likely to relapse. Avoid self-punishment and abnegation. You are confronting probably the hardest task in your life, and the last thing you need to do is increase the deprivation you already feel in doing so. Treat yourself as much as your finances will allow—now is not the time to suddenly get frugal, give up sweets, renounce sex, and give up trash television. If you have compulsive problems in these areas, you can deal with them later. One exception may be cigarette smoking: If you were forced to quit in an inpatient detox, you may as well try to stick with it because tobacco actually kills more alcoholics than alcohol does. If you didn't quit everything at once, however, you might prefer to postpone quitting nicotine (or switch to the gum or patch or inhaler for maintenance for a while).

Allowing yourself to experience other pleasures is, of course, easier said than done. Your finances may be strained because of your addiction, for one—but if you are creative, you can generally come up with inexpensive but satisfying self-rewards. Some examples are chocolate, hot baths, a new CD or tape, library books, a nice dinner, a walk through an area you find beautiful, a pet from an animal shelter, and so on.

Unfortunately, early recovery may also be marked by a chemical inability to feel good ("anhedonia"), which is another common cause of relapse. Although for many people, this resolves itself within a few months, it can be one of the hardest things to take. If you find that no matter what you do, you continuously feel joyless, bored, and unable to find any source of pleasure, you should seek psychiatric help. You aren't a "better" or "stronger" person if you tough it out at the risk of increasing your chances of relapse.

Relapse Processes and Awful Acronyms

Many people have noted that relapse is a process. It doesn't start the moment that you pick up the actual substance. Marlatt created the notion of what he first called "apparently irrelevant decisions" (AIDs) but changed the acronym because of the disease association. He now calls them "seemingly irrelevant decisions" (SIDs)—which isn't much better in the grim acronym department (SIDS also stands for sudden infant death syndrome), but there you are.

Seemingly irrelevant decisions are those decisions you make, which don't appear to you to be setting you up for relapse at the time, but which in retrospect are clearly necessary for relapse to happen. Learning relapse prevention means recognizing these decisions earlier—before the chain reaction has started.

Richard describes one of these decisions perfectly. "A guy I know, at 7 A.M. every day, he gets up and goes to cop. I know that he drives up Mace Avenue. So, a few times, I would 'decide' to walk the dog at 6:50. If he comes, it's a sign that I should get high, so I won't turn away. Of course, I'd walk up the block and inevitably the guy would drive by and I'd say, 'OK, let me come with you. I'll put the dog away.'"

Richard didn't realize that he'd made the decision to relapse when he'd decided to walk the dog at that time—because he felt that there was a chance that the guy wouldn't come, and that he could always choose not to flag him down. The earlier you can identify the decisions that prompt a relapse, the easier it is to interrupt the chain of events. As Richard described it, if he didn't see his friend immediately, he would keep walking the dog up and down the block until he did. He'd become committed to the action much earlier than he'd realized.

In order to avoid such situations—which frequently involve such things as going into a bar for a soda or visiting an old friend whom you know will have drugs in his house—you need to spend a great deal of time watching your own thoughts and motivations. If you are honest with yourself, you will find that you can tell when you are "going out to hear music," and when you are going into a bar because you secretly want to get drunk. If you know you are entering a situation where alcohol and other drugs are available, it's important to check yourself—if you are at all upset, stressed, or anxious, it's probably best to postpone the outing.

Another particularly dangerous time can be a celebration or holiday, especially if family members are involved. Seeing your parents can often prompt the return of childhood feelings and roles, for example, which can push you back toward earlier and more dysfunctional ways of coping. Even celebrating with friends can be risky if you aren't yet comfortable with telling people firmly that you don't drink or take other drugs anymore.

It's not necessary to make a big announcement in all cases—you may want to say that you are "taking some time off" or are "unable to do drugs right now for medical reasons," but some people may persist in trying to convince you, and in such cases, you need to be ready to consistently say no, and perhaps explain why. Most often, fortunately, people won't notice that you are not drinking— you can keep a nonalcoholic drink in your hand, and they will think nothing of it. With drugs, friends may actually be happy that you choose not to partake—it leaves more for them, something you can stress to them if they try to tempt you to use. Your best bet, however, is to avoid these types of situations for the most part until you are stable in your recovery, or plan how you will deal with them in advance.

Unfortunately, good times and positive experiences can also trigger relapse cues. Because drinking and other drugs are so often a crucial part of celebratory rituals, you may feel as though it's not a "real" party if you can't drink or get high. Success can also trigger feelings of disappointment if you had expectations that it would "fix" you and solve your social problems—or if you feel as though you don't deserve it. In such situations, it's really important to talk about how you feel to someone sympathetic, and to at least allow yourself some type of treat that you enjoy so that you don't feel deprived.

One special note about alcohol: This drug, more than most others, reduces inhibitions. If your drug of choice is heroin, and you decide to "have a few drinks," you may really be deciding to relapse into heroin use, because once the alcohol is in your system, your resistance to urges can be greatly reduced. It is best to avoid alcohol entirely for this reason. A number of people recovering from other drug addictions may be able to handle it, but why risk finding out that you are in the group that can't, and thereby jeopardize your recovery?

For Family Members and Other Loved Ones: Support Antirelapse Efforts

Relapse prevention and coping with relapse are areas where people who are close to addicts can really help. You can point out things that they are doing, which may lead to relapse, which they may not be aware of. If they do slip, you can offer support and encouragement to get them back on track. Your belief that they can do it will help them feel more capable and less guilty about having slipped. Because guilt over slips is most likely to lead to continued slips, rather than recovery, this can be really important.

Of course, if addicts seem as though they are heading for relapse, they may not want to be told that that's what they're doing. To avoid simply making them angry, you should ask in a very calm and questioning manner whether they think that, say, hanging out every night in a bar, might be a step toward relapse. They may say that they're fine, "Don't you trust me?"—and you can say, "Of course I do, but I also know that these things can sneak up on you." Where they take it from there is up to them, but by pointing out such things gently and just once, you can help them recognize the potential problems and be more conscious of potential relapse processes.

You will probably be angry and upset if someone close to you does slip—and this is certainly understandable. However, if at all possible, you should try to avoid saying such things as "You blew it again—why didn't you listen?" and try to focus on encouraging the person to quickly put down the substance and minimize the length of the slip and its devolution into relapse.

Of course, if people do continue using and fall back into active addiction, you may have to treat them as though they have returned to a place where they can't see the harm done by it (precontemplation) and keep reminding them of the consequences that happen when they use regularly. Support harm-reduction efforts so that when they come back, they're relatively healthy. If relapse happens repeatedly, you may have to end the relationship or minimize contact with them so as to keep your own sanity, but so long as you feel as though you can help without harming yourself or your other relationships, you should continue to try. In alcoholism and other forms of addiction, the moments when it seems most bleak may actually be the moment when things turn around for good.

Joe

Testing Yourself

Another common relapse situation occurs when you try deliberately to test your willpower. Self-tests—such as keeping alcohol or other drugs in the house or hanging out in bars or other drug-related environments—are almost always a bad idea. They make it much more likely that you will fall victim to a momentary impulse, which would have passed if you had to take the time to go get the stuff. It is not "weak" to avoid keeping drugs around or avoid going into places where booze is likely to be—it is simply sensible.

Back to Work

The old saying "idle hands are the devil's playground" could have been written to describe the relationship between unemployment and relapse: If you have too much free time, you are much more likely to return to using drugs than if you keep busy. If you are employed, try to either keep working through your outpatient treatment or return to work as soon as possible after rehab.

Research finds, in fact, that one of the best correlates of long-term recovery is having a job that you like. While you may not be able to get your dream job immediately, it's generally a good idea to find some work that provides a structure for your day, even if you have to volunteer or work for little pay. Structure itself is important. Unless you are extremely self-disciplined and have experience working from home, such work is probably not the right thing to do for your first work experience in recovery. Without having other people around and having a fixed schedule, it can be easier to get off track and to slip out to get high.

Let's Talk about Sex

Many rehab professionals and drug-recovery experts recommend that those who are not already in a committed relationship refrain from entering one in their first year of recovery. This may be sound advice, but in reality, very few people are willing to give up sex when they have just given up drink and other drugs. In fact, men commonly interpret "no relationships in the first year" to mean that they can have casual sex with no emotional involvement—while women interpret it as "no sex." Obviously, this can lead to problems if two newly recovering people of opposite sexes come together!

Some recovering people realize that they have never had sex without being stoned or drunk—and they may be afraid that they won't be able to do it sober. Others find that the emotions aroused by sex are overwhelming and cause urges to use drugs. If this is the case for you, it might be a good idea to refrain for a while, but if you find this impossible, you should do things to protect your recovery, such as avoiding sex with active alcoholics and other addicts and being sure that you have someone (other than your partner) like a fellow support-group member with whom you can discuss the feelings that arise. It's important to be sure to take safer sex precautions—if you are sleeping with other people in recovery, you are sleeping with people at high risk for HIV and for hepatitis C.

In New York, for example, 40% of people entering treatment are HIV-positive, and some estimates say that 90% of IV drug users carry the hepatitis C virus. If you dodged the bullet while using, it would be terrible to pick up one of these illnesses as you start your recovery. If you are unsure or are uncomfortable about your ability to negotiate condom or dental dam use, try to abstain until you are sure you will do it—or at least try to do only the least risky activities. Resources for safer sex information are listed in the appendix.

While we're on the subject of sexually transmitted diseases such as AIDS, the question of when to get tested is often a sticky one for people who may have been exposed while drinking or using other drugs. Rehabs often encourage testing, and with the availability of medications that dramatically prolong life, it probably makes sense to know sooner, rather than later. However, if you are unsure whether a positive result would lead you to relapse, postpone the test until you feel that you could handle either outcome. If you are HIV-positive, using alcohol or other drugs can increase the progression of the disease (cocaine actually makes HIV reproduce 20 times more frequently!), so it's even more important to maintain your recovery.

Chronic Pain

Serious, chronic pain can also trigger relapse. It's crucial to see a pain specialist as early as possible and to be honest about your drug problem with him or her. Pain specialists will not deny you medication because you have abused drugs, but they will work with you to maximize pain control while minimizing addiction risk. Regular doctors who do not specialize in this area often dismiss any need for pain medication by addicts or ex-addicts as drug seeking. Don't let yourself suffer this outcome!

Relapse can be one of the most trying experiences for people in recovery and their loved ones. Try not to let it get you down, and be aware as much as possible of what you can learn from it if it does occur. The more you learn, and the more you pay attention to potential relapse-provoking situations, the easier it will get. Remember that any amount of time spent clean and sober counts. It is not erased by relapse. Also, keep in mind that a slip doesn't mean that you are no longer "in recovery." You are in recovery so long as you are making an honest attempt to deal with your problem.

It's like learning to ride a bicycle—at first you tend to fall frequently, but over time, the falls become vanishingly rare. You haven't stopped being a bike rider when you have had a fall, and bike riding is not a skill that you forget once you've learned it. Research bears this out—the more times you try to quit, the more likely you are to become clean and sober. Most people think the opposite is true—that if they have tried many times and failed, they are doomed forever. Don't give in—if you keep at it and try a variety of approaches, you will probably eventually get it.

Knowledge Is Power

- Distinguish between slips—where you just have a small amount of a substance and stop yourself—and full-fledged relapses, where you return to whole days of compulsive behavior. Neither a slip nor a relapse is an end to your recovery, but a slip where you self-correct quickly is much less dangerous.
- If you do slip or relapse, don't be hard on yourself about it. Congratulate yourself for returning to your recovery process instead.
- In early recovery, avoid people, places, and things that can increase your urges to use drugs and that give you opportunities to do so.
- Don't test yourself by deliberately creating dangerous situations.
- Watch out for seemingly irrelevant decisions—such as deciding to walk your dog when your drug connection will be out.
- Be nice to yourself, and allow yourself as many nondrug pleasures as possible.
- If hungry, eat. If tired, sleep. If lonely or angry, talk to someone about it, or do something such as exercising, watching TV, listening to music, or going to a support group, to distract yourself.
- Take it one day at a time. The less you give in to urges, the weaker they get.
- If you feel consistently lousy, seek help.
- Family conflict is often a source of stress, which can lead to relapse. If it doesn't diminish, family therapy can be helpful.
- Work or other ways of structuring your time can be crucial to preventing relapse. The more you like your work, the better you will do—so try to go after the kind of work you really want.
- Don't ever give up. The more you try, the more likely you are to achieve a stable, lasting, comfortable recovery.

CHAPTER 22

Emotional and Psychological Problems in Recovery

Clara, a 28-year-old woman with three children, came to see me after having been discharged from a psychiatric hospital. A month earlier, she had been suicidal and had been hospitalized as a result. The night before she was admitted to the hospital, she had been drinking and found herself in a dangerous part of the city. She walked past the apartment of one of her exes, an abusive crack addict who was the father of one of her children. Clara didn't know what drew her to this neighborhood, but at 3 A.M. it was definitely not a place to be walking alone. At the time, she didn't care. She felt numb—a relief, in contrast to the anxiety and distress that usually consumed her.

Unfortunately, her sense of detachment didn't last. Three men grabbed Clara, raped her, and stole her wallet. When the police found her and took her to the emergency room, she said she wanted to die. After a month in the hospital, however, Clara was no longer suicidal, she was taking antidepressant medication, and while hospitalized, she had been completely drug free.

When Clara saw me, she said she had been abusing alcohol since age 15. She occasionally used crack to improve her chronically low mood and feelings of worthlessness. Alcohol was her drug of choice, however. It was alcohol that allowed her to sleep a few hours each night. Clara had been sexually abused by her stepfather when she was 12 years old, and about 3 years later, she left home to live with a man about 10 years her senior. By age 17, she delivered her first child and became increasingly involved with alcohol and cocaine. During the next decade, Clara found herself in and out of psychiatric hospitals and drug-rehabilitation programs. She lost custody of her children and survived by prostituting herself. Clara's friend, Linda—who had known her since infancy and had been her best friend for years—brought her to my office for help.

Addiction and Psychopathology

Among people who come for treatment for addiction, more than half have emotional distress significant enough to warrant a psychiatric diagnosis. It is a matter of much debate among health-care providers whether the psychological distress

248

is a consequence of addiction, or whether the psychological distress leads to the addiction. There are certainly cases where one seems more true than the other. More often than not, however, as in Clara's case, psychological distress and addiction are so intertwined that it is impossible to separate them, no matter what the chronological sequence was.

Unfortunately, just as three blind men touching different parts of an elephant may report feeling a rope, a tree trunk, or a wall, treatment programs are often only able to see the aspect of the problem they are designed to deal with. An important consequence of this selective focus is that people such as Clara often fall through the cracks of the health-care system.

Clara's experience illustrates the problem. When she was in treatment for depression, her psychiatrist paid little attention to her alcoholism. She was prescribed medications but often forgot to take them or missed appointments because she was high. An additional problem is drug interactions: Antidepressants have reduced effectiveness when mixed with alcohol, cocaine, marijuana, or heroin. Also, if taken with alcohol or other downer drugs, most antianxiety medications can have serious, potentially fatal interactions.

In the psychotherapy she received, Clara was not able to deal with her feelings of inadequacy or anger. She used alcohol and cocaine to blunt unpleasant emotions, and, as a result, she had trouble even identifying what she was feeling. Not surprisingly, Clara made little progress in programs that focused solely on her depression and anxiety.

When one of her therapists discovered that Clara was abusing alcohol and cocaine, she was referred to a 28-day inpatient addiction program. The attitude of the staff was quite different here. Clara realized this immediately when she was escorted to a locked ward and thoroughly searched by a staff member. The focus was entirely on abstaining from alcohol and other drugs. Any complaint was dismissed with, "That's part of your addiction. It will get better over time." While in this rehab, Clara remained clean and sober because she was locked up, but her desire to use remained high. She began to experience a variety of strong feelings, including shame, anxiety, and depression. She started having distressing flashbacks. As a result, within a week of leaving the center, she returned to drinking and feeling hopeless about the future.

Psychological Distress and Recovery

The staff of Clara's rehab program were right about one thing: It is quite common for people in recovery to experience a range of distressing feelings during their early weeks and months drug free, and it is hard even for professionals to tell whether someone at this time will improve without additional help. Many treatment centers have begun to dispense with the debate over whether the symptoms will pass if left alone and have decided to help relieve them if the patient reports extreme distress.

It comes down to one's philosophical feelings about medication, basically. If you don't worry that being on a medication is a sign of "weakness" or of being crazy, then you may not mind taking one, even if, perhaps, you could have stuck it out without it. Because these medications don't cause dependence, there is no reason not to try to go for comfort. On the other hand, some people find the idea of psychiatric medication depressing in itself—if this is your view, you may wish to wait and see whether your symptoms improve within a month or so. If you hold this latter view, however, and you don't feel better as your recovery progresses, you may want to reevaluate your position. Why suffer and risk relapse if you can be comfortable and happy on safe, nonaddictive medications?

Feelings and Symptoms

The following are some of the feelings and symptoms people frequently experience in early recovery and some of the ways you can determine whether they signify a disorder for which you may need additional help. At the end of this chapter, you will also find a self-diagnostic test (the Psychological Distress Inventory), which can help you determine whether you should be evaluated further by a professional.

Low Self-esteem

In AA, there is a saying, "Poor me, poor me, pour me a drink." Self-esteem is often a casualty of addiction, and when you stop using alcohol and other drugs and realize how much they have taken from you, it is easy to become angry with yourself over lost time and missed opportunities. This anger is not productive and can be addressed by reminding yourself that placing blame for your addiction won't change what has happened. Remember that people who use drugs and don't get addicted aren't better people, just biologically luckier. Focus on what you can change, and work on that.

Low self-esteem can also be a symptom of clinical depression. If this is the case for you, antidepressants can help by reducing repeated negative thoughts, or by allowing you to do the things (e.g., helping others or using cognitive techniques) that may elude you when depression is overwhelming.

Paranoia

Suspiciousness and overt paranoia can accompany the use of stimulants such as methamphetamine and cocaine. Perhaps on your last binge, you felt that everyone was out to get you and that you couldn't trust anyone. Maybe you believed the police or the Drug Enforcement Agency (DEA) were after you (and maybe they were!), but the paranoia caused by stimulants (and sometimes alcohol) is usually just a result of their pharmacology. Schizophrenia, which is frequently accompanied by paranoia, is believed to result at least in part from an excess of dopamine—which is exactly what occurs when you take too much of these drugs. If these symptoms don't improve rapidly (within days, usually hours), it is very important to seek additional help.

Panic Attacks

Panic attacks are among the most distressing experiences possible. People who have been in combat and have also experienced panic attacks often report that the sheer terror of a panic attack is worse. Panic attacks are marked by the following symptoms: difficulty breathing, heart pounding, sweating, trembling, "jelly legs," intense fear, a foggy sense of reality, thoughts of "going crazy," and an overwhelming desire to flee. Often withdrawal from alcohol and sedatives can lead to panic attacks. It often helps to be reassured that panic attacks in these situations are usually just withdrawal related and will pass. Relaxation techniques, such as slow breathing (which moves your belly, not just your chest, like the way a baby breathes) or breathing into a paper bag, can also be soothing. If panic attacks or extreme fear of panic attacks continue beyond the first month or so of recovery and interfere with your ability to function, seek professional help.

Fear, Worry, or Obsessiveness

The early stages of recovery are often associated with fear that you will not be able to cope without alcohol and other drugs. Other common worries include fear of failure at work, concerns about relationships and sex, and, of course, fear of relapse. If you have a history of previous failures, you may think you are doomed to repeat them. You can easily be overwhelmed by all your new challenges and responsibilities. However, by having realistic expectations of yourself and focusing on the here and now, you can gradually regain your confidence, which addiction may have stolen from you.

This may mean moving more slowly than you might like—starting out perhaps with an easy, part-time job, for example, and then gradually returning to more difficult work. The keys here are to have faith in yourself and not view setbacks as signs of personal unworthiness. Examine your goals carefully, and take manageable steps toward achieving them. Don't be afraid to ask for help.

If you find yourself paralyzed by worry, if your mind is constantly filled with obsessions that you can't shake, or if you find yourself getting stuck checking things, counting things or events, or repeating little rituals, you may have a condition called obsessive-compulsive disorder (OCD). Both cognitive therapy and medication for this condition can be very effective, so don't let the shame that often accompanies OCD keep you from getting help. Obsessions and compulsions have nothing to do with how you were raised or toilet-trained: They are a brain disorder.

Mood Swings

In the early stages of recovery, most people report wild fluctuations in their moods. Fear and despair quickly follow a moment full of enthusiasm and optimism. Laughter and tears run together. Maia's mood swings were so extreme while she was in rehab that she was diagnosed as manic-depressive, although it later turned out that the problem for her was just withdrawal. For most people, like Maia, these mood swings reflect the dynamic changes their brains are going through as they adjust to the absence of drugs. For others, however, mood changes predate drug use and reflect actual manic-depression (also known as bipolar disorder), which they may have tried to self-medicate. If this is the case for you, as you recover from addiction, the mood changes may become more severe, rather than less. If you find that you are experiencing euphoric, giddy, overwhelming highs, followed by falls into the black pit of total despair, you probably should seek further help.

Please note: Many people with bipolar disorder avoid treatment because they enjoy the early parts of the highs—however, this can result in relationships and a work life as disrupted as one marked by active addiction. When mild euphoria slips into full-on mania, behavior becomes uninhibited and often extremely destructive. Spending sprees, staying up for days, drinking binges, promiscuous and unprotected sex are some of the common occurrences. When mania becomes extreme, people may become incomprehensible and psychotic. Bipolar disorder increases the odds of alcoholism, and unless it is brought under control, relapses are a likely consequence, particularly during manic phases.

Depression and Sadness

During the first few weeks of recovery, at times, you will probably feel low, weepy, lethargic, unable to concentrate, and unable to feel much pleasure, and you will probably either sleep too much or too little, or have trouble falling asleep or staying asleep. These are also signs of clinical depression. If you feel suicidal, or if these feelings do not pass within three weeks, seek professional help. Antidepressants really can work miracles here, although sometimes it may take some time before you and your doctor find the best one—and the best dosage—for you.

Anger

Irritability, frustration, and anger are especially dangerous emotions for people in recovery. Common themes are anger related to early childhood experiences such as emotional, physical, or sexual abuse; anger toward unsympathetic people who have abandoned you during your addiction; and even anger at those who pushed you into treatment. A lifetime of slights and disrespects, which you ignored while high, may come up and leave you furious for no discernible present reason. This section suggests some tips for coping with anger.

First, recognize that anger may be appropriate and justified because of past mistreatment. Second, like an alarm that continues to go off even though there's no burglar, the source of the false alarm may need to be addressed before it will stop bothering you. Recognizing that what you are feeling is appropriate and that is it OK to feel this way in response to hurt can go a long way, but often, some resentment remains. For some, peace can be gained through meditation, AA's steps, exercise, or prayer. Others find that if they allow themselves to understand what happened and why, they can move on and even forgive. The cycle of abuse usually didn't start with your own parents or whoever caused you pain, but you can take comfort in the fact that you can be the one to stop it. For those whose anger relates to injustice, there is nothing like activism.

If you find that you are consistently angry and worry about exploding or damaging your relationships, the problem may be that you have not learned to express yourself early enough in your anger cycle. Say something when someone does something you don't like the first time—not when they have done it so many times that you feel so angry you can't see straight. Relationships become much easier when you can tell people what you want before you have become furious. Of course, this new skill usually takes some practice.

Depression, particularly in men, can manifest itself as extreme irritability or rage—so again, be sure you are checked for mood disorders. Without other symptoms, anger alone is rarely a sign of serious mental illness, but if you cannot control it and have been violent in the past, it is certainly a good idea to seek help. Recent research has found that sometimes just expressing your anger can intensify it rather than diminish it, so the best type of treatment may be cognitive therapy focused on dealing with particular situations now, rather than just those in the past.

Flashbacks to Painful Experiences

Because so many alcoholics and other addicts have been victims of childhood or other traumas, when they enter recovery, many find that they are suddenly overwhelmed by memories of what happened earlier. They may even feel as though they have "blacked out" or lost periods of time, or they may have a prevailing feeling of numbness. All of these are signs of posttraumatic stress disorder (PTSD), and if you experience any of them, you should be seen for further therapy. PTSD is much more common in alcoholics and other addicts than in the general population. In fact, one study of female addicts in Harlem found that over 90% had been severely traumatized—either by witnessing people close to them being killed, or having been severely beaten or sexually abused. When you hear their stories, you are frequently amazed that anyone could live through such things and retain any shred of sanity. Drug use seems a rational response.

As a result, recovery can be difficult. Harm-reduction approaches may be needed because a sudden shift to abstinence can cause people to reexperience trauma. People with PTSD are often only able to completely give up the drugs when they have first found a place where they feel safe and trust others, which is—not surprisingly—pretty difficult for them. For opiate addicts, long-term methadone maintenance is often advisable.

Other symptoms of PTSD include panic attacks, flashbacks to the traumatic experience, dissociative states ("spacing out"), and sometimes profound detachment and lack of emotion. This can alternate with paranoia, anxiety, a hair-trigger temper, and hypervigilance, particularly among those who lived in traumatic situations for long periods of time.

Because some of these symptoms can be confused with the symptoms of schizophrenia, be sure that you tell as much as possible about your past as clearly as possible to the psychiatrist who is evaluating you.

Treatment of Dual Diagnoses

Increasingly, specialized programs are designed to treat both addiction and other mental disorders simultaneously. By addressing both issues at once, the problems that Clara had going from one type of treatment to another can be avoided. Also, because both mental illness and addiction can be caused or at least aggravated by past trauma, this issue can be better dealt with in a program that is skilled at handling both disorders.

While we have consistently stressed the importance of empathy, nowhere is this attitude more important than in the treatment of people with dual diagnoses. Dual-diagnosis programs are specially designed to address the conflicts between the attitudes of substance-abuse professionals and mental-health-care providers—such as differing views on the use of medication. Dual-diagnosis programs recognize that the treatment of mental illness often requires the use of medication and that symptoms of mental illness are often completely beyond the patient's control. As a result, their attitudes toward relapse are more forgiving, and they use more one-on-one counseling so that individual problems can be specifically addressed.

Please note: Dual-diagnosis patients who attend 12-step support groups should be very cautious about talking about their medications and their mental illness in meetings. Although the program doesn't officially oppose psychiatric medication, many individuals do, and they often tell people to "stop taking that junk." Suicides have resulted. Dual-diagnosis patients who don't want to deal with such pressures but want peer support may want to attend MICA (Mentally Ill/Chemically Addicted) meetings, "Double Trouble," or Dual Disorders Anonymous. In big cities, there are also frequently specialized AA meetings for people with both problems, in which medication use is encouraged, not stigmatized.

FOR FAMILY MEMBERS AND OTHER LOVED ONES: ACTION STEPS YOU NEED TO TAKE

If you are trying to help someone with a dual diagnosis, you may feel frustrated by the slow pace of progress. For the reasons mentioned previously, the combination of mental disorders and addiction is extremely difficult to treat. Three important principles apply to helping anyone with an addiction problem and are especially important for helping those with dual problems:

1. Take care of yourself first.
   When Linda brought Clara to see me that first time, I recognized that Linda was emotionally depleted. She had given Clara a place to stay,

lent her money (never repaid), and spent countless hours finding different treatment programs for her. Although Linda herself was not addicted to drugs, her life centered on taking care of Clara to the detriment of her other relationships and even her own emotional health. When the needs of others become more important than your own health, it is important to take a step back and ask yourself about why you are in such a situation.

If you are helping a friend or relative deal with a substance problem, you should also check your own emotional health by taking the self-test at the end of this chapter. A frequent scenario is a support person who grew up with alcoholic or other addicted parents. Often, too, such people have a history of physical, emotional, or sexual abuse. People who have grown up in disturbed environments tend to marry people with similar backgrounds.

If you are suffering from significant emotional distress, do not feel ashamed about getting additional support for yourself. Groups such as Al-Anon can help put your needs into perspective. A therapist or counselor could also help you identify additional ways to better take care of your needs. If your tank is running on empty, it is unlikely you will be able to drive yourself or anyone else to health.

2. Set limits, not fires.

If you find yourself constantly making excuses for an addicted partner, you may become increasingly angry and frustrated. Often, I see a pattern in which a support person alternates between "overgiving" with overwhelmingly strong support and harsh emotional withdrawal. As you might imagine, it is confusing for anyone to be subject to such swings, but for a person with a dual diagnosis, these inconsistencies can make a bad situation worse.

Linda's story provides a classic example. One evening, after a night of heavy drinking, Clara wandered home at 2 A.M. She vomited on the living room rug, then passed out. Linda immediately cleaned up the mess and dragged Clara to the couch. She even wrapped a blanket around her friend. The following week, Clara did it again. This time, Linda decided to kick her out. Of course, after Clara had spent several days on the street, Linda couldn't help but worry and invited her back.

To prevent such situations, try to set clear limits. For example, decide on whether you can live with the person based on her or his behavior over time, rather than one particular incident. If you decide you cannot stand what's going on, give the person a realistic date to move out by, and stick to it. With severe mental disorders, you may have to be a bit flexible, however, as some of the behavior may really not be under the person's control. Whatever you do, decide based on your own health first, so that any help you do provide will be freely, rather than resentfully, given.

3. Have realistic expectations.

How do you cope with frequent relapses and numerous failed treatment attempts? Along with the first two suggestions, you have to keep in mind that severe addictions and mental disorders each carry a serious risk of fatal and near-fatal complications. Together, the risk increases dramatically. Rather than looking for someone to blame, you need to remember that the person you are supporting has a unique set of problems that are likely to be chronic. A rocky course is the norm, and while improvement is a likely outcome for many people, some may never recover. If both conditions are severe, you may have to consider your loved one as if he or she had cancer: Treatment might help, permanent remission is possible, but death is also always a possibility. Treasure the good times, and try to stay in the moment, rather than worrying about the future.

Joe

A Guiding Principle for Dealing with Stress and Trauma

In the 1970s, Martin Seligman and his colleagues began a series of experiments showing that exposure to bad events per se did not lead to significant emotional distress. Rather, trauma caused serious emotional harm largely if those who experienced the trauma felt they had no control over the situation and over their ability to deal with it. Being unable to control traumatic situations and experience was associated with a variety of adverse effects, including behavioral passivity, difficulty learning, and biochemical changes such as a rise in certain hormones that indicate a serious, sustained stress response and that can actually harm your body.

Seligman termed the syndrome resulting from uncontrollable trauma "learned helplessness." During my training in graduate school, I worked with Seligman as we extended these findings to physical disorders and addiction. In one dramatic demonstration of the physical effects of learned helplessness, we first exposed rats to controllable shock (they could push a lever to get away), uncontrollable shock (nothing they did made a difference), or no shock, then we injected the rats with cancer-causing cells. In the group of rats that were not exposed to the shock, the immune systems of about half of the rats were able to destroy the cancer cells. For rats that had control over the shock, nearly two-thirds survived, but only 27% of the rats that had received the equivalent amount of shock, but had no control over it, survived the cancer challenge. In addition, conquering stress actually led to a health improvement for the rats that had learned control.

My career in addiction research began as I continued studying learned helplessness. I found that after an experience of uncontrollable stress, rats dramatically increase their preference for alcohol—though not during the stressful situation. As we've seen, increases in drinking following trauma do not occur if the opioid receptors in the brain are blocked by naltrexone. Research increasingly confirms what occurred to me when I did the experiment: that traumatic stress causes the brain to release a natural painkiller, endorphins. Immediately following trauma, you may feel emotionally (as well as physically) numb and detached. High levels of endorphins cause the numbness, as if you had suddenly been injected with heroin or morphine. As the endorphins return to their prestress levels, you start to feel the full emotional and any physical pain of the trauma.

For example, after the Oklahoma City bombing in 1995, the town was initially a state of shock. Despite the best efforts of trauma experts, many people felt worse and worse as time went on. Depression among survivors was common. Symptoms of survivor's guilt, depression over the loss of friends or loved ones, and chronic irritability and fear continued to haunt the people who lived through it. Even among rescue workers who constantly deal with life-and-death situations, huge tragedies such as Oklahoma City often raise suicide rates, as the full impact of the trauma unfolds over time.

Of course, alcohol and other drugs are often used to kill such pain. However, when use is stopped, the pain returns, often even more severe than before, creating the familiar addictive cycle. Some people, like Clara, can also become "addicted" to certain behaviors that can lead to enhanced endorphin release. Perhaps Clara felt relief walking in that dangerous neighborhood because the stress of the high-risk behavior led to a high endorphin level. The dissociation that resulted helped quell her chronic anxiety. Viewed in this way, it is easier to understand why abused children often end up with abusive mates. Rather than reflecting some underlying masochism or self-defeating behavior, the person may actually be using the physical pain and stress to distract herself or himself from earlier emotional problems.

The relationship among stress, endorphins, addiction, trauma, and PTSD has led us to consider novel approaches to the problem. First, we now know that the more control you can give people under stress, the better they will do, both emotionally and physically. Sometimes, even in a situation where there is nothing you can actually change about what is happening, you can change your response to it. For example, someone who is seriously ill can respond to it by fighting, searching for all the options, living every moment to the fullest, and, if hope of a cure is lost, taking control over treatment and pain-management decisions. Someone who has to go to jail can respond by using the time to read everything he or she always meant to get to—or to get into better physical condition. Though both situations are still inherently stressful, those who respond as though they have some power over them tend to do better. You can use this principle to reduce stress during your recovery.

While some people in AA may find this research antithetical to their notion of surrendering control to God, there are ways in which both are actually similar. When you surrender to God, you ask to do His will—and you believe that good will come of it. Such faith can also be a type of control over the situation because when you believe, you believe that you will be taken care of and safe, not abandoned by God to unbearable pain.

There are also new pharmaceutical approaches to the problem. Naltrexone can reduce the numbing effects of your brain's endorphins, and if this is done in a safe and caring environment, someone experiencing PTSD can gradually learn to cope with traumatic memories without resorting to alcohol or high-risk behavior to avoid them. As they gain control over their feelings, they begin to experience true relief from their symptoms—and to work through, rather than around, their problems.

Researcher Bruce Perry, director of the Civitas Child Trauma Program and professor of child psychiatry at the Baylor College of Medicine in Texas, has begun using both naltrexone and clonidine (a drug used to reduce the physical symptoms of anxiety during opiate withdrawal) to treat children who have been recently traumatized and who are just developing the PTSD style of alternating between hyperanxiety and numbness. Though he has not yet done controlled studies, initial results seem promising. It may someday be possible to treat trauma survivors immediately after the traumatic event in a way that prevents the memory from being recalled so vividly and harmfully. We hope that this would reduce the odds of later addiction or other disorders.

Though the picture of dual diagnosis we've presented is somewhat bleak, there is wide variation in the severity and intensity of both aspects of the problem. Someone may have mild depression and addiction, and treatment here can have impressive results. The outcome for people with psychoses such as schizophrenia is less promising, but there are some remarkable new drugs for this condition in the pipeline. Some drugs that are already on the market have been miracles for this disorder because they don't have the deadening, pleasure-killing side effects that earlier drugs did. Having a dual diagnosis, or loving someone with one, is a real challenge—but we now have much more hope and more options for dealing with this condition than ever before.

Psychological Distress Inventory (PSI-32)

Following is a list of problems and complaints that people sometimes have. Please read each one carefully, and circle the number that best describes how much you were bothered by that problem during the past week. PLEASE CHOOSE ONLY ONE. For the past week, how much were you bothered by

	Not at all	A little bit	Moderately	Quite a bit	Extremely
1. Nervousness or shakiness inside	0	1	2	3	4
2. Unwanted thoughts, words, or ideas that won't leave your mind	0	1	2	3	4
3. Loss of sexual interest or pleasure	0	1	2	3	4
4. Trouble remembering things	0	1	2	3	4
5. Worrying about sloppiness or carelessness	0	1	2	3	4

	Not at all	A little bit	Moderately	Quite a bit	Extremely
6. Feeling easily annoyed or irritated	0	1	2	3	4
7. Feeling low in energy or slowed down	0	1	2	3	4
8. Thoughts of ending your life	0	1	2	3	4
9. Crying easily	0	1	2	3	4
10. Feeling shy or uneasy with the opposite sex	0	1	2	3	4
11. Feelings of being trapped or caught	0	1	2	3	4
12. Suddenly feeling scared for no reason	0	1	2	3	4
13. Blaming yourself for things	0	1	2	3	4
14. Feeling blocked in getting things done	0	1	2	3	4
15. Feeling lonely	0	1	2	3	4
16. Feeling blue	0	1	2	3	4
17. Worrying too much about things	0	1	2	3	4
18. Feeling no interest in things	0	1	2	3	4
19. Feeling fearful	0	1	2	3	4
20. Having your feelings be easily hurt	0	1	2	3	4
21. Feeling that others do not understand you or are unsympathetic	0	1	2	3	4
22. Feeling that people are unfriendly or dislike you	0	1	2	3	4
23. Having to do things very slowly to ensure correctness	0	1	2	3	4
24. Feeling inferior to others	0	1	2	3	4
25. Having trouble falling asleep	0	1	2	3	4
26. Having to check and doublecheck what you do	0	1	2	3	4
27. Difficulty making decisions	0	1	2	3	4
28. Having to avoid certain things, places, activities because they frighten you	0	1	2	3	4
29. Having your mind go blank	0	1	2	3	4
30. Feeling hopeless about the future	0	1	2	3	4
31. Having trouble concentrating	0	1	2	3	4
32. Feeling tense or keyed up	0	1	2	3	4

To score, add up the numbers related to the answers you gave. If you score over 30, you should see a professional for further evaluation.

Knowledge Is Power

- Many people with addictions also have mental disorders.
- Not all psychological distress represents a mental disorder. Such symptoms are common in early recovery, as the brain recovers from the drugs.
- Persistent or severe symptoms of psychological distress require treatment that addresses both the addiction and the mental disorder.
- Both substance-abuse and other psychological disorders can have fatal complications. It is important to recognize the severity of the condition and not to blame yourself if a loved one's illness is intractable.
- New medications are in the pipeline for both addictions and other mental illnesses, which offer more hope than ever before.

CHAPTER 23

A New Life: Maintaining Recovery in the Long Run

The police delivered Martin—who was so drunk he was barely able to stand—to the Treatment Research Center. He looked all of his 54 years and more, as he had been living on the streets for more than 20 years. Martin was known throughout the region as a particularly difficult patient. He had had dozens of failed attempts at sobriety. Typically, during an inpatient treatment stay, he would leave against medical advice just before he was to be discharged. He would be back drinking, often moments after leaving. On his last admission to the VA hospital, he threatened to "blow up the building, if I don't get something to stop the shakes." Martin was discharged immediately. During a binge, he began to swing wildly at a police officer who knew him well. It was at this time that he was carried to our center.

Normally, we would not try to treat this type of patient in an outpatient setting, but I had just given a talk to the treatment staff stating that nearly anyone can be safely and effectively treated without having to be hospitalized. I also encouraged my staff to never give up on someone who was asking for treatment. When Martin showed up, the staff looked at me and challenged me to back up what I had said, so I personally began to treat him. After helping him detoxify from alcohol (he needed 10 times the dose of Serax I normally prescribe), I began to see Martin once a week and offered him naltrexone to reduce the alcohol craving. Also, I encouraged him to return to attending daily AA meetings, which he said he had liked in the past. I referred him to a shelter, and thus began a remarkable year.

Martin stopped drinking and began a complete turnaround. He was polite and friendly. Physically, he looked a decade younger once he shaved and dressed neatly. Martin saw me every week for six months and then every other week after that. In many of our later sessions, we talked mostly of our mutual love for golf, as he related stories from his days as a caddy. He assured me that everything was going fine, that he felt wonderful. He began to work part-time at the shelter, and with the money he earned, he rented an apartment and bought insurance for a car his aunt had given to him. As you can imagine, both Martin and I felt quite good about ourselves for most of this year. It was the first time in nearly 30 years he had experienced sobriety for more than a month—and that month had been spent in a rehab.

Toward the end of the year, however, things began to fall apart. With his new car and apartment, Martin's friends from the street began to depend on him to drive them around and to use his place to party and crash for the night. He began to resent them, and he was losing enthusiasm for working at the shelter. In my enthusiasm to prove a point to the treatment staff, I failed to notice that Martin was not happy. He began to feel bored with his new lifestyle and all the attendant responsibilities. Also, at this time, I started to see him less frequently—just once every month or so. Martin began to hint that he was not prepared to leave treatment. At one session, Martin joked that he might be better off drinking because "at least you have less people bugging you to do things all day." Not long after that, Martin came to my office intoxicated, angry, and demanding to see me. When told I wasn't in, he angrily knocked over a tray of cookies and began to charge toward one of the counselors. Once again, the police came to the center, this time to take Martin away to another treatment program.

What happened to Martin holds lessons for people in recovery and their loved ones—not just for overconfident treatment providers like me. While Martin had broken his addiction to alcohol, he never really found alternative sources of pleasure or skills for coping with other people's demands. Martin continued to have a hard time relating to people without alcohol. His friends and his identity remained tied to his days on the street. In retrospect, while he appeared to be moving forward in his recovery, he was really just doing what he felt was expected of him and trying to please others. He chauffeured his aunt to appointments, he opened his apartment to old drinking buddies, and he got a job, perhaps to please me. During his drinking days, Martin depended on his aunt, friends, and shelters for support. Now the roles were reversed, and Martin found himself taking care of everyone around him. Looking back, I can see that even with me, he began rapidly to tell me what he thought I wanted to hear and to pretend that he was feeling better than he was.

In addition, as the year drew to a close, I was gradually withdrawing my support. I didn't see the warning signs that Martin needed more help if he was to sustain his recovery.

Stages of Recovery

The stages of recovery have not been as neatly delineated as the stages of change for starting it, but in general, the first step is to get off alcohol or other drugs, the second is to avoid relapse, and the third stage is to develop a well-adjusted functional lifestyle that doesn't involve the use of alcohol or other drugs. We know a lot more about how to achieve the first two stages than the third, but there are several important principles to keep in mind.

Recogizing That Giving Up Drugs Does Not Ensure Happiness

In the early stages of recovery, once withdrawal has passed, most people find themselves happy (often euphoric) that they have quit. During this phase, treatment providers, family members, and society in general, offer a lot of support. The New Testament story of the prodigal son comes to mind. Someone lost to addiction has been found, let us kill the fatted lamb for our lost brother. This attention can be intoxicating in its own right. Over time, however, the euphoria is replaced by an expectation that the lost son will assume a place in society with appropriate responsibilities. As Martin discovered, as he moved further from drinking, other pressures increased. For someone who had spent most of his adult life intoxicated, dealing with social responsibilities was a new experience and one for which he was not prepared.

There is also another, even more insidious side to giving up a relationship to alcohol and other drugs. Besides the obvious pleasure that drugs can cause, the chaotic lifestyle of an addict in the midst of addiction is quite exciting. For family members and significant others, it may seem incomprehensible that there could be anything positive about that life, but the thrill of evading consequences can be its own reward. Just as war veterans miss the excitement and camaraderie of escaping death, an addict may miss the thrills that came from living life in the fast lane. While dodging bullets may not seem to be much fun, lounging around becomes boring very quickly. Chasing drugs can give you a purpose and an identity just as deep as chasing success or relationships can—and it is really hard to change that part of yourself that involves your values and goals.

Finding Strategies for Recovery

During addiction, almost all your time is spent searching for drugs, getting high, or trying to avoid or cope with withdrawal. Booze and other drugs become the answer to anger, pain, hopelessness, celebration—everything. There is no magic formula for replacing such a powerful part of your life. Also, because treatment is so dependent on individual values and goals, research can't help much here. The various treatment programs discussed in this book have their own terminology for coping with this stage, but we can distill the essential elements into the following strategies: understanding, social support, self-nurturing, and developing new interests.

Understanding

The first and perhaps most important step for those in recovery and those who wish to help is to understand the natural ambivalence toward giving up addiction. People may not admit to themselves or others that they are unsure whether a clean and sober lifestyle is really better. If there is unresolved pain from a mental disorder, using drugs may be more comfortable than recovery, and stable abstinence will be difficult to achieve until the pain is relieved; similarly, if someone has nothing and no one "to live for," drugs may seem a rational choice. It's like the end of a love affair—whether the affair has been healthy or unhealthy, when it's over, you will miss it.

Viewed in this way, it is understandable that someone would be ambivalent about giving up addiction. A void is created where once intense passion existed.

By understanding this ambivalence, you can help to resolve it in favor of continued recovery. Acknowledging it and not judging yourself (or the person in recovery) for it is the first step in this process.

Social Support

Because of decreased access to treatment, family members and friends are increasingly important in teaching recovering people how to use coping skills and helping them to reinforce these skills. The most important message you can convey is that it is OK to ask for help. Sometimes a sympathetic ear is all that is needed. At other times, direct advice for dealing with a specific challenge is important. In any case, as the recovering addict experiences and works through each challenge, her or his confidence will grow, and the chance of relapse will lessen.

As a support person, you may have to be patient, as initial attempts to deal with problems may be inappropriate or short-sighted. In Martin's case, he was unable to speak up for himself and say no to the demands of his family and friends. Also, once he stopped drinking, he found it hard to ask for help in dealing with other fears and frustrations. Rather than ask for assistance, Martin lashed out at those close to him. Fortunately, after the incident where he came to our center drunk and attacked the staff, we realized what the problem had been. Following a brief hospitalization, Martin lived in a halfway house with other recovering addicts, where he was taught that it was OK to assert his needs and to ask for what he needed. The halfway house provided an ideal, safe environment where he could learn by trial and error how to cope without resorting to alcohol or threats of violence.

Self-nurturing

Let's face it—part of life is dealing with serious problems. Kids get in trouble at school, parents become ill, and businesses downsize, leaving you without a job. Through no fault of your own, bad things happen. How you respond to these challenges, however, is under some personal control. The ability to master a stressful situation depends largely on your perception of the event. People who tend to blame themselves, who see the whole world in a negative light, and who believe that the future looks bleak are less able to cope with negative circumstances. Those who are more hopeful—who blame the problem on rotten luck and figure it will be better next time—are much more successful. While people have inborn temperamental predispositions that shape how they see the world, research finds that you can actually teach yourself optimism and improve your ability to handle stress. Numerous studies have found that pessimists are more likely to suffer emotional and physical distress, whereas optimists bounce back following negative experiences. The key is to learn to nurture yourself during stressful times. The following tips can help:

- *Do not blame yourself for a bad event.* While it is important to take appropriate responsibility, it serves no useful purpose to beat yourself over what happened. Guilt is not an effective way to motivate yourself.

- *When bad events occur, do not overgeneralize.* For example, if you are criticized by your spouse, it does not mean you are a bad person or a bad spouse. Look at the specifics of the criticism, and address the particulars. Making one mistake doesn't make you a mistake, and behaving poorly occasionally doesn't make you a bad person. You can do better next time. Another key: When something goes wrong in one part of your life, don't pile it on by thinking about problems in other areas. Deal with what's in front of you now.

- *When bad events occur, do not project more bad events into the future.* If you lose a job, it does not mean you will never get another. Often, job loss opens up new possibilities—your next job may be better paying, more enjoyable, or both. You have no way of knowing the future, but as AA puts it, "When one door closes, another opens up (but it can be hell in the hallway!)."

- *Treat yourself as you would treat a beloved friend.* When feeling down, ask yourself what you would tell a friend, how you would encourage your friend, and what healthy activities you would suggest you and your friend do together. Then engage in these healthy activities, such as exercise, meditation, listening to music, and so on.

- *Coach yourself.* Often, calling a "time out" can break the momentum of a losing situation and give you time to regroup. A time out can make a real difference to the outcome of the game, and it is just as important to be a good coach for yourself.

- *Don't listen to your inner voices of blame and self-hate.* Lifting the burden of self-hate, and recognizing the validity of your own desire to feel OK are among the most important tasks of recovery. One good technique for doing this is again, to detach yourself from the voice in your head that speaks it: If you feel that "nobody loves me, everybody hates me, I'm going to go eat worms," as the song goes, it can really help to recognize that this is just a thought in your head, not a vision of the truth. The more you tell the voice, "Thanks for sharing, now shut up," the better you will feel, and the weaker it will get. Another good technique is to visualize exiting the "obsess" or "urge" or "self-hate" program as if it were on a computer. Think of moving the mouse to the file menu, choosing exit, then opening a better or more interesting program. Turn your mind to something else. You may need to do this a few times before it clicks in, but the more you do it, the easier it gets.

Developing New Interests

Because quitting drugs leaves a huge hole in your life, it's important to find something equally large to fill it. Otherwise, over time, you may forget the pain and the horrors of your addiction and begin fondly to recall the pleasure and the fun parts of drug use. This is where your dreams come into play. Remember what you longed for as a kid? Remember the crazy ideas you had when you were younger? Now is the time to start seriously thinking about taking action on them.

Everyone needs to feel important and as though they matter in life. Some do this primarily through their relationships—with their partner, family, friends, and children. Others do it through their careers or through volunteer work, which makes them feel as though they are giving something back to society. Yet others find that God and religious or spiritual practice offer meaning. It doesn't matter what anyone thinks, whether you succeed in worldly terms or not—it just matters that you find something worth pursuing that makes you feel challenged, engaged, and worthwhile when you participate in it. Research finds that the happiest people are those who pursue nonmaterialistic goals, who seek things like "being of service" or "being the best spouse/partner/parent/friend I can" or "creating beauty."

Don't exclude any idea—people have returned to college in their 50s and 60s and made important contributions; some haven't written a word until they reach their 40s and then become successful writers. If you use just half the energy you devoted to getting high and avoiding getting in trouble for it, you will probably do very well in most things you put your mind to. Also, if one thing doesn't work out, there are always others. If you are not anhedonic, the world should be infinitely interesting and full of possibilities, and if you are anhedonic, you should seek help so that you feel better.

A SPIRITUAL AWAKENING

I am often asked, "What does one need to be successful in treatment?" I respond, partly joking, "a competent doctor, an understanding therapist, good friends, a supportive partner (or failing that a good lawyer!), and a forgiving priest/rabbi/etc." While the doctor, therapist, friends, and partner are obvious, I am increasingly impressed with the need for reconciliation in the process of recovery. Some people refer to spiritual awakening, or finding meaning in life, but from my perspective, it is your relationships to others, the environment, and yourself that defines long-term recovery.

A couple of years ago, we invited women who were in our treatment program for crack-addicted women with young children to come to an open house to celebrate the success of the program. Several women with two or more years of being clean were asked to make a few remarks. When asked what the most important factor in their recovery was, they thanked the treatment staff, supportive friends, and spouses, but most importantly, they uniformly thanked God or some higher power for helping them stay away from crack. Now, I have come to expect such a response from recovering addicts who are involved in a 12-step program, but many of these women didn't participate in AA, NA, or CA. When I talked to the women in greater depth, the consistent theme of long-term success was the ability to form loving relationships in the world again. To them, success in treatment felt like a rebirth, a miracle—something that could only come from God.

When describing their lives now, most admitted that they continued to make mistakes and suffer consequences, but I noticed that they could describe these events and continue to smile. Despite mistakes, they felt an inner peace and a sense of being loved and accepted. It was truly amazing to see this in women who several years earlier had fallen into one of society's most despised groups: crack-addicted welfare mothers.

I suspect that the biggest casualty of addiction is the severing of connections to other people, the world, and oneself. I do not believe that addicts start out with some spiritual deficit, but the long-term consequences of addiction can lead to one. While I have discovered medications to reduce drug craving and relapse and have written manuals to enhance psychosocial treatment, it seems to me that recovery is more than simply the absence of drug use. It is about reconciliation. I think about one patient, Jane, who was reconciled with her daughter whom she hadn't seen in 15 years. The joy and gratitude expressed in that reunion remind me why I am in this field and of the mysteries that still remain in recovery.

Joe

Final Thoughts

To replace the passionate attachment to drugs, an addict needs to redirect these feelings to mending severed relationships and to establishing new ones. If the choices in life are like a breakfast buffet, the person in recovery must learn that there is more to life than the scrambled eggs, you might say. With the help of supportive friends, family members, lovers, therapists, and/or spiritual or religious counselors, you can learn to sample various foods from the buffet table. Try different activities, explore new relationships, call old friends, and forgive yourself and your family. Passion itself is not bad, but be passionate about things that enhance your life, not diminish it.

We hope that you have found these tips and our thoughts on finding and choosing treatment helpful. Recovery can be a long and difficult journey—but don't ever give up. The farther you get from alcohol and other drugs, the better your life tends to become. We can't stress enough how much better you will feel once your active alcoholism or other addiction is truly behind you. The early stages may feel like self-denial, but once you've got a handle on recovery, you'll realize that it's probably one of the best things you've ever done for yourself. As they say in AA, don't quit before the miracle!

APPENDIX:
Treatment and Self-help Resources

Suggested Reading

Alcoholics Anonymous, *Alcoholics Anonymous: The Story of How Many Thousands of Men and Women Recovered from Alcoholism.* New York: Alcoholics Anonymous World Services, 1976, third edition. The "Big Book": the original.

Alcoholics Anonymous, *Twelve Steps and Twelve Traditions.* New York: Alcoholics Anonymous World Services, 1988. The AA guide to the steps.

Fisher, Carrie, *Postcards from the Edge.* New York: Pocket Books, 1987. An accurate and hilarious look at life inside a Minnesota rehab.

Greenberger, Dennis, and Christine Padesky, *Mind over Mood: A Cognitive Therapy Treatment Manual for Clients.* New York: Guilford Press, 1995. A useful book of cognitive-therapy techniques, which can be used on your own or with a therapist.

Hallowell, Edward, and John Ratey, *Driven to Distraction: Recognizing and Coping with Attention Deficit Disorder from Childhood through Adulthood.* New York: Touchstone, 1994. A good guide to living with ADD.

Harris, Judith Rich, *The Nurture Assumption: Why Children Turn Out the Way They Do.* New York: Free Press, 1998. For all parents who think they caused their children's problems: You didn't!

Horvath, T. *Sex, Drugs, Gambling and Chocolate: A Workbook for Overcoming Addictions.* California: Impact Publishers, 1998. Another good cognitive-therapy recovery workbook.

Jamison, Kaye Redfield, *An Unquiet Mind.* New York: Random House, 1997. An autobiographical account of a psychiatrist's own experience with manic-depression—and why even with all she knew, she had a hard time convincing herself to stay on medication.

Kirkpatrick, Jean, *Turnabout: New Help for the Woman Alcoholic.* New York: Barricade Books, 1999. The basic text for Women for Sobriety.

Kishline, Audrey, *Moderate Drinking: The Moderation Management Guide for People Who Want to Reduce Their Drinking.* New York: Crown, 1996. The basic text for Moderation Management.

Klein, Donald, and Paul Wender, *Understanding Depression: A Complete Guide to Its Diagnosis and Treatment.* New York: Oxford University Press, 1993. A good, short book on depression and its treatment.

Kramer, Peter, *Listening to Prozac*. New York: Penguin, 1997. The classic book on the new antidepressants and their psychological and philosophical impact.

McGovern, George, *Terry: My Daughter's Life and Death Struggle with Alcoholism*. New York: Plume, 1997. The former presidential candidate's memoir of his daughter's fatal struggle with alcoholism and the problems his family had dealing with it.

Miller, William, and Reid Hester, *Handbook of Alcoholism Treatment Approaches: Effective Alternatives*. Boston: Allyn and Bacon, 1995. A book for professionals in the field, but readable enough and informative enough for anyone who wants more data about the best treatment for alcoholism.

Peele, Stanton, *The Meaning of Addiction*, Boston: Lexington Books, 1985. If you are curious about the nature of addiction and can't understand why everyone isn't enamored of the disease model, check out this lucid and fascinating account. Peele's later work is a bit off-putting, but this is brilliant.

Peele, Stanton, and Archie Brodsky, *Love and Addiction*. New York: Penguin, 1991. Another classic. Peele and Brodsky set out to depathologize addiction by comparing it to love, and they wound up pathologizing love and inadvertently helping spur the codependency movement; readable and informative about addiction and relationships.

Prochaska, James, John Norcross, and Carlo DiClemente, *Changing for Good: A Revolutionary Six Stage Program for Overcoming Bad Habits and Moving your Life Positively Forward*. New York: Avon Books, 1994. The discoverers of the "Stages of Change" give their own account of their research and how you can apply it to changing any bad habit or addiction.

Rapoport, Judith, *The Boy Who Couldn't Stop Washing: The Experience and Treatment of Obsessive Compulsive Disorder*. New York: Signet, 1991. Anyone with obsessive-compulsive disorder (OCD), or with a loved one with this disorder, should read this book.

Robertson, Nan, *Getting Better: Inside Alcoholics Anonymous*. New York: Ballantine, 1988. Robertson's memoir of her own alcoholism, her recovery through AA, and the history of AA.

Schwartz, Jeffrey, *Brain Lock: Free Yourself from Obsessive Compulsive Behavior*. New York: Regan Books, 1996. Another good book on OCD, but a bit repetitive and slightly antimedication.

Secular Organizations for Sobriety, *Sobriety Handbook, the SOS Way: An Introduction to Secular Organizations for Sobriety/ Save Ourselves*. Oakland, CA: Lifering Press, 1997. The main text for SOS.

Snyder, Solomon, *Drugs and the Brain*. New York: Scientific American Library, 1996. If you want to know more about how drugs affect the brain, it's hard to do better than to read this account by the Nobel laureate who not only discovered the endorphin receptor, but also took LSD and describes the experience here.

Trimpey, Jack, *The Small Book: A Revolutionary Alternative for Overcoming Alcohol and Drug Dependence*. New York: Delacorte Press, 1992. The original main text for Rational Recovery.

Trimpey, Jack, *Rational Recovery: The New Cure for Substance Addiction.* New York: Pocket Books, 1996. The second, revised main text for Rational Recovery.

Weil, Andrew, and Winifred Rosen, *From Chocolate to Morphine: Everything You Need to Know about Mind-Altering Drugs.* Boston: Houghton-Mifflin, 1993. A great drug-education book for teens, which tells the truth, rather than the myths.

Zimmer, Lynn, and John Morgan, *Marijuana Myths, Marijuana Facts.* New York: Lindesmith Center, 1997. If you want to find out what the research really says on marijuana, check out this book.

Other Resources

Please note: We have listed these resources here in order to help you get further information about treatment. A listing here does not mean an endorsement from the authors. Where we have noticed biases, we have mentioned them, but this does not mean that there aren't some we haven't spotted.

University of Pennsylvania
http://www.med.upenn.edu/recovery/
(215) 222-3200

This is our website and program! Includes information on naltrexone, live chat, a self-test, links to the sites listed here, and updated, new material not available at publication time.

Accreditors of Treatment Centers

CARF
The Rehabilitation Accreditation Commission
4891 E. Grant Road
Tucson, AZ 85712
(520) 325-1044 (Voice/TDD)
www.carf.org

A smaller accreditor, with a less consumer-friendly website.

JCAHO
Joint Commission on the Accreditation of Healthcare Organizations
One Renaissance Boulevard
Oakbrook Terrace, IL 60181
www.jcaho.org

This website includes a searchable quality-check database. You can put in the name of the center you are considering, and its status and how to read the information will be located for you. Facilities for alcoholism and other forms of addiction are under the category "behavioral health." Note: If a center isn't listed, it doesn't mean that it is necessarily of low quality, but simply that it hasn't attempted accreditation.

AIDS Information

CDC AIDS Hotline
(800) 342-AIDS (toll free)
http://www.ashastd.org/nah/nah.html

Dual Diagnosis Information

Dual Diagnosis Website
http://www.erols.com/ksciacca
This site, run by a psychologist with her own private practice, includes directories of treatment programs for people with both addiction and another mental disorder.

National Alliance for the Mentally Ill
http://www.nami.org/helpline/disord2.htm
(800) 950-NAMI (toll free)
This advocacy group for the mentally ill has information on its web page about those who have both substance-abuse problems and other mental illnesses, as well as information on the latest medication developments and treatments. NAMI is also a good source of information about how to deal with abusive treatment.

Therapist Information Network
http://www.mental-health.com/PsychScapes/tin.html
A searchable directory of therapists, including their self-described specialties and approaches.

Methadone

Advocates for Recovery through Medicine (ARM)
P.O. Box 164
Davison, MI 48423
(615) 354-1320
www.ARM-advocates.org
A new patient-focused methadone advocacy group, which recently received funding from the Drug Policy Foundation.

American Methadone Treatment Association
217 Broadway
New York, NY
(212) 566-5555
Organization of methadone providers, which lobbies for better and more methadone treatment.

NAMA
National Alliance of Methadone Advocates

435 Second Avenue
New York, NY 10010
(212) 595-NAMA
www.methadone.org

This website includes two national lists of methadone providers, links to other methadone information websites, and information on both travel for people on methadone and consumer advocacy; also offers links to needle-exchange and harm-reduction sites; best place to start for methadone information.

Miscellaneous

EPRA
Employment Program for Recovering Alcoholics
225 W. 34th Street
New York, NY 10001
(212) 947-1471

A unique New York State program, which helps recovering alcoholics and those addicted to both alcohol and other drugs (not for nonalcoholic drug users only) find satisfying work; helps people get scholarships, linked to New York State rehabilitative services; 12-step oriented.

Sobriety High School in Minnesota
5250 W. 73rd Street
Edina, MN 55439
(612) 831-7138

Sobriety High, Minnesota, is a public school for teens recovering from alcohol and other drug problems.

Sobriety High, Marin County
P.O. Box 4925
San Rafael, CA 94913
Contact: Mary Jane Burke
(415) 499-0581

A charter public school in California for teens recovering from alcohol and other drug problems.

Plano, Texas has created "Serenity High," which was set to open in October 1999. It is modeled on the Minnesota Sobriety High. For information, contact Juli Ferraro at (972) 569-6530.

National Hotlines and Websites
with Treatment Center Referral Databases

Alcoholism and Addiction Resource Guide
www.hubplace.com/addictions

A searchable database of mostly 12-step-oriented treatment facilities. Created by a parent with an addicted child and a treatment-center owner, this site is sponsored by various for-profit treatment facilities. Advantages: It lists the specialties offered by each center and the center's self-reported philosophy on confrontation. Disadvantages: Because treatment centers advertise here, they shape the information about themselves.

The Drug and Alcohol Prevention Network
www.drugnet.net
Don't let the hideous design of the homepage for this site deter you — its links page is the mother of all addiction-links pages and is a good one to bookmark for clicking onto other pages; links to treatment, self-help groups, national and local organizations, research journals, and news organizations. Note: These links are not screened — some disreputable organizations are listed.

Drug and Alcohol Recovery Network (DARN)
www.darnweb.com
This website has a searchable national database, including a variety of treatment types with no discernable bias except perhaps in favor of those who advertise on it.

National Clearinghouse for Alcohol and Drug Information
Substance Abuse and Mental Health Services Association Treatment
http://www.health.org/search/treatdir97.htm
This database is searchable by location and treatment type. Some information may be out of date. No particular bias, but also no information on the quality of care at these centers.

National Recovery Network
http://www.recoverynetwork.com/links/linksdrugabuse.html
A television and radio network focused on dealing with addictions; includes another listing of drug-treatment centers and organizations — primarily, but not exclusively 12 step.

Phoenix House Foundation's National Helpline
(800) HELP-111 (toll free)
www.drughelp.org
Provides referrals to treatment facilities, self-help groups, and family-support organizations. Has a searchable database on its website. Because it is run by a major therapeutic community, it may be biased toward this type of treatment (a search of New York for treatment comes out with Phoenix House as the first listing, for example) — but it includes and refers to all types of care.

Practical Recovery
http://www.practicalrecovery.com
A site offering low-cost non-AA treatment and referrals.

Needle Exchange and Other Harm Reduction

National List of Needle Exchange Programs
http://www.safeworks.org/Programs/
  This list isn't complete, but it's a good place to start until there is a better one.

The Lindesmith Center
www.lindesmith.org
  Funded by George Soros, this site has a great deal of information about harm reduction, methadone, needle exchange, and drug-policy options.

Notable Minnesota Model Treatment Centers

Betty Ford Center
(800) 854-9211 (toll free)
(760) 773-4100
www.bettyfordcenter.org
  Website lists affiliated centers and counselors in other states, as well as information on the Betty Ford Center Program, a pioneer of Minnesota Model treatment; also includes a list of professionals who help families do the "Johnson style" intervention.

Hazelden
15245 Pleasant Valley Road
P.O. Box 11
Center City, MN 55012-0011
(651) 213-4000
(800) 257-7810 (toll free)
www.hazelden.org
  Facilities in Minnesota, Florida, Illinois, and New York, including specialized teen treatment and women's treatment.

High Watch Farm
62 Carter Road
P.O. Box 607
Kent, CT 06757
(888) HWF-KENT (toll free) or (860) 927-3772
  The very first residential AA center. Provides low-cost AA counseling and meetings.

Religious Recovery Organizations

CHRISTIAN

Christians in Recovery, Inc.
http://www.christians-in-recovery.com
    Currently constructing a directory of Christian treatment centers nation-
wide—includes directory of Christian counselors. (Note: This organization
includes an e-mail list for 12-step groups for "overcoming homosexuality.")

Glide Memorial Church
United Methodist Church
330 Ellis Street
San Francisco, CA 94102
(415) 771-6300
www.glide.org
    This largely African-American church has long focused on helping people in
its community deal with substance abuse, poverty, and homelessness. It offers
support groups, meals, shelter, and treatment in conjunction with the Haight-
Ashbury Free Clinic, which is designed to be culturally sensitive; includes separate men's and women's groups; may be able to provide information on other
churches with similar programs.

National Association for Christian Recovery
P.O. Box 215
Brea, CA 92822-0215
(714) 529-6227 (Voice)
(714) 529-1120 (fax)
www.christianrecovery.com
    This group links many Christian, 12-step-oriented support groups and
churches. (Note: This group also supports 12-step groups for "overcoming
homosexuality.")

Recovery Options
(800) 662-8273 (toll free)
    Offers referrals to Christian programs.

JEWISH

JACS (Jewish Alcoholics, Chemically dependent persons, and Significant others)
http://www.jacsweb.org/
426 West 58th Street
New York, NY 10019
(212) 397-4197
    A 12-step-focused self-help group for Jewish people dealing with substance
problems; lists local meetings and information about how to integrate Judaism
and the steps.

Research Universities with Addiction Programs

The National Institute on Drug Abuse (NIDA) is currently setting up a national network for clinical trials, which will be similar to the cancer-treatment network run by the National Cancer Institute at some of the best hospitals in the country. It is not known yet when it will be up and running. For information, check out the NIDA website at www.nida.nih.gov, or call (301) 443-1124.

Note: The research that the following centers are doing varies from time to time, and there may or may not be any open treatment studies that meet your needs when you call. Instead, they may be studying something like "how the brain looks during craving" and may need subjects but not offer treatment. Be sure to ask precisely what a researcher is studying and what this entails, to make sure that it meets your needs when you consider any research participation.

Most of the centers listed here do have ongoing treatment research programs—and if they don't have anything open when you call, they may be able to refer you to quality care in the community.

Also, unfortunately, most of these websites are oriented toward students and other researchers more than they are to people seeking to participate in studies. The information you want may be a little hard to find—even if it's actually there somewhere. We've tried to include the best URLs and phone numbers, but it may take a little digging and transferring around to get to the right place.

CenterWatch Inc.
http://www.centerwatch.com/
(617) 247-2327
This is a searchable index of current clinical trials—including those at research universities and the National Institutes of Health (NIH, which includes NIDA). It is not always complete, however, but is a good place to start.

Brown University Center for Alcohol and Addiction Studies
Box GBH
Providence, RI 02912
(401) 444-1800
http://www.caas.brown.edu/

Drug Abuse Research Center
University of California—Los Angeles
1640 S. Sepulveda Boulevard, Suite 200
Los Angeles, CA 90025
(310) 445-0874 (voice)
(310) 473-7885 (fax)
http://www.medsch.ucla.edu/som/npi/DARC/

The Ernest Gallo Clinic and Research Center
Department of Neurology
University of California, San Francisco

http://egcrc.ucsf.edu
(888) 805-UCSF (toll free)

Drug Dependence Research Center
University of California—San Francisco
Box CPR-0984
Langley Porter Psychiatric Institute
San Francisco, CA 94143-0984
(415) 476-7216 (administration)
(415) 476-7471 (clinical laboratory)
http://itsa.ucsf.edu/~ddrc/
    This one includes a directory of free and low-cost treatment in the San Francisco area.

University of California—San Diego
http://www.attc.ucsd.edu/

The Center for the Neurobiology of Addiction
UCSF Box 0984
San Francisco, CA 94143-0984
415/476-7878
http://www.ucsf.edu/~cnba/

Columbia/New York Psychiatric Institute
Columbia-Presbyterian Medical Center
Office of Clinical Trials
622 West 168th Steet
PH 15 Center
New York, NY 10032
(212) 305-5063 (voice)
(212) 305-5065 (fax)
E-mail: mil7@columbia.edu

Addiction Research and Treatment Services
University of Colorado School of Medicine
UCHSC
4200 East 9th Avenue
Denver, CO 80262
(303) 372-0000 (main university number)
(800) 621-7621 (toll free)
http://www.uchsc.edu/sm/psych/dept/research/arts.htm
    Research-based adolescent treatment is one of the specialties here.

University of Maryland College Park
Center for Substance Abuse Research (CESAR)

4321 Hartwick Road, Suite 501
College Park, MD 20740
(301) 403-8329 (voice)
(301) 403-8342 (fax)
E-mail: CESAR@cesar.umd.edu
http://www.cesar.umd.edu
This site includes a cute cartoon, which offers referrals to treatment both on campus and across the state.

The University of New Mexico Center on Alcoholism, Substance Abuse and Addictions (CASAA)
2350 Alamo SE
Albuquerque, NM 87106
(505) 768-0100 (For information on entering treatment at UNM, try 505-768-0150.)
http://casaa.unm.edu
State-of-the-art alcoholism and substance-abuse treatment. CASAA is directed by William Miller, a pioneer in alcoholism treatment research and co-author of the alcoholism treatment effectiveness review, *Handbook of Alcoholism Treatment*.

Information on CRAFT Family Therapy
www.unm.edu/~craft
This site contains citations and abstracts on CRAFT and information about participation in studies of it at the University of New Mexico; somewhat technical, though.

University of Pittsburgh Adolescent Alcohol Research Center
http://www.pitt.edu/~paarc/paarc.html
Presently conducting research on teen drinking problems and their treatment. Also at the University of Pittsburgh:
Center for Education and Drug Abuse Research (CEDAR)
Western Psychiatric Institute and Clinic
3811 O'Hara Street
Pittsburgh, PA 15213
(412) 624-1060

CEDAR Research Center
St. Francis Medical Center
45th & Penn Avenue
10th Floor East Building
Pittsburgh, PA 15201
(412) 622-6178 (fax)
(412) 622-6174 (voice)

Kay Ryan, Director of Clinical Trials
New York University
(212) 263-7961
http://www.med.nyu.edu/IRB/res-subjects.html

Rutgers University
P.O. Box 969
Piscataway, NJ 08855-0969
(908) 445-0941
    Pioneer in alcoholism research; moderate drinking, CBT, and MET
approaches available; treatment available through outside studies, as well.

Alcohol and Drug Abuse Institute
University of Washington
3937 15th Avenue NE
Seattle, WA 98105-6696
(206) 543-0937
http://weber.u.washington.edu/~adai/index.html

Alan Marlatt
Addictive Behaviors Research Center
University of Washington
(206) 685-1395
E-mail: marlatt@u.washington.edu

Addiction Research Unit
Department of Psychology
University at Buffalo, SUNY-Buffalo
Buffalo, NY 14260-4110
(716) 645-3801 (fax)
http://wings.buffalo.edu/aru/

Research Institute on Addictions
1021 Main Street
Buffalo, NY 14203
(716) 887-2566

Institute of Behavioral Research
Texas Christian University
TCU Box 298740
Fort Worth, TX 76129
(817) 257-7000 (university main number)

Brookhaven National Laboratory
P.O. Box 5000
Upton, NY 11973

(888) BNL-RING (888-265-7464) (toll free)

Medications development for cocaine and other addictions; currently request-ing approval from the FDA to use the NMDA-receptor-blocking drug, gamma-vinyl-GABA (vigabatrin) in cocaine-addiction treatment. Clinical trials may be open by the time you see this listing.

Emory University
http://www.emory.edu/WHSC/MED/PSYCHIATRY/GADrug/gadrughm.htm

Clinical Neuroscience Research Unit
Yale University School of Medicine
Connecticut Mental Health Center
34 Park Street
New Haven, CT 06519
(203) 974-7560
(888) 622-CNRU

Self-help Group Listings

American Self Help Clearinghouse
(973) 625-9565
(212) 586-5770
http://www.cmhc.com/selfhelp/

Online database of self-help groups for everything from "Aarskog syndrome" (whatever that is!) to xeroderma pigmentosum. Includes listings of 12-step groups for professionals such as doctors, lawyers, pharmacists, even Realtors, as well as alternative groups.

National Self Help Clearinghouse
(212) 354-8525
http://www.selfhelpweb.org

Maintains a comprehensive list of self-help organizations and contacts for them, though the list itself is not accessible on the Web.

Recovery Alternatives Page
http://www.atlcom.net/night

This site links to many non-12-step self-help groups and is a good place to start if you are checking them out and don't know which one might suit you best.

Self-help Groups

Al-Anon Family Groups / Alateen
(800) 586-9996 (toll free)
www.al-anon.org

Offers 12-step support for families of alcoholics.

Alcoholics Anonymous
(212) 870-3400
http://www.alcoholics-anonymous.org/
   To find AA in your community without the Web, look for "Alcoholics Anonymous" in your local phone book. The website includes the full text of several AA pamphlets and local contact numbers around the world.

Chemically Dependent Anonymous
http://www.cdaweb.org/
   For the person who can't decide what her or his primary addiction is—or just wants one 12-step group to deal with them all.

Cocaine Anonymous
(800) 347-8998 (toll free)
http://www.ca.org
   The 12-step program for those whose drug of choice is cocaine.

Dual Recovery Anonymous Central Service
1302 Division Steet
Nashville, TN 37203
(888) 869-9230 (toll free)
http://dualrecovery.org
   A 12-step program for people with alcohol or other drug problems and mental illness.

Marijuana Anonymous
(212) 459-4423
http://www.marijuana-anonymous.org/
   For pot smokers who can't quit—a 12-step program. Local phone numbers and meeting times are available on the website.

Moderation Management
(425) 844-8228
(212) 330-7094
(212) 635-8157
http://comnet.org/mm
   Self-help group for those who want to moderate their drinking.

Narcotics Anonymous
(818) 773-9999
http://www.na.org
   The website includes basic information on NA and contact information for meetings around the world.

Rational Recovery
(530) 621-4374

http://www.rational.org/recovery/?plain

The RR site includes information on becoming involved with RR and plays a nice jazz tune to boot. However, if you have limited memory on your computer, it's likely to crash.

SMART
(216) 292-0220
www.smartrecovery.org

Not as jazzy as RR's but easier to load; includes an online real-time meeting, material on the program, and a list of treatment programs and counselors that refer people to SMART and use cognitive-behavioral and motivational-enhancement therapy in their treatments.

SOS
(310) 821-8430
www.unhooked.com

This site includes a great deal of material about the SOS program, including meeting information, online meetings, a tool-kit for recovery, and a link to a full-text downloadable version of an SOS book on recovery.

Women for Sobriety
(215) 536-8026
www.womenforsobriety.org

A feminist alternative (for women only) to 12-step programs. Website contains basic information on the program, use the phone number for local meeting information.

Specialized Rehabs and Referrals to Hard-to-Find Organizations and Information

GAY AND LESBIAN RESOURCES

Pride Institute
101 Fifth Avenue, Suite 10D
New York, NY 10003
(800) 54-Pride (toll free)
(212) 243-5565

A 12-step-based treatment center exclusively for gays, lesbians, bisexuals, and transgendered people.

Project Connect
Lesbian and Gay Community Services Center
One Little West 12th Street
New York, NY 10014
(212) 620-7310
www.gaycenter.org

Free counseling and treatment referrals for lesbians and gays with substance-abuse problems. Many 12-step meetings (including one for sadomasochists in 12-step recovery from substance addiction!) are also held at the center.

SUCE (Substance Use Counseling and Education) Program
Gay Men's Health Crisis
119 West 24th Street
New York, NY 10011
(212) 367-1350
www.gmhc.org
Harm-reduction counseling for gay men who use drugs—particularly those concerned with the impact of drug use on their sexual behavior.

RR-Based Treatment: Inpatient and Intensive Outpatient Rational Recovery Rehabs

There are three of these: one in Sacramento, one in Chicago, and one in Orange County, California. For further information, call (916) 484-STOP, (847) 328-0100, or (916) 621-2667.

Referrals to Therapists Who Work with MET/CBT and Moderation for Alcohol and Other Drugs

Behavior Therapy Associates
http://www.behaviortherapy.com/
This site is run by Reid Hester, who co-authored the seminal review of alcoholism treatment efficacy, *Handbook of Alcoholism Treatment Approaches*. It includes a list of therapists who will work with patients to achieve moderation (they all do MET/CBT work, as well) and free software to monitor your drinking on a personal digital assistant. See also the SMART recovery website listed previously.

Referrals to Oxford Houses

Oxford House
ICA Group Foundation
P.O. Box 994
Great Falls, VA 22066-0994
(703) 450-6501
(800) 486-6488 (toll free)
www.icagroup.org

The group's website has a national and an international directory of hundreds of Oxford houses, which are self-managed houses for 12-step program members.

General Information

Web of Addictions
http://www.well.com/user/woa/
Offers many links and lots of information about substance problems.

Join Together
www.jointogether.org
An organization for activism related to substance-abuse problems, but the activism is geared toward banning liquor ads and preventing drug use in schools, rather than the "AIDS won't wait: Needle Exchange Now" type of activism.

Notes

Chapter 1

1. Beer and its relationship to civilization: Vallee, Bert, "Alcohol in the Western world," *Scientific American*, (June 1998), pp.79–85.
2. Humans throughout history and even animals get high: Siegel, Ronald, *Intoxication*, New York: E.P. Dutton, 1989, pp. 11, 16.
3. Chukchee drink urine of mushroom takers: Ibid., pp. 66–67. Actually, the Chukchee apparently discovered this connection because reindeer are connoisseurs of these mushrooms, and they are also attracted to human urine, so much so that visitors to the area must be warned against urinating outside if reindeer are present.
4. Percentages of people who get hooked: The National Institute on Drug Abuse (NIDA) estimates that 10% of cocaine users become addicted. NIDA household survey comparisons show these figures when you compare people using now to ever used; Epidemiologic Catchment Survey finds these percentages also. Heroin figures from NIDA and also derived from Lee Robins's studies of Vietnam veterans. About 20% of U.S. soldiers used heroin in Vietnam: Of those who became physically dependent while in the military, only 12% remained addicted after they returned to the United States, despite access to heroin, and, in some cases, occasional use of it. Robins, Lee, "Vietnam veterans' rapid recovery from heroin addiction: A fluke or normal expectation?" *Addiction* (1993), 88:1041–1054.
5. Caffeine second to water as a drink most consumed: Braun, Stephen, *Buzz: The science and lore of alcohol and caffeine.* Penguin, 1996, p. 108.
6. Cocaine no more addictive than potato chips: Van Dyke, Craig, and Robert Byck, "Cocaine," *Scientific American* (Mar 1982), p. 140.
7. For a description of the validity and reliablity of the screening tests, see Saunders, JB, OG Aasland, TF Babor, JR de la Fuente, and M Grant, "Development of the Alcohol Use Disorders Identification Test (AUDIT): WHO Collaborative Project on Early Detection of Persons with Harmful Alcohol Consumption," *Addiction* (1993), 88:791–804; and King, M, "At risk drinking among general practice attenders: Validation of the CAGE questionnaire," *Psychological Medicine* (1986), 16:213–217; modified drug version not yet tested.

Chapter 2

1. Same brain changes with therapy as with drugs for obsessive-compulsive disorder treatment: Baxter, LR, Jr, J. Schwartz, et al. "Caudate glucose metabolic rate changes with both drug and behavior therapy for obsessive-compulsive disorder," *Arch Gen Psychiatry* (Sep 1992), 49:681–689.
2. Klein's theory on the pleasures of the hunt and the feast, described: Kramer, Peter, *Listening to Prozac*, New York: Penguin, 1997, p. 232.

287

3. Among U.S. residents, 47.2% drink coffee daily: Bloomberg News, "Survey: Coffee still hot in U.S." *Newsday* (July 17, 1998), p. A53.
4. Among coke addicts, 80–90% are alcoholics: Julien, Robert, *A primer of drug action*, New York: Freeman, 1995, seventh edition, p. 127.
5. Six percent of schoolchildren have attention deficit disorder: Ibid., p. 148.
6. Treatment for ADD reduces addiction among kids with ADD by 85%: Biederman, J., T. Wilens, et al., "Pharmacotherapy of attention-deficit/hyperactivity disorder reduces risk for substance use disorder," *Pediatrics* (Aug 1999), 104(2):20.
7. Negative effects of alcohol and smoking: Julien, op. cit., pp. 108–114, 165–179. Among all smokers, 90% are physically dependent: U.S. Surgeon General, *Health consequences of smoking: Nicotine addiction*. Rockville, MD: Department of Health and Human Services, 1988.
8. Among Americans, 74 million tried pot; other figures on American drug use: Substance Abuse and Mental Health Services Administration, National Household Surveys on Drug Abuse (1995–1997).
9. Among marijuana users, 5% are addicted: Nadelmann, Ethan, "Drug prohibition in the United States: Costs, consequences, and alternatives," *Science* (Sep 1, 1989), 944.
10. Marijuana sampling and strength now versus the 1960s and 1970s: Zimmer, Lynn, and John Morgan, *Marijuana myths, marijuana facts*. New York: Lindesmith Center, 1997, pp. 135–141.
11. Amotivational syndrome not due to marijuana: Ibid., pp. 63–69.
12. Kaiser Permanente study of marijuana and lung cancer: Sidney, S, JE Beck, IS Tekawa, CP Quesenberry, GD Friedman, "Marijuana use and mortality," *Am J Public Health*, (Apr 1997) 87(4):585–590.
13. Among LSD users, 15% have flashbacks: Julien, op. cit., p. 317.
14. LSD "freakouts" less frequent, though use still just as frequent: Zinberg, Norman Earl, *Drug, set, and setting: The basis for controlled intoxicant use*, New Haven, CT: Yale University Press, 1984.
15. Negative effects of Ecstasy: Peter McDermott, personal communication, May 1999.

Chapter 3

1. One third to one half of the risk for alcoholism is inherited: Pickens, RW, DS Svikis, et al., "Heterogeneity in the inheritance of alcoholism: A study of male and female twins," *Arch Gen Psychiatry*, (1991), 48(1):19–28.
2. Odds of becoming an alcoholic for children of alcoholics: Begleiter, Henri, and Benjamin Kissin, *The Genetics of Alcoholism*, New York: Oxford University Press, 1995. Also, Schuckit, Marc, "Alcohol, anxiety and depressive disorders," *Alcohol Health and Research World* (1996), 20(2):83.
3. Research on levels of endorphin in children of alcoholics: Gianoulakis, C, B Krishnan, and J Thavundayil, "Enhanced sensitivity of pituitary beta-endorphin to ethanol in subjects at high risk of alcoholism," *Arch Gen Psychiatry* (1996), 53:250–257.
4. Trauma (i.e., child abuse, deaths of parents, other tragedies, etc.) leads to more addiction; for review: Stewart, SH, "Alcohol abuse in individuals exposed to trauma: A critical review," *Psychological Bulletin* (1996), 120:83–112.
5. Dropout rate for AA: Makela, Klaus, et al., *Alcoholics Anonymous as a mutual help movement: A study in eight societies*, Madison: University of Wisconsin Press, 1996, p. 112.
6. Statistics on brief interventions: Fleming, M, et al., "Brief physician advice for problem alcohol drinkers: A randomized controlled trial in community based primary care practices," *JAMA* (1997) 277:1039–1045.

7. Therapeutic community versus incarceration study: Institute of Medicine, *Treating Drug Problems: Vol 1*, Washington, DC: National Academy Press, (1990), p. 178.

Chapter 4

1. Addiction is not an ordinary biological illness. . . . There is a moral dimension. . . : DuPont, Robert, *The selfish brain: Learning from addiction*, Washington, DC: American Psychiatric Press, 1997, p. 25.
2. Surgery with Dr. Bob, "you bet your ass": Robertson, Nan, *Getting better: Inside Alcoholics Anonymous*, New York: Ballantine, 1988, p. 20.
3. "My depression deepened unbearably. . . ": Alcoholics Anonymous, *Alcoholics Anonymous comes of age*, New York: Alcoholics Anonymous World Services, 1957, p. 63; also, *Alcoholics Anonymous: The story of how many thousands of men and women recovered from alcoholism*, New York: Alcoholics Anonymous World Services, 1976, third edition, p. 14.
4. "Anything is better than the way you were . . .": *Alcoholics Anonymous*, p. 14.
5. "An addiction is an experience that takes on meaning and power . . .": Peele, Stanton, and Archie Brodsky, *Love and addiction*, New York: Penguin, 1991, p. v.

Chapter 5

1. Chart summarized from presentation by Thomas McLellan, University of Pennsylvania.
2. Top 10 and bottom 10 treatments from data from Miller, William, and Reid Hester, *Handbook of alcoholism treatment approaches*, Boston: Allyn and Bacon, 1995, p. 18.
3. Two large studies on 12 step vs. CBT: Project MATCH Research Group, "Matching alcoholism treatments to client heterogeneity: Project MATCH posttreatment drinking outcomes," *Journal of Studies on Alcohol*, (1997), 58(1):7–29. Also, Project MATCH Research Group, "Matching alcoholism treatments to client heterogeneity: Treatment main effects and matching effects on drinking during treatment," *Journal of Studies on Alcohol*, (1998), 59:631–639. Oimette, PC, JW Finney, and RH Moos, "Twelve step and cognitive-behavioral treatment for substance abuse: A comparison of treatment effectiveness," *Journal of Consulting and Clinical Psychology*, (1997), 65:230–240.
4. Other research reviewed in Hester and Miller: Ibid.
5. Research on effectiveness of brief interventions: Fleming, M, et al., "Brief physician advice for problem alcohol drinkers: A randomized controlled trial in community based primary care practices," *JAMA*, (1997), 277:1039–1045.
6. "The best antidotes to addiction are . . .": Peele, S, and A Brodsky, *The meaning of addiction*, Boston: Lexington Books, 1985, p. 157.
7. Quote on "urge surfing" from National Institute on Alcohol Abuse and Alcoholism, *Cognitive-behavioral coping skills therapy manual*, Project Match Monograph Series, U.S. Department of Health and Human Services, 1992, pp. 28–29.
8. Therapeutic community, compared with prison, effectiveness as treatment: Institute of Medicine, *Treating drug problems*, Vol. 1, Washington, DC: National Academy Press, 1990, p. 179.
9. Rand Institute study, $1 on treatment is worth $7 on enforcement: Rydell, CP, and S Everingham, *Controlling cocaine: Supply versus demand programs*, Rand Drug Policy Research Center, 1994.
10. DATOS data: www.datos.org.

Chapter 6

1. Background and charts: Prochaska, James, John Norcross, and Carlo DiClemente, *Changing for good: A revolutionary six stage program for overcoming bad habits and moving your life positively forward*, New York: Avon Books, 1994.
2. Fifteen million alcoholics . . . : Grant, Bridget F., et al., *Alcohol Health & Research World*, (Vol. 18, No. 3), NIAAA's quarterly research journal, 1995.
3. Less than 10% in treatment: Substance Abuse and Mental Health Services Administration *Overview of the National Drug and Alcoholism Treatment Unit Survey (NDATUS): 1992 and 1980–1992*, Office of Applied Studies U.S. Department of Health and Human Services Public Health Service, Advance Report Number 9, Washington, DC: Superintendent of Documents, U.S. Government Printing Office, 1995.
4. Wilk, AI, NM Jensen, TC Havighurst, "Meta-analysis of randomized controlled trials addressing brief interventions in heavy alcohol drinkers," *Journal of General Internal Medicine*, (1997), 12(5):274–283.
5. Kübler-Ross, Elisabeth, *On death and dying*, New York: Macmillan, 1969.
6. McGovern, George, *Terry: My daughter's life and death struggle with alcoholism*, New York: Plume, 1997.
7. Research on CRAFT Family Therapy: Hester and Miller, op. cit., pp. 251–256.
8. Questions to determine stage of change: Prochaska, et al., op. cit., p. 68.
9. Nar-Anon should not be confused with the similarly named Narconon, which is a treatment program run by the Church of Scientology.
10. Research on CRAFT Family Therapy, compared to Al-Anon: Miller, W, RJ Meyers, and JS Tonigan, *Engaging the unmotivated in treatment for alcohol problems: A comparison of three intervention strategies* (forthcoming).

Chapter 7

1. "People are so afraid that the fun will go away . . . ": Dodd, David, *Playing it straight: Personal conversations on recovery, transformation and success*, Deerfield Beach, FL: Health Communications, p. 230.

Chapter 8

1. Detox method makes no difference in outcome: Institute of Medicine, *Treating drug problems, Vol. 1*, Washington, DC: National Academy Press, 1990, p. 176.
2. "To the doubters, we could say, 'Perhaps you're not an alcoholic after all . . .' ": Alcoholics Anonymous, *12 steps and 12 traditions*, Alcoholics Anonymous World Services, 1988, p. 23.
3. Most people who choose moderation ultimately wind up abstinent, choice of treatment increases success rate: Hester and Miller, op. cit.
4. Halfway houses and Oxford houses are unlikely to be accredited or even state-licensed since they are not officially treatment. The best way to check them out is to talk to former and current residents.
5. Among women in treatment, 40–80% were sexually abused as children: Wadsworth, Rick, et al., "The role of sexual trauma in the treatment of chemically dependent women: Addressing the relapse issue," *J Counseling and Development*, (Mar/Apr 1995), 401.

Chapter 9

1. Research on empathetic counselors doing best, and choice of treatments improving outcomes: Miller, William, and Reid Hester, *Handbook of alcoholism treatment approaches: Effective alternatives.* Boston: Allyn and Bacon, 1995.
2. Research data showing how the BRENDA approach improves treatment retention and compliance with taking medications, relative to standard addictions counseling: Pettinati, HM, JR Volpicelli, JD Pierce, and CP O'Brien, "Improving naltrexone response: An intervention for medical practitioners to enhance medication in alcohol dependent patients." *Journal of Addictive Diseases* (1999).
3. Some reasons why people are not compliant with taking medications, and strategies for improving compliance: Forman, L, "Medication: Reasons and interventions for non-compliance," *Journal of Psychosocial Nursing & Mental Health Services*, (1993), 31(10):23–25. Keck, PE, SL McElroy, SM Strakowski, SP Stanton, DL Kizer, TM Balistreri, JA Bennett, KC Tugrul, and SA West, "Factors associated with pharmacologic noncompliance in patients with mania," *Journal of Clinical Psychiatry*, (1996), 57(7):292–297.

Chapter 10

1. "One night I was sitting in the lab alone . . . ": *Alcoholics Anonymous: The story of how many thousands of men and women recovered from alcoholism*, New York: Alcoholics Anonymous World Services, 1976, third edition, p. 427.
2. "Most of them are here for cocaine or freebase . . . ": Fisher, Carrie, *Postcards from the Edge*, New York: Pocket Books, 1987, p. 11.
3. "My friend calls the [crack] pipe the devil's dick . . . ": Williams, Terry, *Crackhouse: Notes from the end of the line*, Boston: Addison-Wesley: 1992, p. 25.
4. Ultra rapid opioid detox information: Szalavitz, Maia, "Detox dilemma: Hopeful or hoax?" *Newsday* (Feb. 17, 1998), C3.

Chapter 11

1. People generally don't like taking Antabuse, and it is generally not effective when given without a support person to ensure compliance: Fuller, RK, L Branchey, DR Brightwell, RM Derman, CD Emrick, FL Iber, KE James, RB Lacoursiere, KK Lee, I Lowenstam, I Maany, D Neiderhiser, JJ Nocks, and S Shaw, "Disulfiram treatment of alcoholism: A Veterans Administration cooperative study," *JAMA*, (1986), 256(11):1449–1455.
2. Rats increase their alcohol preference after stress, and the poststress increases in alcohol drinking are blocked by naltrexone: Volpicelli, JR, MA Davis, and JE Olgin, "Naltrexone blocks the post-shock increase of ethanol consumption," *Life Sciences*, (1986), 38:841–847.
3. The use of naltrexone reduces relapse rates by 50%: Volpicelli, JR, AI Alterman, M Hayashida, and CP O' Brien, "Naltrexone in the treatment of alcohol dependence," *Arch Gen Psychiatry*, (1992), 49(11):876–880.
4. The group at Yale replicates the finding that naltrexone reduces alcohol relapse: O'Malley, S, AJ Jaffe, G Chang, and R Schottenfeld, "Naltrexone and coping skills therapy for alcohol dependence: A controlled study," *Arch Gen Psychiatry*, (1992) 49:881–887.

5. Among diabetics, 58%: Meichenbaum, D, and D Turk, "Treatment adherence," cited in Fumento, Michael, *The fat of the land*, New York: Viking, 1997, p. 26.

6. In less compliant subjects, naltrexone is no better than placebo, but in patients taking more than 80% of their pills, placebo patients were three times more likely to relapse: Volpicelli, JR, KL Rhines, JS Rhines, LA Volpicelli, AI Alterman, and CP O'Brien, "Naltrexone and alcohol dependence: Role of subject compliance," *Arch Gen Psychiatry*, (1997) 54:737–742.

7. Most people using buprenorphine report mild withdrawal symptoms when switching from heroin to buprenorphine; buprenorphine is a safe and effective alternative to methadone for the treatment of heroin addiction; addicts can't tell methadone from buprenorphine: personal communication with Tom Kosten, Yale University.

8. The use of antidepressants to treat cocaine addicts has not be found to be useful, when compared with placebo: Arndt, IO, L Dorozynsky, et al., "Desipramine treatment of cocaine dependence in methadone-maintained patients," *Arch Gen Psychiatry* (1992) 49(11):888–893.

9. Medications that stimulate the GABA system may even reduce cocaine's effect on the dopamine system and lead to effective treatments: Dewey, SL, AE Morgan, et al., "A novel strategy for the treatment of cocaine addiction," *Synapse* (1998), 30(2):119–129.

10. Antabuse significantly reduces both cocaine and alcohol abuse: Carroll, KM, C Nich, et al., "Treatment of cocaine and alcohol dependence with psychotherapy and disulfiram," *Addiction* (1998), 93:713–727.

11. An open trial of naltrexone reduced cocaine and alcohol abuse: Oslin, DW, et al., "The effects of naltrexone on alcohol and cocaine use in dually addicted patients," *Journal of Substance Abuse Treatment* (Mar. 1999), 16:163–167.

Chapter 12

1. "Alcoholics Anonymous is a fellowship . . . ": Alcoholics Anonymous, *Preamble*, Alcoholics Anonymous World Services.

2. Percentage of population that has attended a 12-step program meeting: Room, R, and TK Greenfield, "Alcoholics Anonymous, other 12-step movements and psychotherapy in the US population, 1990," *Addiction* (1993), 88:555–562.

3. Dropout rate of AA—40% stay: Makela, K, et al. *Alcoholics Anonymous as a mutual help movement: A study in 8 societies*, Madison: University of Wisconsin Press, 1996, p. 112.

4. Among AA members, 42% are addicted to other drugs, in addition to alcohol: Makela, Klaus, et al., *Alcoholics Anonymous as a mutual help movement*, Madison: University of Wisconsin Press, 1996.

5. Average meeting attendance of AA members: Alcoholics Anonymous World Services, "AA membership survey," 1996.

6. Twelve Steps of Alcoholics Anonymous . . . . What an order . . . : *Alcoholics Anonymous: The story of how many thousands of men and women recovered from alcoholism*, New York: Alcoholics Anonymous World Services, 1976, third edition, pp. 59–60.

7. Random assignment to AA doesn't work, affiliation may help: McCrady, B. and S. Delaney, "Self Help Groups," in William Miller and Reid Hester, *Handbook of alcoholism treatment approaches: Effective alternatives*. Boston: Allyn and Bacon, 1995, p. 174.

8. Men do better than women in AA: Tonigan, J. Scott, and Susan Hiller-Sturmhofel, "Alcoholics Anonymous: Who benefits?" *Alcohol Health and Research World* (1994), 18(4):308.

Chapter 13

1. SOS Guidelines, from SOS website: www.unhooked.com
2. Deputy Sheriff's story, from SOS website: Ibid.
3. "You didn't save my life . . . ", from Rational Recovery website: www.rational.org
4. SMART recovery information, SMART website: www.smartrecovery.org
5. Women for Sobriety, New Life Acceptance Program, from website: www.womenforsobriety. org

Chapter 14

1. Data from CATOR on outcomes of Minnesota Model treatment: Hoffman, Norman, and Norman Miller, "Treatment outcomes for abstinence-based programs," *Psychiatric Annals* (Aug 1992), 402–408.
2. DARP and TOPS are summarized in Institute of Medicine, *Treating drug problems*, Vol. 1, Washington, DC: National Academy Press, 1990. DATOS data are at www.datos.org.

Chapter 15

1. Completion rate of 10%: Institute of Medicine, *Treating drug problems*, Vol. 1, Washington, DC: National Academy Press, 1990, p. 164.
2. TCs graduates success rate: Ibid., p. 162.
3. Average abstinence rates: Hubbard, Marsden, et al. *Drug abuse treatment: A national study of effectiveness*. Chapel Hill: University of North Carolina Press, 1989, p. 125. See also DATOS website, www.datos.org.
4. Success of TC versus plain incarceration: Institute of Medicine, op. cit., p. 179.

Chapter 16

1. Review of research on moderation (including information on Miller's moderate-drinking guide, with confrontational versus empathetic versus no therapist, and on similar outcomes in moderation and abstinence programs over the long term): Hester, R.,"Behavioral self control training," in William Miller and Reid Hester, *Handbook of alcoholism treatment approaches: Effective alternatives*. Boston: Allyn and Bacon, 1995, pp. 148–157.

Chapter 17

1. "I kept going back and interviewing clients and interviewing outreach workers . . .": Drug historian William White, interviewed by Bill Moyers, for PBS TV in *Moyers on addiction: Close to home*, 1998.
2. HIV prevalence in cities with and without needle exchange: Hurley, SF, "Effectiveness of needle-exchange programmes for prevention of HIV infection," *Lancet* (1997) 349:1797.
3. San Francisco versus New York AIDS rates and needle exchange: Szalavitz, Maia, "Point counterpoint: Why IV users deserve clean needles," *Village Voice* (Mar 27, 1990). See also San Francisco Department of Public Health (SFDPH) AIDS Office, *AIDS Surveillance Report* (Sept 30, 1997).

4. Data on states with over-the-counter availability, compared with those without: Szalavitz, Maia, "Clean needles saved my life," *New York Times* Op-ed (June 8, 1996) sect. 1 p. 19. See also Normand J, D Vlahov, LE Moses, eds., *Preventing HIV transmission: The role of sterile needles and bleach*, Washington, DC: National Academy Press, 1995.

5. Study of the ARRIVE program: Harry K. Wexler, et al. "ARRIVE: An AIDS/relapse prevention model for high risk parolees," *International Journal of the Addictions*, (1994) 29(3):361–386.

Chapter 18

1. Methadone cuts death rate among addicts: Gearing, MF, "Methadone maintenance in the treatment of heroin addicts in New York City: A ten year review," in L. Roizin, et al., eds., *Neurotoxicology, Vol 1*, New York: Raven Press, 1977, pp. 71–79.

2. Methadone is best treatment for heroin addiction: Institute of Medicine, *Treating drug problems, Vol. 1*, Washington, DC: National Academy Press, 1990, p. 187; see also, Institute of Medicine, Rettig, Richard A. and Adam Yarmolinsky, eds., *Federal regulation of methadone treatment*, Washington, DC: National Academy Press, 1995.

3. Methadone is the most researched addiction treatment: Ibid.

4. Methadone cuts use over time: Ibid.

5. Methadone reduces incarceration: O'Brien, C, and J McKay, "Psychopharmacological treatment of substance use disorders," in *Treatments that work* (in press).

6. Methadone cuts crime in New York: Herman Joseph, "The criminal justice system and opiate addiction: A historical perspective," in National Institute on Drug Abuse, *Compulsory treatment of drug abuse: Research and clinical practice*, Rockville, MD: National Institute on Drug Abuse, 1988.

Chapter 19

1. Acupuncture effectiveness for addiction: "Acupuncture," *NIH Consensus Statement Online*, (Nov 3–5, 1997), 15(5):1–34.

2. Study on diet and alcoholism cited to back diet-book claims: Biery, Janet Reid, et al., "Alcohol craving in rehabilitation: Assessment of nutrition therapy," *Journal of the American Dietetic Association*, (Apr 1991), 91(4):463–466.

3. Glutamine and alcoholism: Rogers, Lorene, Richard Pelton, and Roger Williams, "Amino acid supplementation and voluntary alcohol consumption by rats," *J Biological Chemistry* (May 1956), 220(1):321–323.

4. Recovery diet books mentioned: Larson, Joan Mathews, *Seven weeks to sobriety*, New York: Fawcett, 1997; Powter, Susan, *Sober and staying that way: The missing link in the cure for alcoholism*, New York: Fireside, 1999.

Chapter 20

1. Teens who experiment are more healthy than abstainers or heavy users: Shedler, Jonathan, and Jack Block, "Adolescent drug use and psychological health: A longitudinal inquiry," *American Psychologist* (May 1990), 612–630.

2. Teen treatment increases crack and alcohol use, doesn't cut other use: Substance Abuse and Mental Health Services Organization, Office of Applied Studies, *Services research outcomes survey*, U.S. Department of Health and Human Services, DHHS Publication Number: (SMA) 98–3177, 1998.

3. Heavy teen users don't necessarily grow up to be addicts: Bates, Marsha E., and Erich W. Labouvie, "Adolescent risk factors and the prediction of persistent alcohol and drug use into adulthood," *Alcoholism: Clinical and Experimental Research* (1997), 21: 944–950.

4. Cognitive and behavioral family therapies are best treatments for teens: De Graffenreid Riggs, Paula, and Elizabeth Whitmore, in Chapter 4, "Substance use disorders and disruptive behavior disorders," *Review of psychiatry series, 1999: Disruptive behavior disorders in children and adolescents*, Washington, DC: American Psychiatric Press, 1999.

5. Review of teen treatment literature, which concluded that some may be better than none . . . : Catalano, RF, JD Hawkins, et al., "Evaluation of the effectiveness of adolescent drug abuse treatment, assessment of risk for relapse and promising approaches for relapse prevention," *International Journal of the Addictions* (1991–1992), 25(9a,10a): 1085–1140.

Chapter 21

1. Review of relapse literature and techniques: Dimeff, Linda, and G. Alan Marlatt, "Relapse prevention," in William Miller and Reid Hester, *Handbook of alcoholism treatment approaches: Effective alternatives*. Boston: Allyn and Bacon, 1995, pp. 176–194.

2. Having a good job is well correlated with recovery: McLellan, AT, JC Ball, et al., "Pretreatment source of income and response to methadone maintenance: A follow-up study," *Am J Psychiatry* (1981), 138(6):785–789.

3. Success rate improves with number of times you try: Prochaska, James, John Norcross, and Carlo DiClemente, *Changing for good: A revolutionary six stage program for overcoming bad habits and moving your life positively forward*, New York: Avon Books, 1994, p. 50.

Chapter 22

1. PTSD data: Van der Kolk, BA, M Greenberg, H Boyd, and J Krystal, "Inescapable shock, neurotransmitters and addiction to trauma: Toward a psychobiology of post-traumatic stress," *Biol. Psychiatry* (1985), 20:314–325.

2. Rat research stress and cancer: Visintainer, MA, JR Volpicelli, and MEP Seligman, "Tumor rejection in rats after inescapable or escapable shock," *Science* (1982), 216: 437–439.

Index

About the Authors

Joseph Volpicelli, M.D., Ph.D., is Associate Professor of Psychiatry at the University of Pennsylvania and Senior Research Scientist at the University of Pennsylvania Addiction Treatment Research Center. He developed the medication naltrexone for the treatment of alcoholism and has been studying and treating addictive disorders for more than a quarter century.

Maia Szalavitz is a journalist and former addict who specializes in covering health, science, and drug policy. She served as series researcher and associate producer for the acclaimed PBS documentary, *Moyers on Addiction: Close to Home*. She has also been a segment producer for *Charlie Rose* and has written for the *New York Times*, *New York Magazine*, *McCalls*, the *Washington Post*, and *Newsday*.